# Sri Vijnana
# Bhairava Tantra
### The Ascent

*With kind regards,* ॐ *and prem*

Swami Niranjan

# Sri Vijnana Bhairava Tantra
## The Ascent

Swami Satyasangananda Saraswati

*Under the Guidance of*
**Swami Satyananda Saraswati**

Yoga Publications Trust, Munger, Bihar, India

Published by Yoga Publications Trust
    First edition 2003
    Reprinted 2004, 2006, 2008

ISBN : 978-81-86336-32-8

Publisher and distributor: Yoga Publications Trust, Ganga Darshan, Munger, Bihar, India.

Website: www.biharyoga.net
        www.rikhiapeeth.net

Printed at Thomson Press (India) Limited, New Delhi, 110001

# ABOUT THE AUTHOR

I initiated the author, Swami Satyasangananda Saraswati, into sannyasa in the year 1982. All the knowledge she has gained in this short time about the spiritual sciences, their profound philosophies, as well as untold practices, has not been through a process of intellectual study, but through an unfoldment from within. Her intellectual growth and subjects of study prior to sannyasa were in no way related to this subject, yet she astutely mastered each and every aspect of this complex knowledge, as if it were her natural heritage. This should be a pointer to others, as it affirms the proclamation of my guru, who said to me in the early years of my ashram life, "You do not have to bring the light from outside. Work hard and purify yourself; the light will unfold from within." Others before and after him have also said this.

The life of a sannyasin should be dedicated to two goals. The first is to live in the service of others and the second to arouse in oneself the experience of transcendental knowledge. If one does not work towards this end, sannyasa becomes hypocrisy and a sham. Swami Satyasangananda has been sincere to both these ideals of sannyasa. Therefore, this work is much more than a translation of *Vijnana Bhairava Tantra* by a student or scholar of tantra; it is a work based on the personal experience of a sannyasin who has dared to uphold the lofty values of *tyaga* (renunciation), *vairagya* (non-attachment) and *samarpan* (surrender). These are the *kavach* or armour of a sannyasin, with which he marches ahead towards the fragrance of *atma anubhuti* or self-realization.

*Swami Satyananda*

# Dedication

*In humility we offer this dedication to
Swami Sivananda Saraswati, who initiated
Swami Satyananda Saraswati into the secrets of yoga.*

# Contents

| | | |
|---|---|---|
| **Preface** | | *xv* |
| **Introduction** | | 1 |
| **Commentary** | | 93 |

*Inquiry into the nature of reality*

*Sloka*

| | | |
|---|---|---|
| 1 | Rudrayamala and Trika | 95 |
| 2 | Reality of Bhairava | 99 |
| 3 | How the Bhairava reality is perceived | 101 |
| 4 | By what experience this reality is known | 104 |
| 5 | Transcendent or immanent | 107 |
| 6 | Indivisible and indefinable | 109 |
| 7 | Essence of tantra | 110 |
| 8 | Forms of Bhairava | 111 |
| 9 | Sakara aspect of Bhairava | 116 |
| 10 | Purpose of sakara meditation | 119 |
| 11 | What Bhairava is not | 121 |
| 12 | Essence of Bhairava | 123 |
| 13 | What has been told about Bhairava | 125 |
| 14 | Immeasurable and without attribute | 127 |
| 15 | Atman of Bhairava | 129 |
| 16 | Nature of highest reality | 132 |
| 17 | Bhairava is known by Paradevi | 134 |
| 18 | Dharma and the possessor of dharma | 136 |
| 19 | Dualism is a preliminary step | 138 |
| 20 | Shakti is the face of Shiva | 140 |
| 21 | Shiva is revealed by Shakti | 142 |
| 22 | Bhairava state of consciousness | 144 |
| 23 | Means to achieve Bhairava consciousness | 146 |

**Dharanas**

| Sloka | | Page |
|---|---|---|
| 24 | Dharana on the two generation points | 148 |
| 25 | Kumbhaka dharana | 157 |
| 26 | Perfection of kumbhaka | 160 |
| 27 | Kumbhaka leads to inner peace | 163 |
| 28 | Kundalini jagran dharana | 165 |
| 29 | Piercing of the chakras | 167 |
| 30 | Kundalini becomes shiva | 169 |
| 31 | Mind transcends thought | 172 |
| 32 | Shoonya panchaka dharana | 175 |
| 33 | Mindful awareness | 178 |
| 34 | Dharana on the crown of the head | 180 |
| 35 | Sushumna dharana | 182 |
| 36 | Shanmukhi mudra | 184 |
| 37 | Dissolution in the cave of the heart | 186 |
| 38 | Dharana on shabdhabrahman | 188 |
| 39 | Pranava dharana | 190 |
| 40 | Dharana on Aum matras | 193 |
| 41 | Nada dharana | 195 |
| 42 | Bija mantra dharana | 197 |
| 43 | Dharana on the directions | 199 |
| 44 | Sushumna and daharakasha dharana | 201 |
| 45 | Sushumna, daharakasha and hridayakasha dharana | 203 |
| 46 | Antarakasha dharana | 205 |
| 47 | Antarakasha dharana (cont.) | 207 |
| 48 | Antarakasha dharana (cont.) | 208 |
| 49 | Dharana on the mantra in the heart space | 209 |
| 50 | Dharana on dwadashanta | 210 |
| 51 | Result of dharana on dwadashanta | 212 |
| 52 | Dharana on Kaalagni | 214 |
| 53 | Result of dharana on Kaalagni | 216 |
| 54 | Tattwa dharana | 218 |

| *Sloka* | | *Page* |
|---|---|---|
| 55 | Dharana on the indriyas or senses | 220 |
| 56 | Dharana on universal dissolution | 222 |
| 57 | Shiva tattwa dharana | 224 |
| 58 | Vishwa shoonya dharana | 226 |
| 59 | Dharana on an empty pot | 228 |
| 60 | Dharana on a deserted place | 230 |
| 61 | Dharana on the space in between two objects | 232 |
| 62 | Dharana on one object | 234 |
| 63 | Dharana on all existence as consciousness | 236 |
| 64 | Dharana on the fusion of vayus | 238 |
| 65 | Dharana on ananda | 240 |
| 66 | Dharana on austerity | 242 |
| 67 | Dharana on the ascent of pranashakti | 245 |
| 68 | Dharana on manipura and anahata | 247 |
| 69 | Dharana on union with shakti | 249 |
| 70 | Dharana on sexual bliss in the absence of shakti | 251 |
| 71 | Dharana on joy | 254 |
| 72 | Dharana on enjoyment of food and drink | 256 |
| 73 | Dharana on sensual pleasures | 258 |
| 74 | Dharana on satisfaction of mind | 260 |
| 75 | Dharana on the threshold before sleep | 262 |
| 76 | Dharana on the luminous space | 264 |
| 77 | Dharana on the tantric mudras | 266 |
| 78 | Dharana in relaxed asana | 271 |
| 79 | Dharana on shoonya yantra | 274 |
| 80 | Dharana on an object | 276 |
| 81 | Dharana on 'Ha' | 278 |
| 82 | Dharana on suspension of the body | 280 |
| 83 | Dharana on swinging the body | 282 |
| 84 | Dharana on the sky | 284 |
| 85 | Dharana on chidakasha | 285 |
| 86 | Dharana on reality | 287 |
| 87 | Dharana on the darkness of night | 289 |

| Sloka | | Page |
|-------|--|------|
| 88 | Dharana on the dark form of bhairava | 292 |
| 89 | Dharana on restraint of the senses | 294 |
| 90 | Dharana on akaara | 296 |
| 91 | Dharana on visarga | 299 |
| 92 | Dharana on oneself in the form of space | 301 |
| 93 | Dharana on piercing of the skin | 303 |
| 94 | Dharana on no-mind | 305 |
| 95 | Dharana on the nature of the elements | 308 |
| 96 | Dharana on ending desires | 310 |
| 97 | Dharana on 'Who am I?' | 312 |
| 98 | Dharana on desire | 314 |
| 99 | Dharana on knowledge | 316 |
| 100 | Dharana on undifferentiated consciousness | 318 |
| 101 | Dharana on the negative qualities | 320 |
| 102 | Dharana on the illusive nature of life | 323 |
| 103 | Dharana on the middle path | 325 |
| 104 | Dharana on 'I am everywhere' | 327 |
| 105 | Dharana on higher knowledge | 329 |
| 106 | Dharana on the subject-object relationship | 331 |
| 107 | Dharana on consciousness | 333 |
| 108 | Dharana on the unsupported mind | 335 |
| 109 | Dharana on identification with Shiva | 337 |
| 110 | Dharana on identification with the source | 339 |
| 111 | Dharana on whirling around | 341 |
| 112 | Dharana on erroneous perception | 343 |
| 113 | Dharana of steady gazing | 346 |
| 114 | Dharana on anahad nada | 349 |
| 115 | Dharana on a deep well | 351 |
| 116 | Dharana on the omnipresent reality | 353 |
| 117 | Dharana on poornatva | 355 |
| 118 | Dharana on the state of Brahma | 357 |
| 119 | Dharana on memories | 359 |
| 120 | Dharana on unmani | 361 |

| Sloka | | Page |
|---|---|---|
| 121 | Dharana on intuition | 363 |
| 122 | Dharana on a particular object | 366 |
| 123 | Dharana on purity | 367 |
| 124 | Dharana on the non-dual reality | 369 |
| 125 | Dharana on equality | 371 |
| 126 | Dharana in between two opposites | 373 |
| 127 | Dharana on bhairava as the unknowable void | 375 |
| 128 | Dharana on outer space | 377 |
| 129 | Dharana on thoughtlessness | 378 |
| 130 | Dharana on the word bhairava | 380 |
| 131 | Dharana on Tat (that highest reality) | 383 |
| 132 | Dharana on divine attributes | 385 |
| 133 | Dharana on the illusory nature of the world | 386 |
| 134 | Dharana on the changeless atman | 388 |
| 135 | Neither bondage nor liberation | 390 |
| 136 | Withdrawal of the senses | 392 |
| 137 | Dharana on knowledge and knower | 394 |
| 138 | Dissolution of the set of four | 396 |

**Conclusion**

| 139 | Means of cessation | 398 |
|---|---|---|
| 140 | Perfection of one dharana | 400 |
| 141 | Master of yogis and siddhas | 401 |
| 142 | Liberated while living | 402 |
| 143 | Who is the worshipper and who is worshipped? | 403 |
| 144 | Gross forms of worship | 405 |
| 145 | Japa dharana on the supreme consciousness | 407 |
| 146 | Verification of meditation | 409 |
| 147 | True worship | 410 |
| 148 | Complete fulfilment or satisfaction | 411 |
| 149 | Real oblation | 412 |
| 150 | Saviour of all | 413 |
| 151 | Highest contemplation | 414 |

| *Sloka* | | *Page* |
|---|---|---|
| 152 | Real purification | 416 |
| 153 | What is worship? | 417 |
| 154 | Supreme place of pilgrimage | 418 |
| 155a | Blissful sacrifice | 420 |
| 155b | Hamsa dharana | 422 |
| 156 | Continuous japa of the breath | 424 |
| 157 | Need for secrecy | 425 |
| 158 | Qualification for tantric practice | 427 |
| 159 & 160 | Tantric initiation | 429 |
| 161 | Never give up this knowledge | 431 |
| 162 | Devi's understanding | 432 |
| 163 | Union of Shiva and Shakti | 433 |

**Appendices**
| | | |
|---|---|---|
| A: Sanskrit Text | | 437 |
| B: Translation | | 452 |
| **Glossary** | | 473 |
| **Index** | | 494 |

# Preface

The knowledge of history, geography, astrology, astronomy, languages and other subjects that we study is recorded in their respective texts. Similarly, the knowledge of the mind and consciousness is recorded in the texts of the Tantras, Vedas and Puranas. These texts were written in Sanskrit, which was the language of their time, but this factor now limits the access to information contained within them to a very small minority who know that language. However, there are students of the science of the mind who have studied these texts and explained them in modern languages so that sincere seekers can avail themselves of this valuable information. This is not an easy task as these texts are written in a coded and abbreviated way, which only the discerning and enlightened can shed light on. On account of this limitation very few texts are available today that elucidate these ancient forms of spiritual knowledge.

It is often said that when the student is ready the teacher appears, and also when the time is right conditions conducive to spiritual dissemination arise. In that sense the subject of dharana, or concentration, which is the theme of *Vijnana Bhairava Tantra* (VBT), is most relevant today. Spiritual seekers the world over, who have maintained personal disciplines for the evolution of consciousness, are now in need of this knowledge. For this reason the time is now ripe to introduce the tantric system of dharana as it was practised by the ancients. Of course, the techniques of dharana are not new to practitioners of meditation, yet very few are aware of the full scope of the tantric system and its application.

Whether one is a materialist or a spiritualist, it is important to realize that the practice of dharana is most vital for progress in all spheres of life. Even the materialists pay homage to energy, because they realize that this whole world is nothing but a play of energy. The materialists exploded the atom through a physical process in order to harness its immense energy for the benefit of mankind. In the same way, the practice of dharana explodes the atom of energy within the mind through a spiritual process, so that it can be harnessed to accelerate the evolution of individual consciousness. For this reason dharana is as valuable as the nuclear sciences and should, therefore, receive the same recognition and status.

Very few translations and commentaries of VBT are currently available. Therefore, the publication of this work is very significant as it will shed a great deal of light on the practice of dharana, which until now has been revealed only by peripheral explanations. The main aim of this text is to convey the relevance of dharana and the means or techniques to incorporate it into one's life. It also reassures that this can be done quite easily, even if one does not have any expertise in this field. Although dharana is a practice intended for a practitioner whose mind is steady and controlled, this book provides a way even for those of unsteady mind to gradually develop one-pointedness.

All the wealth, assets, luxuries and comforts that one can have in this world are of no use if the mind is uncontrolled and dissipated. In this sense a mind that travels on the desired path is the most valuable asset that a man can possess. If one has such a mind, nothing more is needed.

The great poet-saint Kabir Das has rightly said, *"Mein to un santan ka daas jinhone man maar liya"*: I bow only before that saint who has conquered his mind. Although we may not realize it, we are all slaves to our minds. Throughout the day we do whatever the mind directs us to do. If the mind is worried, we feel anxious; if it is happy, we are pleased; if it is envious, we are ridden with jealousy; if it is furious, we become violently angry. Is there ever a moment in our life when we put our foot down and say, "No, I will not be angry, or happy, or vengeful?"

We simply cannot put an end to this process without knowing the practice of dharana. There is no other way to gather the vagrant tendencies of this powerful substance known as mind, except by the practice of dharana, the path of concentration. Dharana is a practice which generates the momentum to override the dissipated energies of the mind and convert them into a stream of awareness. Therefore, we are very happy to present this work, which is the result of an in-depth study of dharana in relation to the tantric view of meditation, substantiated by the personal experience of the author.

# Introduction

The loftiest dictum pronounced by the sages and seers of the upanishadic and vedic era was *Aham Brahmasmi,* "I am That." Their search was within; they explored the vast dimensions that constitute the inner life. Mentally they dissected the body and discovered its subtle essence to be the senses. Through meditation on the senses they discovered the corridors and avenues of the mind. By reflecting on the mind they realized the potential energy that was dormant within. By awakening that energy they discovered consciousness, and by uniting the inherent energy with the individual consciousness they realized that they were indeed intimately connected to and a part of the cosmic consciousness. This was realized by the tantrics a long time ago, even before the vedic era. The entire spectrum of vedic and tantric philosophy is based on this realization; whether Shaivism, Vaishnavism or Shaktism, the subject is exploring the substance that man is composed of.

Several hundred thousand years later, the unified field theory which physicists talk about uncannily points in the same direction. According to this theory, the entire creation is one composite whole and all of life, whether animate or inanimate, manifest or unmanifest, is intimately connected. In other words, whatever you think, feel, say or do spreads like ripples into unending space, mixing, merging and

1

colliding with ripples from other sources. This is a very dynamic idea, which lends universality to each and every human being and gives life an importance and status that goes far beyond one's imagination and expectation. Through the dark ages of history, the average man has found himself severely limited whenever he has tried to delve into areas of life that extend beyond what the senses can see, hear, taste, touch and smell. The range of human perception is limited to this dimension.

Although man has amassed enormous wealth, luxuries and comforts, and has fortified himself with immense power to protect himself from enemies, imaginary or real, he still finds himself unprotected and vulnerable. He knows that the span of life is short. When he has to bid farewell, he cannot take the armour which has protected him throughout life; he has to go empty-handed. So this proclamation of *Aham Brahmasmi* gives man hope and sustenance. Not only that, the vedic and tantric sages have generously shared their meditative experiences with mankind, revealing vital clues about the real purpose of human life. Although man lives to amass wealth, power and status, these goals give only limited satisfaction. There is no permanence in the joy derived from material gains. The real joy and everlasting bliss can be had only when man realizes himself.

### Realize the self

What does it mean to realize the self? I know that I am male or female, Indian or American, Hindu or Muslim, Christian or Jew, rich or poor, beautiful or ugly, intelligent or dull, black or white, educated or illiterate, saint or sinner, atheist or believer, compassionate or cruel, generous or mean. However, the tantric and vedic sages say that all of these criteria are irrelevant, immaterial and unimportant as far as the quest for the self is concerned. In this quest one's sex, nationality, class, creed, social status, dogma and religious beliefs hold no sway. The self relates to a different dimension altogether. Exploring the self, they say, is not a social, cultural or religious affair.

The emphasis of the sages was on the innate qualities of man, not the acquired ones. They realized that the spectrum of human awareness ranges from demonic to human to divine, on account of the interplay of the three qualities, or *gunas*, which constitute his being. These three qualities are known as sattwa, rajas and tamas. *Sattwa* denotes divinity, *tamas* the demonic quality, and *rajas* the human endeavour. Of course, this is a very broad classification, but it is true that all of these traits are a part and parcel of our nature. The three gunas are present in each one of us and continually direct our thoughts, actions, feelings and, in fact, the totality of our lives. They determine the temperament of each one of us as well as our inclinations in life. We make all of our choices on the basis of these gunas.

However, no matter what choices we make in life, we should not forget the purpose for which we have come into this world. That purpose is to realize the self. Human birth has been given great importance, because it is only as a human being that we can know our true essence. It is the seed of individuality that has been sown in human beings which gives us knowledge of our existence. Other forms of creation live without any knowledge of their existence. It is man alone who has knowledge of each and every act that he performs and thereby of his existence.

Man is aware of time, space and object. Although animals, plants and minerals are sentient beings, they do not have this awareness. A dog barks, but he does not know that he is barking. A tree bears fruit, but it does not have the knowledge that it does so. Many forms of life have feelings, likes and dislikes, acute responses and memory as well, yet they do not know of their existence in time and space nor do they have any knowledge of the objects around them. Man is exceptional because he can have knowledge of his existence within time and space and beyond time and space as well. He can voluntarily transcend the objective self and travel into the realm of timelessness to experience the unified awareness of which he is an integral part and from which he has evolved into the gross body and mind that he is. (VBT sl. 97)

## Evolutes of consciousness

Ironically, that same tattwa or principle which gives man the knowledge of individuality and differentiation is responsible for the experience of unified awareness, or knowledge of unity with the rest of creation. That principle is known as ego or *ahamkara*. The word *aham* means 'I am'. Other forms of life, both inferior and superior, do not have ahamkara. In the lower forms of life this principle is latent, and in the higher forms it has been transcended. Therefore, in the vedic and tantric traditions human life is much sought after, even by those who have attained divinity, because only man can know the creator. In that sense the human birth is considered to be most valuable.

According to tantra, the universal consciousness descends towards manifestation as individual consciousness, assuming four states, known as buddhi, chitta, ahamkara and manas. *Buddhi* represents the higher intellect with its activity of *viveka*, or discrimination, and *sadvichara*, or right thinking. *Manas* is the lower mind with its characteristic activity of *sankalpa* and *vikalpa*, or thought and counter-thought. *Chitta*, or memory, is the storehouse of past actions in the form of *samskaras*, or archetypes. Ahamkara, or ego, is the notion of self-existence, conditioned by the above three.

This is the arc of *avaroha*, or the descent of the dynamic universal consciousness into human life. It is only at the human stage of evolution that *unmesha* or *aroha*, the ascent towards higher life, is possible. Inner realization dawns when manas, buddhi, chitta and ahamkara are dissolved into universal consciousness through the medium of *shakti*, or energy. This is the highest *yajna*, or sacrifice, man can offer. (VBT sl. 138) Other forms of life do not have this privilege because they do not have these four aspects, which are collectively known as *antahkarana*, or the inner instrument.

The ascent of consciousness from its association with gross matter and base emotions to the effulgence of spirit is the focal point of tantric and vedic thought. Other philosophies speak of the descent of universal consciousness, whereas tantric and vedic thought upholds that ascent from matter to spirit is the inherent design which prakriti or nature has woven into all creation. Tantra says that the descent of universal consciousness in its pure form is a possibility which occurs very rarely. This descent of universal consciousness into matter while retaining its pure form is known as avatar. The avatar represents universal consciousness on earth and, therefore, the laws of nature are well within his control. Sri Krishna was such an avatar and so was Sri Rama. However, very few such persons have descended to earth. So, it is the ascent and not the descent of consciousness that we have to understand in relation to our meditative practices and spiritual evolution.

The supra-mental state which Sri Aurobindo, the twentieth century yogi, often referred to also points in this direction. At present, man is functioning with a mere fraction of the potential power of the brain. It is only the tip of the iceberg. The higher faculties of the brain, which are latent, have to be illumined and awakened through two important practices of tantra, known as dharana and dhyana. These two practices strengthen the electro-magnetic circuits of the brain so that it becomes accustomed to handling the high voltage energy that is a consequence of inner illumination. These practices form channels and pathways for the energy to be transmitted to all points of the brain, leading to total illumination. If illumination occurs before these preparations are complete, short circuits may occur and fuses may blow, as the 'wiring' of the brain cannot withstand the influx of powerful currents generated by total illumination of the dark recesses.

Different vedic and tantric traditions offer lucid and incisive dialogues and debates on this very subject. Their enquiries were both subjective and objective, leaving no stone unturned. They dissected thoughts, ideas and experiences, analyzed feelings and emotions, and subjected themselves to intense and rigorous scrutiny in search of the real and the permanent. In the science of alchemy a substance is rarefied until it becomes pure and refined. Similarly, through the alchemical process of meditation the mysterious ocean of thoughts, desires and passions surging within is churned by the practice of dharana. In this way, the yogis uncovered layer after layer of mind stuff and with each uncovering they discovered more and more refined substances. Each degree of refinement brought greater illumination and the discovery of a new set of attributes. Technically, these attributes are classified as *siddhis*, or perfections. Sage Patanjali, who gave us the invaluable aphorisms, or *sutras*, on yoga, calls them *vibhootis*, or accomplishments of yoga. These special attributes are the hidden potential within man that makes him more and more perfect.

By this inner process, the yogis discovered that the source from which the gross body has evolved is pure consciousness, reverberating with energy. This consciousness is cosmic in nature and has no limitations. It is neither bound by time nor confined to any particular space. It pervades each and every form of life and is present in each and every being. The yogic alchemists were also curious to know which part of the body this consciousness inhabits, so they searched further and found that it is the indweller of all

6

hearts. As *jivatman*, or individual consciousness, it rests in the heart cavity, or *anahata chakra*.

The form of individual consciousness is three-dimensional, luminous, laser-like light, which oversees everything and awaits the moment when it can reunite with shakti or energy from whom it has separated for the purpose of creation. At the transcendental level it exists as *bindu*, the primal point, and *nada*, the primal sound, which reverberates through the stratosphere as cosmic vibration and within us as *anahad nada*, the unstruck sound. (VBT sl. 38) The yogis experienced this nada in many forms, such as the melodious notes of the flute (VBT sl. 41), the call of the peacock, the roaring of thunder and also in the various mantras. There are countless descriptions of their experiences in the tantric texts from which it is clear that the consciousness has many degrees of manifestation, whereby it can be experienced as sound, light, form and idea.

When a substance refines itself by separating from or uniting with another substance, either inherent or apart from itself, this is known as alchemy. The tantric seers were the most proficient alchemists of all time. They refined highly subtle forms of matter, such as the human mind, intellect, ego and individual consciousness. The product that emerged from such internal refinement was an experience. This form of experience was so subtle that the human mind could not comprehend it until the attention was turned completely away from matter and focused on spirit. This experience superseded all the varying stages of realization that the ascending shakti had passed through before reuniting with consciousness.

**Principle of reunification**

This reunification led to the realization of oneness of jivatma with *paramatma*, the cosmic consciousness or highest spirit, which inhabits the cranium at a psychic centre known as

7

*sahasrara chakra*. When the jivatma, or individual consciousness residing in the heart cavity, unites with *mahashakti*, the
highest energy, which inhabits the cavity at the base of the
spine known as *mooladhara chakra*, it sets the ground or
foundation for this reunification. It is mahashakti who sets
the wheel of creation into motion at the behest of
consciousness. Her physical form is that of a coiled serpent,
thus she is known as *kundalini*. When she unites with the
individual consciousness in the region of anahata chakra,
the resulting explosion completely overrides the electro-
magnetic circuits of the brain and total illumination occurs
in sahasrara chakra, the abode of Shiva, which has been
described as a thousand-petalled lotus. (VBT sl. 28)

When the matter that constitutes man explodes, an
enormous inner detonation occurs and immense heat is
generated. This inner fire purifies the physical matter to
such a degree that it liberates the inherent energy or shakti,
which in turn frees the consciousness from its clutches. The
equation is thus matter into energy into consciousness, and
vice-versa. The resulting experience of this energy conversion
was so subtle that the yogis were speechless and had no
words to convey it. When asked to describe their experience,
all they could say was, *"Neti, neti"*: not this, not this. The
highest spiritual state cannot be described, explained or
understood; it can only be experienced. Whatever one may
say about that experience, the words fall short. Something
remains unsaid, because there are no words in our vocabulary
to describe that spiritual reality.

The yogis called it light and they were not wrong, but it
was more than that. They also called it *sat-chit-ananda* or
*satyam-shivam-sundaram*, which mean truth, consciousness
and bliss. However, these remain just words until we
transform ourselves and attain that experience. Therefore,
the aim of human life is not mere intellectual understanding
of these sublime truths, but to expand the frontiers of the

mind and liberate the energy in order to have the experience of that supreme consciousness. The source from which all matter has evolved is consciousness. The body is gross matter, the mind is subtle matter and each vibrates with energy. However, on account of their mundane state, the potential to experience that pure consciousness from which they have evolved is lost.

**Expansion and liberation**

In order to achieve this experience, the science of tantra postulates two theories: expansion and liberation. By boiling water, the particles of hydrogen and oxygen are expanded and liberated from the gross form of water and become subtle vapour. In the same way, by expanding the awareness tantra liberates the energy that is locked up in the body and mind. Energy is the link between matter and consciousness. Once it is released from the clutches of matter, it unites with consciousness and a resulting awakening occurs.

In physics the same principle is applied to explode the atom bomb. Through the process of fission or fusion the energy is released from matter and united with its opposite polarity to create this explosion. When the scientist and philosopher, Oppenheimer, watched this event for the first time, he was moved to tears and spontaneously recited aloud a verse from the *Bhagavad Gita*, in which Sanjaya describes this same cosmic experience to the blind monarch, Dhritarashtra.

*Were a thousand suns to light up the sky,*
*still they could not match the light of absolute consciousness.*
(11:12)

Although these two types of explosions are remarkably similar, the difference between them is vast. One takes place externally and the other internally. One destroys, the other creates. One is a part of nature's plan for the destiny of mankind, the other is man's plan for the destiny of mankind. But one thing is clear: the process of alchemy that the tantric and vedic seers employed for this experience was taken from the laws of nature, which are perfectly scientific and apply to all levels of creation. Matter is continually breaking up and transforming into different forms and substances. For example, over a period of time coal changes into diamond and fossils into petroleum and gas. The practices of tantra have been derived through strict observance of these natural processes and their application to man, who is also a product of nature.

Man is destined to awaken this experience at some point of evolution, even if no conscious effort is made to liberate the energy and expand the awareness. This is the natural heritage and birthright of every human being, but without applying a specific procedure it will take a long, long time. The practices of tantra hasten the natural process of evolution and allow that experience to unfold in this life itself, here and now, at this very moment. This experience bestows *ananda* and *jnana*, bliss and knowledge, which man seeks through external objects, but never finds. On account of this, human life is full of misery, frustration and depression. The experience that arises through expansion of consciousness and liberation of energy is the only permanent solution to human suffering.

### Sadhana, the means to realize oneself

In order to liberate the mind from the clutches of matter and turn towards the effulgence of spirit, tantra lays great emphasis on *sadhana*, or practice. Sadhana is a process of internal refinement, which allows man to move towards perfection. What exactly does sadhana refine? Does this process refine just the body or does it extend beyond the body as well? What is the level of perfection that can be attained through sadhana? What is the level of perception of a person who attains that perfection? These are some of the questions that VBT answers. But these answers are not explained; they are provided through a set of practices which leads you to the answer. Each of these practices is complete in itself. One practice does not necessarily lead to another. Each is independent and, at times, even completely different to the preceding or following practice. Often they complement each other, but never do they contradict one another.

It has been the experience of all who have practised sadhana in its pure form that this refinement takes place on several levels. Even on the physical level there are many degrees of refinement. What can be said of the mental and supra-mental levels of perfection? The sadhanas prescribed by tantra are said to bestow the three qualities of omnipotence, the power to do all, omnipresence, the power to be everywhere, and omniscience, the power to know all. These are the qualities of that highest reality. Tantra says that these qualities are attained only when the inner awareness is streamlined and refined. Every form of life is continuously refining itself and moving towards perfection. Sadhana is a way of hastening this process and ensuring that it takes place in a controlled manner.

The basis of sadhana is *abhyasa*, which means regular and uninterrupted practice. If sadhana is interrupted for any reason, it has to be commenced right from the beginning, and not where you left off. This is because the area that you are trying to reach through sadhana is beyond your control. It does not listen to your mind or intellect. How are you going to interact with that which is beyond you? This interaction is only possible through abhyasa. Remember the saying, "Practice makes perfect." Just as you master material knowledge, or *apara vidya*, through constant practice, in the same way, *para vidya*, or transcendental knowledge, is mastered through constant, unbroken practice. The principle is the same, although the subjects differ.

11

## VBT, a text of transcendental knowledge

There are two kinds of knowledge in this world, para and apara, material and transcendental. Sri VBT teaches the practices you need to master in order to gain transcendental knowledge. Mundane knowledge such as physics, chemistry, science, geography astronomy, astrology, mathematics, history, music and the arts all come under the banner of material knowledge, or apara vidya. But do you know what transcendental knowledge or para vidya is? It is a very specialized form of knowledge, for it cannot be known through the medium of words; it can only be realized in the realm of experience. (VBT sl. 6)

No words can fully describe the transcendental experience. In a beautiful Sanskrit ode to Shiva, it has been said that even if Saraswati, the most eloquent goddess of speech, were to use all the paper and ink in the world to describe that transcendental knowledge, she would not be able to describe it to its fullest extent. The words 'paper' and 'ink' would fall short. That transcendental knowledge is beyond words, but it is not beyond experience. This makes VBT very significant for sadhakas, as it is not a book of philosophy but of practice. It does not go into high-sounding philosophies to convince the reader. Instead it lists practice after practice, describing one hundred and twelve different ways to have that transcendental experience. The spectrum these practices cover is so vast that there is a practice for each and every sadhaka, no matter what his inclination and temperament may be.

## Tantra, a unique philosophy

After realizing the principles for achieving this experience, the founders of tantra applied them to every facet of man's personality and explored means and ways to make this sacred knowledge applicable to all who wished to tread the inner path. No matter what kind of person you are, whether sattwic, rajasic or tamasic, tantra offers a way to bring you closer to enlightenment. This is the uniqueness of tantra; it never seeks to reform. Instead it says there is a path for you, whether you are a saint or sinner, religious or atheist, enlightened or ignorant, sensual or abstemious, emotional or intellectual, attached or detached. Even if you are in the clutches of anger, jealousy, hatred, delusion, doubt or hypocrisy, do not wait for the day when you conquer these qualities, but start where you are. Utilize these very same forces that cause you agony to raise your awareness. (VBT sl. 101)

No other philosophy in the world has ever said this. Other systems say that in order to tread the spiritual path you have to be good, kind, noble, merciful, compassionate, disciplined, religious, charitable, and so on. Only then can you be inducted into the path that leads to enlightenment. Tantra says the opposite; it accepts you as you are and does not ask you to do the impossible. Can the average person conquer anger, jealousy and hatred? No, but all the religions ask you to do so. In this way your entire life passes trying to overcome your base nature, and ultimately you are left floundering due to your inability to accomplish that.

Tantra claims that the whole universe is based on the principles of duality. These dual principles of night and day, sun and moon, love and hate, cruelty and compassion, heat and cold, birth and death, are as old as creation itself. One cannot exist without the other. Would it then be correct to deny one and accept the other, to suppress one and express the other, to defame one and glorify the other? Anger is just as much a part of you as love. They are both intimate facets of your personality. How can you ignore either of them?

Tantra does not advocate suppression either, as it leads to severe abnormalities and mental illness. If society today is ailing, it is on account of the suppression imposed on man

13

by his environment. To create a healthy society man should not suppress the base instincts; rather he should transform them by becoming aware of himself. Tantra asks you to awaken the seer within. Human beings alone have the potential to do this. All other forms of life are governed by instinct. It is humans who have the capacity to perform an act and simultaneously know that they are doing so.

Although humans have this potential, they have yet to awaken it. Most people live life unaware. Their actions are performed without awareness. Their lives are mechanical and they remain in the realm of instinct as animals do. For example, few people can remember where their awareness was in a heated situation. Was it on the event or on the emotions that it generated? Most get caught up in the event and lose awareness of themselves. The anger bursts forth and overwhelms them and they cannot stop it. Later, if asked about it, they may even deny their anger.

**Awareness**

There is simply no awareness of the acts performed twenty-four hours of the day. To be aware of an act means to be a witness to what you do, say, think and feel. No matter what you do, there is a part of you that is watching and overseeing everything. This awareness gives you a greater understanding of yourself. You begin to know yourself, your responses and your feelings, which form the inner core of your being. Tantra says the greatest achievement of man is to know oneself. Many philosophies and religions also proclaim that man should know himself, but they seek to reform him, while tantra seeks to educate him by developing the awareness.

What is this awareness? Is it different to the mind and intellect? Where does it dwell? How can it be awakened? Is it inherent in man? These are the questions that tantra deals with and for which it also offers some excellent answers.

14

According to tantra, the mind and awareness are two distinct entities. Just as there is an individual mind and a cosmic mind, there is also an individual awareness and a cosmic awareness. Both are inherent in man. He is born with them and they live on even after the body decays and the mind disintegrates. This individual awareness is known as *chetana*, also defined as individual consciousness. The most significant quality of chetana is illumination.

Chetana is described as self-illumined because it does not require any outside agency for illuminating the jnana, or knowledge, inherent within it. Thus it is the sum total of what you are and acts as the propelling force that unites you with the cosmic awareness. This cosmic union is a unique experience which completely transforms the mind by exploding the atom of knowledge and bliss within it. The entire effort of tantra has always been to achieve this transformation. Every practice prescribed is solely for this purpose and no other.

### Agama and nigama

Tantra is known as agama, as opposed to the Vedas which are known as nigama. *Agama* means 'to carry on' or 'go forward'. The agamas are older than the Vedas. In fact, they are as old as man himself. The birth of agama took place with man's first appearance on this earth, as he passed on the knowledge and experiences he had gained. Agama is not opposed to change and adaptation according to the circumstances and situations that confront man. It readily accepts new ideas or thoughts that are beneficial in man's quest to know himself. Thus many ideas have been added down through the ages as man became more and more aware of the world around him, thereby increasing the vibrancy and dynamism of the agamas. Sage Atharvan classified and coded the agamas that existed under the name of tantra and consolidated them in the *Atharva Veda*, which was named after him. Prior to that, there were only three Vedas. He is responsible for the fourth. He lived in Haryana, and Rishi Vyasa, who was his contemporary, often visited him.

On account of its antiquity tantra has always had a primitive quality and a purity too. In order to practise tantra, one has to shed many of the conditionings acquired as a social animal. Many tantric practices are shunned by society and religion because they leave no room for compromise. The tantric faces life squarely. Can science make any compromises with its discoveries? No, the scientist is ready to give up everything he has believed in, in the event that it is proved wrong. So too is the approach in tantra. The scientist is aware of the complexities of the universe, and the tantric of the complexities of man. New revelations are always being made about man and the universe and, at the same time, they both remain forever a mystery. In this way tantra and science leave room for both eventualities.

The word tantra is made up of two syllables, *tanoti*, which means 'expansion', and *trayati*, 'liberation'. Thus the word tantra has vast connotations. It signifies the expansion of mind and liberation of energy from the clutches of matter, whereby the light of consciousness illumines the entire being. What exactly is expansion of mind? Ordinarily you see, hear, feel, think and act through the medium of the senses. But there is a dimension where you can experience sound, smell, form, taste and touch in the absence of any external object, without the medium of the senses, and that is known as expansion of mind. (VBT sl. 55)

When the mind disassociates from sensory perception through the practice of *pratyahara*, or sensory withdrawal, and turns its attention to the chetana, or awareness residing within that watches and oversees everything, then all the finite boundaries are broken and it assumes the quality of consciousness, which is expansion. In Sanskrit, consciousness is known as *Brahman*, which is derived from the root *bri*, meaning 'to expand'. Consciousness is forever expanding and reaching out everywhere. It is not limited or restricted in any way. Thus it gives the experience of the physical world that exists in time and space as well as the metaphysical world which exists beyond time and space. As consciousness expands everywhere, it knows everything and thus has been defined as absolute knowledge. The final aim of tantra is to give man absolute knowledge. Imagine a society where men and women have attained this state. Is this not a solution to many of our problems? So, through the practices of tantra man seeks his own individual liberation, but society and the world are liberated as a consequence.

**VBT, a tantric text of the Shaiva tradition**

The practices described in VBT are all methods for expanding the mind or awareness, thereby releasing the energy locked up in the gross matter which constitutes the body. Thus it is classified as a tantric text of the Shaiva tradition, not as a text of yoga, although many of these practices are also taught in yoga. Actually, tantra and yoga are one and the same. Yoga is 'union' and tantra is 'expansion' through that state of union.

The sacred tradition of Shiva is known as Shaivism. Shiva's antecedents are so remote that it is difficult to separate fact from fiction. However, it is certain that he was a yogi who attained the highest spiritual eminence, that of supreme consciousness, through intense and rigorous spiritual life. Today he is worshipped throughout the length and breadth of the Indian subcontinent and far beyond as the supreme awareness into which everything merges and dissolves. He is the bestower of boons. His followers are known as *Shaivites*, just as the followers of the sacred tradition of Vishnu are known as *Vaishnavites*, and those of the Shakti tradition are known as *Shaktas*.

17

Apart from these three traditions, in ancient times there were two more which still exist today in some regions of India. They are *Ganapatya*, worshippers of Ganesha, found in Maharashtra, and *Saura*, worshippers of the sun, found in Bihar. Thus you have Shaiva Tantra, Vaishnava Tantra, Shakta Tantra, Saura Tantra and Ganapatya Tantra. The underlying beliefs of these traditions are derived from tantra, which is the mother of all philosophies, traditions, sects, beliefs and practices. Tantra is the oldest spiritual culture in the world, even older than the Vedas.

Within these traditions there are further divisions that can be identified by three distinct systems of thought. They are: *Advaita*, knowledge of the one supreme reality, *Dvaita*, knowledge of one supreme reality that appears as duality in the relative world, and *Traita*, where the one supreme reality appears as three-fold. This is the age-old question: whether the supreme reality is one, two or many. Sri VBT resolves this question by asserting that it is all of these. It postulates one reality, or consciousness, which has two aspects: transcendental and immanent. The former is beyond manifestation and the latter pervades the universe of manifest phenomena in a multiplicity of forms. Both are real, says VBT, for the effect cannot be different from the cause.

This supreme consciousness eternally alternates between two phases, 'rest' and 'action', i.e., transcendent and immanent. The transcendental phase is a period of potentiality, technically described as the state of *pralaya,* or dissolution, when matter becomes dormant in the bosom of consciousness. The immanent phase, where matter becomes manifest, is technically called *srishti,* creation. In this way consciousness is eternally expressing itself through its passive and active phases.

Shaivism too is further divided into two main systems: *Kashmir Shaivism,* which flourished in Northern India, and *Shaiva Siddhanta,* which flourished in Southern India.

Kashmir was the birthplace of Shaivism. Eminent scholars, saints and pandits born there expounded its philosophy as well as codifying and explaining its practices. It is a sublime philosophy classified as the *Spanda Shastras*, doctrine of vibration, and *Pratyabhijna*, doctrine of recognition. In very classical and technical terms it describes the root of creation as *spandan*, vibration, and how the individual can once again recognize his true nature or the essence of reality. VBT is a text of Kashmir Shaivism and forms a part of the *Rudrayamala Tantra*. This literally means the tantra of the union between Rudra and his Shakti, which in modern terms represents the union of consciousness and energy. This text expounds the Trika philosophy, which relates to the Traita system of thought and is the basis of Shaivism as it flourished in Kashmir in the seventh century. (VBT sl. 1)

Trika, as the name implies, deals with the three-fold principle of shakti or energy: para, parapara and apara. The first principle, *para*, is the reality perceived as transcendent. The second, *apara*, is the reality perceived as immanent. The third, *parapara*, is the intermediate stage when traces of both are perceived. These three divisions of shakti or energy are expressed through the triple division of shiva, shakti and nara, or consciousness, energy and matter. VBT, being essentially based on the Trika philosophy, describes how to experience that supreme state of consciousness which is transcendental and immanent in its pristine purity.

**Author of VBT**

As the awareness increases through sadhana, varying stages of consciousness are experienced. Although these experiences are perceived by the mind and remembered by the chitta (memory), they belong to a higher realm of existence. These states are classified as the *sapta bhumikas,* or seven levels of existence. The first is *bhuh*, which corresponds to the gross physical awareness, followed by *bhuvah*, which is

19

the intermediate plane between the physical and the divine. Beyond bhuvah is *svahah,* which corresponds to the plane of divinity where the experiences are full of luminosity, radiance and light. The next plane is *mahah,* the abode of realized beings, the saints and siddhas. *Janah* is the next plane of the seers or rishis, who can create worlds and manifest matter. This is followed by *tapah,* which is the plane of liberated souls, and the highest is *satya,* the level of absolute truth.

These planes of existence are like a ladder with seven rungs which the awareness must ascend in order to experience the ultimate truth. Tantra says that these sapta bhumikas, or seven states of consciousness, are enshrined within each one of us, and describes in meticulous detail the different experiences a sadhaka undergoes on this journey. These different states of awareness have been clearly defined, categorized and explained in the tantric texts and they are also represented by the different tantric sects. For instance, the *Aghoras* are a sect of tantrics whose consciousness is described as being totally attuned with nature. They can understand, converse with, influence, as well as control all natural phenomena. Nothing in nature or creation is abhorrent to them because they experience total and complete unity with nature.

The *Paramahamsas* are a sect whose consciousness is established beyond the state of duality. The word *paramahamsa* means the 'great swan'. It is a befitting word to describe this state of awareness, as here the consciousness is so refined that it begins to separate the essence from the form in much the same way as the swan is able to separate milk from water. At this point the awareness is three-fold, sometimes inner, sometimes outer, and often both simultaneously. The *Vairagis* are another sect of tantric practitioners, who experience intense detachment from the material phenomena and an attraction or pull towards the spiritual. The word *vairagya* means 'non-attachment' and the vairagis are known to transcend matter, which is a very rare and elevated state of awareness. Very few people in this world have true and constant vairagya.

Sannyasa is also an ancient order whose roots are found in the tantric tradition and it represents a state of consciousness where there is total surrender to the universal consciousness. The totality of one's being: the body, mind and soul, is offered to the will of the divine. This is a choiceless awareness and very difficult to attain. To become constant in this state of awareness, one must seek a guru or illumined being and live in total surrender in order to imbibe this awareness from him. The word *sannyasa* means 'trustee'. A sannyasi is a trustee of all that he is, and entrusts himself to the higher will to use as He wants. The basis of surrender is inner faith, without which surrender does not flourish and blossom as it should.

*Bhairava* is another tantric sect which represents a higher state of consciousness where the awareness is able to perceive and experience the three principles of creation, sustenance and annihilation. This is an epithet of Shiva, who is Bhairava, and his consort Parvati is Bhairavi. Just as sannyasa is both a state of mind and an order, known as Dashnam, so too there is an order, or *sampradaya*, known as Bhairava. In this tradition there are eight Bhairavas, known as: Batuka Bhairava, Kaala Bhairava, Shanta Bhairava, Ananda Bhairava, Vijnana Bhairava, and so on. Perhaps they were disciples of Shiva who attained that state under his tutelage and were given that epithet, just as sannyasins today have ten names, such as Saraswati, Puri, Giri, and so on. In that sense, it may not be wrong to surmise that *Vijnana Bhairava Tantra* is an epithet on Tantra, written by a person known as Vijnana Bhairava. Just as you have the *Yoga Sutras* by Patanjali, the *Dharmashastras* by Jaimini, etc., so too you have the Tantra by Vijnana Bhairava. Perhaps the dialogue between Shiva and Parvati took place in his presence.

VBT was evidently written when this philosophy was at its zenith or pinnacle. Each philosophy has a life that can be divided into three periods: growth, establishment and decline. The directness and strength of the assertions made by the author point to the fact that VBT was written when this philosophy was fully accepted and very popular. At the time of growth and decline a philosophy is compelled to add unnecessary ideas and beliefs in order to survive. But when it is at its peak, it does not have to compromise and can say exactly what it wants to. The book itself is a masterpiece and every sadhaka will realize that. Without fuss and fanfare, it describes many different ways to focus and hold the awareness so that inner illumination can occur. It is an encyclopaedia on tantra; as it sums up its multifaceted philosophy through simple and clear instructions on practices that lead to expansion of mind and liberation of energy. VBT is an invaluable text for anyone who wants to know what tantra really is and what it has to offer.

The text is presented in the form of a dialogue between Shiva and his consort, Parvati, and in the very first sloka we eavesdrop on a conversation between them. This is an exchange between two lovers, who also happen to be husband and wife as well as guru and disciple, and represent the universal principles of consciousness and energy. They are extraordinary in the sense that they have attained luminosity and shine with knowledge. At one time they must have walked on this earth like you and me, but today they are worshipped as *devata* and *devi*, the illumined ones. This divine couple often have such dialogues. Parvati, the kinetic energy principle, raises some high-sounding metaphysical and philosophical questions, and Shiva, the conscious or intelligent principle, answers them. These dialogues are the basis of the agamas. They were revealed to enlightened sadhakas and then passed down through successive ages.

Tantra says these revelations are the birthright of each one of us. This knowledge is inherent in us, but we cannot avail ourselves of it until and unless there is expansion of mind and liberation of energy. Then we too can overhear the dialogues between Shiva and his consort, Parvati. One may wonder why Parvati, who is illumined herself, needs to ask these questions of Shiva. Surely she must know all the answers, as she is not different to Shiva. They are both knowledge personified, and it is their *anugraha*, or grace, that compels them to present this knowledge to us for our evolution. It is their love for humankind and intense desire for their upliftment that motivates them to discuss these matters. She is primordial energy and he is primordial consciousness. He is grace and she is receptivity. As an evolute of consciousness, she is a part of him. Still there is a need to raise this question because he is the principle of knowledge and she is the principle of experience.

**Creation**

Classically there are no barriers of knowledge between Shiva and Shakti as long as they are united. However, when Shiva sends Shakti forth to create the manifest world through her three attributes of *jnana* (knowledge) *kriya* (action) and *iccha* (will), the limitations appear in the form of doubts on account of the separation. This is the same plight which the *jiva*, the individual soul, finds itself in when it is separated from the cosmic soul. Doubts and dissensions appear as the experience of unity with the cosmic soul fades into memory and only a dim recollection of it remains. It is similar to losing something very precious and striving to find it once again. The jiva spends the entire life doing just that. But on account of this lapse of awareness, he looks for his counterpart in the objects of the world rather than within.

Just as Shakti initiates the dialogue, we raise questions as to the nature of the highest reality, *Paramshiva*. It is not that

23

we do not know the answers, but we have forgotten and need to be reminded. So, Shiva reminds Parvati of his true nature, and through her we too are reminded. Shakti is the medium of Shiva. She transmits his grace, knowledge and compassion to us. Without Shakti, Shiva remains inert, motionless and immersed in self-contemplation. She is the doorway to Shiva and brings him alive for us. She creates that experience in us, for she is the creative matrix, or Mother of the universe.

In the doctrine of Kashmir Shaivism, the source of VBT, Shiva is described as the ultimate reality in which there is no distinction of subject or object. He is *prakasha*, the eternal light, which illumines everything. His cosmic counterpart, Shakti, is described as vimarsha, the *svabhava,* or nature of Shiva. *Vimarsha* is that aspect of prakasha by which it knows itself. Shakti is the mirror, so to speak, in which Shiva realizes his own grandeur. This is why the feminine principle, or Shakti, is most important in tantra. Without her consent the experience of Shiva is just not possible. He reveals himself only through her, thus initiating the process of evolution. (VBT sl. 20 & 21)

At the cosmic level she remains forever by his side, entwined around him, seated in his lap in a loving embrace. But when Shiva has the will to create, he sends Shakti forth with her three attributes: jnana shakti, kriya shakti and iccha shakti, which are transformed into sattwa, rajas and tamas, the three gunas or qualities of nature. The interplay of these gunas gives rise to the manifest world, and they are present in each and every speck of creation in differing proportions. Tantric philosophy postulates that the universe of matter and energy has evolved out of primordial nature or Shakti, who represents pure energy. Her cosmic counterpart and co-creator is Shiva, or pure consciousness, who exists as conscious intelligence, distinct from her and her derivatives. In the original state Shiva is forever immanent

24

and eternal but inactive, as opposed to Shakti, who is forever immanent and eternal but active.

Although Shiva and Shakti separate momentarily, giving rise to the individual consciousness, in their cosmic manifestation they forever exist side by side. So there are both cosmic and individual aspects of Shiva and Shakti. In the individual aspect Shiva and Shakti appear as dual forces only due to the obscuring power of *maya*, the illusory force, inherent in the shakti principle. Shiva and Shakti together give rise to the *avyakta*, or unmanifest cosmos, as well as the *vyakta*, or manifest universe. The first manifestations of the cosmic process of creation are known as nada, bindu and kalaa. *Nada* literally means 'vibration'. As a part of the unmanifest creation, it exists as the cosmic vibration or spandan. In the vyakta, or manifest creation, it exists as sound of varying frequencies. *Bindu* represents a point or nucleus, and *kalaa* is a ray or force which emanates from the nucleus, or bindu, due to vibrations created by nada.

The cosmic manifestations of Shiva and Shakti as nada, bindu and kalaa interact and give rise to the gross and subtle elements of which man is composed. It is considered that the human being is composed of thirty-six tattwas, or elements, that cover the entire spectrum of human existence and experience on the gross, subtle and causal levels. So, on the one hand, we are pure, untainted consciousness and, on the other hand, we are also gross, tangible matter. In order to realize our source, we will have to refine the perception of ourselves. While most religions and philosophies have advocated moral and spiritual disciplines to accomplish this refinement, tantra advocates *abhyasa*, or constant, unbroken practice.

**Four upayas or processes**

The range of sadhana according to tantra and more specifically Kashmir Shaivism has been broadly classified under four heads, known as *upayas*, means or processes. These four upayas are: anupaya, anavopaya, shaktopaya and sambhavopaya. Although these classifications may coincide with the sadhana traditions according to other philosophies, they are distinctly related to the system of Trika philosophy, which forms the basis of Kashmir Shaivism.

*Anu* means 'little' and *anupaya* occurs when the spiritual state is attained through little or no means; just a casual hint from the guru is enough for the aspirant to enter the mystic state. Such a rare case is known as anupaya and naturally it is intended only for the advanced aspirant. Anava, shakta and sambhava upayas are definite techniques through which inner realization dawns, but anupaya has no technique. It just happens on account of grace which is showered on the sadhaka. The practices in VBT all fall under these four upayas; however, they are not watertight compartments. The aspirant has to pass from anava to shakta and finally to sambhava. One upaya leads to another, and the realization of sambhavopaya is the highest.

In *sambhavopaya*, the means of approach to the Divine is alertness, which is passive not aggressive. The alertness is fully directed to the present moment, not the past or the future. This upaya is amply illustrated in VBT. Many of the practices employ this upaya to raise the awareness. VBT advocates awareness of the present moment and what one may be experiencing at that time. There is a sense of choicelessness in this upaya, as there is no object or support on which the awareness is to be steadied or fixed. Rather the awareness is withdrawn and ceases to play an active role, thereby becoming supportless. When the awareness loses its accustomed support it turns within, but as it does not know what to expect there, it has no choice. There is an element of spontaneity in this state, and it is highly creative as the alertness becomes steady and vigilant. This is the state of watchful awareness.

In *shaktopaya* too, the awareness is not steadied on any object; there is no concentration or meditation on anything. In this upaya the awareness is used for seeking the source from where it has arisen, and for seriously turning the philosophical attention towards what exactly is meant by the 'I' or self. It is used to experience and thus understand the deeper significance of mantras and the supreme consciousness, which is the source of all mantras. By focusing on this upaya, the awareness is elevated through the bhavana of faith, sanctified and ultimately transformed by the energy of the mantra, so that the aspirant intuitively realizes the supreme reality, which is his own self. Shaktopaya is also not possible for everyone; it is intended for those who are already spiritually oriented. It is a process of self-enquiry. Ramana Maharishi is the best example of shaktopaya. The *alambana*, or support, of the awareness in shaktopaya is the essential self, which is a very fluid support.

In *anavopaya* the case is different. Here anu, the limited, conditioned individual, takes up some limited aspect, such as buddhi, prana, or some object in space, from which he starts his practice of dharana. He uses this as a support in order to concentrate the full potential of his awareness on one specific thing. Most practitioners come under this category. They are unable to focus the awareness on the present moment unless they have an alambana, or support. This support is selected on the basis of one's swabhava, the innate or inherent nature which one is born with, not on the social, moral or religious nature which one picks up as one goes along.

### Awareness of the present moment

The innate nature has spontaneous likes and dislikes, and the support is chosen on the basis of what one is naturally drawn to, so that the awareness is completely absorbed by it and thereby drawn to the present moment. This is a very important factor in meditation. Every practitioner has to know that unless he can remain in the present moment, the awareness cannot enter the area of timelessness. In this state the past, present and future become one timeless eternity, transcending time, space and object, wherein the Self, which is beyond these three aspects of material existence, is experienced.

In actual fact, to progress in sadhana what the sadhaka has to realize is that the divisions of time which we have created are not real. Time is absolute, but it exists only in the present. As far as the dimension of time is concerned there is no past or future, just the present which we experience every moment. Past and future are a fallacy in relation to time. If they appear real to us, it is only because we relate time to events, but this is an absolutely wrong understanding of time.

Past and present exist only in relation to events. It is the mind that associates past experiences within an imaginary time frame. In actual fact the past does not exist nor does the future. But we imagine them to be real because the mind continues to relive past impressions of events that have created a strong impact on it, or projects itself into the future and hallucinates about what will happen, say ten years from now. This does not mean that the future is real, for you may cease to exist before that. It is only the mind that perceives it as such, because it is habituated to brooding over events that have occurred, and on the basis of past experience it projects into the future.

In Sanskrit, time is known as *kaala*, that which devours and consumes everything in creation. Shiva is known as *Mahakaala*, the great time, and his consort is *Kali*, the destroyer of time. She is depicted standing on top of Shiva, wearing a garland of skulls. Her tongue hangs out, dripping with blood, and she holds a noose and sharp weapons in her hands. Kali symbolizes the death or eradication of our false

28

notions of time relating to past and future, while Mahakaala symbolizes timelessness. So when VBT says to live in the present, what it actually means is that the sadhaka has to separate the mind from events and connect it to time in the absolute sense, or kaala. (VBT sl. 52)

Therefore, the sadhaka is asked to fix his mind on an object so that he remains focused in the present. The mind may repeatedly wander and stray to events that have happened in life, but he has to bring it back to the object. With practice, the awareness becomes steady, fixed and focused on the object and on the space that it occupies in the present moment or time. Gradually the three: time, space and object, merge into one another and there is an explosive experience at the nucleus, or bindu, of the psychic centres where they meet. These centres are within the physical body and are vortexes of nadis, or pranic currents, that carry the flow of vital energy throughout the body. (VBT sl. 29)

## Role of dharana in VBT, tantra and yoga

The sutra of sambhavopaya is: *chaitanyam atma*, the awareness is light. In shaktopaya it is: *chittam mantra*, the awareness is mantra. In anavopaya, the first sutra is: *chittam atma*, the awareness is atma. In shaktopaya, jnana is emphasized, and in anavopaya, kriya. These upayas can be classified as dharana, which means total focus on any one object, thought, idea, feeling, remembrance, person or act. The word *dharana* literally means 'to hold' or 'to possess'. The state of dharana is attained when you are able to hold or possess something to the exclusion of all else in *chidakasha*, the space of consciousness. Success in dharana leads to *dhyana*, or meditation, which is the state of complete and spontaneous absorption in the object of dharana. Then you are led without any effort to the state of consciousness known as bhairava.

The upayas or means of approaching the enlightened state as described in VBT all come under the practice of dharana. Most yoga sadhakas or practitioners are familiar with this term. It is the sixth stage of *ashtanga yoga*, the eightfold path of yoga, which immediately precedes dhyana or meditation. Dharana is one-pointed focus on something and dhyana is the state of total, unbroken awareness of that. Total awareness means awareness of only one thing and no other, whether it is a form, an idea, a feeling, an act or an experience. To attain this state you can choose anything that can spontaneously, effortlessly and totally absorb you: body, mind and soul. This absorption leads to *samadhi*, or total illumination. From this it can be understood how important the practice of dharana is in the path to enlightenment. Without perfection of dharana, no progress can be made in this direction. In fact, once dharana is mastered, the aspirant does not have to make any further effort to attain enlightenment. Dhyana, or meditation, and samadhi, inner illumination, follow as a natural consequence of dharana. If any effort at all has to be made, it is only to sustain that experience in our daily lives.

In yoga, the aspirant is asked to master the disciplines of *yama* and *niyama*, which are codes of conduct for the body and mind. Then he has to master *asana*, the body postures, and *pranayama*, the breathing techniques, which stimulate the flow of energy, balance and direct it to the higher centres. After this he has to achieve the enormous task of pratyahara, withdrawal of the senses and awareness from the external stimuli and directing them within. Then in dharana the awareness is focused on whatever object he chooses to create mentally. The only difference is that the object he creates within is not comprised of matter, but of consciousness. Later, when the aspirant becomes proficient in this art, he can even recreate the same thing in the tangible world for all to see. Many yogis have attained this state and become co-creators. In relation to yoga, the system of tantra, and more specifically VBT, takes up the spiritual journey from a higher point. It does not impose the codes of conduct and other preliminary steps of yoga, but simply asks one to select a point of dharana and dive deep into it.

## Obstacles in sadhana

We are all subject to the pull of gravity on account of which we forever rotate in the cycle of creation. We are unable to get out of that pull because of our material existence, which makes us heavy and tamasic in a physical as well as spiritual sense. Quite literally, in the meditative process we have to become light. When this lightness pervades our being, then it becomes possible to break out of the pull of gravity and experience luminosity, radiance, knowledge and peace. There is a transition period for the awareness when it leaves the field of gravity and enters other dimensions. Difficulties can occur before the awareness becomes accustomed to and stabilized in these dimensions. Then again if there is some fault in the process of sadhana, these difficulties obstruct the success of the sadhaka's endeavour.

This is because *prakriti*, or nature, steps in and prevents the sadhaka from making further progress by creating *samshaya* (doubt), *alasya* (laziness), *nidra* (sleep), *bhaya* (fear) and *dosha* (disease). These obstructions are in-built and natural. Often you may not even realize that nature is trying to tell you that something has gone wrong. Perhaps you are doing too much sadhana or your diet is in incorrect or you have not received or followed the instructions from the guru. You have to learn to read the signals, so that when obstructions occur during sadhana, you are aware of them and can take the appropriate measures. For instance, excess practice, wrong diet, arising of deep-rooted samskaras, and purification on subtle and causal levels may cause imbalance for a time. Success depends on unflinching allegiance to the practices at this point. If you falter, the awareness once again drops. If you do not falter, the awareness is elevated.

Along with commitment to the practices, another important expedient for overcoming obstructions in sadhana is to live amongst people who have a raised awareness. This helps a great deal as their heightened awareness uplifts all those who come in contact with them, resolving many obstacles effortlessly. This contact is possible in an ashram where the environment is built up over the years by the positive vibrations of the people who inhabit it, so that even a chance visit to such a place is very uplifting and resolves many difficulties and obstructions in one's sadhana.

**Awareness in dharana**

In relation to sadhana, dharana represents the transition to a higher dimension, where the awareness is completely withdrawn from the senses and crystallized at one point. At other times it is scattered and dissipated, fixing itself on whatever catches its fancy, then dropping that for something else. Dharana trains the awareness to hold onto whatever object has been chosen without fluctuation. It is not a process of thinking, but of seeing. The mind plays no part in this process. If the mind is active, then dharana does not take place. In dharana the faculty of chetana, or awareness, which is subtler than the mind, becomes active. Chetana has the ability to illumine the object on which it is focused. You can try it for yourself. Whenever you have to solve a problem, quieten the mind and focus the awareness on it. You will surely find the solution.

Dharana utilizes that very same awareness that you focus on solving day-to-day problems. You have to train that awareness to focus inwards and crystallize on one point. Once you are able to do that, the inner path you are to traverse and later the destination are gradually revealed. At first, the inner point may appear hazy and unfamiliar, but later it will attract your awareness like nothing has attracted you before, on account of the *anandam*, or bliss, it generates

32

within. At this point you will be pervaded by feelings of well-being, love, oneness and totality, but until this arises you must continue practising, for it is well worth the effort. Dharana is an invaluable accomplishment that surpasses all others; it is the epitome of human achievement. All other achievements pale in comparison.

## Perception

Your mind is the mirror through which you see the world. Whatever your mind perceives becomes the truth for you, as you see it that way, but that may not be the ultimate perception. As your mind grows the perceptions change, and they keep changing all the time. Perception is actually a quality of the higher mind. The mind that perceives is pure awareness. Knowledge filters through it easily, as there are no barriers of time, space or object to hinder the free flow of knowledge. In fact, it can be said that pure knowledge is nothing but homogenous, unbroken awareness. Based on perception, the awareness keeps sending information to the mind to guide you.

On the conscious plane the mind has another source of information, the *indriyas*, or organs of knowledge and action. Sometimes the two sources contradict one another, and at other times one source of information is clearer or more convincing than the other, so that becomes your perception. Sensory perception is severely limiting and often an inaccurate way of perceiving things. This is because the senses are finite; their existence depends on time, space and object. The senses cannot exist if these three factors are absent. The senses have limitations because of their finite nature. Moreover, they are not independent sources of knowledge; they need the cognizing powers of manas, the rational mind, to understand the information they receive and the discriminative powers of the intellect, or buddhi, to determine truth from falsehood. Apart from the mind and

33

intellect, the senses are also governed by the ego, or ahamkara, which assesses the knowledge in relation to oneself. Awareness, on the other hand, is infinite, having no beginning and no end. It is totally independent of the mind, senses, intellect and ego. The awareness, or chetana, is present in each and every one of us. How to develop this awareness is the subject matter of VBT. This is a very important subject because our performance in life depends on it at every level, whether physical, emotional, intellectual or spiritual. If you analyze carefully, you will discover that the sum total of life is not the number of years you have lived, but what you have perceived of it. Your awareness of life is, in fact, the reality of your life, more so than your muscles, bones and body. Without awareness or perception, the body would be of no use to you at all.

So then the question arises: if this awareness exists independently of the body and mind, where does it reside and what is its link with the body and mind? The abode of awareness is best described through a beautiful analogy of the lotus flower that is born and lives in muddy water, yet remains unsoiled and untouched by it. Awareness is all pervading within and without you. It exists in each and every cell, atom and molecule that you are made up of. It is present all around you too in each and every form. Nature is sentient and ripe with awareness.

**Establishing the pranic link**

Tantra asserts that the link between the body, mind and awareness is prana, which is a direct evolute of consciousness and is described as the medium for the awakening and ascent of consciousness. Our being or existence as an individual entity can be categorized into five sheaths or bodies. The physical body is known as *annamaya kosha*, the food or material energy sheath, and the mind as *manomaya kosha*, the mental energy sheath. In between these two is an electro-magnetic field known as *pranamaya kosha*, which is the vital energy sheath. This field of vital energy surrounds, pervades and sustains the physical body and acts as a vital link between the body and mind. Therefore, prana is the bridge between the body and mind, and it also connects the mind to the psychic field, or causal body, which is known as *vijnanamaya kosha*, the sheath of special or higher knowledge. The fifth sheath is the blissful body, or *anandamaya kosha*, where prana remains in its pure state of harmony, bliss and luminosity. Thus prana is most important as it sustains all dimensions of existence.

According to tantra, the subtle nature of prana is spandan, or pure vibration, at a very high frequency. Consciousness is not yet trapped in matter at this level, so cosmic prana, or spandan, is the vibratory field of pure consciousness. Just as consciousness has varying states of manifestation, prana too evolves through three different levels of energy in its descent from pure consciousness by which it can be known, intensified, channelled and merged back into its source, consciousness. These three levels of prana are also characterized by their quality of spandan or vibration on account of which the electro-magnetic field of prana surrounding the body is continuously expanding and contracting. It is this perpetual activity of expansion and contraction in the pranic field that is responsible for all dimensions of experience in life. When this activity diminishes or ceases, life itself is extinguished and all individual experience and perception retreats into the causal body, or vijnanamaya kosha.

In relation to creation the first level of emanation is *Pranashakti*, or cosmic prana, which is the creative aspect of pure consciousness. It is the energy inherent within consciousness which sets the evolutionary cycle into motion and brings forth all animate and inanimate beings. Pranashakti is responsible for the entire creation: sun, moon,

35

stars, animals, vegetables, trees, rivers and mountains; they are all evolutes of Pranashakti. In the absence of Pranashakti, all of creation would disintegrate and cease to exist. Pranashakti is represented in the physical body as kundalini, also known as the serpent power, lying in three and a half coils at the base of the spine. This dormant power is the main focus of tantra, which claims that spiritual experience commences only when it is awakened. The experiences prior to that belong to the physical, mental or psychic plane. The awareness becomes internalized only when Pranashakti is aroused, begins her ascent and crosses manipura chakra at the navel.

In VBT the first set of dharanas are devoted to this event (VBT sl. 24–31) because without this achievement the dharanas that follow will remain purely mental exercises. In order to attain the experiences described in the later dharanas on *nada* (primal sound), *shoonya* (void), *bhavana* (intense emotion), *japa* (spontaneous repetition of mantras), *kshobha* (mental agitation), *vikalpas* (thoughts), it is necessary that the Pranashakti moves out of her abode at the base of the spine into the sushumna nadi to unite with Paramshiva. The esoteric traditions of tantra that relate to individual practice deal purely with this event, which they ascribe to the control, restraint and reversal of two important pranic flows of the body, known as *prana* and *apana*. These pranas are evolutes of that Pranashakti and are controlled by her.

This brings us to the second level of that cosmic prana where it manifests as an individual force. This evolute of Pranashakti is also known as Prana, which can be understood as prana with a capital 'P', as it is responsible for the entire individual existence, which includes the five energy bodies described above. This individual prana draws sustenance from the cosmic prana at all times, as the link between the two is never severed. You may say that the individual prana is connected to its source, the cosmic prana, through anandamaya kosha, which acts as an invisible umbilical cord in much the same way as a foetus is connected to its mother in the womb for nine months. In this sense the cosmic prana is the original mother from whom we draw nourishment throughout our lives.

The individual prana is responsible for all the mental and physical functions as well as the pranic field, which is divided into five main categories: prana, samana, apana, udana, and vyana. This five-fold manifestation of prana is under the voluntary control of the individual prana and is guided by its counterpart, the conscious principle. Prana is generated in the individual through various means, such as *anna*, or food, which generates physical prana; *shvasa*, or breath, which generates vital prana; *vichara*, or thoughts, which generate mental prana; and *bhakti bhavana*, or higher feelings, which generate spiritual prana. These pranic flows form the basis of the first set of dharanas in VBT. The claim of tantra is that Shakti is the doorway to Shiva (VBT sl. 17). It is through the medium of Shakti that we can know Shiva. Thus it is easy to understand why VBT employs the pranic flows in the body, which are the manifestation of Shakti, to reach this experience. You cannot know the source from which they have sprung until and unless the pranic flows merge.

The third manifestation of prana is the breath which you involuntarily breathe 21,600 times each day for the entire span of life, thereby oxygenating and energizing all the cells and tissues of the body. The link between body and mind can be established very easily through awareness of the breath, which is the gross medium of prana. The pulsation of prana within the breath emits the subtle sound of '*So*' during inhalation and '*Ham*' during exhalation. As this sound accompanies each breath, it is the *ajapa japa* mantra, or the spontaneous mantra, which never ceases. (VBT sl. 155b) The mantra of the breath can be perceived at varying levels, ranging from the audible to the inaudible, unstruck sound. Dharana can be done on the mantra of the breath at all of these levels.

Along with the pranic flows, the breath too is an important base for dharana in VBT and also in other tantric and yogic practices. This is understandable as breath is life, and it is also the very force of creation. Thus awareness of the upward flow of prana and downward flow of apana can be accentuated by following the movement of the breath in the body. This is done through the practice of pranayama by becoming aware of the inward and outward breath, as well as the point when the breath stops before it turns from inward to outward and from outward to inward. When the breath stops, either inside or outside, that is known as *kumbhaka*. The point where the breath stops is known as *dwadashanta*, which literally means 'the end of twelve'. The dwadashanta for internal kumbhaka is at the heart centre and for external kumbhaka is an imaginary point twelve fingers away from *nasikagra*, or tip of the nose.

Through dharana on the dwadashanta, one gradually regulates the *ayama,* or 'length', of prana to twelve *angulas,* or finger-widths, internally and twelve angulas externally from the body. Thus VBT offers a vital clue as to the precise ayama of prana required for heightening the awareness. These two points are the ideal distance for the prana to travel externally away from the body as well as internally into the body. By this form of dharana the loss of prana is controlled and with practice even stopped altogether. When loss of prana ceases, its intensity doubles and triples. This heightened prana halts degeneration and illumines the entire being. (VBT sl. 64) This is why the breath plays a very important role in the practices of tantra as well as the dharanas of VBT.

The breath has to be regulated in such a way that it gains maximum potency. Sometimes the breath regulates itself spontaneously without effort. At that time we will feel calm, relaxed and blissful. But this does not happen unless we flow with the natural body rhythms, which are the rhythms of nature. We are so out of tune with these rhythms that the breath is irregular all the time. The influence of the breath on the mind is so great that dharana will not take place if the breath is disturbed. Irregularities in breathing are reflected in the body as disease and in the mind as turmoil and disturbance. Any impurity or obstruction in the nadis or pranic channels will also affect the mind and cause disturbance and disruption of dharana. Therefore, it is necessary to regulate the breath and purify the pranas and nadis throughout the body in order to attain the full experience of dharana. In many of the dharanas, although prana is not the point of focus, it still plays an underlying part in the practice.

It is also possible to connect with the cosmic consciousness by awakening the chakras, or psychic energy centres in the body, which function as pranic generators and accumulators. The chakras are connected to the brain and have a very strong link with the awareness, a sort of hotline, you may say. One of these centres is mooladhara, situated at the base of the spine, where the latent spiritual energy resides. When fully activated, this energy shoots up to sahasrara, the highest centre at the crown of the head. After uniting with the cosmic awareness in this centre, the spiritual energy descends along the same route back down to mooladhara, irrigating all the psychic centres one by one, before returning to her abode.

After regulating and purifying the prana, it is important to channel or direct it to the appropriate psychic centres where consciousness is high, so that an experience occurs which can totally transform your being and take you to an enlightened state of consciousness. (VBT sl. 29) The tantric and vedic texts contain numerous dialogues, discourses and debates, which describe examples and experiences of people who have attained this state. From these we learn that it is possible to reach that state, as others before have done, through constant, unbroken practice under the guidance of a guru.

## Transmission of knowledge

The tantric guru is more of a transmitter than a teacher. His method of teaching is very subtle and refined. The transmission of knowledge takes place directly between the guru and disciple, if there is a connection between them. Although the guru does teach through the medium of speech, the real lessons take place on a different dimension where there are no barriers. In this way his knowledge reaches the disciple immediately, pure and intact. It is like turning on a switch and at once light appears. Great importance has been given to the guru factor in any spiritual practice. In fact, it has been said that sadhana does not bear fruit without the blessings of a guru. It is, therefore, necessary to emphasize this point so that you do not waste your time and wonder why you are not able to progress.

In Sri VBT the entire dialogue between Shiva and Parvati takes place between them as guru and disciple. They assume these roles before knowledge is imparted primarily because it is only through discipleship that one receives any form of knowledge, whether it is material or transcendental, para or apara. A disciple is one who has surrendered himself to the guru. He is pure receptivity, and presents no barrier to the transmission of knowledge, because through surrender he has become egoless. This is a prerequisite for the transmission of knowledge between guru and disciple, and we can easily understand why. It is only through egolessness that one can connect with the channel through which knowledge is transmitted. That transmission is very subtle and ego is too gross to receive it.

40

The knowledge that is transmitted reaches the higher mind, or chetana, and there is illumination within the disciple. Knowledge is flowing freely through very subtle channels all around you, so too are negative feelings, emotions and thoughts. You have to tune in to the right frequency so that you catch the transmission you want. Just as radio and sound waves are transmitted through various frequencies, measured in kilohertz and megahertz, there are sounds of higher frequencies which are inaudible to the human ear, but perceivable by the chetana, awareness or higher mind residing within. These are the sound waves that radiate knowledge of each and everything that is conceivable. However, this knowledge is not received through words, but in the form of an experience which is perceived directly. The practice of dharana is the pivot on which spiritual illumination depends because it refines the perception, enabling you to tune into these higher frequencies.

Attuning with higher frequencies is an important achievement in spiritual life, but it is not the ultimate goal. The destination of individual consciousness is to merge with the supreme or collective consciousness that pervades each and every speck of creation as a unified whole. The unified field theory says the same thing in figures and equations. The unification of consciousness is a great accomplishment and can be achieved through practice, but one should not seek it until dharana has been perfected. This is a precondition existing in the very nature of consciousness. In fact, one cannot gain ascent of awareness without mastery of dharana. Another precondition is that the process of unification has to be guided by a guru who has become a receptacle for the divine grace to filter through and flow to the aspirant.

In this light, there is a mythical analogy of Lord Shiva receiving the tumultuous river Ganga in his matted locks, as she flowed down from the higher realms before reaching the earth. Ganga here represents the descent of a river of divine knowledge and grace. If the matted locks of Lord Shiva had not buffered the fall of this river, the full force of her descent would have crushed the earth. Shiva was the first guru to become a vessel for the descent of divine grace, therefore, he is known as Adi-guru. The guru lineage begins with him and includes all those who have qualified as gurus or enlightened beings within the tantric and vedic traditions. Swami Sivananda was of that lineage. So too is my guru, Swami Satyananda, who spoke to me of Vijnana Bhairava Tantra in much the same way as Shiva did with Parvati.

### Refining the receptivity

*Antahkarana* means 'inner tool' or 'instrument of perception', and it has four aspects or functions: manas, chitta, buddhi and ahamkara. Although separate and distinct identities, they correlate with each other in such a magnificent way that it is hard to distinguish between them. Thus they appear as a composite whole, which we commonly refer to as the mind. Manas is thought and counter-thought. The word *manan* means 'to contemplate'. In order to think, manas draws on information received through the senses. Afterwards it makes an extremely quick assessment of it according to related information, which is stored in the chitta as memory. Then an understanding of this information is derived through the discriminatory powers of buddhi. Finally, the information is identified in relation to the individual ego through the medium of ahamkara, and thereby the mind arrives at a conclusion.

The speed of the mind is fantastic, faster than the speed of light. The fastest speed recorded by man is the speed of the mind. A thought and the transmission of that thought occur simultaneously. There is no difference in speed between the two. The time gap which occurs is on account of receptivity. If there is delay or absence of transmission, it is on account of faulty, defective or unrefined receptivity. To improve the receptivity you will have to refine the four inner tools of perception, known as antahkarana, so that they vibrate at the frequency of consciousness or chetana. This is possible because the antahkarana is also a form which consciousness has assumed. The four tools are varying stages of consciousness that manifest as it evolves into matter.

Dharana is the way prescribed to refine the antahkarana. Through dharana the scattered forces of the mind, forever swinging from thought to counter-thought, are trained to focus on one thing to the exclusion of all else. As you progress, at one point you will transcend yourself. You will cease to exist, and only the experience of consciousness or pure awareness will remain. Spiritual experience begins only when dharana has been perfected and the state of dhyana dawns. The experiences you have in meditation prior to that are drawn from your conscious and subconscious mind. But the realm of mind influenced when dharana merges into dhyana is the causal or unconscious state.

Dharana is achieved after perfecting pratyahara, or withdrawal of the awareness from the external to the internal perception. You can say that dharana is the natural consequence of pratyahara. When the awareness is internalized and fixed on one point for a period of time, the consciousness begins to flow freely. When there is no break, obstruction, diversion or distraction, the flow of consciousness gains intensity and dhyana or meditation occurs. So, just as pratyahara develops into dharana, in the same way, dharana develops into dhyana, which develops into samadhi, or inner illumination. This is as natural a consequence as the development of a child into an old man.

## Necessity of mental training

An important factor to remember regarding the process of meditation and the experience of higher consciousness is that dharana is an essential stage in order to avoid uncharted flights of awareness. Just as the pilot of a plane or the captain of a ship takes the aid of compasses, maps and charts to reach the destination and avoid losing the way, similarly, the sadhaka also needs a plan and direction for the flight of consciousness, where to turn left, right, about turn or apply the brakes. Without a defined path and milestones to guide the consciousness, accidents may take place or one may be diverted or lost and never reach the destination.

The mind and consciousness is an immense power which must be managed correctly. In the hands of an adept the mind is directed to become a luminous and positive force, but if it is misused or misdirected, this same mind can plunge into darkness and despair. Therefore, the mind is not something to play around with. Directing the mind is a serious matter, which requires understanding and attention. Dharana is most important in this sense, because it gives training and a direction to the mind and awareness.

At present the mind is directed by the indriyas, the ten organs of action and knowledge, known as the karmendriyas and jnanendriyas. Wherever they lead, the mind follows. If the indriyas are trained, then the awareness is focused and directed. But if they are not, which is usually the case with most of us, it is as if the mind is mercilessly driven by an untrained animal. Dharana is a process of mental training that enables the aspirant to focus and direct the awareness as he desires, without any interference from the indriyas or senses.

If you want to progress in sadhana, you have to first fix the awareness at one point, so that it has a specific direction in which to travel. In other words you must train the awareness before allowing it to roam freely. Until the awareness is firmly established at one point, it must not be allowed free flight. This is not only damaging, in some cases it may also be irrevocable. It is for this purpose that different symbols are used in meditation, and some are more efficacious than others. The tantric symbols utilized for dharana are mantra, yantra and mandala. They are purely scientific as they depend on the influence of sound, form and light to create an effect on the energy within the body and mind. *Mantras* are mystic sounds that reverberate with tremendous energy, *yantras* are perfect geometric formations of the sounds emanating from the mantras, and *mandalas* are three-dimensional forms of the same mantras.

The following parable aptly illustrates the path of dharana and the importance of symbols as a basis for the mind in meditation. One day it began to rain and the rain continued for days and months on end. Everything was submerged under water and there was no land or landmark of any kind in sight. A lone bird was hovering over this vast expanse of water and seeing no landmark anywhere became lost and could not return to its home. Then the water gradually receded a bit and a log of wood came into sight. The bird at once landed on the wood and, using it as a base, flew back and forth from there in order to find food and whatever else it needed. Each time the bird flew off in any direction, it kept the piece of wood in sight and, in this way, always returned to the same base without any difficulty.

Similarly, in dharana the awareness flies high and travels over vast expanses of consciousness, which are untracked and have no visible markers to identify them. But again and again the awareness returns back to the object which it is focused on, recognizing it to be the base for all of its flights. That way the awareness does not go astray or get lost. It makes forays into the unknown, but is guided back in the right direction. This is why the object of dharana is important and should be one that you are naturally drawn to. If you have a natural attraction for the object of dharana, the mind will remain fixed on it and will not be distracted easily.

45

Otherwise the awareness tends to wander from the base for long periods and may eventually become lost in the uncharted dimensions of consciousness.

## Paths of darkness and light

The state of dharana, which is the basis of all the practices in VBT, is also described in the textbooks of yoga. Patanjali says: "Binding the mind at one place is dharana." This is necessary in order to focus the awareness, which is normally scattered due to external perceptions. Dharana can be practised on any object, image or person, as well as on different psychic centres, nadis, or on a thought, idea or feeling. Through one-pointed concentration the hidden power of the chosen symbol is revealed and we enter a different dimension where a new awareness dawns. It is as if a curtain has been lifted and we can see what was concealed until that moment.

There are many levels of awareness, and as they are unveiled, new powers are revealed that we were not aware of before or whose existence we could not have imagined. At present we are only aware of the conscious and dream state, and even these are not in our control. In fact, we spend most of our time grappling with the perplexities of these dimensions. We get confused, agitated, elated, depressed, anxious, worried and fearful just by what is revealed to us in these most ordinary states of awareness. What would happen if we were to become aware of subtler and deeper dimensions of existence?

These deeper dimensions are just as real as our everyday awareness, but we regard them as imaginary and unreal. We are not accustomed to them because they cannot be experienced through the senses, which we mistakenly regard as the ultimate source of knowledge. For instance, when we have an intense dream, we wake up feeling that it actually happened. Of course, there is always an element of doubt, because the moment we wake up the dream disappears and fades from memory. There is nothing tangible to ensure that what occurred in the dream actually happened on some dimension. If we practise dharana on our dreams, however, we can perfect the art of understanding them as well as train our awareness to have certain dreams of our choice. Then we will realize that, in fact, our dreams are as real as our experiences in the waking state. (VBT sl. 75)

In the same way, when we go deep into the state of dharana, what we experience there is also real. Whatever image we conjure in dharana is as real as the objects we see outside. The only difference is that we see one with our eyes open and the other with our eyes closed. In the first stage of dharana we may focus on the image of Rama, Christ, Devi, a flower, a beautiful gem, a mountain or a river, with our eyes open. When the image has saturated our mind, we can then recreate it within. Both the outer and inner images are real, but the stuff they are made of differs. One is made of paper, stone or clay, and the other is made of consciousness. The external light illumines one, and the other is self-illumined. As the consciousness becomes lighter and lighter, the effulgence begins to grow from within. This light is known as *jyotsna*.

On the path of meditation there should always be light within, not darkness. If you see darkness, smoke or blurred images, this is an indication that the practices are taking you on a wrong path from which you will have to come back and return to normal awareness. If instead you see luminosity, radiance and brilliance, then know that you are on the right track and that the awareness has gained ascent. These two paths of meditation are called *uttarayana* and *dakshinayana*, the northern and southern paths. Dakshinayana is the southern path by which one returns to the state of ignorance and attachment to the things of the world, so it is associated with darkness.

47

Uttarayana, or the northern path, is associated with illumination and freedom from worldly attachment, so it is the favoured way for dharana and meditation. It elevates the consciousness to such a great extent that the aspirant need not return to normal consciousness. If he so chooses, he can operate from that elevated state and become a channel for the flow of higher knowledge and bliss. In technical terms that state is known as *jivanmukta,* or total liberation of the consciousness from the clutches of embodied matter in this physical body itself. Of course, jivanmukta is an extremely high state, which is rarely attainable and destined only for the most purified souls. But mention of this is made to indicate what can be achieved through dharana and dhyana, and the indications that signify one is on the right track.

Through focused concentration on any object, the consciousness is directed towards that. As concentration is perfected, a state of total, inner absorption without any break arises. It could happen even for a split second. It does not have to go on for hours or even for minutes. It may only last for the blink of an eye, so that you may wonder whether it happened at all. But this state of meditation penetrates through the veils of consciousness, which open before you, one by one, and reveal different levels of awareness and existence. There the same matter that you see all around you exists in subtler and subtler forms.

To what height can the awareness ascend? What is the final destination of awareness and under what conditions does it return to the state of consciousness you were familiar with before the ascent began? Many seers have experienced higher states, and that is why they could explain them to a large degree, but at some point they were unable to convey this experience through the medium of speech. (VBT sl. 6) So they became channels and began to transmit the experience to others who were receptive. Even now, those transmissions are available if you can attune the frequencies of your antahkarana to receive them. This is what is achieved through dharana when the aspirant traverses the path of illumination in a guided and controlled manner, as opposed to the path of darkness.

## Mantra

Mantra is another important base for dharana in VBT. All the vedic and tantric mantras have been realized by seers in deep states of dhyana. They are the seers of the mantras. The word mantra means, 'that which liberates by contemplation'. Every sound is not a mantra. Only a sound that has been realized or heard by an enlightened seer in a deep state of awareness is a mantra. In other words, the mantra may be perpetually echoing in different subtle strata of the atmosphere, but it is only heard and revealed to others by someone who is tuned into that frequency. Such a person thus becomes the seer of that mantra. The sage Vishwamitra realized the Gayatri mantra and thus became its seer. There are several such examples.

The tantric mantras have no literal meaning; they simply have sound and form. Of course, the underlying meaning can be inferred through intellect. But, in fact, mantras are beyond meaning; they are pure vibration. Every mantra has a secret power that unlocks the energy residing in it. (VBT sl. 42) Therefore, any meaning that a mantra may have would be purely metaphysical and could only be revealed in the form of an experience. The most common way to access this energy is by repeating the mantra continuously until the sound arises spontaneously in your awareness. You may not even realize that you are repeating it. A mantra can also be realized by focusing on its corresponding yantra or mandala. Or else it can be realized by the benevolent grace of guru.

The practice of mantra is so ancient that it is a part of man's primordial origins. Most, if not all, of the tantric and vedic mantras have been practised for hundreds and

49

thousands of years. Mantra is an integral part of the science of tantra, wherein sound is considered to be the first evolute of consciousness after the primary impulse of creation. This sound is known as nada, which exists as the cosmic nada in the mantra *Aum,* and as the microcosmic nada in all sound vibrations of varying frequencies.

*Aum* is the primal sound. (VBT sl. 39) All the other sounds in the universe are contained in and emanate from this one sound. It is the simplest and most natural sound formation conceivable. When you open your mouth the sound that emanates is *Aaa,* and when you close your mouth the sound you make is *Mmm.* In that brief moment when the mouth is neither fully open nor fully closed, there is an intermediary sound of *Uuu.* (VBT sl. 40) This is the mantra *Aum.* The mantra *Soham,* which is the inherent sound of each breath, is another natural mantra which we repeat consciously or unconsciously throughout the day, every moment of our lives.

Another important aspect of mantra is *matrika,* which are also known as the 'little mothers' of creation. They represent the inherent sound vibration of each *akshara* or indelible sound vibration contained within the letters which make up words and language. (VBT sl. 2) Mantra is the source of matrika, or creative energy. In fact, they are so closely linked that another name for mantra is matrika. In the *Shiva Sutras,* an important text of Kashmir Shaivism and Trika philosophy, Shiva states that matrika is concealed in the mantra and does not reveal itself unless he commands, thus showing the interdependence of energy and consciousness. When the awareness is focused through the medium of mantra, the energy awakens from its slumber. Until that is done, the energy remains asleep.

In the process of dharana, the awareness is not focused on energy directly, but indirectly through the medium of the mantra. Dharana takes place within the dimension of

50

time, space and object, so these are the three players in this arena. Here time represents energy, space represents consciousness and object represents the mantra chosen for dharana. When the awareness is focused on the mantra, it stirs up the energy. As the concentration deepens, consciousness and energy move towards each other from opposite directions and collide at the nucleus. The impact of their union causes a great explosion, which reverberates not just on the physical dimension, but also on the subtle and transcendental dimensions.

Therefore, the power of mantra should not be under-estimated. Mantra is not the name of God, nor is it important to know its meaning. Mantra simply has to be repeated for the vibration to be effective. Mantra is *dhvani,* or sound vibration, which creates similar sound frequencies in different parts of the body and mind. Moreover, the *akshara,* or letters, from which these mantras are derived correspond to the different energy centres located in the body. Each of the akshara, which are fifty in number, is written on the different lotus petals of the chakras, which indicates their intimate connection. Just as an iron smith repeatedly strikes a piece of hot iron with a strong hammer to mould it into the shape he wants, similarly, through constant repetition of the mantra you are able to strike the corresponding energy centres in your body related to that mantra. With regular practice the mantra resonates with the chakras, which are activated and energized to their optimum potency. (VBT sl. 30)

During the practice of mantra the sound should be repeated first at the *vaikhari,* or spoken level, where the dhvani is projected outwards, then at the *madhyama,* or middle level, where the dhvani is directed inwards, and finally at the *pashyanti,* or mental level, where it gains momentum. Gradually, through repeated practice the awareness will become fully saturated with the mantra. At this point the vibrations that emanate from your being will reach out

51

towards that very same mantra which is reverberating throughout the universe as a part of the cosmic nada, without anyone repeating it. This is how the mantra liberates the mind and becomes a gateway to enter the domain of cosmic experience. Apart from bestowing spiritual illumination, many mantras also have healing effects and ward off illness, accidents and calamities.

## Crystallization of consciousness

Another important concept utilized in the dharanas of VBT is *shoonya,* or the void. This is a classic example of dharana without any alambana, or support. In dharana on mantra, time or energy is the criteria for entering deeper states of awareness; however, in dharana on shoonya, space is the criteria for achieving the same objective. If you have ever gazed into vacant space with an empty mind, devoid of any mental formations, then you may have noticed that the mind begins to dissolve and the inner awareness crystallizes on a bindu, or point in that empty space, which is the void or shoonya. (VBT sl. 58)

In the practice of chidakasha dharana, when you gaze into the empty space behind the forehead, suddenly a point of light, or bindu, appears. (VBT sl. 85) When you see that, you are having a glimpse of your consciousness crystallizing at one point. As this experience deepens, the light becomes brighter and engulfs you, so that you may even experience yourself as light. When the poet-saint Mirabai sang devotional songs, she would transcend her body, which glowed with light for all to see. This is no ordinary light, like that which lights up your room. It is the light of the soul, which is effulgent and complete in itself. It is luminous, all pervading and unbroken. It is not confined to one point, but spreads equally in all directions at the same time.

Sometimes while gazing into the vacant space, instead of light, a thought or idea may gain momentum so that your awareness turns towards it. This may be any thought, but in order to crystallize your consciousness on it, that thought should remain constant and unbroken. That is the only precondition that VBT gives for crystallization of consciousness. However, because of that requirement, it can be understood that dharana is the key for any progress in this direction, because unbroken and constant awareness of one object or idea, to the exclusion of all else, can only be attained through one-pointed concentration.

**Bhavana, a concept for dharana**

Another concept utilized in VBT as a focus for dharana is *bhavana*, which means 'innermost feeling'. The most intrinsic part of our nature gives rise to bhavana and no person on earth is devoid of it. This feeling is a very powerful substance as it rules our emotions, which influence each and every experience in our lives. If this force can be harnessed through dharana and channelled towards the path of enlightenment, it will bring us very close to that ultimate experience. Furthermore, VBT reveals that not only can the positive emotions be utilized for this purpose, but the negative as well, because all emotions are forms of energy, or shakti. Emotions, thoughts, feelings, inner turmoil and mental agitation are the forms of bhavana utilized in VBT to explode the higher awareness within.

Now the question arises, who is eligible to practise dharana? (VBT sl. 158) Classically, if you analyze the depth of the practice and its consequences, it stands to reason that dharana is for one who has already made some headway in curbing and controlling the mental fluctuations, or *chitta vrittis,* as they are responsible for the entire spectrum of behaviour, personality, desires, ambitions, wants and needs. One who can manage them without being compelled by them is ready for the practice of dharana. But for most people that may never happen. So one begins the practice in a guided and controlled manner, allowing the consciousness to gradually focus and crystallize.

Each time the mental fluctuations draw the consciousness away from the object of focus, one again brings it back. In this way, through repeated practice the mental fluctuations will gradually become less and less forceful and in time they will diminish. In the classical system of raja yoga only a person who has mastered pratyahara, or withdrawal of the awareness from outer sense perceptions, is considered to be ready for dharana. However, tantra allows every individual to dive into this practice by indicating how the base emotions and instincts can be transformed and guided towards enlightenment. The energy is the same, says tantra. It is up to you whether you want to direct it towards the sensory perceptions that lead to enjoyment or towards the extra-sensory perceptions that lead to enlightenment. (VBT sl. 73)

Tantra is a science that does not exclude any individual from the possibility of experiencing higher awareness and has also shown the way whereby we can start this ascent of awareness. At the same time, in order to have profound inner experiences, the sadhaka must be of a high calibre and have an awakened kundalini. Some people are born with an awakened kundalini due to their attainments in previous lives. Others may have this awakening through personal effort and the divine grace of guru. It is these persons who are ready for the practice of dharana. If the process of dharana is achieved effortlessly and you are able to exclude everything except the point you have chosen for concentration, even for a short time, then you are ready for the higher practices of dharana and dhyana.

**Basis of inner conceptualization**
What is dharana? If you think about it, dharana is simply a process where you create a thought, feeling or image within you. You imagine a light, a shivalingam, Rama, Krishna,

Christ or any of nature's attributes, and simultaneously generate a feeling of faith and devotion towards it. Faith is the basis of inner conceptualization, and without faith dharana is incomplete and difficult to master. Faith is the stuff which nourishes and unfolds the experience of dharana. Without faith our practice will falter, because faith is that quality which creates an experience. Faith is different to dogma or belief; it is alive, vibrant and experiential. Faith has the power to transform, like nothing else can. To develop faith it is not necessary to search outside; faith arises from within. We are all born with this quality, but it has not developed in us as the intellect has, due to our education and training. The power of faith is revealed through the practice of dharana, and creates a strong basis for the mind in the process of inner conceptualization.

Through faith the scattered and dissipated mental energy is focused and crystallized at one point. This brings enormous clarity of perception and enables you to conceptualize whatever you focus the mind on and create it within. The same object which is seen outside can be seen inside with the same clarity, as if it were as real as the object outside. Once this has been mastered, and that object alone remains in the awareness, the ego begins to dissolve. At this point the awareness merges with the object; you and the object become one. This leads to the state of dhyana, or inner illumination.

**How to choose the object for dharana**

There are hundreds and thousands of symbols, mantras, objects and ideas to choose from, but there are two important points to consider first. The first is that the object should be one which you are naturally drawn to, and the second that you should be able to conceptualize it easily. In terms of human evolution, no two people are the same. What one can conceptualize easily may be difficult for another. For instance, there are people who cannot conceptualize an abstract thought or idea and need something more tangible, while others cannot conceptualize an objective form and find it easier to focus on an abstract idea, like a formless and nameless God.

In that sense tantra is no different from Vedanta, but tantra takes into account that most people cannot conceptualize formlessness, void or emptiness. For this reason the concept of symbol was introduced because one must start somewhere. It is necessary to direct the awareness voluntarily, rather than allowing it to move involuntarily. At present the mind is scattered, dissipated and lacks direction. This is why the thoughts, actions, speech and emotions, the four facets of personality that constitute the external self, are always in disharmony. To harmonize them it is essential that the awareness should be focused and streamlined as well as steady and balanced. It should not be erratic and whimsical.

Regarding the concept of symbol and its necessity in dharana, the point in question is not whether the ultimate reality or God should be perceived as formless or with form. The question is: what is a person to do if he cannot conceive of formlessness? Is he to give up the idea of evolving his consciousness or is there another way for him? In the first slokas of VBT, Shiva says that form is only an aid for the aspirant. It is not the supreme consciousness or ultimate reality which he has set out to perceive, but it is a necessary and invaluable aid all same. (VBT sl. 9–10)

In fact, aspirants should not fall into the trap of trying to establish whether form or formlessness is the ultimate. One should ignore this point altogether and instead make intense efforts to focus the awareness and direct it to the higher centres in the physical body. Even if one is able to establish whether form or formlessness is true, it will only be a logical exercise borrowed from books or other persons. After achieving dharana, one will know the answer and will not need to ask anyone, because his own experience will guide him.

## Not a religious affair

For perfection in sadhana you must give greater attention to the practice of dharana. The subject of God plays no part in this process. Whether you believe in God or not, whether your God is tall or short, fair or dark, male or female, with form or formless, these factors are not at all important for the practice of dharana. When you learn to drive a car, it is not important to know its maker. It is not important how Mr Ford of Ford Motors looks or acts. For you to drive your car successfully you need to know about its parts: the clutch, brake, accelerator, and how they work.

In the same way you need not worry about the creator of consciousness during meditation; you simply have to know the nature and behaviour of consciousness so that you can direct it for self-knowledge and enlightenment. In the entire text of *Yoga Sutras*, which deals with the science of the mind, the Sage Patanjali does not even talk about God. Similarly, in VBT the emphasis is on practical methods to focus the mind and not on any form or philosophy of God. For training the mind and awareness it does not matter whether you believe in God or not. You may deny God, but you cannot deny the mind, chetana or awareness. The mind, and not God, is the subject matter of VBT and all the texts on tantra and yoga.

This is why the symbol for dharana can be anything. It does not have to be drawn from religious iconography. Of course, it is true that certain symbols are more potent catalysts for focusing the awareness, as they have been taken from the collective unconscious and correspond with the archetypes present in man. But still you may choose any symbol that the mind is spontaneously drawn to and it will be effective. Ideally, however, the symbol is chosen according to the psychic temperament and inclination of the aspirant, and it is always recommended that it be received from an enlightened person or one who is an expert in this science. However, once the symbol is decided it should not be changed, as this may destabilize the inner consciousness and cause imbalance.

## Science of today

*Atma chintan*, or reflective thinking, elevates the awareness, because this too is a form of dharana that is practised in jnana yoga. To give philosophical attention to something is also dharana. The greatest discoveries of mankind have been possible only through this means. Apples fall from trees every day, but only Newton could derive the law of gravity when he saw this because he could give philosophical attention to that event. You bathe in the tub everyday, but unlike Archimedes you could not discover the principle of buoyancy. Can you imagine how focused the awareness must have been of the man who gave electricity to the world?

This is the quality of awareness which dharana develops. Any great artist, musician, mathematician, scientist, business-man, sportsman, politician, statesman, siddha or saint attains perfection in their field only because they are adept in dharana. Great achievements would not be possible unless they were able to focus the awareness on their chosen field. Without concentration and focus of mind, it is not possible to accomplish even the day-to-day tasks. How then could the great task of enlightenment be accomplished without steady and sustained concentration?

It does not matter what your religious, social or political beliefs are. It does not matter what country you belong to or whether you are male or female, young or old, literate or illiterate. It does not even matter if you are good or bad, important or insignificant. The practice of dharana is useful for all, irrespective of their station in life. Whatever success one may have, whether material, emotional, professional or spiritual, depends on the ability to concentrate the mind on the task at hand. This system of mental training as described in tantra and yoga is not a religious doctrine. It is the science of today, although it was revealed long ago by the rishis and munis. Can you imagine the level of evolution that society had attained where men and women described the workings of the human body, mind and consciousness with such amazing clarity and precision?

Yoga and tantra are not religions, says Swami Satyananda. They are sciences which influence all the dimensions of man: physical, mental, psychic and spiritual. They contain highly evolved systems of inner knowledge and practices, which are so powerful and pertinent to our needs, they can resolve all the problems we face today, whether they be related to physical disease, mental stress, depression, emotional imbalance, lack of confidence, and many other maladies we are subject to, while simultaneously activating the evolution of consciousness.

### Therapeutic application of dharana

Have you ever compared the behaviour of an agitated and restless mind with that of a mind that is focussed and concentrated? Try to imagine a pendulum swinging wildly left and right and then gradually settling down at the centre with no movement at all. While the pendulum is moving, there is intense activity, just as the agitated and restless mind is in constant motion. When the pendulum stops moving there is stillness, just as the quiet mind experiences emptiness, void or shoonya. That state of emptiness and stillness is known as turiya, where transcendental knowledge pours in and illumination occurs.

Dharana is important, not only because it brings about this experience, but also because it prepares the aspirant to

59

receive it. Although the transcendental experience takes place beyond the body, its effects are felt on the body in a very acute way. The different organs of the body are affected by this experience, as it filters down to every level. The practice of dharana, therefore, affects all the levels of our being: physical, mental, emotional, psychic as well as spiritual. It removes the blocks and obstacles from every level so that the experience of turiya consciousness can unfold. On account of this, we also derive a feeling of well-being, dynamism, confidence and immense power within from the practice.

So we can say that dharana is very important for our spiritual evolution as well as total well-being. In this sense, the practice of dharana can be understood as a form of physical and mental therapy as well. Dharana has already been applied successfully in Australia and America for the treatment of life threatening diseases such as cancer and AIDS. These patients were asked to focus their awareness through a process of visualization on the diseased cells being destroyed and replaced by healthy cells; in much the same way as one army destroys and takes over another.

Dharana is a therapy at the mental level also as it harnesses, focuses, energizes, directs and ultimately liberates the mind. Swami Satyananda has said that we should always befriend the mind. This means that the mind should never be opposed or suppressed. Of course, we may wonder how on earth it would be possible to live in society without opposing the mind, which can suggest anything. For instance, if a thought comes to injure someone through harsh words or actions, should we suppress it or express it? Swami Satyananda says we should do neither; instead we should learn to harness the mind through dharana.

Through this practice the mind is directed away from negativity towards positive experiences and expression. Is this not a therapy for the mind? The agony that the mind faces due to negative ideas is dispelled without confrontation, suppression or expression. Today we talk of harmony, brotherhood and peace, but these positive expressions are only possible if the mind is transformed. The negative qualities of the mind cause separation, sorrow and affliction; there is no feeling of unity. Each individual feels himself to be separate from another. Through dharana the mind overcomes these barriers which divide man from man. This gives us a new outlook and view of things which is more balanced and allows us to be more harmonized within our environment and within ourselves.

## Transformation of the genetic structure

The major diseases rampant in the world today are caused by genetic defects, which are inherited from the parents, not by virus and bacteria. These defects are deeply encoded in the DNA, and no medicine can correct them. Medical science has found no cure for many metabolic diseases, such as diabetes, arthritis, multiple sclerosis, heart failure, cancer and aids. At best it can provide temporary relief, but no permanent solution.

However, genetic defects can be influenced, altered and corrected by a thought, idea, feeling or emotion. A deep feeling can alter the genetic structure in a way that no medicine can. This is why the practices of dharana are invaluable to mankind, for dharana can be effective where medicine has failed. This was realized a long time ago by the tantric and vedic seers, who completely altered the structure of their DNA by utilizing these very same practices of dharana and dhyana.

This is a very important point for the welfare of mankind because in this lies the root of our problems. People the world over are suffering on account of disease and disharmony. Despite the advancements of modern science, no answers have been found. It is time now to look within

61

for the answer. We have the power to correct all of our genetic and metabolic defects. It is just that no one has ever taught us how to access it. This power is revealed through the practice of dharana. Therefore, dharana is important, not only for spiritual experience, but also for our day-to-day life, so that we can be healthy, happy and balanced individuals.

Through the process of dharana a complete transformation of the genetic structure takes place in order to convert the mundane and gross awareness into spiritual awareness. The only difference is that this transformation takes place in a far more refined dimension than the physical. As dharana is perfected, the genetic structure, which was previously influenced at the physical level, comes under the influence of the practice at the pranic, mental, intuitive and spiritual levels as well. Thus the entire being is transformed by the practice, and one may even become a totally different person.

In living memory, we have such examples as Ramakrishna Paramahamsa, Swami Vivekananda, Swami Sivananda, Swami Satyananda, Anandamayi Ma and Sai Baba of Shirdi. In vedic history also we have the splendid example of numerous rishis and munis who developed great physical, mental, intuitive and spiritual prowess through the mastery of dharana, dhyana and samadhi.

### Altered states of consciousness

From the dawn of civilization, it was noticed that some people were born with special abilities which were considered to be supernatural powers. Some could see into the future and predict events; others could heal or influence nature. A deep study of such persons revealed that, in fact, they had an altered state of consciousness. Thus man's inner quest began and with that the birth of tantra took place. We should not equate tantra with religion, because tantra is very ancient and predates all the known religions of the world. Tantra is an all-encompassing, evolutionary science which comprises the different ways that man has developed down through the ages to experience altered states of consciousness. Within the science of tantra different states of consciousness have been explicitly defined and mapped, along with definite ways to experience those states. Moreover, the indications or manifestations that arise as a consequence of those altered states have also been elucidated in great detail. This is why the science of tantra is so unique and valuable for the evolution of mankind.

In modern psychology we learn of three states of consciousness: waking, dreaming and sleeping; or *jagrat*, *swapna* and *sushupti*. But tantra speaks of a fourth state of consciousness, known as *turiya*, which is experienced when the consciousness is trained to look inwards rather than outwards, and is focused on the higher centres in the body. However, within these four states there are many more intermediary states that the consciousness passes through on its journey from the outer to the inner dimensions. Dharana is the bridge which makes it possible to cross over from the external to the internal reality without any mishaps. If the psychologists and religious teachers of today understood the purpose and significance of concentration on a symbol, then this important tool would be accepted and utilized for man's inner development.

A symbol is a crutch or aid which is used until the consciousness can walk on its own, without any support, along the unknown and mysterious inner path. Without the help of a symbol to keep the mind focused, it is possible for the consciousness to enter the twilight zone unguided, leading to complete disorientation with the surroundings, and perhaps even to madness. You may enter an inner dimension from which the consciousness is unable to disentangle itself and return to the normal conscious state.

In this case you could become a totally different person, not recognizing your surroundings or the people intimately known to you. Even the experience of inner realization can be completely disorienting for the aspirant who has not mastered the art of going deep within and then returning to the symbol. There are many realized beings who have no control over their external functions. They require someone to feed and clothe them and direct their physical movements, because they remain immersed in a trance-like state, unaware of the body and its needs.

In the second chapter of the *Bhagavad Gita*, Lord Krishna explains to Arjuna that a realized being is one who is established in *sthita prajna*, or stabilized consciousness. Arjuna then asks him how a man who has attained sthita prajna looks, behaves, acts, thinks and speaks. Krishna replies that there is total uniformity in his personality. His actions, thoughts, words and feelings express total equipoise, and there is no conflict between their outer and inner expression. In other words he is in total control over all the activities of his life and personality. There is no aberration in thought, speech, action or behaviour. This stabilized state can be attained by following certain rules regarding the training of the mind, and one should not be in a hurry to achieve realization without fulfilling them. One doesn't dive into the deep end of a swimming pool without knowing how to swim; rather a rubber float is used as an aid until one can swim safely to the other side.

Suppose you are feeling extremely happy, so happy that you are bursting with joy and bliss. Perhaps this euphoria is too great to contain and it spills over into your behaviour. Would you not appear a bit strange and perhaps abnormal to others at that time? If this happiness were to continue until you could stabilize your external behaviour, despite your inner experience of overwhelming happiness, your day-to-day life would be disturbed. You could even find

64

yourself in the loony bin, as others may think you have gone insane. The same would apply if you had an overwhelming feeling of depression, and could not rebalance your external behaviour.

The symbol of dharana acts as a catalyst to draw the consciousness back to normality in such cases. Abnormality does occur and unfortunately one cannot predict where, when and how. Therefore, it is better to take precautions, which act as an antidote to such conditions. Spiritual literature and art have profusely depicted this abnormality as a type of intoxication, similar to the union of two intimate lovers who have been pining for one another. Do lovers not behave abnormally? They forget to eat, sleep or converse, and think only of their beloved, in much the same way as the individual consciousness pines for union with the cosmic consciousness. The *Rubaiyat* of Omar Khayam and also the poem *Madhushala* by Harivansh Bachchan beautifully describe this intoxication as an intense yearning of the soul.

This inner journey reveals many stages of consciousness. Each stage manifests differently and also bestows a different degree of illumination in the form of experiential knowledge. You learn though experience, not through books or words, because you actually feel what is happening to you. The inner experience does not just take place mentally, intellectually or emotionally. It completely supersedes the body, mind and psyche, and you become that experience. As a result, at that moment inner knowledge or jnana is born, which not only enlightens but transforms as well. It could transform you into a saint, poet, musician, philosopher, artist, or into a good human being with a touch of excellence, a special quality that will set you apart from others.

## Speciality of tantra

In actual fact, the process of dharana is natural for us. There are hundreds of tasks in our day-to-day lives which we accomplish through concentration, whether it is reading, writing, studying, singing, talking, cooking, romancing, watching films, dancing, planning, working, painting, sculpting, acting or memorizing. Our success in these acts depends largely on how well we are able to focus and channel the mind on whatever we are trying to do. In this way the practice of dharana is reflected in our external life, and similarly our external life reflects on our practice.

There are also many emotions or expressions arising in the mind that we can practise dharana on. Happiness, sorrow, anxiety, jealousy, passion, lust, restlessness, turmoil, hatred, love, desire, craving, enmity, impatience, irritability and greed are just some of them. VBT prescribes this form of dharana for those who can conceptualize their emotions, feelings or *bhava*. For example, when the mind is totally saturated with inner turmoil and you are so obsessed with it that even while talking, eating, sleeping or any of the hundreds of acts performed daily this turmoil still lurks somewhere in your mind, that is spontaneous dharana. But it is involuntary and goes on without control or awareness. That very same experience has to be recreated and experienced voluntarily with awareness. When you are successful at focusing your awareness on the turmoil within, at some point you will find that calmness descends. This calmness need not extend for very long; it could be just for a split second, but in that moment illumination dawns.

Thus tantra utilizes the very same forces by which we fall to elevate the awareness. This is the speciality of tantra. It does not ask you to negate your enjoyments or weaknesses; instead it provides a way to utilize them to experience the state of bhairava consciousness. (VBT sl. 70–72) This is a very important revelation, as it means that we do not have to overcome our base nature before we set out on the spiritual journey. We can start the practice of dharana wherever we are and proceed from there. This makes the application of

66

tantra universal, as it does not exclude any type of person from its practice. There is something for each one of us.

An interaction took place in the ashram which illustrates this point. One day I happened to pass by a French girl and a young swami who were engaged in a conversation. The girl was a painter and she was seated in the sun under a mango tree, brush in hand, painting with fine strokes. The swami was keen to impress on her the importance of practising yoga, to which she answered, "But that is exactly what I am doing." The swami said, "No, you are having fun." She said, "Yes, you are absolutely right. I am having fun but I am also practising yoga. If you don't believe me, look at this." She held her painting to the sky. He looked up towards it and was simply amazed to see the exact replication of the sky in her painting. The same cloud formations, the gorgeous colours, the exact light, the lone bird and even the hint of a breeze.

The swami thought to himself, what a good demonstration of a concentrated mind. Such a mind grasps every detail, as it is able to focus itself on whatever it chooses. That quality of mind will excel, no matter where it is applied, whether it is art, music, science or even in the transcendental quest. That is purely a matter of choice. But the swami still had the last word when he told her that despite her excellence there was a practice called dharana which would be very useful for her to develop greater skills in concentration, so that, being an artist, she could have a wider range of expression.

### Importance of perseverance

One day a young English boy came to the ashram to see Swami Satyananda. He had a problem. The moment he closed his eyes he would see clear and vivid pictures of people, places and events that he had never encountered in his life and did not recognize. It was as if he had switched on

67

a television set. His main concern was that he did not know how to switch it off because these inner visions were spontaneous and involuntary. In the case of dharana, however, the inner vision must be voluntary, according to the will of the practitioner and the symbol he has chosen, and no other.

When you start the practice of dharana, many thoughts and visions will draw your awareness in different directions as soon as you sit down and close your eyes. Often you may find that you could not visualize your symbol at all for the entire duration of your session due to these disturbances. When you open your eyes again, you will be surprised that so much time has elapsed, as you had become totally immersed in these visions or thoughts. This should not alarm or discourage you. Let it happen, but each time wilfully draw your awareness back to the symbol or basis of dharana which you have chosen.

Gradually the visions or thoughts will diminish by themselves and the vision of the symbol will become clearer and last for a longer duration. The time it takes to accomplish this will differ from person to person. However, you should not abandon the practice, even if you are unable to attain one-pointed awareness of the symbol after long years of training. Once your destination is determined, you should not waste energy and willpower worrying about how long it will take to reach it. Have faith that one day you will surely reach the goal, if you persist in your efforts. You should also be confident in the symbol you have chosen and not change it, thinking that another symbol may bring quicker results. That is not the case.

### Rewiring the brain

The practice of dharana reinforces many channels and pathways in the brain which may not be in use at present, although they existed beforehand. When a car travels over

68

an unused path several times, it creates a track which can then be used by others. In the same way there are many centres in the brain that are in a state of dormancy because they were not connected with the other nervous circuits, and you have not created new paths that connect them. Through the repeated practice of dharana on the same symbol, day in and day out, new pathways or grooves are formed which ultimately link one centre to another. The moment this happens, an electro-magnetic circuit is created in the brain, which is self-luminous and lights up whatever there is along that path. In this way, you begin to see many new things during the practice.

Similarly, if the car changes its track, that path will be washed away after some time unless it is deep. In the same way, the grooves or pathways which are reinforced in the brain through the practice of dharana have to become deeply embedded or else they too may fade away. For this reason, the practice of dharana has to be repeated over a long period of time. Then gradually the brain gets rewired due to the electro-magnetic circuits created through dharana, and all the parts of the brain become illumined, revealing its full potential, which is a treasure house of gems. That English boy mentioned previously had somehow got wired up, but because he did not have a base for his awareness, he did not know how to manage it.

There is a beautiful analogy in the tantric texts which relates this rewiring of the brain with the *jata,* or matted locks, of Shiva. Just as the strands of his matted hair are all entwined together, the circuits of the awakened brain are also totally inter-connected. But the unawakened brain is like unmatted hair, consisting of loose strands. The circuits are all there, but the energy does not flow through them because the channels or grooves which connect them are faded or not yet formed. Repeated practice, or abhyasa, is the secret for forming these grooves. When you were born you did not know anything, but gradually you learned and remembered many things, which you do not forget for your entire lifetime. This is because those grooves have been formed, and they remain active due to their constant use. As you grow older you may discard the repeated use of certain knowledge and in time that will be forgotten. This happens because the grooves disintegrate due to disuse.

At present the grooves formed in our brain are those of apara vidya, knowledge of the phenomenal or material world. In order to gain para vidya, we will have to form new grooves or circuits, which will allow the transmission of transcendental knowledge. This is accomplished through the practices of dharana and dhyana, which activate those circuits that are capable of carrying high voltage energy. These practices should be regular and continuous over a period of time in order to strengthen the grooves you have carved out, otherwise they may fade, causing short circuits, and your brain may blow a fuse.

There are billions of electro-magnetic circuits in the brain, and as they are rewired and switched on they illumine everything on their path from one part of the brain to the other. In this way, many visions and experiences arise. However, you have to remember that these things are just part of the psychic scenery which lies along the way; they are not the ultimate destination. Similarly, when you travel from one place to another, you see many things on the way, but you do not stop until you reach the point you had set out for.

**Witnessing attitude**

As the practice of dharana progresses you will see many things within you, but these visions do not come under the category of spiritual experience. They belong to the realm of the psyche and are known as psychic experiences. When these begin to manifest, you will know that the brain circuits and pathways for inner illumination are being formed and you should persist in your efforts. Do not get carried away or mistake psychic experiences for the real stuff. It is easy to do that, because sometimes these visions are so attractive and breathtaking. But you must continue with the practice of dharana on your symbol, despite these inner experiences, just as you would continue on any journey, despite whatever you may see on the way, because you have to reach your destination. For this reason the attitude of a witness or *sakshi bhava* should be developed from the very start, so that you do not lose yourself in the inner experiences.

The word sakshi means 'witness'. This attitude is emphasized in the practices of yoga and tantra as a means to maintain the awareness. In order to develop the witnessing attitude, you have to divide your awareness. While one part is doing the practice, another part is watching you do the practice and witnessing all that you are experiencing. In this way, your experiences become subjective as well as objective. This witnessing attitude is very important and will help you progress in sadhana. If you get immersed and lost in every experience, your progress will be delayed or obstructed, and in some cases lost altogether. But if you can become a witness to the experiences you are having, this will not happen. You will be able to rise above them easily and return to the symbol of dharana.

**Dual awareness**

This witnessing principle in dharana leads to the development of dual awareness. This is an extremely difficult state to attain and also to maintain. Here the awareness observes the external as well as the internal events simultaneously and with the same clarity of perception. So, although one sees the world outside with the eyes open, at the same time the gaze is also turned inwards and one also experiences everything going on within in the same manner. Dual awareness can also be extended to perceive different dimensions of consciousness simultaneously, and eventually leads to expansion of consciousness at all levels.

Swami Satyananda has emphasized in his teachings that every serious practitioner of meditation should develop the ability to split the awareness in this way, having total control over both inner and outer experience. He has also said that to lose awareness of the outer and immerse oneself in the inner experience is not the aim of meditation. Dhyana or meditation is homogenous awareness. This indicates that every kind of experience is included in the state of dhyana. Therefore, exclusion of the outer experience and development of the inner dimension only does not result in a total or homogenous awareness. If omnipresence, omnipotence and omniscience are the attributes of the supreme reality, then that would include the experience of all realms, not just the outer or the inner. By merging with that reality in the state of dhyana, the practitioner acquires those attributes and gains complete knowledge of both inner and outer simultaneously. Then dharana becomes the means to go deep within oneself whilst still retaining the outer awareness of the symbol.

### Experience of Bhairava

Bhairava is one such state that the consciousness passes through during the journey from the outer to the inner experience. It is that state which just precedes the experience of the universal consciousness or Shiva. You may have noticed that all Shiva temples have a Bhairava shrine at the entrance, where one worships first before worshipping Shiva. This is a very subtle way of allegorizing this very secret as well as sacred truth. Bhairava is known as the security officer of Lord Shiva, who screens everyone about to enter his domain. Unless you pass through Bhairava's infra-red check, you cannot enter that zone of pure consciousness.

You first have to pay obeisance to Bhairava and then to Shiva.

At the ancient city of Ujjain, where the famous jyotirlinga known as Mahakaleshwar is enshrined, there is also a famous Bhairava temple at the outskirts where worship is done of Kaala Bhairava. There is a curious story about this shrine. The deity here is appeased by liquor, which he downs by the gallons, and always appears intoxicated. During the British rule, the authorities dismissed this as a hoax and had the shrine excavated to check if there was a secret channel through which the liquor flowed when it was poured into the mouth of the deity. But they found nothing, and even today devotees flock there to offer alcohol to Bhairava, which he consumes and then grants their wishes.

Instead of dismissing this custom as superstition, one may discover exactly what it indicates to the devout and faithful, if one ponders over it deeply. Of course, logic and reason tell us there is no need to offer alcohol to a statue made of stone or clay. However, if we understand bhairava as a state of intoxicated bliss, where the individual consciousness has realized its true identity and experiences intense longing to unite with the supreme consciousness of which it is an intimate part, then this ritual takes on a very significant meaning.

The word bhairava is derived from the Sanskrit word *rudanti*, meaning crying, wailing or howling. *Rudra* is also an epithet of Shiva, and signifies yet another state of consciousness, derived from the same word. (VBT sl. 1) Some scholars have interpreted the word bhairava as creation, sustenance and withdrawal. They are not entirely wrong, because it represents that state where the consciousness is very close to the experience of the creator in whom these three qualities are inherent. However, in the state of bhairava individual consciousness is still at the threshold, although it realizes its proximity to the universal consciousness. So it lets out a loud wail or howl, similar to the howling of a dog pining for his mate. This is why the vehicle of Bhairava is a dog.

That bloodcurdling sound of a dog howling into the night is the wail emitted on the subtle and causal plane by the consciousness that is pining for union with its source. It is a very intense psycho-emotional state. Perhaps it is not a coincidence that the jiva's first action on gaining entry into the world is to let out a loud wail. This happens at the exact moment when the ties with the cosmic prana are physically severed by the cutting of the umbilical chord. As he breathes his first individual breath, he too perceives this separation and craves for union.

There are eight Bhairavas, each of which denotes a state of consciousness. They are *batuka*, meaning 'little'; *kaala*, meaning 'time' in the absolute sense or eternity; *shanta* meaning 'tranquil'; *vijnana,* meaning 'essential truth', and so on. Out of these, vijnana bhairava is the state where the knowledge that is special and sacred begins to flow freely and spontaneously into the individual consciousness, thus signifying that it is united and connected with the cosmic consciousness, which is the source of all knowledge.

Bhairava is a state of total and complete surrender. This manifestation, although a trifle fearful due to the psychic sounds of wailing, howling and crying that are heard by the causal body, is extremely benevolent and full of radiant knowledge. This is why surrender is regarded as the highest quality in a spiritual aspirant. In the state of surrender there is very high receptivity, and knowledge is received without any obstruction or disturbance.

**Four feet of atma**

The consciousness has four feet, which are like the four fractions of a single coin. They are a unified and homogenous part of the consciousness, not separate or broken off. These four aspects are responsible for the different experiences of consciousness as it undergoes manifestation in the dimension of matter. These four fractions of consciousness exist in the microcosm as individual consciousness and in the macrocosm as cosmic consciousness, both of which can be experienced by each individual.

The first stage of consciousness is known as *Vaishvanara,* whose sphere is the waking state, or *jagrat,* where the consciousness is associated with physical matter. Jagrat means 'awake' to the world. Philosophically, however, it is a state of avidya, where we are in deep slumber, because we identify with the material body and not with pure consciousness, which is the source of our existence. Vaishvanara has awareness of the external objects and receives knowledge by means of its seven limbs and nineteen mouths through which it enjoys and feeds on the gross objects. These limbs and mouths represent the lokas, tattwas, indriyas, pranas and antahkarana, and they form the avenues of knowledge and experience.

*Virat* is the cosmic counterpart of *vishwa,* the individual consciousness. The sum total of vishwa is virat. The word virat literally means 'enormous' and rightly so, because in this state the consciousness is experienced as the sum total of all that exists. Only something very enormous can contain the totality of the gross universe, which includes humans, vegetables, minerals, rivers, oceans, mountains, sun, moon, stars, galaxies, planets, comets, earth, water, fire, air and ether. Whatever exists in one's own body also exists in the universe. The whole universe is the body of virat. Your physical body is included in virat as are those of all others. The microcosm as well as the macrocosm is virat. This experience is described in chapter eleven of the *Bhagavad Gita* where Arjuna requests Lord Krishna to assume his virat form on the battlefield. Arjuna saw the magnificent sight of everything that has been created or yet to be created, emerging and being absorbed in virat.

The second stage of consciousness is known as *tejas*, whose sphere is the dreaming state, or *swapna*, where the consciousness is associated with the internal objects perceived through its seven limbs and nineteen mouths. It enjoys the subtle objects, feeding on the leftover remnants from the waking state. The word tejas means 'bright', and tejas is the essence of light through which it illumines the subtle objects. Just as virat is one with vishwa, so also the cosmic counterpart of tejas is *hiranyagarbha*, the cosmic womb, which holds the subtle impressions of the entire creation that is contained in virat. Hiranyagarbha is therefore the sum total of all subtle existence. In this sense, it is the cosmic mind. The individual mind is linked to this cosmic mind through the subtle body. On account of this link the mind is a very powerful substance and the range of its attributes is enormous.

Thought is an expression of the mind which translates itself into speech and action. Thought, speech and action generate emotions such as happiness or unhappiness, and also give rise to other attributes such as clarity of thinking, accurate perception, proper understanding, right action and so on. Every thought has weight, colour, shape, smell, size, quality and momentum. Thoughts are not a static substance. Once they come into existence, they begin to move outwards as vibrations. They keep moving, creating ripples wherever they go, influencing and affecting others and connecting you with them, not on the conscious plane but on the unconscious plane. In fact, you may never realize how deeply you are connected with others until you study the science of the mind.

The individual mind is an evolute of *mahat*, the cosmic intelligence, which is an evolute of Shiva, the pure cosmic consciousness. During the process of evolution the individual mind manifests in five stages. In the first, where it is in close proximity to supreme intelligence, it manifests as *niruddha*, total cessation or perfect control. In the second it becomes

76

*ekagrata*, or one-pointed, but not totally controlled. From one-pointed it becomes *vikshipta*, oscillating between steadiness and distraction. From oscillating it becomes *kshipta*, or totally dissipated, and from there it enters the last phase of *moodha*, which is dull and forgetful.

The third state of consciousness is *prajna*, or intuitive knowledge, whose sphere is *nidra*, or deep sleep. Prajna enjoys pure bliss, where there is no thought, desire or dream. In this state mind and ego, subject and object are absent. But there is *avidya*, the veil of ignorance, for in deep sleep the mind involutes into its cause, *moola-ajnana,* or the root of non-awareness. This veil of ignorance prevents the individual consciousness from knowing its source, and unless this veil is pierced through, avidya remains.

Prajna is the causal body and the experiencer of bliss in deep sleep. Its cosmic counterpart is *Ishvara*, which means 'non-destructible' or permanent reality, and represents the sum total of all the causal bodies. Your causal body is included in Ishvara as are the causal bodies of others. Although prajna is associated with avidya, it is still described as a very powerful state where the source of knowledge is neither the senses nor the remnants of past impressions, but the cosmic storehouse. Here everything is stored that has come into existence or is waiting to come into existence, that has been destroyed and consumed or is waiting to be destroyed and consumed, that has been spoken or is waiting to be spoken, that has happened or is waiting to happen. It is the mythical Pandora's box or the skeleton in the closet.

Prior to this state, the source of knowledge was controlled by the individual mind, discriminated by the intellect and identified by the ego. But now the source of knowledge is beyond the gambit of the individual mind in the realm of intuition, thus it is called prajna. (VBT sl. 121) This form of knowledge is derived from a cosmic source and is very powerful. Some of the experiences of prajna can be mind

77

blowing and difficult to handle. Moreover, as the individual faculties of mind, ego and intellect are absent, one has no control over those experiences. Therefore, they can be completely overwhelming and override the normal jagrat awareness, where one is guided by instinct and intellect, but not by intuition.

One who has entered the state of prajna consciously may appear strange and abnormal to others, as he will act on the knowledge he is receiving from the causal plane, which corresponds with Ishvara, the sphere where all the causal bodies are stored. Today Ishvara is translated as God, but in fact, Ishvara is that consciousness which is cosmic in nature and contains the cosmic storehouse of all karmas, samskaras and past impressions. Your karmas are also stored there in much the same way that information is stored on a super computer. Your file so and so.doc would be stored in it, and at the time of birth, the individual soul, or jiva, collects all the data from there and is born on the physical plane as embodied matter.

The fourth state is *turiya*, where the individual conscious-ness merges with the cosmic consciousness. Transcendence is experienced in this state because the consciousness goes beyond matter and becomes liberated from its clutches. Here the only source of knowledge is knowledge itself, for turiya is pure, untainted jnana, which is absolute and cosmic in nature. The sphere of turiya is the pure *atman*, or that which pervades everything. Today the atman is translated as 'soul', but in fact, it means 'all pervading', that which exists everywhere in all spheres of time and space and beyond as well. It is neither external nor internal awareness; neither is it absence nor presence of awareness. It is the experience of the sum total of all that exists, both manifest and unmanifest, in its most sublime and refined state. This experience is indefinable, unthinkable, unknowable, and can never be experienced by the ego, so say the Upanishads.

It is a state of awareness which is attained spontaneously and not by any practice.

Dharana and dhyana lead to savikalpa samadhi, the third state of consciousness, which is prajna, and leave you at the threshold of the fourth. They cannot unlock the door to turiya, but they bring you to the exact point where you get a glimpse of that fourth door, even if it is closed. When savikalpa samadhi occurs, a few chinks of light sometimes escape from behind that closed door, giving a glimpse of what lies beyond. But that awareness is still fragmented and broken; it is not unified and continuous. Only in turiya, with the dawning of nirvikalpa samadhi, does that the unified and effulgent experience become total, when subject and object merge completely into the one supreme awareness.

## Negotiating the mega-merger

Vijnana bhairava consciousness is savikalpa samadhi and shiva consciousness is nirvikalpa samadhi. All the practices of VBT bring you up to the experience of savikalpa samadhi. Beyond that, there is no practice by which you can attain the highest state of shiva consciousness. When savikalpa samadhi .is broken, all you have to do is continue the practice of dharana. Gradually, nirvikalpa will happen by itself as savikalpa becomes steady for extended periods of time. Through prolonged periods of savikalpa samadhi, the awareness makes a quantum leap which propels it out of the pull of gravity into a different dimension altogether. In that dimension the electro-magnetic pull of the supreme awareness is so strong that it draws the individual consciousness into its bosom, where they unite and become one.

Vijnana bhairava is that state where special knowledge, which is untainted and pure, is accessed for the first time. That is why this book is titled 'Vijnana Bhairava'. It could have been called jnana bhairava instead of vijnana bhairava, because jnana also means knowledge. However, what these

79

practices in VBT reveal is not just knowledge, but specialized and absolute knowledge which is so pure that the only other name for it is Truth. Up to this state the aspirant can subject his experiences to verification, scrutiny and intense examination, for the subject-object awareness is still present. Thus, this knowledge is known as vijnana bhairava because it has been scrutinized. After this stage, however, the subject and object merge and themselves become the experience, so there is no possibility of scrutiny, for who will scrutinize whom, as the experiencer and experience have collaborated to form the biggest merger of all times. In modern language it can be called the mega-merger.

Vijnana is bhairava and both are identical. They are one in nature. *Vi* is shakti and *jnana* is shiva or bhairava. So, by attaining the state of vijnana, one can know bhairava. What has been called vijnana bhairava consciousness in tantra is the equivalent of prajna and ishvara in the upanishadic analysis of consciousness. Both have been described as states of bliss, where there is no mind and no ego, but traces of avidya still remain. So, although the supreme reality is known and perceived, the awareness is still negotiating the collaboration and the final stages are yet to be worked out before the mega merger takes place.

This experience belongs to the causal body where all information is stored in coded form as archetypes. These archetypes reveal themselves in the form of experiences, both abstract and tangible. For instance, you may see someone in your room whom others present with you cannot. Swami Satyananda has described his personal experience of this stage as follows. While meditating in his room at Munger, he suddenly saw a snake lying on the floor, and as he rose to protect himself, it vanished into thin air. On another occasion a lady with a large red dot on her forehead appeared at his window and stood there staring at him, and each time he went to close the window she would disappear. This happened so many times that he had to permanently block the window in order to proceed with his meditation.

This signifies that the aspirant develops the psychic powers which manifest matter in the state of savikalpa samadhi. The mind becomes cosmic and assumes the form of a *kalpa vriksha,* or wish-fulfilling tree. Whatever one thinks at that time happens. Thus, although there is still avidya, the Upanishads describe this as a state when the mind assumes immense power. This is an attribute or quality of Ishvara, the name given to this state of consciousness.

## Quantum leap

VBT teaches the scientific principles of tantra, which gather the scattered waves emanating from the mind and fix them at one point. This, in turn, leads to the experience of bhairava consciousness, where you are just about to enter the domain of the ultimate reality. When the train is about to pull into your final destination, you cannot see the place as you have not yet reached there, but you begin to get an idea about it from the smells, sounds, air and vibrations that emanate from the approaching station. In the same way, when you experience the state of consciousness known as bhairava, the attributes of Shiva begin to show up and surround you from all sides, but you are not yet face to face with him. It is a moment of intense excitement, anticipation and longing. This agony of separation is similar to two lovers who are about to meet after a long separation, but it is of the nature of bliss, not sorrow; of knowledge, not ignorance.

Vijnana, by its name, implies that during this state of consciousness the aspirant experiences a free flow of specialized and pure knowledge within. However, despite access to the supreme knowledge, still the highest reality has not been experienced in its totality. In philosophical terms it is said that this is on account of avidya, or lack of

81

knowledge. In technical terms this is because of the fact that at this point the consciousness is suspended in the twilight zone where dawn has set in but the night has not fully gone. From this point the consciousness is within the purview of darkness as well as light. On one side it views matter and on the other spirit. Suffice it to say that, as the consciousness is not fully rid of its material shell, it is still within the gravitational pull that surrounds the physical body. In order to get out of that circuit, it will have to take a quantum leap into the unknown to enter the range of influence created by the most subtle, pure and effulgent consciousness.

What this actually means is that in order to transcend matter, you have to transcend gravity. It is gravity that holds matter together and pulls the awareness down to the material level. Try to imagine the scenario if one day while sitting in the practice of dharana, your mind were to attain such intense concentration that dhyana occurred and then you entered samadhi. Transcending gravity momentarily, your consciousness would leave the body and become all pervasive, all knowing, all seeing and all-experiencing. At that moment your physical body might begin to rise into the air and float. Depending on your prowess, you may be fully alert or enter into a trance-like state. If the awareness is trained in dharana, it will remain alert and follow the correct path on its flight without being diverted or lost.

At the point when you emerge from the pull of gravity, finding the correct spandan or vibration is very important. Your consciousness has left its cage and is about to take flight. What path should it follow and who or what will guide it at that time? Will it turn back or will it go forward on the right path? Apart from dharana the only other factor that can guide the consciousness at this stage is the guru's grace. That is why the spiritual master is known as guru, for he dispels the darkness by steering the disciple's consciousness onto the narrow path which leads to the light.

## Classification of practices in VBT

Having understood the ultimate goal, VBT tells us that the same mind which functions in everyday life is transformed through the practice of dharana into the most heightened state of awareness. Let us now take another look at the general modes of practice it prescribes to achieve this task of enlightenment. These methods, or upayas, can be classified as sthoola, sukshma and karana. The *sthoola upayas* are physical in nature and belong to the jagrat state. They include those methods that relate to the breath, such as pranayama, and to the nadis, such as mudras. The *sukshma upayas* are subtle in nature and belong to the swapna state. They include methods of dharana that relate to the psyche, such as japa, trataka and concentration on a symbol. The *karana upayas* are abstract in nature and belong to the sushupti stage. They include those methods that relate to the causal body, such as dharana on ideas, emotions, thoughts and feelings. As stated earlier there is no technique or upaya to reach turiya. It just happens spontaneously by itself at a certain moment in time.

Although the practices have been classified, they have not been graded. Each practice is complete in itself and can lead you to that heightened state of awareness. The practices do not depend on each other to progress towards that awareness. The sthoola upayas are no less potent and effective in achieving that experience than the sukshma or karana. They have been classified so that the aspirant may choose the practice suited to his temperament. If his consciousness is in jagrat awareness, he should choose the sthoola sadhana. If his consciousness is in swapna, he should choose the sukshma sadhanas, and if it is in sushupti, he should choose the sadhanas that influence the karana sharira.

Only one who knows this science and has an understanding of the inner mind can assess the level where the consciousness is functioning. Therefore, it is mandatory

83

that these practices are chosen and performed under the direction of an adept or guru who has mastered this path of tantra. Although certain practices are termed sthoola, they should not be rejected as inferior, because they can take the aspirant to the sukshma and karana awareness quite effectively. So, one should not choose the karana practices over the sukshma or sthoola practices with the idea that these will give the experience faster. The correct upaya is that which one is spontaneously comfortable with and which totally absorbs the mind so that concentration occurs without much effort and is not broken time and again.

Dharana is not a sthoola sadhana. It actually comes under the category of karana sadhana because its area of influence spreads over three realms: physical, subtle and causal. Dharana is the bridge by which the sadhaka crosses from the outer to the inner realm. Therefore, it is important to perfect this practice before proceeding further, as the path becomes more difficult to follow in the subtler dimensions and the abysses into which one can fall are deep and unknown.

The common underlying factor in all the practices of VBT is your own awareness, which must be directed towards one single object to the exclusion of all else. In each practice your awareness must be directed, only the object differs. The objects specified in different practices range from prana and breath, to matrika and mantra, as well as nada and chakras. If these do not suit you, there is another whole range of practices that directs your awareness to emotions and feelings of pain and pleasure. Then again there is a range of abstract dharanas on ideas and thoughts, and yet another range of even more abstract dharanas on shoonya, void, emptiness and stillness.

VBT says that it is possible to reach the most heightened state of consciousness by directing your total awareness, not fragmented awareness, to any of these points. Logically, this ought to be true because the supreme awareness is all pervading, so it should be everywhere and we can discover it anywhere. Vedanta says Brahman is everywhere in the manifest and unmanifest too. In that case, every thought, idea and feeling, as well as everything seen and unseen, should have Brahman as its source and destination.

Tantra also advocates the same idea. In theory Shiva, the supreme consciousness, is omnipresent and pervades every atom, molecule and cell of all beings. The phrase in Hindi is: *"Kan kan mein bhagavan."* VBT says that if you focus your full awareness on any point, you will discover the power residing within it. That power is energy, or shakti, which is none other than shiva. Shiva is *shaktiman,* the holder of shakti. How can the holder of shakti be different from it? There is nothing in this world or out of it that is made up of shiva or consciousness alone. Wherever there is consciousness, there is energy; they are inseparable. (VBT sl. 19)

If you hold love in your mind, you become love, and it can be said that you are love. Or if you hold greed or hatred, you become that. Just as these feelings pervade you, in the same way shakti pervades shiva and vice-versa. Even when they separate in order to manifest matter, they still remain as one at the cosmic level. Shakti is that principle or phenomenon by which the consciousness of shiva can be known. (VBT sl. 20) Without shakti, shiva remains inert, inactive and unseen. The practices of dharana are aimed at awakening the power or energy within matter. They act as a mirror in which your consciousness can see its own splendour. Shakti, or energy, has the passport and visa to travel freely whenever and wherever the awareness is directed. Thus by awakening shakti one becomes all-pervasive and whatever one wishes is fulfilled.

**Preparation for higher practices**
It is significant to mention here that Swami Satyananda has taught all the practices of VBT to his disciples and students

as hatha yoga, kriya yoga, kundalini yoga, laya yoga, nada yoga, raja yoga, jnana yoga, bhakti yoga and karma yoga. The similarities will be highlighted whenever they occur in the practices. In fact, they are the very same practices that you may already be doing, but there is a subtle difference. That difference is in awareness.

The ABCs that are learned in nursery school form the basis of all that is learned later in life. Without that foundation you could never grasp the knowledge you receive in an MSc. In the same way, all that you have done until now has prepared you for the higher stages of practice. In teaching all the yogas, Swami Satyananda has prepared us for this promotion into the higher class of dharana and dhyana. Those who have sincerely followed the practices will find it easier to slip into the higher class than those who have not.

VBT is a higher class or stage in the sense that the practice of dharana uses mental faculties rather than physical ones. All of these experiences are self-created in the absence of objects by conceptualizing forms, thoughts, ideas, feelings, emotions, sounds and even the movement of the breath. In VBT the idea of form is transcended up to the point where you can recreate it within yourself in the absence of an object. In other words you are allowed to dwell on a form so long as you have created it yourself without any external stimuli. This is a big leap which will crystallize the energies in a manner that no other practice can.

**Imposing the symbol on the body**

Unlike asana, pranayama, mudra and bandha, dharana is not a physical exercise. There is no physical movement during dharana. Steadiness of body is a prerequisite for any form of dharana. The faculties that you require for dharana are imagination and visualization. Even the dharanas which ask you to utilize practices of asana, pranayama, mudra and bandha are intended to be done on the mental plane. You have to imagine the entire process and superimpose it on your body. For example, in the second dharana in sloka 25, when you are asked to restrain the pranas from their respective points of return, instead of actually performing the kriya you are supposed to imagine it through the process of visualization, and superimpose it on your body. In actual fact, nothing is happening, but you are imagining that it is happening. This process will lead you to a very vital discovery, that you can influence your body and mind just through the process of imagination.

Gradually the mind will become so refined that you can perform all the sensory acts through its medium, without actually having to go through the process. (VBT sl. 70) You can smell the scent of sandal, taste your favourite food, see the face of your beloved, touch the softness of silk or even hear the sound of a flute. Those experiences that you normally have through the senses are accessible to you even without the presence of the sense objects. As explained earlier, this is the result of a mind that has expanded its boundaries. When this happens you can completely alter the structure of your being. In other words, your DNA can be restructured and you can be born again in the same physical body as an illumined being.

Moreover, as these practices are mental in nature, they can be done at any place and at any time, whenever you are not occupied. For example, you can practise when you are sitting in the park, riding on the train or bus, relaxing in your armchair, standing in a roomful of people, waiting for your turn at the dentist, or sitting on your meditation mat in the perfect posture. Dharana can even be practised with the eyes open once you become proficient at turning the gaze inwards.

In the course of your daily activities you are often practising dharana without your knowledge. There is an unknown process of consciousness that goes on subliminally, even when you are totally extroverted. You may have noticed that often while having a conversation, listening to music or doing some work, for a split second you are not there. If asked about it, you may not even be able to recall what happened in that split second. This is because in that moment your attention was pulled inwards without your conscious awareness. It touched that on which it was subliminally focused and then again reverted back to the extroverted awareness that was present before it happened. If you are attentive at such a moment, you can dive into an area that can reveal something to you. Artists are very proficient at diving deep within and bringing up some form of expertise, which shows up as talent or genius in them.

This subliminal process of dharana is an important stage in the process of growth and development of awareness, but it has to be trained and guided so that it remains within your voluntary control. Otherwise it may result in talent or genius, but it will never culminate in spiritual ecstasy. Without mental training, these subliminal experiences will never take you to a greater height. Your awareness will simply remain at that level. Just as there is a known process or path of consciousness, there is an unknown one too. Dreams are one manifestation of that unknown process, but there are many others, such as thoughts, feelings, likes, dislikes, temperament and tendencies. However, in these processes the normal awareness has the upper hand and the subliminal awareness is subdued.

When the subliminal awareness gains the upper hand in an untrained mind, problems may arise, such as erroneous perception, distorted outlook, faulty judgement and even insanity. This is because the area of consciousness that the subliminal process covers is in touch with the unconscious. It is very hard to know, understand or direct the unconscious; a completely different set of rules applies there. It is neither the realm of logic and reason, nor of emotion and feeling. It is the realm where everything is stored in codes and symbols which require interpretation. It is very hard to interpret these symbols through the rational mind; you need an intuitive mind for that. The mistake many aspirants make is to approach spiritual experience with logic and reason, because these do not apply here.

## Continuity of consciousness

As consciousness evolves into the manifest world and assumes form and substance, it loses its continuity. This continuity of consciousness is the secret for attaining higher states of awareness. If you can stop the mental fluctuation and revive the experience of continuity of consciousness, then you will attain the goal you set out to achieve. It is as simple as that. You can have that experience here and now, this very moment, says VBT, because you do not have to introduce any extraneous factor from outside. That unbroken, untainted and pure stream of consciousness is already flowing within you, but you are unaware of it on account of the external and fragmented focus of the mind.

The *Srimad Devi Bhagavatam* describes the abode of that supra-mental consciousness as surrounded by mountains, creeks, rivers, trees, nooks and crannies. Today scientists have correlated this description with the two hemispheres of the brain, along with the different layers which surround it. Although this text has camouflaged the supra-mental consciousness so beautifully, the discerning and enlightened can pick up the similarities. The barrier between you and that sublime experience is your own mind and the quality of awareness it generates. You are the victim or the victor of your own mind.

The same mind which causes distraction, dissipation, turmoil, insecurity, delusion, hatred, anger, fear, panic and dread can create courage, stability, confidence, security, love, one-pointedness and calmness within you. External

89

circumstances are not at all responsible for the quality of your experience. That depends entirely on what is stored within you in the different layers of your mind. It is not the spouse or the job, the home or the children, the riches or poverty, health or sickness, gain or loss that determine your happiness or despair. It is simply the quality of your mind that generates what you experience. The secret, therefore, lies in harnessing the mind through the practice of dharana and steering it onto the path of transcendental knowledge.

However, a word of caution is also necessary at this point so that sadhakas are not misled by the idea that para vidya, or transcendental knowledge, can be achieved so easily. One will have to qualify for it, just as one must qualify for apara vidya, or material knowledge. As para vidya is more profound than apara vidya, it is natural that the preparations required to receive it will have to be more intense, and the examination more demanding and difficult. A quick comparison between the faculties and qualities required for attaining apara and para vidya reveals that. For apara, or material knowledge, greater emphasis is laid on the intellect, whereas for para, or transcendental knowledge, it is intuition, or prajna, that has to be touched.

More than that, it is startling to learn that for transcendental experience one has to unlearn everything that one has learnt while qualifying for apara, or material knowledge. Apara is acquired knowledge, which is brought in or borrowed from outside, and para is innate knowledge, which unfolds from within. Apara is the realm of the head, which is the domain of logic, and para that of the heart, which is the seat of experience. Transformation occurs only through experience and not by discussion and debate. Thus it would be correct to surmise that you have to pay greater attention to the heart in order to attain transcendental knowledge. You will have to cherish and nurture the qualities of childlike innocence, spontaneity in action, purity of feeling, faultless honesty, positive outlook and cheerful disposition, and side by side develop the ability to separate the real from the unreal. Then whatever you think, speak or do will come from the heart and not the head.

Para vidya can be revealed only to the sadhaka in whom faith is alive and compassion has blossomed and borne fruit. If the tenderness of compassion and the cool fragrance of shraddha and bhakti are absent, the sadhaka will burn himself out by the brilliance of that knowledge. The qualities of the intellect are too gross to handle that kind of brilliance. So, in order to manifest brilliance, the sadhaka requires softness and subtlety, not rigidity and crudity. Receptivity and openness of heart will also enable the sadhaka to live in harmony with that transcendental experience, so that he can become an indivisible part of its homogeneity and experience the everlasting bliss of bhairava.

# Sri Vijnana Bhairava Tantra

# Commentary

*Bhairon Yantra*

# 1. Rudrayamala and Trika

श्री देव्युवाच
श्रुतं देव मया सर्वं रुद्रयामलसम्भवम् ।
त्रिकभेदमशेषेण    सारात्सारविभागशः ॥ 1 ॥

*Shree Devyuvaacha:*
*Shrutam deva mayaa sarvam rudrayaamalasambhavam;*
*Trikabhedam asheshena saaraat saaravibhaagaashah.* (1)

## Anvay

*Shree devee*: auspicious goddess; *Uvaacha*: says; *Shrutam*: heard; *Deva*: divine one; *Mayaa*: by me; *Sarvam*: all; *Rudrayaamala sambhavam*: that has emerged from Rudrayamala Tantra; *Trika*: group of three; *Bhedam*: divisions; *Asheshena*: complete; *Saaraat saara*: quintessence; *Vibhaagashah*: section-wise.

## Translation

Sri Devi says:
O Deva, I have heard in detail all that has been revealed through the union of Rudra and his shakti or what has emerged from the Rudrayamala Tantra. I have also understood Trika, or the three divisions of Shakti, which forms the quintessence of all knowledge.

## Commentary

Satya, or truth, is eternal. It is forever existent in the cosmos at the paravak level in latent form. Yogis, rishis and munis, the scientists of yore, have known these truths, not by the mind, but by raising their awareness to that level. In order to make these truths available to man at his present level of evolution, in a manner that he can grasp, Shiva, as a part of his anugraha, or grace, reveals satya at the vaikhari, or spoken level, in answer to questions posed by his shakti. She knows all that has emerged from the Rudrayamala and Trika, which form the quintessence of all the doctrines dedicated to the quest for truth. This tradition of tantra, where Shiva expresses himself through the medium of his Shakti, has higher connotations too. For it is through the medium of energy (shakti) that consciousness (shiva) reveals itself. Without shakti, shiva remains unmanifest and inert.

*Trika* literally means 'three' and is the name given to the doctrine of Kashmir Shaivism which upholds the triple divisions of existence: shiva, shakti and nara; consciousness, energy and matter; para, apara and parapara; time, space and object. Trika here has been called the quintessence of all the scriptures, as it speaks of one reality which is both transcendental (monistic) as well as immanent (dualistic). It is in this sense that Kashmir Shaivism and Vedanta are both unique. One gave the doctrine of unity in diversity; the other extended it to diversity in unity.

The basic premise of Trika is that energy, or shakti, is the link between matter and consciousness. The experiences obtained during the process of evolution from matter to consciousness denote the triple divisions of shakti from which this philosophy gets the name Trika. These three experiences are apara, purely gross experience, parapara, both gross and transcendental experience, and para, purely transcendental experience.

When the energy is locked up in matter, it gives rise to the apara, or gross experience. The analogy given in tantra for this experience is that of kundalini lying asleep in three and a half coils at the base of mooladhara chakra in the region of the cervical plexus. When the energy awakens and begins to ascend, it gives rise to the parapara or gross and transcendental experience, which is sometimes gross and sometimes transcendental. When the energy reaches its destination in sahasrara chakra and unites with consciousness, it gives rise to para, or transcendental experience.

Trika philosophy is called the quintessence of all the scriptures because it enumerates all three dimensions of existence.

Rudra is derived from the Sanskrit word *rudanti*, which literally means 'to weep'. *Yamala* means 'pair' or 'couple'. Rudrayamala is the union of Rudra and his shakti, *prakasha* and *vimarsha*. Rudrayamala Tantra is an important tantric text, parts of which are now in obscurity. It deals mainly with the interplay of consciousness and energy, which gives rise to a wide range of experience from jagrat to turiya.

Primarily, the tantra shastras are divided into three sections: agama, tantra and yamala. Each has its own characteristics. The yamalas throw light on creation down through the ages in a sequential order, with specific emphasis on sadhana or methods of perfection. These sadhanas are not restricted to aspirants belonging to any particular race, social strata or religion, but can be availed of by any sincere sadhaka who qualifies for them. These sadhanas come under the category of *Kaula Tantra* and are intended for vira sadhakas. They are most secret and this condition of keeping them confidential should not be violated. If they are practised as instructed, they will certainly lead to perfection in all spheres of life.

The *Varahi Tantra* names Adiyamala, Brahmayamala, Vishnuyamala, Rudrayamala and Ganeshyamala. Out of these only the *Uttara Tantra* of Rudrayamala is available. The subject matter of Rudrayamala Tantra is devoted entirely to esoteric sadhanas, such as smashan sadhana, kumari pooja, bhairavi pooja, chakra bhedan, pancha makara, sushumna jagran, etc. It also details the different categories of sadhakas or aspirants, conditions of sadhana and importance of guru. Vijnana Bhairava Tantra is a part of the Rudrayamala Tantra.

Rudra is an epithet of Shiva. Mention of Rudra is found in the Vedas, and as tantra is more ancient than the Vedas, it is quite evident that Rudra is a deva of great antiquity. Devas are defined as luminous beings who have attained luminosity by sheer dint of their sadhana. In the *Yajurveda* a splendid hymn, known as *Rudri*, is entirely devoted to this deva, where he is named as one who presides over the eight quarters of space, and also as the lord who protects. These eight quarters or directions of space are extremely important in any tantric sadhana or esoteric practice. If they are not taken care of, hindrances may occur. It is for this purpose that Rudra manifested as *ashta*, or eight, Bhairavas, so that each quarter of space would be protected for the sadhaka who endeavoured to enter the realm of transcendence. Therefore, it may be inferred that anyone who embarks on this journey has to invoke Bhairava, who then acts as the guardian of that aspirant.

The agama literature is very extensive, as it includes all that comes under the banner of experiential knowledge or is related to existence and creation. Although the tantras contain the very same information as the agamas, they are a more classified literature in that they deal with specific topics. In this way the tantric texts eliminated the unnecessary and kept what was important. There are sixty-four tantras, a number which relates with the *chausath shaktipeethas,* or sixty-four places of Shakti in various parts of India.

## 2. Reality of Bhairava

अद्यापि न निवृत्तो मे संशय: परमेश्वर ।
किं रूपं तत्त्वतो देव शब्दराशिकलामयम् ॥ 2 ॥

*Adyaapi na nivritto me samshayah parameshvara;*
*Kim roopam tattvato deva shabdaraashikalaamayam.* (2)

### Anvay

*Adyaapi*: even today; *Na nivrittah*: not dispelled; *Me*: my;
*Samshayah*: doubts; *Parameshvara*: O Supreme Lord; *Kim
roopam*: what form; *Tattvatah*: in essence; *Deva*: O Divine
One; *Shabdaraashi*: multitude or garland of letters;
*Kalaamayam*: creative energy of the divine.

### Translation

O Supreme Lord, in spite of everything that I have heard,
even today my doubts are not dispelled. What is your reality,
O Divine One? Are you the power or energy contained in
sound from which all the mantras have originated?

### Commentary

If Rudrayamala and Trika are the quintessence of all the
scriptures, then one wonders why Devi still has doubts after
hearing and understanding them in detail. This is because
the writer wants to emphasize that mere understanding of
the scriptures is not enough to realize the supreme reality.
One has to experience it in order to know that phenomena
fully. Until then it is merely intellectual knowledge and
doubts will thus prevail. It is experience alone that can
transform the awareness and turn doubt into faith, as
experience is above the realm of intellect.

According to tantra, nada, or cosmic sound, is the first
evolute in the scheme of creation. When Shiva, the supreme
consciousness, wants to create, he sends forth his creative

power, or shakti, who creates a spandan, or vibration, through her inherent attributes of jnana (knowledge), kriya (action) and iccha (will). This vibration gives rise to nada, or cosmic sound, from which mantra, akshara and all forms of sound originate. The concept of akshara is peculiar to this philosophy, which considers it to be full of the creative energy of the divine. This creative energy is the power residing in the mantras, known as matrika, which is realized only when the mantra or sound becomes efficacious and reveals its hidden power to the aspirant. The etymology of the word akshara suggests that it is an indestructible power and, therefore, it is also called *akshara brahman*.

Therefore, Devi is curious to know if the supreme reality is the same as the hidden power of mantra.

## 3. How the Bhairava reality is perceived

किं वा नवात्मभेदेन भैरवे भैरवाकृतौ ।
त्रिशिरोभेदभिन्नं वा किं वा शक्तित्रयात्मकम् ॥ 3 ॥

*Kim vaa navaatmabhedena bhairave bhairavaakritau;*
*Trishirobhedabhinnam vaa kim vaa shaktitrayaatmakam.* (3)

### Anvay

*Kim vaa*: or else; *Navaatma bhedena*: piercing of the nine atmas; *Bhairave*: in Bhairava (agama); *Bhairava aakritau*: in the form or state of bhairava; *Trishiraha*: three flows; *Bheda*: penetration; *Abhinnam*: different; *Vaa*: or; *Kim*: what; *Vaa*: or; *Shakti trayaatmakam*: three kinds of shakti.

### Translation

Can your reality be perceived through the nine different ways by which one can enter the realm of higher consciousness, as enumerated in Bhairava Agama? Is it different from the procedure in Trishira Bhairava Tantra? Or can it be perceived through knowledge of the triple forms of shakti, ie. para, parapara and apara? These are my doubts, O Bhairava!

### Commentary

Here, Devi refers to procedures that have been enumerated in Bhairava Agama, *Trishira Bhairava Tantra* and the Trika philosophy. Bhairava Agama is not just a tantric text, but encompasses the entire spectrum of knowledge, which has been handed down on the subject of that state of consciousness defined as bhairava. *Navatma* refers to the nine different designs or formations of consciousness that are to be realized in order to attain that state. That state called bhairava, which grants bliss and liberation, is of nine forms. You can utilize any one of these forms to approach that state. The nine forms are as follows: *kaala* (time), *kula* (one that ascends), *naama* (name), *jnana* (knowledge), *chitta* (awareness), *nada* (sound), *bindu* (seed), *kalaa* (wave) and *jiva* (individual soul).

Just as there are nine designs for the supreme consciousness, there are also nine designs for the supreme energy, which is known as bhairavi. They are: *vama* (the energy that flows in ida nadi), *ambika* (the energy that flows in pingala nadi), *jyestha* (the supreme flow of energy in sushumna nadi), *raudri* (protectress of space), *iccha* (energy of will), *jnana* (energy of knowledge), *kriya* (energy of action), *shanti* (energy of tranquillity) and *para* (transcendental energy). These forms react deeply to the intonation of mantras and regulated flow of breath.

*Trishira Bhairava Tantra* is a text which outlines the role of the three flows of prana, known as ida, pingala and sushumna. The word *tri* means 'three' and *shira* literally means 'that which carries'. In this case, trishira refers to the three major nadis that carry the flow of pranashakti or kundalini to the highest centres after piercing the six vital chakras located along the spine. There is another related work of significant importance, known as *Trishiropanishad,* that deals with these three shiras, or flows of vital energy.

The trishira is one of tantra's most unique concepts. In fact, all of the practices of yoga and tantra are aimed at balancing these three flows of energy. It is the claim of both yoga and tantra that when the flow of prana in ida and pingala nadis is balanced and equalized, a tremendous awakening takes place, whereby the dormant serpent power or kundalini begins its ascent through the third nadi, known as sushumna.

Trika, or the triple forms of shakti, is related to the entire gambit of experiences that arise in relation to this awakening on the gross, subtle and causal levels. This whole universe of matter is nothing but energy. This field of energy extends from the manifestation of matter to the transformation of matter into energy and consciousness and finally into pure spirit. The range of energy includes both matter and spirit, and in this sense energy is gross as well as transcendental. Therefore, materialists pay homage to energy and so do the spiritualists. This is proof in itself that shakti, or energy, is not limited to any one sphere, but is present in all the *lokas,* or realms of existence.

In this sloka Devi outlines three very important procedures for attaining higher states of awareness. The first is the penetration into navatma, or the nine states of higher awareness mentioned earlier, the second is piercing awareness of the flows of ida, pingala and sushumna, and the third is deep awareness of the three realms of shakti. Each of these can be experienced through the awareness of breath, or mantras, or both together.

Devi asks if that supreme reality can be realized through these procedures.

## 4. By what experience this reality is known

नादबिन्दुमयं वापि किं चंद्रार्धनिरोधिका: ।
चक्रारूढमनच्कं वा किं वा शक्तिस्वरूपकम् ॥ 4 ॥

*Naadabindumayam vaapi kim chandraardhanirodhikaah;*
*Chakraaroodham anachkam vaa kim vaa shaktisvaroopakam.* (4)

### Anvay

*Naada bindu mayam*: full of the forms of nada and bindu; *Vaa
api*: or else; *Kim*: what; *Chandra ardha*: half moon;
*Nirodhikaah*: obstructor; *Chakra*: psychic centres; *Aaroodham*:
ascending; *Anachkam*: unstruck sound; *Vaa*: or; *Kim vaa*: or
else; *Shakti svaroopakam*: form of shakti.

### Translation

Is it nada and bindu or can it be known by concentrating on
the ascending psychic centres or the unstruck sound which
emanates without any vibration? Or is it the form of the
obstructing half moon or else is it the form of shakti?

### Commentary

Nada, or primal sound, is the first evolute to emerge from
the spandan, or vibration, of that supreme consciousness.
Bindu is the nucleus from which this vibration emerges.
The six main chakras, or psychic centres, along the path of
kundalini in the spinal column are mooladhara, swadhisthana, manipura, anahata, vishuddhi and ajna. But there
are many more minor centres which are not as well known.
Below mooladhara are said to be two chakras known as
vishu and adha-sahasrara, and above ajna in the skull there
are nine centres known as bindu, ardhendu or ardhachandrika, nirodhika, nada, mahanada or nadanta, shakti,
vyapika, samani and unmani.

Bindu is the point where the descending consciousness bids goodbye to the experience of unity and steps down into the experience of multiplicity and diversity. It is also the point where the nectar, or *amrita*, is held before it drips down to irrigate the entire body. Thus, it is also known as *bindu visarga*, which literally means 'falling of the drop'. On account of this, the system of tantra regards bindu as an extremely important point for the experience of transcendence. In his book *Kundalini Tantra*, Swami Satyananda has called bindu 'the point which contains the blueprint for life'.

*Ardhachandrika*, meaning 'half moon', is a psychic centre which corresponds so closely with bindu that they are often referred to as the same centre. The symbol of bindu is also depicted as a crescent moon. *Nirodhika* is the psychic centre where the experience of form is obstructed. *Nada* is the centre where cosmic sound manifests, and *nadanta* is the centre where the difference between the sound and the experiencer dissolves, or the end of sound. *Shakti* is the centre where intense waves of bliss permeate the entire being. *Vyapika* is the centre or abode of shoonya, which can be pierced or transcended only by the appearance of *jyotsna*, or light. *Samani* is the centre where samprajnata samadhi is experienced, which is samadhi with illumination, or the pratyabhijna consciousness. *Unmani* is the centre beyond mind or thought, where the gaze is completely turned inwards.

Patanjali has described the various states of samprajnata samadhi which can be correlated with these higher centres, i.e., nirvitarka and nirodhika, nirvichara and nadanta, ananda and shakti, asmita and samani.

*Chakra aroodham* relates to the great ascent of kundalini, as it pierces through the six major psychic energy centres on its journey from mooladhara chakra at the base of the spine to sahasrara chakra at the top of the skull.

Anahata chakra, or the heart centre, is the seat of the unstruck sound, or anahad nada, where it resounds without any objective cause and without any interruption. From the anahad nada originate all the akshara, or letters of the alphabet, which are formed by the varying frequencies of vibration produced by this nada. These vibrations produce *dhvani,* or sound, as well as jyotsna, or light.

Devi is curious to know if that supreme reality is any of these states of awareness.

## 5. Transcendent or immanent

परापराया: सकलम् अपरायाश्च वा पुन: ।
पराया यदि तद्वत्स्यात् परत्वं तद्विरुध्यते ॥ 5 ॥

*Paraaparaayaah sakalam aparaayaashcha vaa punaha;*
*Paraayaa yadi tadvatsyaat paratvam tad virudhyate.* (5)

### Anvay

*Paraaparaayaah*: transcendent cum immanent; *Sakalam*:
complete; *Aparaayaashcha*: also the immanent; *Vaa*: or; *Punah*:
again; *Paraayaa*: transcendental; *Yadi*: if; *Tadvatsyaat*: be like
that; *Paratvam*: transcendence; *Tat*: that; *Virudhyate*:
contradicted.

### Translation

(Is your reality) transcendent and immanent or is it completely immanent or completely transcendental? If it is
immanent (then the very) nature of transcendence is
contradicted.

### Commentary

Devi next inquires about the nature of reality. The immanent
reality is perceived as form and the transcendent reality is
beyond form. This relates to the age-old question in the
quest for truth: whether the reality is with form or without,
sakara or nirakara; or is it both sakara and nirakara? Different
philosophies and religions have developed theories to resolve
this question. However, the tantric approach is more
experiential. It does not give much importance to specula-
tion, but advocates a sincere effort to experience the reality
for oneself.

In fact, at the very outset Devi has expressed her
apprehensions in calling that ultimate reality immanent,
because in transcendence there is no room for immanence

107

at all. When you transcend something, you leave it behind. That reality is the ultimate transcendence which has left behind all the familiar associations of name, form and idea, along with the sensory perceptions of sight, sound, smell, taste and touch, which connect us with the external world, or the immanent reality.

## 6. Indivisible and indefinable

नहि वर्ण-विभेदेन देहभेदेन वा भवेत् ।
परत्वं, निष्कलत्वेन, सकलत्वे न तद्भवेत् ॥ 6 ॥

*Nahi varnavibhedena dehabhedena vaa bhavet;*
*Paratvam, nishkalatvena, sakalatve na tadbhavet.* (6)

### Anvay

*Nahi*: not; *Varna*: colour; *Vibhedena*: divisions; *Dehabhedena*: division of forms; *Vaa*: or; *Bhavet*: exist; *Paratvam*: transcendence; *Nishkalatvena*: indivisibility; *Sakalatve*: composite parts; *Na*: not; *Tat*: that; *Bhavet*: to be.

### Translation

Paratva, or transcendence, cannot exist in the divisions of varna (colour), shabda (sound) or roopa (form). If transcendence is indivisible, then it cannot be defined or co-exist with composite parts.

### Commentary

The immanent reality, or finite world, is made up of *shabda*, *varna*, and *roopa*, or sound, colour and form. We know this experience very well, as we have ample experience of it in our daily life. It is the transcendent reality that we are unfamiliar with. Here it has been described as indivisible, undefinable and unmanifest. Therefore, these three aspects of sound, colour and form, which together shape our perception of the manifest or finite world, have no existence or role to play in transcendence.

## 7. Essence of tantra

प्रसादं कुरु मे नाथ निःशेषं छिन्धि संशयम् ।
भैरव उवाच
साधु साधु त्वया पृष्टं तन्त्रसारमिदं प्रिये ॥ 7 ॥

*Prasaadam kuru me naatha nihshesham chhindhi samshayam;*
*Bhairava uvaacha:*
*Saadhu saadhu tvayaa prishtam tantrasaaram idam priye. (7)*

### Anvay

*Prasaadam*: grace, blessings; *Kuru*: do; *Me*: to me; *Naatha*: O Lord; *Nihshesham*: completely; *Chhindhi*: remove, cut; *Samshayam*: doubts; *Bhairava*: Bhairava; *Uvaacha*: says; *Saadhu saadhu*: good, auspicious; *Tvayaa*: by you; *Prishtam*: asked; *Tantrasaaram*: essence of tantra; *Idam*: this; *Priye*: O dear one.

### Translation

O Lord, by your blessings, please destroy all my doubts completely. Then Bhairava says: Good, well spoken, O dear one! What you have asked about is the essence of tantra.

### Commentary

Shakti propitiates Bhairava to dispel her doubts regarding the views she has expressed on transcendence in the previous slokas. She asks him as he represents the transcendent state, and only one who has realized this state can confer its experiential knowledge and understanding. Furthermore, she acknowledges and reaffirms the role of grace in the transmission of this knowledge. Bhairava is pleased with her question, as what she has asked is the very essence of tantra, a science dedicated to the realization of the truth behind existence.

Thus Devi asks a most auspicious question, which can completely eradicate the doubts and delusions within the seeker.

## 8. Forms of Bhairava

गूहनीयतमं भद्रे तथापि कथयामि ते ।
यत्किञ्चित्सकलं रूपं भैरवस्य प्रकीर्तितम् ॥ 8 ॥

*Goohaneeyatamam bhadre tathaapi kathayaami te;*
*Yatkinchit sakalam roopam bhairavasya prakeertitam.* (8)

### Anvay

*Goohaneeyatamam*: most secret; *Bhadre*: noble one (lady);
*Tathaapi*: yet; *Kathayaami*: I will speak; *Te*: to you; *Yat kinchit*:
whatever; *Sakalam*: composite part; *Roopam*: forms;
*Bhairavasya*: of Bhairava; *Prakeertitam*: expounded.

### Translation

Noble lady, although this is the most secret part of the
tantras, yet I will speak to you about what has been
expounded regarding the (defined) forms of Bhairava.

### Commentary

All esoteric sciences the world over are diligently kept secret,
and so too is tantra. This is not because there is anything to
hide, but because this science is so powerful that it is meant
only for a sadhaka or practitioner who has faith in the
practice, motivation to practise it and the self-control not to
misuse the power accruing from it. You would certainly not
put dynamite in the hands of a child. Similarly, the tantric
practices, which detonate the inner experiences, should not
be exposed or made accessible to the undiscriminating seeker.
Devi, however, is fully authorized to receive this secret
knowledge, as she is most noble, high-minded and sincere.

At the very outset there is a word of caution, and very
rightly so, because mental powers may be acquired through
the practices of tantra that are beyond the scope of the
ordinary person. The practitioner who has not developed

sattwic qualities will eventually be destroyed and consumed by those powers, as was Bhasmasura. In the Puranas there is a story about Bhasmasura, who performed great austerities to receive a boon from Shiva. The boon he received was that whomever he placed his hand over would turn to *bhasma*, or ashes. That was how he got his name.

Bhasmasura was so intoxicated with power that his mind became deluded and he began to think he could destroy anyone, even Shiva, the one who had given him the boon. So he went after him with that intention, but Shiva engaged Bhasmasura in a dance where he had to imitate his every step. Gradually, as Bhasmasura became immersed in that dance, Shiva danced a step in which his hand was placed over his head. Bhasmasura did the same and was immediately burnt to ashes.

So, the system of tantra is not just philosophical teachings; it is a science by which immense power can be generated. It is power that you are dealing with here, the power of consciousness! The Upanishads declare: *Kshurasya dhara nisita duratyaya durgam pathastat kavayo vadanti*, meaning "the wise say this path is as sharp as the edge of a razor and thus very difficult to walk." Therefore, one who treads such a path has to proceed carefully and with caution.

The phrase *sakalam roopam bhairavasya* indicates the forms of bhairava consciousness that have been expounded in tantra. After emphasizing the limitation of rites and rituals, form and substance, it may seem a contradiction that this sloka speaks of the defined forms of Bhairava. In tantra, however, every abstract phenomena and subtle experience has been categorized. It is this unique categorization that makes tantra so sacred and special, because these forms have been empowered to generate the experience which they represent.

To develop these states of awareness tantra employs the tools of mantra, yantra and mandala, which are based on the primordial principles of sound, light and form. Tantra says that every object and experience has a sound vibration, which is called mantra. From sound vibration emanates laser-like light that is linear and geometrical in form, which is called yantra. These geometrical forms result in a three-dimensional reality, which is called mandala. Concentration, or dharana, on any one of these tools will replicate and lead you to that very same experience which is enshrined in it. Thus each level of awareness has a mantra and a corresponding yantra and mandala.

The Rudrayamala Tantra, which is the source of VBT, provides a list of sixty-four mandalas of Bhairava. These mandalas are in eight groups, consisting of eight Bhairavas in each group, and each one has a corresponding mantra and yantra. Tantra says that these mantras, yantras and mandalas can be used very effectively to induce the level of awareness that they indicate.

The groups are distinguished by body colours, ornaments and weapons. The first group of Bhairavas is headed by Asitanga (the sword bearer); they are all yellow in colour and have well formed limbs. In their hands they carry a trident, hand drum, noose and sword. The second group, led by Ruru, is pure white in complexion, bedecked with ornaments, carrying a rosary, goad, book and lute. The third group has Chanda as its leader; they are of blue complexion, charming and carry fire, shakti, a mace and pot (kunda) in their hands. The fourth group is headed by Krodha; they are smoky-grey in complexion and carry a sword, shield, spear and axe. The fifth group is led by Unmattabhairava; they are white-complexioned, good-looking and carry a pot (kunda), shield, club (parigha) and bhindipala. Kapala heads the sixth group, which are of yellow complexion and carry the same weapons as the previous group. The seventh group is led by Bhishana; they are red in complexion and carry the same weapons.

113

Samhara Bhairava leads the eighth group; they resemble lightning and carry the same weapons.

Apart from the tantras, descriptions of the forms or mandalas of these eight Bhairavas are found in many of the Puranas, i.e., *Vamana Purana* (ch. 57), *Brahmavaivarta Purana* (ch. 61), *Kalika Purana* (ch. 44) and *Vishnu Dharmottara* (ch. 3.59). The Puranas do not describe these groups as elaborately as the tantras, but they ascribe the origin of Bhairava to Shiva's fight with the asuras or demons and list the number as ashta, or eight. Vishnu Dharmottarra adds a curious detail where Bhairava is shown as frightening Parvati with the serpent in his hand.

These eight Bhairavas rule over the eight quarters or directions of space, namely: north, south, east, west, northeast, northwest, southeast and southwest. Armed with their respective weapons, they prevent unauthorized entry into the domain of Shiva, as well as protection to those who have gained access into this sacred zone. These ashta Bhairavas actually signify eight states or manifestations of consciousness which, although a trifle fearful in appearance, are extremely benevolent and full of radiant knowledge.

In fact, Bhairava is regarded as one of the violent forms of Shiva associated with his fights against demons. The term demon is used here to personify characteristics or traits that one encounters on one's journey from gross to subtle spheres of consciousness. These Bhairavas personify states of awareness that the consciousness assumes during its ascent from darkness to light in order to ward off any dangers that may befall the aspirant.

As one studies tantra it is simply astonishing to discover that not only have different states of consciousness been explicitly defined, but definite ways to experience those states have also been given. Even the expressions that arise as a consequence of those altered states have been elucidated in the finest detail. It is these countless experiments in times gone by that gave birth to formulated, codified and defined tantric practices in the most minute detail, which we can still avail ourselves of today in such authentic texts as VBT.

*Bhairon Yantra*

## 9. Sakara aspect of Bhairava

तदसारतया देवि विज्ञेयं शक्रजालवत् ।
मायास्वप्नोपमं चैव गन्धर्ववनगरभ्रमम् ॥ ९ ॥

*Tadasaaratayaa devi vijneyam shakrajaalavat;*
*Maayaasvapnopamam chaiva gandharvanagarabhramam.* (9)

### Anvay

*Tat*: that; *Asaaratayaa*: unsubstantial; *Devi*: O Devi; *Vijneyam*: know; *Jaalavat*: like the magical web; *Shakra*: Indra; *Maaya svapna upamam*: illusion, dream-like; *Chaiva*: and also; *Gandharva*: celestial musician; *Nagara*: city; *Bhramam*: delusion.

### Translation

O Devi, the sakara aspect of Bhairava is insubstantial and of no spiritual value, like the illusory dream-like web of Indra, and is also like the delusion of celestial musicians.

### Commentary

This is a very important sloka in the context of philosophy, as it completely undermines sakara and by inference upholds nirakara. This is the essence of Vedanta, a philosophy that attempts to define transcendence with utmost honesty and sincerity. Vedanta means 'the end of knowledge' and its final proclamation in this regard is: "Neti, neti", not this, not this. Thus, it has ostensibly argued that the supreme reality is formless, or nirakara. By describing the sakara aspect as illusory and having no substance, this text reiterates the claims of Vedanta, showing the similarity of views.

Indra is the Lord of devas, who rules over the heavens. He stood foremost in the vedic pantheon and was invoked and worshipped in all the hymns of the Vedas. The Gandharvas are celestial musicians who reside in heaven.

Through their musical expertise they create the magical intoxication and perpetual bliss of the heavenly sphere, for which it is much sought after by the *devas* and their opposite counterparts, the *daityas*. The devas and the daityas are experts in creating maya, or an illusory effect on the mind. This is why those who reside in heaven are all complacent and content.

The common afflictions of man, such as illness, old age, death, worry anxiety and unhappiness, are unknown to those who dwell in heaven. But the heavenly bliss which they enjoy is also an illusion because it does not last forever. It is said that those who live according to dharma attain heaven by their meritorious acts. However, when their quota of merit runs out, the soul returns to *samsara*, or the cycle of birth and death. Heaven is only for the enjoyment of the merits one has earned on the earthly plane. It is not possible to earn more merit there, so that is the Catch 22 situation of heaven.

This sloka firmly states that sakara has no spiritual value; rather the association with form keeps you deluded about the real bhairava nature. You can never experience transcendence as long as you are under the spell of sakara, or form. What does this mean in the context of all the pooja, or worship, and dharana, or concentration on the symbol, that we have been doing over the years? Does it imply that all of these sadhanas are of no spiritual value and that we have been deluding ourselves? The answer is yes and no.

Sakara sadhana may have no spiritual value in the ultimate sense, but without going through sakara you cannot reach nirakara, or that which is of spiritual value. Sakara is a preparation and it teaches you the skills you will require when you dive deep into the waves of spiritual bliss. All that you have been doing until now is a preparation for that great evolutionary leap. However, without this preparation you cannot even think of taking this leap, for you would surely fall into the abyss.

After cautioning the sadhaka about the limitations of sakara at the very outset of this discourse, Bhairava will describe the type of sadhaka for whom sakara sadhana is useful. Later he will give the ways to realize the formless reality, which is the basis of spiritual experience. This text offers many means to reach that highest point of awareness, not only the tools of mantra, yantra and mandala. After all, if you are travelling from a cold to a hot place, you will have to abandon your woollens at some point on the journey. But just because you discard them along the way does not mean they were useless because you did require them when you set out. Without those warm clothes you may have fallen ill and not have been able to complete the journey. They protected you until you reached the point where you could continue on without them.

Moreover, there is a deeper significance to this statement. By cautioning the sadhaka about the illusory nature of sakara, he should realize that eventually he has to become an adept at recreating that very object which he has employed for sakara worship, even in the absence of the object. In other words he has to transcend the object made of clay, stone or metal, as it is finite in nature, being subject to decay, and instead realize the infinite reality of that very same object through dharana and dhyana.

So, when Bhairava speaks of sakara as being illusory and of no spiritual value, it really means that the experiences which you have in relation to the object are of no spiritual value as long as they belong to the mental and psychic realm, which relate to the conscious and subconscious levels. It is only when you transcend that object made of clay and are able to replace it with one made up of energy and then of consciousness that you enter the domain of the spirit. Whatever objects you see outside have their own images in the mind, says Swami Sivananda in *Mind: Its Mysteries and Control*, where this mystifying process is described with immense clarity and detail.

118

## 10. Purpose of sakara meditation

ध्यानार्थं भ्रान्तबुद्धीनां क्रियाडम्बरवर्तिनाम् ।
केवलं वर्णितं पुंसां विकल्पनिहतात्मनाम् ॥ 10 ॥

*Dhyaanaartham bhraantabuddheenaam kriyaadambaravartinaam;*
*Kevalam varnitam pumsaam vikalpanihitatmanaam.* (10)

### Anvay

*Dhyaanaartham*: for the sake of meditation; *Bhraanta*:
deluded; *Buddheenaam*: intellect; *Kriyaa*: action, rites;
*Aadambara vartinaam*: ostentatious rituals; *Kevalam*: only;
*Varnitam*: described; *Pumsaam*: to these people; *Vikalpa*:
dichotomizing thought patterns; *Nihataa*: prey; *Aatmanaam*:
people.

### Translation

(The sakara sadhanas) are described for those people of
deluded intellect, who are prey to distracted thought patterns
or are inclined towards the performance of action and
ostentatious rituals to traverse the path of meditation.

### Commentary

After denying the reality of sakara in the spiritual sense,
Bhairava explains its role in sadhana for those who are bound
by their thoughts and actions. The path of knowledge is not
accessible for those who are deluded or distracted. This path
is also obstructed by rites and rituals performed with arrogance
or ostentation. The purpose of sakara methods of meditation
is to guide and propel such seekers onto the path of
realization. Other than that, sakara sadhana has no spiritual
value. It is only intended to get the seeker on to the right path
and then from one point on the path to another.

In this sense, sakara sadhanas are like the different
rungs of a ladder, while nirakara is the topmost rung, where

119

you can climb off the ladder and then dispense with it altogether. But without the rungs of the ladder, how could those who are weak and infirm reach the top? So, sakara meditation is a necessary and important aid to sadhana and spiritual realization because most people would never get started without it. Moreover, as stated earlier, sakara meditation develops the skills needed to steer your way through deeper and deeper levels of consciousness into spiritual experience.

So, for this reason the vedic and tantric systems have accepted sakara sadhanas, even while proclaiming that the spiritual experience is nirakara.

## 11. What Bhairava is not

तत्त्वतो न नवात्मासौ शब्दराशिर्न भैरव: ।
न चासौ त्रिशिरा देवो न च शक्तित्रयात्मक: ॥ 11 ॥

*Tattvato na navaatmaasau shabdaraashirna bhairavah;*
*Na chasau trishiraa devo na cha shaktitrayaatmakah.* (11)

### Anvay

*Tattvatah*: in reality; *Na*: not; *Navaatmaasau*: nine forms;
*Shabdaraashih*: garland of letters; *Na*: not; *Bhairavah*:
Bhairava; *Na cha*: not even; *Asau*: this; *Trishiraa*: three flows;
*Devah*: divine being; *Na cha*: and is not; *Shakti trayaatmakah*:
three powers of shakti.

### Translation

In reality (the essence) of Bhairava is not the nine forms, nor
the garland of letters, nor the three flows and not even the
three powers of shakti.

### Commentary

One by one all the suppositions of Devi are negated. This
does not imply that these powers are insignificant; it just
means that the highest reality is something other than these.
Navatma, described in sloka 3, are the nine forms through
which the supreme atman, or indweller of all, can be realized.
Shabdarashi, the garland of letters, is the indestructible and
ceaseless source of sound, or mantra, referred to in sloka 2.
Trishira are the three manifestations of subtle energy, and
*shakti trayatmakam,* the three levels of subtle experience, also
described in sloka 3.

The rays of light emanating from the sun and the heat
produced by the sun are essential aspects of the sun, but
they are not the sun itself. In the same way, the energy fields
within the physical existence, as well as the different states

of awareness and experience, are *anshas,* or parts of that transcendental reality, but not transcendence itself. When you experience heat, you can infer that there must be some source from which it emanates. Similarly, when you experience subtler dimensions of existence, you can infer that they too have a source which is different from and greater than the experience.

Your son, although born from your body, is not you. By looking at him one may infer who his parents are, but still he remains an offshoot of you, and not you. In the same way, the evolutes of consciousness can give some idea of the power of that ultimate reality, but they are not the totality of that experience. Shakti, nada, bindu, the nine states or navatma, ardhachandra, nirodhika, trishira, are all the subtle forms that consciousness assumes in its descent from spirit to matter, and due to this the experience of that highest reality can only be inferred, not realized, by these states.

## 12. Essence of Bhairava

नादबिन्दुमयो वापि न चंद्रार्धनिरोधिका: ।
न चक्रक्रमसम्भिन्नो न च शक्तिस्वरूपक: ॥ 12 ॥

*Naadabindumayo vaapi na chandraardhanirodhikaah;*
*Na chakrakramasambhinno na cha shaktisvaroopakah.* (12)

### Anvay

*Naada bindu mayo*: full of nada and bindu; *Vaapi*: or else; *Na*: not; *Chandraardha*: of half moon; *Nirodhikaah*: obstruction; *Na*: nor is; *Chakra krama*: series of chakras; *Sambhinnah*: piercing; *Na cha*: not even; *Shakti*: power; *Svaroopakah*: of the nature.

### Translation

His (Bhairava's) form (cannot be perceived) in nada and bindu nor even in the obstructed half moon, nor in the piercing of successive chakras, nor does shakti, or energy, constitute his essence.

### Commentary

Now the suspense is building. If that highest reality is not all of these, then what is it? Because nada, bindu, crescent moon, chakras and shakti or kundalini are in themselves seats or storehouses of divine power and, according to tantra awakening of any of these centres induces extremely heightened states of awareness that can induce the experience of omnipotence, omnipresence and omniscience in the aspirant. Each of these centres has the cosmic experience enshrined in them. If it is none of these, then that experience must be very special, the ultimate experience.

This verse refers to the previous statement made in sloka 4, where Devi is curious to know whether nada, bindu, chandrardha, nirodhika, chakrakram and shakti are the

123

essential reality. Tantra asserts that these are evolutes or emanations of that transcendental reality, as well as actual points in the physical body through which one can experience that transcendental reality which is above and beyond them all. An experience points to the fact that there must be an experiencer. One is not possible without the other. However, if that transcendental reality is devoid of duality, subject and object, then how can it be perceived in these emanations of sound and light?

## 13. What has been told about Bhairava

अप्रबुद्धमतीनां हि एता बालविभीषिका: ।
मातृमोदकवत्सर्वं    प्रवृत्त्यर्थमुदाहृतम् ॥ 13 ॥

*Aprabuddhamateenaam hi etaa baalavibheeshikaah;*
*Maatrimodakavatsarvam pravrittyartham udaahritam.* (13)

### Anvay

*Aprabuddha*: immature; *Mateenaam*: intellects; *Hi*: also; *Etaa*: these; *Baala vibheeshikaah*: frightful talk to discipline children by fear; *Maatri modakavat*: like a sweet given by a mother; *Sarvam*: all; *Pravrittyartham*: to induce; *Udaahritam*: have been told.

### Translation

These things have been told (about the form of Bhairava), like the tales used to frighten children, to induce people of immature intellect to follow the spiritual path, just as the mother entices her child with sweets.

### Commentary

The average man is still living very much in the world and therefore can only respond to concepts and ideas which relate with form. Because of his belief in the reality of material existence and associations, he must be guided through spiritual analogies, which are told in the form of myths and stories relating with creation and divinity. Such stories are used to influence the minds of ordinary persons, just as frightening tales are told to influence children. In this way, the worldly-minded person gradually becomes attracted towards the path of sakara worship, although he still cannot conceive of a formless reality.

Those who are established on the spiritual path can understand how important it is to transcend name and

125

form in order to dive into the richness and power of inner experience. However, this sloka describes the way for people of immature intellect who are not established on the spiritual path. Those people who live in the material realm must be guided and instructed with stories and examples, like a child. In actual fact, isn't that the state of most of us? Despite all of our efforts in sadhana and spiritual discipline for years at a time, how many of us have transcended the gross and material world of the senses?

Bhairava speaks about sakara from an enlightened viewpoint because nirakara is his reality. He negates sakara and calls it an immature form of worship in relation to nirakara, the ultimate experience. Although, we may understand nirakara as a concept, still it is not our reality. Therefore, sakara meditation offers an immediate way that we too can traverse the path by using form as a support until we are able to enter the nirakara dimension. It is important to start the journey at the point where we are and not where we think we should be.

## 14. Immeasurable and without attribute

दिक्कालकलनोन्मुक्ता देशोद्देशाविशेषिणी ।
व्यपदेष्टुमशक्यासावकथ्या      परमार्थत: ॥ 14 ॥

*Dikkaalakalanonmuktaa deshoddeshaavisheshinee;*
*Vyapadeshtum ashakyaasaavakathyaa paramaarthatah.* (14)

### Anvay

*Dikkaala*: direction and time; *Kalanah*: measure; *Unmuktaa*: free from; *Deshah*: space; *Uddesha*: designation; *Avisheshinee*: not attributed by; *Vyapadeshtum*: can neither be indicated nor described; *Ashakyaasaau*: not possible; *Akathyaa*: beyond the reach of; *Paramaarthatah*: ultimately.

### Translation

Ultimately (that state of bhairava) cannot be measured in terms of time, space or direction, nor can it be indicated by any attribute or designation.

### Commentary

Here the state of bhairava is described as immeasurable. That which can be measured pertains to the finite dimension, whereas bhairava consciousness belongs to the infinite. Time, space and direction are measured by the finite mind. They are constantly changing and, therefore, are not permanent or eternal. As soon as the sadhaka transcends the mind, he enters into a different dimension altogether, the zone of timelessness and eternity. Past, present and future are imaginary concepts created by the mind in relation to the events it experiences. Similarly, space and direction do not exist independently, but can only be perceived in relation to the objects which are positioned within them in a particular time frame.

Furthermore, the supreme reality is absolute and unqualified, having no particular attributes or qualities by which it can be indicated, experienced or known as being of one genre or another, either manifest or unmanifest. Being free from all possible attributes or qualities, this state can have no name or designation. Therefore, the only way to describe it is by negating all that it could possibly be, and the only way to know it is through experience.

## 15. Atman of Bhairava

अन्तः स्वानुभवानन्दा विकल्पोन्मुक्तगोचरा ।
यावस्था भरिताकारा भैरवी भैरवात्मनः ॥ 15 ॥

*Antah svaanubhavaanandaa vikalponmuktagocharaa;*
*Yaavasthaa bharitaakaaraa bhairavee bhairavaatmanah.* (15)

### Anvay

*Antah*: inner; *Sva*: own; *Anubhava*: experience; *Aanandaa*: bliss; *Vikalpah*: dichotomizing thought constructs; *Unmuktah*: free; *Gocharaa*: know, experience; *Yaavasthahaa*: that state which; *Bharitaakaaraa*: form of fullness; *Bhairavee*: bhairavi; *Bhairava aatmanah*: atman or consciousness of bhairava.

### Translation

One can have this inner experience for oneself when the mind is free from modifications or thought patterns. The atman of bhairava, which is known as bhairavi, is then experienced as the bliss of one's own inner awareness, a state whose form is fullness, free from all contradictions (which is the abode of the entire universe).

### Commentary

Although the state of bhairava is beyond description, it is not beyond experience. This sloka is most important as it clearly states that one can experience this consciousness for oneself, describing the experience in detail. It reinstates the importance of transcending the finite mind in order to experience that highest state. This has always been the claim of tantra and yoga, as well as the Vedas and Upanishads. You simply cannot have that ultimate experience through this mind. You will have to retire the mind if you want to have spiritual experience.

In the *Raja Yoga Sutras*, Maharishi Patanjali states in the second and third sutras that the definition of yoga is: *chitta vritti nirodaha,* or cessation of the mental modifications, on achieving which, *tadah svarupe avasthanam,* the sadhaka is established in his real nature. Today yoga has been defined as 'union' or 'yoking', but in fact, yoga means *pranavaprasuti,* or 'withdrawal'. *Prasuti* means 'to send forth' and *pranava* is 'to retrace' or 'to withdraw'. Yoga teaches how to withdraw the different thoughts which the mind sends forth, as well as how to obstruct their formation. Patanjali has been acclaimed because he taught the method of separation and called it yoga, or union!

The Vedas and Upanishads are full of vidyas that teach the same principle. There are gayatri vidya, panchagni vidya, ashwamedha vidya and so on. Throughout the ages the root *vid,* from which the word vidya is derived, has meant 'inner knowledge'. Today we use the word meditation, but in the vedic era it was called vidya. These vidyas taught how to experience that highest state by stopping the mental patterns or formations of the mind.

Tantra, which is much older than the Vedas, also teaches this science. Tantra means to stretch the mind, and in doing so to remove and liberate it from its bondage. Different names have been given for this process during different periods in history; however, the outcome is the same. It is not as if tantra says anything different from vedanta or yoga; it simply uses different terms which point in the same direction.

The mind is continually sending out waves in the form of thoughts. These thoughts have weight, quality, frequency and outward movement. They drag the mind to the outer experience. If these thought patterns are obstructed, which is possible with effort and practice, stillness occurs. Then the mind, having no *alambana,* or support, enters into a void. If this experience is sustained and deepened, the highest awareness is experienced, which is a state of fullness. Although that state is known as bhairava, it is no different from bhairavi, because both are one and not dual. They only appear to be two on account of avidya and outer identification with the gross senses and physical forms to which the mind is accustomed. The term *bhairavi bhairava atmanaha* refers to this.

So, although sakara is the prop by which your awareness evolves, the trick lies in dropping sakara and focusing on nirakara to have the ultimate experience. The same is true for everything that you identify with and experience as 'I', me or mine. The mind, ego intellect, memory, samskaras, and physical body are all props for the evolution of awareness. All of these drop momentarily when dharana, dhyana and samadhi occur. At that moment the stillness of pure awareness is experienced, composite and whole.

## 16. Nature of highest reality

तद्वपुस्तत्त्वतो ज्ञेयं विमलं विश्वपूरणम् ।
एवंविधे परे तत्त्वे क: पूज्य: कश्च तृप्यति ॥ 16 ॥

*Tad vapus tattvato jneyam vimalam vishvapooranam;*
*Evamvidhe pare tattve kah poojyah kashcha tripyati.* (16)

### Anvay

*Tadvapuh*: entire universe; *Tattvatah*: in essence; *Jneyam*: be known (as); *Vimalam*: free of dross; *Vishva pooranam*: all pervasive; *Pare*: highest; *Tattve*: reality; *Kah*: who is; *Poojyah*: to be worshipped; *Kashcha*: who is to be; *Tripyati*: pacified.

### Translation

The essence of his nature is known to be free of dross and pervades the entire universe. This being the nature of the highest reality, who is the object of worship and who is to be pacified by worship?

### Commentary

Here for the first time we get an inference of his essence, which is *vimalam,* or 'full of purity'. Most religions have a concept of the highest reality or God as being immaculate and pure, but this purity, which is known as vimalam, is not purity in a religious sense. Purity here indicates the homogeneity and wholeness of the supreme awareness that is bhairava. Here purity means absence of duality, or subject and object.

This sloka echoes the verdict of *Aham Brahmasmi,* "I am That", proclaimed by vedanta. So where is the difference between vedanta and tantra? When that highest reality is all pervading, then it must be in me too. If that supreme awareness pervades me, then I am not separate or different from it; I am that. Whatever that supreme awareness is, I am that. That is my real nature, nirakara, not this outer form, which is sakara.

The word *akara* means 'form' or that which is confined within a limited space, and *nirakara* means 'formless', where there is no confinement or limitation. If that supreme awareness is no different to mine, then who is going to worship whom? Because the worshipper and worshipped are one and the same.

## 17. Bhairava is known by Paradevi

एवंविधा भैरवस्य यावस्था परिगीयते ।
सा परा, पररूपेण परादेवी प्रकीर्तिता ॥ 17 ॥

*Evamvidhaa bhairavasya yaavasthaa parigeeyate;*
*Saa paraa, pararoopena paraa devee prakeertitaa.* (17)

### Anvay

*Evamvidhaa*: in this way; *Bhairavasya*: of bhairava; *Yaavasthaa*: that state which; *Parigeeyate*: described, sung; *Saa*: that (she); *Paraa*: highest; *Pararoopena*: by means of the absolute or highest form; *Paraadevee*: highest goddess; *Prakeertitaa*: is well known.

### Translation

In this way the transcendental state of bhairava, which is described or sung of, is known by means of the absolute or highest form that is Paradevi, the highest goddess.

### Commentary

This sloka establishes the intimate relationship between bhairava, the supreme awareness, and his cosmic counterpart, bhairavi, the supreme energy. They are prakasha and vimarsha, which is an important principle of Kashmir Shaivism. Bhairava is prakasha, or light, and bhairavi is vimarsha, nada, vibration or sound. Together they give rise to the manifest phenomena through their interplay.

Although the principle of vimarsha or shakti is foremost in the ascent towards heightened awareness, at the same time it is at the behest of prakasha or shiva, the supreme awareness, that this process is happening. Without the consent of shiva, neither evolution nor involution of individual awareness can take place. In that sense shiva and shakti are intimately connected and cannot function without each other.

This is not just a philosophical truth, but one you experience in your daily life as well. Without awareness one cannot experience the different manifestations of creation, which belong to the sphere of shakti. At the same time, if the principle of energy did not manifest out of that supreme consciousness, it would not be possible to have embodied awareness, nor would the experience of self-realization take place.

Paradevi, whose form is absolute, assumes infinite forms to bring you face to face with you real self. How can you know that which is formless unless you assume a form, because in order to experience formlessness there has to be an experiencer. If consciousness has to be realized, then matter has first to be converted into energy. The experience of consciousness cannot be had by matter, which is regarded as *jada,* or inert, unless and until it is infused with chetana, or awareness.

The basis of this awareness is energy. However, it is not energy as we know it in its mechanical, electrical, magnetic, chemical or mineral form. This energy is *para*, or transcendental, because it is all of these and yet it transcends all of them due to its infinite nature. So the supreme energy is also chetana, just as the supreme consciousness, or awareness, is chetana.

This sloka further reinstates the assertion made in sloka 15, where Bhairavi was defined as the atman, or all-pervading and indestructible force of Bhairava, the supreme consciousness. If, for a moment, for the purpose of understanding this profound truth, you regard Bhairava, the supreme consciousness, as your father or creator, and Bhairavi, the supreme energy, as your creatrix or mother, and yourself as their offspring, then the important role that Bhairavi plays in introducing you to your father would become clear to you. For, it is the mother alone who can identify the father.

## 18. Dharma and the possessor of dharma

शक्तिशक्तिमतोर्यद्वत् अभेद: सर्वदा स्थित: ।
अतस्तद्धर्मधर्मित्वात् पराशक्ति: परात्मन: ॥ 18 ॥

*Shakti shaktimator yadvat abhedah sarvadaa sthitah;*
*Atas taddharmadharmitvaat paraa shaktih paraatmanah.* (18)

### Anvay

*Shakti*: shakti, power; *Shaktimatoh*: power holder; *Yad vat*: like that; *Abhedah*: identical; *Sarvadaa*: always; *Sthitah*: exists; *Atah*: so also; *Tat*: that; *Dharma*: dharma; *Dharmitvaat*: possessor of dharma; *Paraa shaktih*: absolute or highest power; *Paraatmanah*: essence of the absolute.

### Translation

Just as shakti, or power, is not different from shaktimaan, the holder of power, similarly parashakti, the highest power, who is the essence of the absolute (and therefore) identical with dharma, can never be separated from Bhairava, the possessor of dharma.

### Commentary

Just as power and that which holds it are not different, similarly, dharma is not different from that which possesses it. Bhairavi is dharma, the eternal law, which guides the universe, and Bhairava, the one who possesses or holds that dharma, is the lawmaker. Dharma is one of the most important concepts of tantra. Dharma refers to the enduring values or principles of life which never change as they are based on the universal and constant laws of nature. Thus it is known as *sanatana*, or eternal. Has it ever happened that the sun did not rise at dawn or set at dusk, or that the moon changed its course?

Dharma is based on these eternal laws and teaches the principles that hold existence or creation in place. The

136

dictionary defines dharma as 'right conduct'. Instead it should be defined as the values that complement the laws of nature. From sanatana dharma, the eternal values or laws of life, arose the concepts of yuga dharma, or codes that apply to different ages, such as the satya yuga, treta yuga, dwapara yuga and kali yuga. From yuga dharma arose the sectarian dharmas, or the codes of the various religions, and individual dharmas, which apply to the particular varna or class of each person, such as intellectual, warrior, trader and labourer.

This sloka, however, is not referring to the offshoots of sanatana dharma, but to the eternal law itself. Just as alteration takes place as the evolutes of consciousness begin to emerge, in the same way the timeless values that arose from sanatana dharma lost some of that eternal quality, which was its hallmark. Yuga dharma, religious dharma and individual dharma are open to interpretation and application, but sanatana dharma is not.

In VBT the concept of shiva and shakti, or transcendental consciousness and transcendental energy, are represented as bhairava and bhairavi. They are the closest experience to supreme consciousness within us and therefore represent the eternal law of sanatana dharma. It is the claim of tantra that, by uniting these two principles through the practice of dharana and dhyana, the sadhaka can experience the source of all creation from which all experiences have emerged.

## 19. Dualism is a preliminary step

न वन्हेर्दाहिका शक्ति: व्यतिरिक्ता विभाव्यते ।
केवलं ज्ञानसत्तायां प्रारम्भोऽयं प्रवेशने ॥ 19 ॥

*Na vanher daahikaa shaktih vyatiriktaa vibhaavyate;*
*Kevalam jnaanasattaayaam praarambho'yam praveshane.* (19)

### Anvay

*Na*: is not; *Vanheh*: from fire; *Daahikaa*: to burn; *Shaktih*: power; *Vyatiriktaa*: separately; *Vibhaavyate*: imagined; *Kevalam*: only; *Jnaana sattaayaam*: level of knowledge; *Praarambhah ayam*: in the beginning; *Praveshane*: entry into.

### Translation

(Just as) the power to burn is not separate from fire, (similarly parashakti is not different from Bhairava). However, it is imagined as separate in the beginning, as a preliminary step towards entry into its knowledge.

### Commentary

Here, for the first time a hint of dualism arises. In order to know something, you have to view it objectively. That is the basis of all scientific discoveries, and science will settle for no less. Science boasts of objective analysis, not subjective experience, as the basis for its claims. For objective experience it is necessary to divide the awareness into subject and object. The range of objective experience is available only to those who have attained human birth. Other forms of life simply do not have the faculties required to have an experience and simultaneously know they are having it.

The sloka further states that this dual perspective is only relevant in the beginning stages of sadhana before inner knowledge, or vidya, is acquired. This duality of subject and object is responsible for the manifest world. When the dual awareness of subject and object dissolves and becomes one, this world also fades away and becomes non-existent. In this way the experience of duality is ultimately transcended, but in order to transcend it you have to first become aware of what you are transcending. Otherwise how will you transcend it? So, to experience unity you will have to first experience diversity and then direct your awareness back to the source or experience of union.

## 20. Shakti is the face of Shiva

शक्त्यवस्थाप्रविष्टस्य निर्विभागेन भावना ।
तदासौ शिवरूपी स्यात् शैवी मुखमिहोच्यते ॥ 20 ॥

*Shaktyavasthaapravishtasya nirvibhaagena bhaavanaa;*
*Tadaasau shivaroopee syaat shaivee mukham ihochyate.* (20)

### Anvay

*Shaktiha*: shakti, energy; *Avasthaa*: state; *Pravishtasya*: enter (the); *Nirvibhaagena*: without division; *Bhaavanaa*: feeling of identification; *Tadaasau*: then he; *Shivaroopee*: verily like the form of shiva; *Syaat*: becomes; *Shaivee*: shakti; *Mukham*: face; *Ihochyate*: here, in this context; (she) is said.

### Translation

One who enters the state of shakti has the feeling of identification with Shiva, without division. Then one verily becomes like the form of Shiva. In this context, it is said that Shakti is the face of Shiva.

### Commentary

This sloka actually carries on from the previous verse and completes the concept regarding duality and unity expressed there. With the dawning of knowledge, one enters the state of shakti, or pure energy, where identification with Shiva, or pure consciousness, is experienced without any separation or division. At this point, the awareness of duality is transcended and the experience of unity begins. This is referred to in the sloka where it says that one then assumes the form of Shiva. Finally the verse says that Shakti is the face or outward appearance of Shiva.

Every individual or object has a face or appearance by which he, she or it is known. That face belongs only to him, and wherever he goes it goes with him. The face and the

140

person to whom it belongs are never separated, even for a moment. He is recognized only by his face and by no other means. Whenever you see his face, you are reminded of him. In the same way the face of Shiva, or transcendental awareness, is Shakti.

In order to experience the presence of Shiva, you have to know what the experience of Shakti is. How does Shakti manifest and how does she appear? VBT says that without knowledge of Shakti, Shiva cannot be known. That is a precondition of the transcendental experience. Therefore, the main effort of the sadhaka should be to awaken Shakti, because when that happens Shiva is sure to be experienced.

When you enter the realm of transcendental energy, you get a whiff of transcendental consciousness, thus affirming that they are not different to each other. In the same way, when you are driving to a hill station, as soon as you begin to smell a certain kind of air you know that soon the hills will appear. Or when you are nearing the sea, you can tell by the breeze that you are approaching the shore.

Nature has many signs and signals, which are governed by certain laws that tell us when something is going to take place. This applies at all levels of life, both internally and externally. If you are attentive, you can recognize those signs. Gradually, as a sadhaka you will be able to apply this understanding to your inner journey, because nature is active there too and will guide you along the way.

This sloka emphasizes the experiences of Shakti as indications of knowing Shiva. Similarly, all the upayas of VBT are for awakening the kundalini energy and taking the aspirant to the savikalpa state. Once the state of savikalpa samadhi is established, nirvikalpa occurs by itself, effortlessly and instantly. Savikalpa is the form of nirvikalpa, just as Shakti is the form and the face of Shiva.

## 21. Shiva is revealed by Shakti

यथालोकेन दीपस्य किरणैर्भास्करस्य च ।
ज्ञायते दिग्विभागादि तद्वच्छक्त्या शिव: प्रिये ॥ 21 ॥

*Yathaalokena deepasya kiranair bhaaskarasya cha;*
*Jnaayate digvibhaagaadi tadvachchhaktyaa shivah priye.* (21)

### Anvay

*Yathaa*: just as; *Aalokena*: by the flame; *Deepasya*: of a candle; *Kiranaih*: rays; *Bhaaskarasya*: of the sun; *Cha*: and; *Jnaayate*: known; *Dik*: direction; *Vibhaagaadi*: parts, etc.; *Tad vat*: so also; *Shaktyaa*: by Shakti; *Shivah*: Shiva; *Priye*: O dear one.

### Translation

Just as space, direction and form are revealed by the flame of a candle or the rays of the sun, similarly Shiva is revealed by the medium of Shakti, O dear one.

### Commentary

In the scheme of creation the birth of form takes place through the interplay of light and sound. Today it is an accepted fact that form is an emanation of sound and light. When they combine, form emerges. This sloka is an apt analogy of this claim of tantra. Until the flame of a candle is lit or the rays of the sun fall on an object, form and direction, the true representation of time and space, are not revealed. In the same way Shiva, or consciousness, is revealed only through the medium of Shakti, or energy.

According to Trika philosophy, which is the basis of Kashmir Shaivism and VBT, shakti has three stages: para, apara and parapara. These three stages are responsible for the name trika, which literally means 'three'. Para is transcendental, apara is immanent and parapara has traces of both. Shiva is para, whereas shakti is para, apara and parapara. In this sense shakti is present in all levels of existence and, therefore, is the most suitable medium through which that *paramtattwa*, Shiva, can be known.

Parashakti is the medium for revealing Shiva. In the physical body parashakti resides at the base of the spine, lying dormant in the form of a three-coiled serpent as kundalini. Her exact location is mooladhara chakra, which corresponds with the cervical plexus. All sadhanas without exception are intended to awaken this sleeping serpent power, which is the seat of Bhairavi. When kundalini awakens and ascends to the crown chakra, it unites with Shiva and pure consciousness is experienced without separation or division. Kundalini can be awakened by different means, such as *janam* (birth), *mantra* (mystic sounds), *aushadhi* (herbs), *guru kripa* (guru's grace) and *tapas* (austerity).

About kundalini, Swami Satyananda says: "Whatever happens in spiritual life is related to kundalini. The goal of every form of spiritual life, whether you call it samadhi, nirvana, moksha, communion, union, kaivalya or liberation, is in fact the awakening of kundalini. Once the great shakti awakens, man is no longer a gross physical body, operating with a lower mind and low voltage prana. Instead every cell of his body is charged with the high voltage prana of kundalini. And when total awakening occurs, man becomes a junior god, an embodiment of divinity." He becomes Shiva.

## 22. Bhairava state of consciousness

श्रीदेव्युवाच
देव देव त्रिशूलाङ्क, कपालकृतभूषण ।
दिग्देशकालशून्या च व्यपदेशविवर्जिता ॥ 22 ॥

*Shree Devyuvaacha:*
*Devadeva trishoolaanka kapaalakritabhooshana;*
*Digdeshakaalashoonyaa cha vyapadeshavivarjitaa.* (22)

### Anvay

*Shree Devee*: Sri Devi, auspicious lady; *Uvaacha*: says; *Deva deva*: O Lord of Gods; *Trishoolaanka*: who bears the trident; *Kapaala*: skull; *Krita*: has made; *Bhooshana*: ornament; *Dik*: direction; *Desha*: space; *Kaala*: time; *Shoonyaa*: devoid of; *Cha*: or; *Vyapadesha*: description; *Vivarjitaa*: free from.

### Translation

Sri Devi said: O Lord of the Gods, who bears the trident and skulls as ornaments, (tell me) of that state (which is) devoid of time, space and direction and free from (any) characteristics.

### Commentary

Although the transcendental awareness is nirakara, it has been personified as Shiva for the benefit of the sadhaka. This is a peculiarity of the vedic and tantric streams of thought, where every experience has been personified in a form with characteristics which can easily be described and understood by the intellect. Without this personification the average aspirant would find it difficult to conceive of the notion of transcendence. Shiva is thus known to his followers by the trishul, or trident, which he holds and the ornament of skulls around his neck. The three-pointed trishul represents the three gunas: sattwa, rajas and tamas, in perfect equipoise, thus signifying a state of no mind or beyond mind. The skulls denote the death of the individual ego.

These symbols are again a powerful reminder that the experience of transcendence is only possible when the individual mind and ego are sacrificed as *ahuti,* or oblations, into the fire generated by the awakening of the kundalini energy. This is the true *mahayajna,* or the great sacrifice, spoken of in the Vedas and Upanishads, where the awareness acts as the ladle by which they are poured into the fire. In this sense, dhyana is the real sacrifice or yajna, but the methods are not yet revealed.

Devi's doubts are still not satisfied, so she repeats her question. The great Lord has told her about that transcendental state, but has not yet revealed the ways to attain that state. It is experience alone that transforms doubt into conviction and reaffirms the faith.

*Shiva Yantra*

145

## 23. Means to achieve Bhairava consciousness

यावस्था भरिताकारा भैरवस्योपलभ्यते ।
कैरूपायैर्मुखं तस्य परादेवी कथं भवेत् ।
यथा सम्यगहं वेद्मि तथा मे ब्रूहि भैरव ॥ 23 ॥

*Yaavasthaa bharitaakaaraa bhairavasyopalabhyate;*
*Kairupaayair mukham tasya paraa devee katham bhavet;*
*Yathaa samyag aham vedmi tathaa me broohi bhairava. (23)*

### Anvay

*Yaavasthaa*: that state; *Bharitaakaaraa*: of the state or form of
fullness; *Bhairavasya*: of Bhairava; *Upalabhyate*: is achieved;
*Kaih*: by which; *Upaayaih*: means; *Mukham*: face; *Tasya*: his;
*Paraadevee*: highest shakti; *Katham*: how; *Bhavet*: becomes;
*Yathaa*: as; *Samyak*: completely; *Aham vedmi*: I shall know;
*Tathaa*: whereby; *Me*: to me; *Broohi*: tell; *Bhairava*: O
Bhairava.

### Translation

By what means can that state of fullness of Bhairava be
achieved, (and) how does Paradevi, the highest Shakti,
become the face (or entrance of Bhairava)? Tell me (this),
O Bhairava, in the manner (whereby) I shall know it
completely.

### Commentary

This sloka demonstrates the practicality of tantra, the science
of consciousness. As in all sciences, tantra emphasizes that
knowledge alone is incomplete unless it is substantiated by
the means and methods to experience it. For tantra believes
that the proof of the pudding lies in the eating. We also get
another important clue about the nature of that transcendental reality. In reference to the bhairava consciousness,
the word *bharitakara* literally means 'of the form of fullness'.

This fullness is experienced as completeness or absence of duality with no divisions.

In the sadhaka this experience of fullness or completeness manifests through the feeling of *santosha,* or inner contentment, which is an indication of higher awareness. Santosha is the basis for vairagya, or non-attachment, because it transcends cravings and desires of any sort. Swami Sivananda has said that santosha is one of the essential qualities of a sannyasin, because renunciation is also a path which leads to the realization of bhairava consciousness.

Devi also raises another pertinent question, which is most important to understand if you want to enter the realm of experience. She asks Shiva to tell us how the supreme energy becomes the entrance to the realm of bhairava. It is only when you realize this that you can know that stage of bhairava completely or fully.

## 24. Dharana on the two generation points

श्रीभैरव उवाच
ऊर्ध्वे प्राणो ह्यधो जीवो विसर्गात्मा परोच्चरेत ।
उत्पत्तिद्वितयस्थाने,   भरणाद्भरिता   स्थिति: ॥ 24 ॥

*Shree Bhairava uvaacha:*
*Oordhve praano hyadho jeevo visargaatmaa parochcharet;*
*Utpattidvitayasthaane bharanaad bharitaa sthitih. (24)*

### Anvay

*Shree Bhairava uvaacha*: Sri Bhairava says; *Oordhve*: upward;
*Praanah*: prana; *Hyadhah*: downward; *Jeevah*: apana;
*Visargaatmaa*: whose nature is visarga or creation;
*Parochcharet*: manifestation of paradevi; *Utpatti*: generation;
*Dvitayasthaane*: at the two places; *Bharanaad*: fixing the mind;
*Bharitaa sthitih*: state of fullness.

### Translation

Sri Bhairava said:
Paradevi, whose nature is visarga, or creation, manifests as
the upward prana and the downward apana. By fixing the
mind at the two points of generation (of prana and apana),
the state of fullness results.

### Commentary

Here the first upaya, or practical method of dharana, is revealed.
This upaya can be treated either as an individual dharana or as
a part of the series of dharanas from slokas 24 to 31 that leads
to the experience of awakening, ascent and merging of
kundalini with Paramshiva. Awareness of the pranic flows is
the medium for these preliminary dharanas. Thus, in order to
understand this dharana it is necessary to know how the
pranic flows are generated within the body, where their source
is and what functions they assume in the process of
manifestation.

Paradevi is the transcendental energy which, as the sum total of all the energy in the universe, is responsible for creation or manifestation. This manifestation goes on all the time; it never stops. If it were to stop, life would come to an end. Paradevi manifests in the physical body as pranashakti, the life force. Pranashakti is one force, but it has many jobs to do. So, at the individual level it assumes five fields or energy bodies, known as koshas, each more subtle than the other. The first is known as *annamaya kosha,* the physical sheath, made up of food. The second is *pranamaya kosha,* the vital energy sheath, forming a fine network through which prana flows. The third is *manomaya kosha,* the mental sheath, which is a more concentrated and subtle form of energy that surrounds the pranamaya kosha. The fourth is *vijnanamaya kosha,* the intuitive sheath, an extremely rarefied field of energy, which is closer to spirit than to matter, surrounding the mental sheath. The fifth is *anandamaya kosha,* the sheath of bliss, where pranashakti is united with the supreme self.

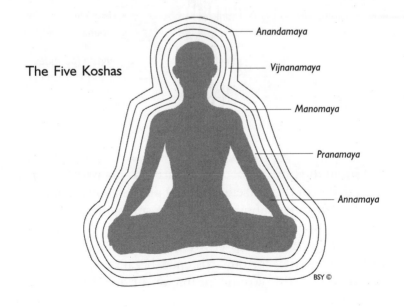

The Five Koshas

Anandamaya

Vijnanamaya

Manomaya

Pranamaya

Annamaya

BSY ©

149

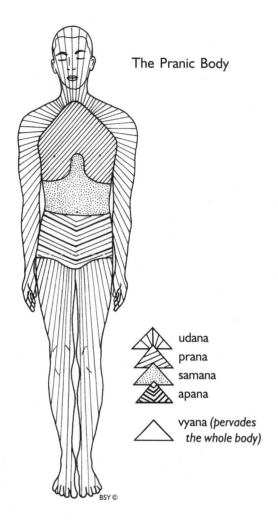

The Pranic Body

udana
prana
samana
apana

vyana (*pervades the whole body*)

BSY©

Within the physical body there are also many roles which pranashakti, or the vital energy, must play. So, the pranamaya kosha mentioned above is further subdivided into five categories or functions: prana, apana, samana, udana and vyana. These five pranas create a pranic field around the body which is vital for our existence, because through it we are linked to the cosmic prana or pranashakti. If our

150

perception were finely tuned to the pranic field, we would see a body of light having the same shape as the physical body, in which there are thousands of delicate wire-like structures conducting shakti, or energy.

The link between the first two koshas, annamaya and pranamaya, is the breath. This is why breathing techniques directly influence these sheaths in such a manner that generates well-being, balance and harmony within. But if the pranamaya kosha is to be activated for the purpose of higher spiritual experience, then the practices of concentration and visualization are necessary. This is because concentration alone can direct the heightened awareness that develops as a consequence of the pranayama practices.

Although pranayama practices are extremely useful for balancing the energy and clearing the pranic pathways, these practices cannot achieve the same results that dharana or concentration can. This is because concentration of mind activates the manomaya kosha and it is the mental rather than the physical energy that is the key to controlling the pranic forces. There is a difference between influence and control. The physical energy of annamaya kosha can influence the vital energy of the pranamaya kosha, but it cannot control it. To do that mental energy is required because the mind is a subtler and superior force.

The first evolute of cosmic prana is also called prana, but these two should not be confused. One is transcendental energy and the other is individual energy, which is its evolute. The individual prana further divides into the five koshas, or energetic bodies, and the pranamaya kosha further evolves into the sub-pranas, which are referred to in this sloka. These subtle sub-pranas which form the pranic body further manifest as the physical breath, and through its medium influence both the body and mind in a very dramatic way, affecting the way we think, feel, act and speak. In fact, neither the body nor the mind can function without prana.

Therefore, by controlling these pranas we can effectively control the body and mind.

Swami Sivananda has said, "Prana is related to the mind, through the mind to the sankalpa shakti, or willpower, through the willpower to the individual soul, and through the individual soul to the supreme being. When the breath is directed by the mind, under the control of the will, wonders can be achieved in all spheres of life, from personality development to healing, as well as spiritual experience." Therefore, if you know how to control the forces of prana flowing through the mind, then the secrets of the universal prana, or Paradevi, will be known to you.

Yogis consider prana to be superior to the mind, as prana is present even when the mind is absent in deep sleep. This implies that prana plays a more vital role in our lives than the mind. Of course, the science of raja yoga teaches control of the fluctuations of the mind whereby the pranas are suspended as a consequence. But it is a very difficult and tedious process to isolate the mind from the ego and senses. In tantra, however, the same result is attained by controlling and awakening the pranas.

This sloka asserts that prana and apana are manifestations of Paradevi, so focusing the awareness on these two forces should lead to the experience of transcendental energy, or pranashakti. If you look at a pair of twins, you are sure to be reminded of their mother who has borne them. They are her evolutes in the same way that prana and apana are evolutes of the cosmic prana. In this dharana prana and apana must be observed closely at the two points where they are generated.

The actual points of generation of prana and apana are at the *nabhi,* or navel centre, and at *bhrikuti,* the eyebrow centre. But we can also say that the original generation point for both is at bindu visarga, because the individual prana, which is unified and whole without any divisions or dualities, begins its descent to the lower centres from this point. During the descent, when it reaches manipura chakra, it emerges as prana and apana and begins to flow in opposite directions.

This idea is further emphasized by the tantric texts that speak of *amrita*, a very potent secretion, dripping down from bindu visarga, a point at the top back of the head. When the amrita falls down into the body, it is consumed by the heat of the sun at the nabhi chakra, and becoming *retas*, it falls down further to the lower centres, causing decay and death. If this process is reversed through certain practices described in tantra, this secretion can be redirected back upwards to the higher centres. Then the yogi experiences a quantum of higher energy which completely alters the awareness, allowing him to become conscious of the transcendental side of his nature.

*Dvitiyasthane* refers to, not one, but two points of generation. The other point can only be bindu visarga, where the individual energy emerges from the cosmic energy and begins its descent into the manifestation of prana and apana. So, in a sense, although prana and apana are not yet born, the point where their source, the cosmic prana, emerges is also their point of generation. The sloka says you should closely observe and gradually fix your mind at those two points: bindu visarga, where energy in the form of amrita is born, and manipura, where the amrita is converted into retas. In this way the dharana includes the entire psychic passage from bindu to manipura. The science of kundalini yoga also reveals these two centres as most important for the generation and distribution of pranic flows in the body.

As you focus on these two points where the prana and apana are generated, you become aware of their flow: apana moving downward and prana upward. Together they represent the inward and outward flow of parashakti, or the supreme energy, from the cosmos to the physical body. You can call them the cosmic umbilical cord by which you are connected to mother nature. They are extremely important for maintaining the life force, as they touch important energy centres during their flow in the body. The energy centres situated along this pathway are intimately connected to the physical organs. For instance, manipura influences the digestive organs and anahata the heart and lungs. As prana and apana pass through, these energy centres are revitalized and they in turn revitalize the corresponding parts in the physical body.

In this dharana the awareness is focused at the two points of origin, and the entire process is carried out on the mental plane. It is presumed here that one is familiar with the areas and directions of flow of prana and apana, and is able to visualize them with accuracy. The focus is not on breathing, which is a physical act, so it is not necessary to perform pranayama or regulate the breath in any way during this process. Dharana is a mental kriya, not a physical practice such as asana, pranayama, mudra or bandha. By physically altering the breath, the kriya would cease to be a dharana and become a pranayama instead.

Therefore, in this process you are not asked to alter the breath in any way, but to become aware of the movement and focus in on it until the breath is experienced as a flow of prana. In this way the movement of prana and apana will gradually be experienced, and then you can concentrate the awareness at the two points where they are generated. In order to practice this, you can imagine that you are seeing yourself and assume a subject-object relationship with yourself, like that of a seer or witness.

This is the case with all the dharanas in VBT which are to be carried out on the mental plane. It also means that they can be done at any time or place and in any posture. However, the practitioner must be totally familiar with the process so that he can visualize it in the finest detail. Any visualization on the mental plane also influences the physical processes dramatically. Thus all the practices of hatha yoga and kriya yoga that you may have been doing until now are only a preparation for the process of dharana. Eventually it is the mind or Indra, the ruler of the senses, that has to be harnessed for higher experience.

The definition of creation, according to tantra, is not just confined to the moment when matter becomes manifest, but to the entire process which takes place unseen and unknown before it actually takes shape as matter. For example, when a man and woman unite, a seed is sown in the womb. Although the product of this union does not emerge until nine months later, the process of creation has started. However, at that point of time it is *adrishya,* or unseen, and therefore, unknown. Similarly, the symbol for creation in tantra is bindu, a point represented by a dot, which is known as visarga. Curiously, in the Sanskrit language, visarga is represented by two dots, which can also be correlated with the two generation points of prana and apana; one at bindu visarga, where the process of creation starts, but is unseen, and the other at manipura, where they actually come into existence.

The generation points of prana are an extremely meaningful concept of tantra, which if reflected on, can lead to a very profound understanding of the link between consciousness, energy and matter. Bindu is the point where consciousness and energy separate in order to create, and manipura is the point where the great energy, which was singular in nature, becomes dual. So, the split of consciousness takes place at bindu and the split of energy takes place at manipura.

*Bharita sthiti* here refers to the state of fullness and completeness where there is no division. This further emphasizes that by focusing on these two points of generation the practitioner gains control over the process

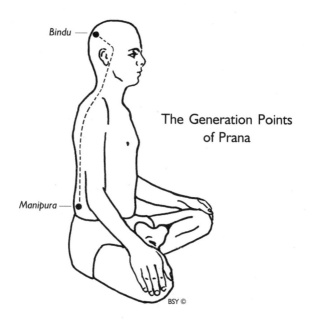

The Generation Points
of Prana

whereby the consciousness splits into subject and object, prana and apana. By mastery of this dharana, one is able to establish the consciousness in the state of fullness or completeness, which is beyond duality.

There is also an explanation of this dharana given by some scholars that correlates the two points of generation with the breath. However, it actually refers to the subtle flows of prana and apana vayus within the body, rather than the breath. Moreover, dharana is a mental action, not a physical one. But in order to perceive or focus on the subtle pranic movement, you may commence this dharana with the breath. Then, as your awareness deepens, you may focus on the movement of prana and apana before they manifest into the breath.

## 25. Kumbhaka dharana

मरुतोऽन्तर्बहिर्वापि वियद्युग्मानिवर्तनात् ।
भैरव्या भैरवस्येत्यं भैरवि व्यज्यते वपुः ॥ 25 ॥

*Maruto'ntar bahir vaapi viyadyugmaanivartanaat;*
*Bhairavyaa bhairavasyettham bhairavi vyajyate vapuh.* (25)

### Anvay

*Marutah*: pranic air, vayu; *Antah*: inside; *Bahih*: outside; *Vaa*: also; *Api*: and; *Viyat*: space; *Yugma*: both, pair; *Anivartanaat*: restrain from return; *Bhairavyaa*: from Bhairava; *Bhairava-syettham*: thus of Bhairava; *Bhairavi*: Bhairavi; *Vyajyate*: manifests; *Vapuh*: essence.

### Translation

When the ingoing pranic air and outgoing pranic air are both restrained in their space from their (respective points of) return, the essence of bhairava, which is not different from bhairavi, manifests.

### Commentary

In this second dharana mental concentration is directed towards the restraint of prana and apana. In the previous dharana the mind was fixed at the two generation points of prana and apana. Here the awareness is focused on the restraint in movement of prana and apana, now described as the ingoing and outgoing airs or vayus. When these vayus are restrained, at that moment there is cessation of all activity and sense perception. The mind becomes steady and calm, as there are no ripples emanating from annamaya or pranamaya koshas to disturb it. In that stillness the essence of bhairava consciousness, which is not different from bhairavi, is experienced.

Prana is the inward and upward moving force, which flows from the nabhi, or navel, to bhrikuti, or ajna chakra, and from there to the higher centres in the brain. Apana is the downward and outward moving force, which flows from manipura downward to the lower centres in the pelvic region. This movement has to be restrained through the process of dharana so that neither of them moves out of their respective space. By restraining the movement of prana and apana, both the incoming and outgoing sensations are also stopped. No outer sensations are perceived inside, nor are any inner sensations created by the samskaras projected outside. Thereby a condition of complete cessation arises and kevala kumbhaka occurs.

The practice of pranayama involves three aspects: *pooraka* (inhalation), *rechaka* (exhalation) and *kumbhaka* (retention). In breath retention, or kumbhaka, the breath is suspended. There are three types of kumbhaka: *antar* (inner), *bahir* (outer) and *kevala* (spontaneous). In antar, or inner kumbhaka, the outgoing breath is restrained, and in bahir, or outer kumbhaka, the ingoing breath is restrained. Antar and bahir kumbhaka may be either *sahita*, performed with conscious effort, or kevala, without effort or spontaneous. Inhalation and exhalation are an integral part of the process, but kumbhaka is the actual phenomenon.

This dharana refers to kevala, or spontaneous kumbhaka, which occurs as a consequence of perfection in restraint of the movement of prana and apana vayus. Sahita kumbhaka is related to the practices of pranayama, which deal with the breath or the physical act of inhalation and exhalation. Kevala kumbhaka, on the other hand, is related to dharana, where restraint of the flows of prana and apana vayus occurs spontaneously. The previous dharana involved awareness of the points where prana and apana are generated, but this dharana involves restraint of their flows so they do not move upward in the case of prana and downward in the case of apana.

Thus in this dharana the awareness of these two vayus becomes more concentrated, because you have to become aware of their flows in order to restrain them. This results in the awareness of the source from which the pranas have evolved, which is Bhairavi or Shakti, who is none other than Bhairava.

*Bhairon Yantra*

159

## 26. Perfection of kumbhaka

न व्रजेन्न विशेच्छक्ति-मरुद्रूपा विकासिते ।
निर्विकल्पतया मध्ये तया भैरवरूपता ॥ 26 ॥

*Na vrajen na vishechchhaktir marudroopaa vikaasite;*
*Nirvikalpatayaa madhye tayaa bhairavaroopataa.* (26)

### Anvay

*Na vrajet*: not having moved; *Na vishet*: nor moving swiftly in a specific direction; *Shaktih*: shakti; *Marut roopaa*: in the form of vayu or pranic air; *Vikaasite*: there develops; *Nirvikalpatayaa*: through a state of nirvikalpa; *Madhye tayaa*: in the middle; *Bhairavaroopataa*: form of Bhairava.

### Translation

When shakti in the form of vayu or pranic air is still and does not move swiftly in a specific direction, there develops in the middle, through the state of nirvikalpa, the form of Bhairava.

### Commentary

Through the restraint of prana and apana, as kevala kumbhaka is established, a concentration of energy builds up and this creates a reverse movement in these pranic flows, so that they begin to move towards each other instead of away from each other. Kumbhaka is a state of animated suspension of prana, which leads to suspension of mind. Suspension of mind leads to laya or dissolution of the jagrat and swapna awareness, so that the sushupti awareness prevails. At that moment the life force, or pranashakti, does not move. As long as there is movement of prana there is sense perception, as the pranic flows influence and activate all the dimensions of perception. But when you stop their movement for any length of time, they reverse their flows and fuse into one another.

160

Reversal of the flows of prana and apana so that they merge into each other is achieved through dharana alone. It cannot be achieved through pranayama or alteration of the breath. Although pranayama can prepare you for the process, it cannot achieve this end. For that you must learn the art of influencing the pranic movement on the psychic plane through dharana. The restraint and reversal of pranas purifies the nadis and chakras and causes the prana to enter sushumna, the medial nadi, which lies between ida and pingala. Moreover, whenever there is fusion of prana and apana, immense heat is generated, which acts as a catalyst for the ascent of kundalini. So, with the awakening of sushumna, the subtle infrastructure is ready for this great event. In this way, as the awareness is further established and deepened through the restraint and reversal of prana and apana, the state of bhairava develops.

This process has been poetically described in the mystical and esoteric traditions of India, which are devoted entirely to sadhana and spiritual experience. They say that restraint, reversal and fusion of the pranas leads to the experience of *trikuti*, the point where ida, pingala and sushumna merge at ajna chakra, and one becomes firmly established in the transcendental awareness. This is also described as *madhye taya*, the middle state, in which there is no experience of night or day, sun or shade. Here the transcendental sounds are heard into which the mind dissolves spontaneously and thereby enters the fourth state, which is known as turiya.

The *Bhagavad Gita* (4:29–30) also speaks along similar lines. Lord Krishna, while elucidating this very vital process to Arjuna, says that fusion of prana and apana is the highest sacrifice, or yajna. Some yogis offer prana to apana and others apana to prana. Yet others, who are disciplined in habits of eating, are able to stop the movement of prana and apana and offer prana as oblation to prana. These yogis are the knowers of yajna and through this process the yogi dwells in the experience of amrita, or nectar, which is the remnant of this great yajna and revealed only to the yogi who can undergo this yajna.

*Hatha Yoga Pradipika*, an authoritative and classical text on yoga, says that prana moves upwards and apana downwards. This is their natural tendency, but if you can reverse this procedure so that prana moves downwards and apana upwards, the ageing process can be reversed. So, this dharana has an important contribution to make in relation to genetics. By focusing the mind on these two pranic flows, you can alter the genetic structure so dramatically that you seem to be younger than you actually are.

Patanjali has called this dharana kevala, the fourth pranayama, which transcends the internal and external object. In his commentary on the Raja Yoga Sutras of Patanjali, Swami Satyananda has said that in fact it is none other than ajapa japa, a practice which he has taught extensively as a preliminary to dhyana or meditation. This concept of fusion of prana and apana is most important in yoga and tantra and ample references are found in these texts, a few of which have been mentioned above.

## 27. Kumbhaka leads to inner peace

कुम्भिता रेचिता वापि पूरिता या यदा भवेत् ।
तदन्ते शान्तनामासौ शक्त्या शान्त: प्रकाशते ॥ 27 ॥

*Kumbhitaa rechitaa vaapi pooritaa yaa yadaa bhavet;*
*Tadante shaantanaamaasau shaktyaa shaantah prakaashate.* (27)

### Anvay

*Kumbhitaa*: kumbhaka or retention; *Rechitaa*: expelling outwards; *Vaapi*: or else; *Pooritaa*: drawing inwards; *Yaa*: or; *Yadaa*: when; *Bhavet*: takes place; *Tadante*: after that; *Shaanta*: tranquillity; *Naamaasau*: by the name; *Shaktyaa*: Shakti; *Shaantah*: peace; *Prakaashate*: revealed.

### Translation

When kumbhaka takes place after pooraka or rechaka, then the shakti known as shanta is experienced and through that peace (the bhairava consciousness) is revealed.

### Commentary

In the practices of pranayama, pooraka is explained as inhalation and rechaka as exhalation. However, in the practice of dharana pooraka relates to the ingoing tendency of prana and rechaka to the outgoing or expelling tendency of apana. In this dharana awareness is directed to the state of retention which occurs when these two movements are controlled.

Kumbhaka stills the mind, which is the main requisite for dharana, or concentration. This is why it is considered a very useful aid for inducing dharana and an effective way to stop the thoughts altogether, preventing the emission of countless thoughts waves into the environment. These thought waves consume a lot of mental energy, as they are continuously being projected from the mind into the

163

environment and from the environment to the mind. You may have noticed that when the mind is agitated with many thoughts, the breathing becomes rapid, and when the thoughts are less, the breathing becomes slow and relaxed. There is deep significance in this interrelation of the flow of prana and apana with the breath, the senses and the mind.

With the cessation of pranic movement, stillness of mind is achieved and the tranquil or motionless form of shakti or energy known as shanta is revealed to the aspirant. This sloka signifies complete balance and equipoise in the flow of the triple energies in ida, pingala and sushumna nadis, which results in stillness. It is this stillness and motionless that sets the stage for the stormy awakening of kundalini and its ascent to the higher centres in the cranium.

Shakti is not a person or form, nor is Shiva; they are both an experience. Just as anger, lust, hatred and deceit conjure up an image of a crooked person, in the same way, there are certain sattwic qualities that invoke the experience of shakti and shiva. One of the foremost of those qualities is tranquillity or peace. When anything moves slowly or not at all, we experience a sense of tranquillity. This is why we feel tranquil in quiet rural places where there is no hustle, bustle and noise. In the same way, when all movement of prana ceases during kumbhaka, tranquillity is experienced. By practising dharana on that moment of tranquillity, the experience of Bhairava takes place.

Tranquillity is not an inanimate substance; it has life and power. That power is very close to the power of the divine, which explains why tranquillity induces a soothing and nourishing feeling. The moment you feel tranquil, you are rejuvenated. That rejuvenation occurs on account of your proximity to the bhairava consciousness. This sloka further develops the dharana on the pranas.

## 28. Kundalini jagran dharana

आ मूलात्किरणाभासां सूक्ष्मात् सूक्ष्मतरात्मिकाम् ।
चिन्तयेत्तां द्विषट्कान्ते शाम्यन्तीं भैरवोदय: ॥ 28 ॥

*Aamoolaat kiranaabhaasaam sookshmaat sookshmataraatmikaam;*
*Chintayettaam dvishatkaante shaamyanteem Bhairavodayah.* (28)

### Anvay

*Aamoolaat*: from the root; *Kiranaabhaasaam*: like the rays (of
the sun); *Sookshmaat*: getting subtler and subtler;
*Sookshmatara-aatmikaam*: most subtle self; *Chintayettaam*:
meditate, concentrate; *Dvishatkaante*: twice six, i.e., twelve;
*Shaamyanteem*: dissolves; *Bhairavah*: bhairava; *Udayah*:
manifest.

### Translation

Concentrate on the shakti arising from the root like the
rays of the sun, gradually becoming subtler and subtler,
until at last she dissolves in the dwadashanta and bhairava
manifests.

### Commentary

Fusion of prana and apana gives rise to the awakening and
ascent of kundalini through sushumna nadi, which is
described in this dharana. Paradevi manifests as kundalini
shakti, and entering the physical body, takes her seat at
mooladhara chakra. A psychic centre, or chakra, is a vortex
of energy, where many nadis converge and then redistribute
this energy to different parts of the body, wherever they go.
There are said to be seventy-two thousand nadis in the
physical body. The word *nadi* means 'flow' or 'channel'; it
does not mean nerve. The nerves are the gross counterpart
of the nadis which carry electrical impulses from the brain
to the different parts of the body. The nadis carry subtle

energy in the form of consciousness, or chittashakti and pranashakti. The nadis are invisible to the outer eyes, but can be perceived in the form of light by the inner eye. It is the power of pure awareness that assumes the form of a nadi.

Dwadashanta means 'at the end of twelve' and here refers to sahasrara, at the top of the head, which is the seat of Shiva, the pure untainted consciousness. It also refers to the twelve chakras, or psychic energy centres, through which the awakened energy passes, gradually becoming more and more subtle until it merges into sahasrara, which is the abode of the most subtle self situated at the end of these twelve chakras. These twelve chakras are: mooladhara, swadhisthana, manipura, anahata, vishuddhi, ajna, lalana, nasikagra, manas, soma, bindu and sahasrara.

Of course, if you cut open the body, you will not see these chakras because they constitute the pranic body and, like the nadis, are too subtle to be perceived by the human eye. However, they form the psychic passage of sushumna, with mooladhara at the base and sahasrara at the top. Pranashakti, who is sleeping at mooladhara chakra in the form of a coiled serpent, is known as kundalini. When the kundalini ascends through sushumna, it opens these twelve chakras, one by one. In this way the experience of consciousness and energy becomes more and more subtle, and the feeling of peace and tranquillity arise.

In this dharana the awareness has to be focused on the kundalini rising from the root and dissolving into the dwadashanta, where it unites with Shiva, or consciousness, in sahasrara. When the kundalini starts to ascend sushumna, it is perceived as luminosity like the rays of the sun, but as it travels up along the spine, it becomes more and more subtle. When the kundalini finally dissolves in dwadashanta, it is no longer perceived as a separate entity. At that moment there is only the experience of Bhairava.

## 29. Piercing of the chakras

उद्गच्छन्तीं तडिद्रूपां प्रतिचक्रं क्रमात्क्रमम् ।
ऊर्ध्वं मुष्टित्रयं यावत् तावदन्ते महोदय: ॥ 29 ॥

*Udgachchhanteem tadidroopaam pratichakram kramaat kramam;*
*Oordhvam mushtitrayam yaavat taavad ante mahodayah.* (29)

### Anvay

*Udgachchhanteem*: moving upwards; *Tadidroopaam*: like lightning; *Pratichakram*: all the chakras; *Kramaat-kramam*: one by one; *Oordhvam*: upward; *Mushtitrayam*: measuring three fists, i.e., twelve fingers; *Yaavat*: until; *Taavadante*: then at last; *Mahodayah*: the great dawn.

### Translation

(Meditate on that shakti) moving upwards like lightning through all the chakras one by one to the dwadashanta. Then at last the glorious form of Bhairava dawns.

### Commentary

The term dwadashanta was referred to in the previous sloka and is used to denote a measure of distance. Literally it means 'at the end of twelve', but this can be understood in several contexts. It can refer to a distance of twelve angulas (finger-widths) or three fists. Angula is both a measure of space as well as of time. For example, the length of prana during inhalation should be twelve finger-widths inside from the tip of the nose to the dwadashanta, which corresponds with the heart centre. The length of prana during exhalation should be twelve fingers from the tip of the nose to the dwadashanta outside. There are many such points of dwadashanta in the body.

This sloka refers to the dwadashanta at sahasrara, which is the supreme abode of Shiva. Kundalini is an electrically

167

charged energy of very high voltage which arises swiftly like lightning and opens each of the chakras, one by one, until it reaches sahasrara, the last chakra. At this point the transcendental experience dawns in the light of which the form of Bhairava is perceived. Just as each dawn gives birth to a new day full of new experiences, *mahodaya*, the great dawn, hints at the birth of a new experience of consciousness.

In the previous dharana kundalini was experienced as luminosity. Here she is experienced as lightning, the high voltage current that can reduce anything to ashes. After the kundalini reaches manipura, it takes the form of lightning. Awakening and ascent of kundalini in the form of lightning eliminates the sensorial experience on account of which the glory of bhairava is experienced.

It is at manipura chakra that the first *granthi*, or esoteric knot, is pierced or untied. Prior to that the kundalini energy is luminous and diffused, like the rays of the sun spreading its light on whatever it falls upon. However, after the piercing of the rudra granthi it begins to travel in a definite direction, which is upwards. In other words the great ascent to sahasrara begins. After this point has been crossed the energy no longer reverts back or recedes to its lower abode. It may halt but not revert. This is a significant achievement in the journey of a sadhaka as it is at this point that the spiritual experiences commence.

## 30. Kundalini becomes shiva

क्रमद्वादशकं सम्यग् द्वादशाक्षरभेदितम् ।
स्थूलसूक्ष्मपरस्थित्या मुक्त्वा मुक्त्वान्ततः शिवः ॥ 30 ॥

*Kramadvaadashakam samyag dvaadashaaksharabheditam;*
*Sthoolasookshmaparasthityaa muktvaa muktvaantatah Shivah.* (30)

### Anvay

*Kramah*: successively; *Dvaadashakam*: twelve; *Samyak*: right understanding; *Dvaadashaakshara*: twelve letters; *Bheditam*: piercing; *Sthoola*: gross; *Sookshma*: subtle; *Parah sthityaa*: being beyond; *Muktvaa muktvaa*: becoming liberated one by one; *Antatah*: finally; *Shivah*: Shiva.

### Translation

The twelve (centres) should be pierced successively through proper understanding of their (associated) twelve letters. Thus becoming liberated from the gross then the subtle, one by one, at the end (of its journey) the kundalini becomes shiva.

### Commentary

According to this sloka, each of the twelve centres is pierced by the kundalini, when there is correct understanding of its corresponding seed syllable or bija mantra. In this sense, mantra is the esoteric key that opens the twelve doors to liberation. The classical definition of mantra is: *Mananat trayate iti mantraha*: "that which liberates the mind is mantra". Each of these twelve chakras has a particular mantra, or akshara, to denote it. These mantras are in bija, or seed form, which means they are pure energy in its potential state.

Just as a seed carries the inherent power to sprout and grow into a giant tree, a mantra has the inherent power to explode gross matter and transform it into energy. The bija mantras are like missiles which travel at lightning speed, carrying the gross physical awareness to subtle and transcendental states. The chakras and their corresponding bija mantra are as follows: mooladhara – *lam*, swadhisthana – *vam*; manipura – *ram*, anahata – *yam*, vishuddhi and lalana – *ham*, and nasikagra – *so*. The bija mantra for all the higher chakras such as ajna, manas, soma, bindu and sahasrara is *Aum*.

The technique used to pierce these twelve centres requires a proper understanding of these mantras in relation to varna, roopa and nada, or colour, form and sound. Each bija mantra is as potent as the chakra it represents. Dharana should be practised on the respective bijas in their various aspects of colour, form and sound to open the chakras. In this way, each chakra can be opened, one by one, and the desired experience attained. As the kundalini ascends, the range of experience changes from gross to subtle. For example, the experience of colour will give way to sound or light, which are subtler forms of the same experience.

All the mantras originate from akshara. The word *akshara* means 'indestructible' or that which never alters or dies. Akshara are made up of dhvani, or sounds of varying frequencies. In order to explode the energy within the mantra, the dhvani has to be separated from the akshara. There are fifty-one aksharas, which correspond to fifty-one energy centres in the physical body. These energy centres are connected to the different centres in the brain. Repetition of the Sanskrit slokas awakens the inherent centres within the brain, because the Sanskrit language is also made up of these fifty-one aksharas.

Different aksharas constitute the different bija mantras, and with repetition they progressively influence the kundalini energy as it pierces through the twelve chakras, one by one. Dharana on the bija mantras is essential at this point, because kundalini also must become very subtle in order to pierce these centres, otherwise she would not pass through. A heightened state of experience arises when kundalini pierces through the twelve centres and is liberated from the clutches of the gross experience. When all the dross is left behind and the involution process is complete, shakti and shiva become one again, and their separation is over.

## The Chakra Location Points

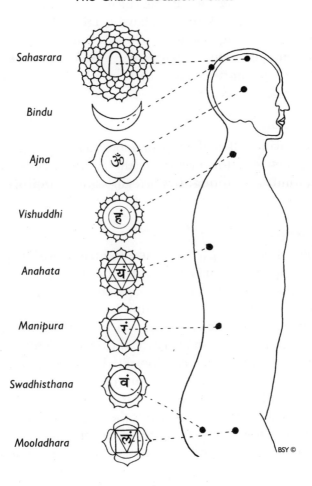

## 31. Mind transcends thought

तयापूर्यांशु मूर्धान्तं भङ्क्त्वा भ्रूक्षेपसेतुना ।
निर्विकल्पं मनः कृत्वा सर्वोर्ध्वे सर्वगोद्गमः ॥ 31 ॥

*Tayaapooryaashu moordhaantam bhanktvaa bhrookshepasetunaa;*
*Nirvikalpam manah kritvaa sarvordhve sarvagodgamah.* (31)

### Anvay

*Tayaa*: then; *Pooryaashu*: having filled; *Moordhaantam*: at the
tip of moordha; *Bhanktvaa*: having crossed; *Bhrookshepa
setunaa*: the bridge between the eyebrows; *Nirvikalpam*:
dichotomizing thought patterns; *Manah*: mind; *Kritvaa*:
having done; *Sarva-oordhve*: above all; *Sarvagah*: omnipresence; *Udgamah*: rise.

### Translation

Then, having filled the tip of moordha and crossed the
bridge between the eyebrows, the mind rises above all
dichotomizing thought patterns and omnipresence
(prevails).

### Commentary

*Moordha* is a minor psychic centre located above the palate,
where it opens into the nasal cavity. It is the point where the
sound *sha* is emitted. In the Sanskrit alphabet there are
three categories for the sound *sha*. One of them is
moordhanya sha, which is emitted from this centre. You
can say that it is the matrika of this centre. This practice
refers to ujjayi pranayama. Moordha is the point which the
breath touches and stimulates through this pranayama.

The bridge of the eyebrows is another minor psychic
centre called *bhrumadhya*, which is the trigger point for ajna.
A web of nadis converge here, some ending and others
redistributing themselves in different directions. The three

major nadis: ida, pingala and sushumna, merge at this point. Ida flows on the left side and influences the right hemisphere of the brain and pingala flows on the right side and influences the left hemisphere of the brain. These nadis originate at the base of the spine and flow upwards, intersecting at the chakras as they pass through them. When the flows of these two nadis are in perfect balance, sushumna is activated and opens.

The kundalini rises through sushumna nadi in her ascent from mooladhara chakra. After the kundalini crosses the bridge between the eyebrows, the mind transcends thought and becomes nirakara, as there are no mental patterns to draw it back into the dimension of sakara. So, the mind becomes supportless at this point, and dissolves into the great void, or shoonya. Now the kundalini is no longer contained within sushumna, but flows freely in all directions, filling every nook and cranny of the *kapala*, or skull. It thus becomes all-pervasive and a sense of omnipresence arises.

Slokas 24 to 31 present a complete range of dharana, whereby the sadhaka can awaken the dormant energy and direct it to the highest centre. These eight dharanas are performed within one's own physical body, rather than on any external object or symbol. In the first dharana (sl. 24), you are asked to focus on two points: one where consciousness and energy separate and the other where energy splits and its first manifestation takes place in the form of the two pranic flows, known as prana and apana. In the second dharana (sl. 25), you are asked to restrain their movement. This leads to kevala kumbhaka, or spontaneous cessation of the pranas, which is the basis of the third and fourth dharanas (sl. 26, 27). This results in an awakening of energy at the base of the spine and its ascent to the higher centres, which forms the basis of the next four dharanas (sl. 28–31).

This first set of dharanas utilizes the tools of breath, psychic centres and mantras. When examined closely you can easily discern the similarities between them and the practices of kriya yoga, kundalini yoga, pranayama and ajapa japa taught by Swami Satyananda. Those very practices are being revealed here as dharanas. So, in actual fact, the practices are the same; the only difference is that now, instead of doing them physically, you have to transform them into a mental process. In other words, you have to make a quantum leap from the physical to the mental dimension, from annamaya kosha to manomaya and vijnanamaya koshas.

## 32. Shoonya panchaka dharana

शिखिपक्षैश्चित्ररूपैर्मण्डलै: शून्यपञ्चकम् ।
ध्यायतोऽनुत्तरे शून्ये प्रवेशो हृदये भवेत् ॥ 32 ॥

*Shikhipakshaish chitraroopair mandalaih shoonyapanchakam;*
*Dhyaayato' nuttare shoonye pravesho hridaye bhavet.* (32)

### Anvay

*Shikhipakshaih*: feathers of peacocks; *Chitra roopaih*: in the form of pictures; *Mandalaih*: in circles; *Shoonya-panchakam*: five voids; *Dhyaayatah*: meditate; *Anuttare*: follow to the end; *Shoonye*: void; *Praveshah*: enters; *Hridaye*: heart; *Bhavet*: becomes.

### Translation

Like the five different coloured circles on the peacock's feathers, one should meditate on the five voids. Then by following them to the end, which becomes the principle void, enter the heart.

### Commentary

The *shoonya panchakam*, or five voids, refer to the five *tanmatras*, which have no concrete form and are abstract evolutes of consciousness. A tanmatra is an abstract quality through which a *tattwa*, or element of the body, is perceived. In the scheme of evolution the five tattwas evolved out of the five tanmatras. These five tattwas are: *akasha* (ether), *vayu* (air), *agni* (fire), *apas* (water) and *prithvi* (earth). Each tattwa has a corresponding tanmatra. For example, akasha is perceived through the tanmatra of *shabda* or sound, vayu through the tanmatra of *sparsha* or touch, agni through the tanmatra of *roopa* or form, apas through the tanmatra of *rasa* or taste, and prithvi through the tanmatra of *gandha* or smell.

# Evolution of the Individual Elements

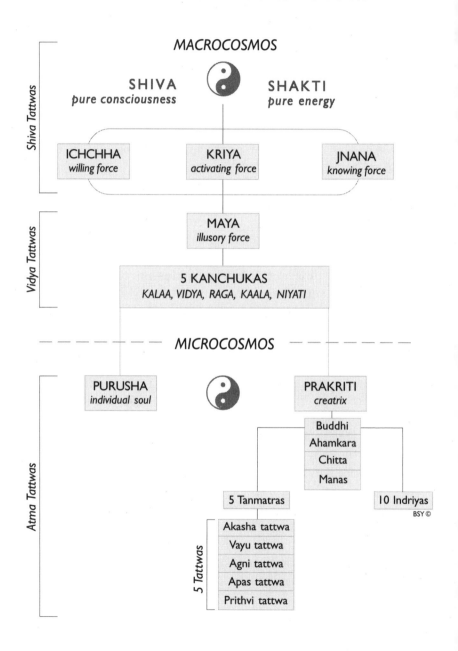

Dharana on the tanmatras will gradually lead to more subtle states whereby the principal void, or source from which the tanmatras have evolved, will be experienced. Through a process of involution the awareness returns back to the source and enters the heart cavity where it resides. In the scheme of creation these five tanmatras evolved out of the *chatushtaya antahkarana*, or the fourfold inner instruments through which the awareness operates, which include: buddhi (intellect), chitta (memory), manas (rational mind) and ahamkara (ego). The antahkarana in turn evolved out of prakriti, which evolved out of shakti, the cosmic energy.

If this process of involution is followed by concentration on the void or source of five tanmatras, ultimately the awareness enters the heart cavity, or anahata chakra, which is the abode of *jivatman*, the individual consciousness. The interplay of consciousness and energy gives rise to matter. The abode of individual consciousness, or jivatman, is in the heart cavity and that of energy is in the sacral cavity. This dharana uses the technique of realizing consciousness by focusing the awareness on its derivatives. While tracing the manifested form of consciousness back to its source, you will enter the heart cavity, which is the abode or the source of the principal void.

## 33. Mindful awareness

ईदृशेन क्रमेणैव यत्र कुत्रापि चिन्तना ।
शून्ये कुड्ये परे पात्रे स्वयं लीना वरप्रदा ॥ 33 ॥

*Eedrishena kramenaiva yatra kutraapi chintanaa;*
*Shoonye kudye pare paatre svayam leenaa varapradaa.* (33)

### Anvay

*Eedrishena*: in this way; *Kramenaiva*: gradually; *Yatra*: wherever; *Kutra api*: there; *Chintanaa*: mindful awareness; *Shoonye*: void; *Kudye*: wall; *Pare*: another; *Paatre*: excellent; *Svayam*: self; *Leenaa*: absorbed; *Varapradaa*: granting a boon.

### Translation

In this way, wherever there is mindful awareness, either on the void, or on another (object such as a) wall, or on an excellent person (such as guru), gradually the boon of absorption into the self is granted.

### Commentary

Dharana means holding something in the mind, so along with concentration on one object or point, conceptualization is also dharana. This sloka says that you can become absorbed in the self, no matter what you conceptualize, whether emptiness or void, an object such as a wall, or even an extraordinary person like the guru.

The object you conceptualize is not the only criteria for absorption into that heightened state of awareness. The quality of your conceptualization and your ability to hold that concept for a sustained period of time to the exclusion of all else also figure largely in determining your success. To improve the quality of conceptualization you should develop mindful or focused awareness. Mindful awareness is a term which signifies that the sadhaka should be aware of each and every aspect related to the object from gross to subtle. This is only possible when the mind is very sensitive and observant and is able to focus on the present moment without interruption.

This sloka provides a wide range of objects on which the awareness can be fixed. The aspirant should choose one according to his temperament.

*Swami Sivananda of Rishikesh*

## 34. Dharana on the crown of the head

कपालान्तर्मनो न्यस्य तिष्ठन्मीलितलोचन: ।
क्रमेण मनसो दाढ्र्यात् लक्षयेल्लक्ष्यमुत्तमम् ॥ ३४ ॥

*Kapaalaantarmano nyasya tishthan meelitalochanah;*
*Kramena manaso daardhyaat lakshayet lakshyam uttamam.* (34)

### Anvay

*Kapaalaantah*: crown of the head; *Manah*: mind; *Nyasya*: fixing attention; *Tishthan meelita*: having closed; *Lochanah*: eyes; *Kramena*: successively; *Manasah*: of the mind; *Daardhyaat*: stable, stability; *Lakshayet*: concentrate; *Lakshyam uttamam*: eminently discernible, towards the highest goal.

### Translation

Having closed the eyes, and fixing the attention at the crown of the head, gradually stabilize the mind and direct it towards the highest goal, which will gradually become discernible.

### Commentary

Dharana on the crown of the head refers to concentration on sahasrara chakra, which is the abode of supreme consciousness. To perfect dharana one should develop attentiveness in thought, word and action. An attentive person will be extremely successful in the practice of dharana because he already knows how to focus his awareness. The process of dharana involves fixing your attention on something, conceptualizing it, and then holding it in the mind for a length of time so that the awareness becomes steady. This steady awareness culminates in a new experience, which could belong to another dimension of the object of dharana.

Here the attention is fixed at the crown of the head where sahasrara chakra is located. *Chakra* means 'wheel' or anything circular. *Sahasra* means 'a thousand' and *ara* means 'spokes'. So, sahasrara chakra is a wheel with a thousand spokes. These spokes have also been poetically conceptualized as the thousand petals of a lotus, and you will find this description in most texts. Other chakras have different numbers of petals or spokes, for example, anahata has twelve and vishuddhi sixteen. These spokes denote the number of main nadis that converge at that chakra.

Sahasrara chakra is the abode of Shiva, the supreme consciousness; it represents the convergence of all the main nadis, so the number one thousand is given. By abode it does not mean that Shiva lives here and nowhere else. Shiva consciousness is all-pervasive. It is everywhere, in every cell, atom and molecule of your body. Sahasrara is said to be the abode of Shiva because this is the point where the supreme consciousness is realized.

This dharana involves closing the doors to sensory perception and fixing the attention at the crown of the head. In this way the mind gradually becomes stable and the mundane thoughts are transcended. As the attention deepens, the highest achievement in terms of inner experience becomes eminent and discernible.

## 35. Sushumna dharana

मध्यनाड़ी मध्यसंस्था बिससूत्राभरूपया ।
ध्यातान्तर्व्योमया देव्या तया देव: प्रकाशते ॥ 35 ॥

*Madhyanaadee madhyasamsthaa bisasootraabharoopayaa;*
*Dhyaataantarvyomayaa devyaa tayaa devah prakaashate.* (35)

### Anvay

*Madhyanaadee*: medial nadi, i.e., sushumna; *Madhyasamsthaa*:
situated in the middle, i.e., in the spinal column;
*Bisasootraabha*: like the fibre of a lotus stem; *Roopayaa*: by
means of the form; *Dhyaataa*: should meditate; *Antarvyomayaa*:
by using means of the inner space; *Devyaa*: by means of
Devi; *Tayaa*: by that, by her; *Devah*: the divine; *Prakaashate*:
is revealed.

### Translation

One should meditate on the inner space of the medial nadi
(sushumna) situated in the central axis of the body (the
spinal column), which is as slender as a fibre of the lotus
stem, and then by the grace of Devi, the divine (form) is
revealed.

### Commentary

Sushumna is the nadi which carries kundalini straight up to
sahasrara chakra. It flows along the spinal column and is
intimately linked to the pranic body, or pranamaya kosha.
Within sushumna there is another thin slender nadi known
as *brahma nadi* which this sloka describes as being slender
like a fibre of the lotus stem. It is this slender nadi that is
equipped to carry the high voltage current of kundalini to
the higher centres.

The yogi aspires for the awakened kundalini to enter
sushumna and no other nadi, to travel upwards. If, for some

reason, kundalini enters ida or pingala nadi instead, there could be either mental or physical imbalance and the spiritual journey of the sadhaka would suffer a setback, as the development or progress would not be total, but conditional. In his book *Kundalini Tantra*, Swami Satyananda says that, "If there is awakening in pingala, one becomes a healer, and when there is an awakening in ida, one becomes a prophet. But when sushumna awakens, kundalini ascends straight to sahasrara and one becomes a jivanmukta, a liberated soul."

Ida and pingala are associated with the left and right nostril flows respectively. They flow separately in the swara, or the breath, throughout the day. Ida flows for one hour and twenty minutes and then the swara changes over to pingala. At the time of changeover the sushumna flows for a few seconds. Through practice the duration when sushumna flows can be increased. This is a moment of heightened creativity, and if you sit down for meditation when this happens, dharana and dhyana can take place without the slightest effort. When sushumna flows, kundalini gets a jolt and it moves. If the sushumna flows for longer periods, then the kundalini can even raise its head, stretch itself and begin to rise.

This is a very important dharana of kundalini-kriya yoga.

## 36. Shanmukhi mudra

कररुद्धदृगस्त्रेण  भ्रूभेदाद्  द्वाररोधनात् ।
दृष्टे बिन्दौ क्रमाल्लीने तन्मध्ये परमा स्थिति: ॥ 36 ॥

*Kararuddhadrigastrena bhroobhedaad dvaararodhanaat;*
*Drishte bindau kramaat leene tanmadhye paramaa sthitih.* (36)

### Anvay

*Kara rudddha*: closing by the hands; *Drigastrena*: all directions;
*Bhroobhedaad*: from the piercing of the eyebrow centre;
*Dvaara rodhanaat*: from the blocking of the entrance; *Drishte*:
is seen; *Bindau*: in the bindu; *Kramaat leene*: gradually
absorbed; *Tanmadhye*: then inside that; *Paramaa*: the
supreme; *Sthitih*: state.

### Translation

By using the hands (as tools) to block the entrances in all
directions, the eyebrow centre is pierced and bindu (or
light) is seen. Being gradually absorbed within that, the
supreme state is realized.

### Commentary

In this dharana the help of shanmukhi mudra is taken. A
mudra is a gesture whereby the hands, face or body are
positioned in a way that focuses and directs the pranic
energy. This gives them power to act as tools to obstruct the
dissipation of pranashakti, so that it may be conserved for
higher experience. Mudras form a very important part of
tantric and yogic sadhana. They are used along with bandhas
to channel the energy and aid concentration.

In shanmukhi mudra the hands are used to block the
sensory apertures in the head. The ears are closed with the
two thumbs, the eyes with the index fingers, the nostrils
with the middle fingers and the upper and lower lips with

184

the ring and little fingers. These entrances are also exit points through which loss of pranic energy takes place. If these points are blocked by shanmukhi mudra, a build up of energy occurs which pierces the eyebrow centre and bindu or light is seen.

Shanmukhi Mudra

Bindu is a point at the top back of the head, which is regarded as the nucleus for spiritual experience. It is at the exact point where the Brahmin priests leave a tuft of hair, known as *shikha,* when they shave. It may look a bit peculiar and outdated, but it is a tradition which has more to it than meets the eye. Bindu is the twilight zone where psychic experience turns into spiritual experience. From this level one gazes at both experiences, but the focus here is on the spiritual. As the awareness perceives bindu it is pulled towards the light emanating from it. At first the light appears as a point, and gradually it grows bigger until it absorbs and illumines everything. In that absorption the supreme state is realized.

## 37. Dissolution in the cave of the heart

धामान्तः क्षोभसंभूतसूक्ष्माग्नितिलकाकृतिम् ।
बिन्दुं शिखान्ते हृदये लयान्ते ध्यायतो लय: ॥ 37 ॥

*Dhaamaantah kshobhasambhootasookshmaagnitilakaakritim;*
*Bindum shikhaante hridaye layaante dhyaayato layah.* (37)

### Anvay

*Dhaamaantah*: condition; *Kshobha sambhootah*: produce after shaking and agitation; *Sookshmaagnih*: subtle fire; *Tilaka*: mark on the forehead; *Aakritim*: in the form of; *Bindum*: bindu (point); *Shikhaante*: at the end of the tuft of hair; *Hridaye*: in the heart cave; *Layaante*: absorption; *Dhyaayatah*: whenever one meditates thus; *Layaha*: dissolution.

### Translation

Whenever one meditates upon the subtle fire, in the form of a tilak (like the mark on the forehead), or on the bindu at the end of the shikha, a condition of agitation and shaking is produced, followed by absorption and dissolution in the cave of the heart.

### Commentary

*Tilak* is a mark in the shape of a flame applied on the forehead with red or vermilion powder. It is applied before any auspicious and important event as a part of ritual worship. In sadhana it is applied to mark the point of dharana and stimulate it by applying a kind of acupressure at that point. The point of bindu chakra is marked by the *shikha*, or tuft of hair, which Brahmins leave at the top back of the head. The word shikha also means 'flame'. *Sukshmagni* refers to the result of this great awakening generated by the fusion of prana and apana and followed by the ascent of kundalini through sushumna. The result is a subtle fire whose form

186

can be perceived as a flame either at a point between the two eyebrows, known as ajna chakra, or at the point of shikha, known as bindu visarga.

This leads to shaking and agitation followed by absorption and dissolution of the awareness in *hridaya*, the cave of the heart, where the individual consciousness resides. Although the shaking and agitation referred to in this dharana can be perceived physically, it is more of a psychic agitation and shaking, which is the consequence of a total restructuring of all the cells, tissues, atoms and molecules on all levels of one's existence, whether physical, mental or spiritual.

This sloka outlines the process and stages of dharana leading to laya, dissolution or shoonya.

## 38. Dharana on shabdhabrahman

अनाहते पात्रकर्णेऽभग्नशब्दे सरिद्द्रुते ।
शब्दब्रह्मणि निष्णातः परं ब्रह्माधिगच्छति ॥ 38 ॥

*Anaahate paatrakarne' bhagnashabde sariddrute;*
*Shabdabrahmani nishnaatah param brahmaadhigachchhati.* (38)

### Anvay

*Anahaate*: unstruck, in anahata; *Paatrakarne*: adept in listening; *Abhagna*: uninterrupted; *Shabde*: sound; *Sarid drute*: rushing like a river; *Shabda brahmani*: Brahman in the form of sound; *Nishnaatah*: adept; *Param*: supreme; *Brahma-adhigachchhati*: attains to Brahma.

### Translation

One who is adept in listening to the unstruck sound in anahata, (which is) uninterrupted like a rushing river, attains the supreme state of Brahma by mastery of shabdabrahman, the form of Brahman as sound.

### Commentary

The word anahata means 'unstruck', and *anahad nada* is the inner sound which is produced without any stroke. Ordinarily all the sounds we hear are produced by two things, an object and something that strikes it. An object lying idle by itself will not produce any sound until someone or something comes along and strikes it. Even the vocal cords produce sound only when the breath passes through and ruffles them. In tantra we learn that this is the grossest form of sound, known as *vaikhari*, or audible sound.

Apart from audible sound there are more subtle frequencies of sound that are inaudible to the human ear. These sounds are uninterrupted and continue ceaselessly, but they go unnoticed as they are beyond the normal range of auditory perception. Nada yoga is a system of dharana which attunes the awareness to these subtle sound frequencies which are heard internally.

Anahata chakra is the point where the unstruck sound, or nada, is produced. In this dharana the nada emanating from anahata flows continuously like a rushing river. This inner sound may be perceived as thunder, the call of a peacock, the melody of a flute or the blowing of a conch. Different aspirants have heard it differently. One has to become adept at hearing the anahad nada in whatever form it comes. This will lead to the experience of *shabdabrahman*, the supreme awareness as sound.

As explained earlier, nada is the first evolute of consciousness. Even the Bible says, "In the beginning was the word and the word was with God." In tantra that word is the mantra Aum. This nada is present at varying frequencies. At the cosmic level it is *para*, followed by *pashyanti* (mental), *madhyama* (whispering) and then the gross spoken word, which is vaikhari. Through repeated practice it is the para sound which we should aim to hear. That para nada is none other than shabdabrahman, the highest consciousness experienced in the form of sound.

This dharana indicates that in the heightened state of awareness you can still experience sound, taste, smell, form or touch, but this is different to the experiences in daily life because it takes place in the absence of any gross object to cause it. Therefore, such experiences belong to a different dimension.

## 39. Pranava dharana

प्रणवादिसमुच्चारात् प्लुतान्ते शून्यभावनात् ।
शून्यया परया शक्त्या शून्यतामेति भैरवि ॥ 39 ॥

*Pranavaadisamuchchaaraat plutaante shoonyabhaavanaat;*
*Shoonyayaa parayaa shaktyaa shoonyataam eti Bhairavi. (39)*

### Anvay

*Pranava aadi*: pranava or aum; *Sam uchchaaraat*: from perfect recitation; *Plutaante*: after protracted; *Shoonya bhaavanaat*: concentrating on void; *Shoonyayaa*: by that void; *Parayaa*: by the transcendental; *Shaktyaa*: shakti or energy; *Shoonyataam eti*: the void; *Bhairavi*: O Bhairavi.

### Translation

O Bhairavi, one who repeats the Pranava (Aum) perfectly, while concentrating on the void for protracted periods, experiences the void, and by that void the transcendental shakti (is revealed).

### Commentary

Pranava is the mantra Aum, the first sound to originate in the cosmos. Thus Aum or Pranava is the para nada, or transcendental sound, which is reverberating throughout the universe at all times. Pranava is synonymous with the pure self, or atman, before it becomes qualified or associated with the manifest nature.

About Aum, Swami Sivananda has said: "All mantras, sounds and letters of the alphabet are contained within the mantra Aum. This mantra represents all three states of awareness: jagrat, swapna and sushupti, or conscious, subconscious and unconscious. These states can be experienced and transcended by repetition of this mantra alone. If repeated for extended periods of time, it induces

190

the experience of turiya, the transcendental state. The mantra Aum is none other than Brahman."

Aum is a tantric as well as vedic mantra. The form of this mantra is the akshara. Research on this mantra has revealed that when it is correctly uttered into a tonoscope, the form of the akshara is produced. If you do not have a mantra, this is the one you may safely practise until you are able to receive one directly from the guru. Aum is the primordial sound which, according to Swami Satyananda Saraswati, one of the foremost authorities on this subject, is able to influence the beta, alpha, theta and delta brain waves, inducing experiences of different dimensions of consciousness.

The term *sam uccharat* gives us an important hint in relation to the practice of this mantra. It tells us two things: first, that the recitation of the mantra should be perfect and second, that it should be balanced. Perfect utterance of the mantra is an important prerequisite of this science if it is to achieve the desired results. This factor alone is responsible for its influence on the corresponding energy centres within the body. This applies especially to the tantric mantras. The second hint relates to its intonation, which should be balanced and not erratic. In other words all three parts of the mantra: the beginning, middle and end, should be of the same length of duration.

The Pranava is more than sound; it is the source of sound. By continuous repetition of the Aum mantra, first at the level of vaikhari (spoken aloud), then at the levels of madhyama (whispering) and pashyanti (mental), the aspirant can realize the great void, which is pure consciousness. Correct repetition of Pranava acts as an aid for the awareness to pierce through the veils that obstruct higher experience. The mantra carries the awareness upward at tremendous speed in much the same way as a supersonic jet carries its passengers up with unmatchable speed.

191

Pranava is the source of all manifest vibration and, therefore, it goes beyond vibration. Ultimately, Aum is anahad, the uncaused or unqualified vibration which is heard in the silence of shoonya. So, in this dharana one should also focus the awareness on shoonya, or the void, for extended periods in addition to repetition of the mantra. In this way the awareness will be led to the experience of the supreme void. While contemplating on the Aum mantra and the void, the focus can also be directed towards the transcendental shakti, or energy, whose essence is revealed by this void.

This dharana indicates that the transcendental energy which is inherent in the great void is revealed through the medium of transcendental sound.

## 40. Dharana on Aum matras

यस्य कस्यापि वर्णस्य पूर्वान्तावनुभावयेत् ।
शून्यया शून्यभूतोऽसौ शून्याकार: पुमान्भवेत् ॥ 40 ॥

*Yasya kasyaapi varnasya poorvaantaav anubhaavayet;*
*Shoonyayaa shoonyabhooto'sau shoonyaakaarah pumaan bhavet.*
(40)

### Anvay

*Yasya kasya*: whoever; *Api*: even; *Varnasya*: matras, letters;
*Poorva*: beginning; *Antau*: end; *Anu bhaavayet*: contemplates;
*Shoonyayaa*: by (meditation) of the void; *Shoonya bhootah-*
*asau*: becomes the void; *Shoonya-aakaarah*: in the form of
void; *Pumaan*: sadhaka; *Bhavet*: becomes.

### Translation

Whoever contemplates even on the matras or letters (of
Aum) from first to last, in the form of void, verily that
sadhaka by meditation on the void becomes the void.

### Commentary

The Aum mantra is comprised of three matras or letters:
'A', 'U' and 'M', which are related to the three states of
consciousness: jagrat (waking), swapna (dreaming) and
sushupti (sleeping) or conscious, subconscious and
unconscious. Even in pronunciation of the three letters,
these three states are discernible. For example, while
pronouncing the first syllable, 'A', you will feel the sound
projecting from the mouth outward and this represents the
jagrat awareness. The second syllable, 'U', projects from the
throat both outward and inward and this represents swapna
awareness. While the third syllable, 'M', comes from deep
down in the chest and is only projected within, representing
the sushupti awareness. So, by focusing on each matra of

Aum separately, the three dimensions of consciousness are awakened, which leads to the experience of the fourth dimension of turiya, the transcendental state. In this way the three matras or letters of Aum combined together represent the entire conscious field, which is the theme of the *Mandukya Upanishad*.

The three matras of Aum also represent the three gunas, or qualities of nature, in the primordial, unmanifest state. The pure vibration of sattwa guna, or total luminosity, corresponds to the letter 'A'; rajo guna, the vibration of dynamic creativity, corresponds to the letter 'U' and tamo guna, the vibration of complete stillness, corresponds to the letter 'M'. The combination of these three matras is thus the pure self, the atman or Brahman. By meditation on each matra, from first to last, as the void, the manifest dimension and all of its possibilities are transcended. In this way the individual mind and awareness is merged back into the source, which is the void, and one becomes the void.

The mantra Aum is meditated on in brahmarandhra, which is the great void in the region of the head. In this dharana one must meditate on oneself as being permeated by this three-syllabled mantra.

## 41. Nada dharana

तन्त्र्यादिवाद्यशब्देषु दीर्घेषु क्रमसंस्थिते: ।
अनन्यचेता: प्रत्यन्ते परव्योमवपुर्भवेत् ॥ 41 ॥

*Tantryaadivaadyashabdeshu deergheshu kramasamsthiteh;*
*Ananyachetaah pratyante paravyomavapur bhavet.* (41)

### Anvay

*Tantryaadi*: stringed, wind and percussion instruments; *Vaadya shabdeshu*: sounds of musical instruments; *Deergheshu*: prolonged; *Krama*: gradually; *Samsthiteh*: established; *Ananya*: one- pointed; *Chetaah*: awareness; *Pratyante*: in the end; *Para vyoma*: the supreme space; *Vapuh*: the body; *Bhavet*: becomes.

### Translation

When one-pointed awareness on the prolonged inner sounds of different musical instruments, such as stringed, wind and percussion, is gradually established, in the end the body becomes the supreme space.

### Commentary

Like shakti, or energy, nada too is para and apara. This sloka describes the para state of nada as inner sound. It further says that when these sounds are prolonged or continue ceaselessly, they lead the sadhaka to the experience of shoonya. By establishing one-pointed awareness on the inner sounds that resemble those of various musical instruments, one can completely transcend the grossness of the body and feel oneself dissolving into time and space. These inner sound frequencies, or nadas, are psychic and are heard with the awakening of the kundalini as the awareness enters the subtle dimensions of consciousness. Although the possibilities are infinite, the most common nadas that are heard during meditation are the sounds of bells, conch, lute, flute, cymbals and drum.

These sounds manifest differently in different individuals and may also be accompanied by visions of light, colour and form, which manifest within the space of consciousness. The sounds that are heard depend on the depth of inner space which the awareness has penetrated. Many different sounds can be heard in the levels of vijnanamaya and anandamaya koshas. In this dharana, as one focuses on the inner sounds and the concentration deepens, there is a moment when one experiences the mind moving at lightning speed into space. It is as if the awareness is not confined to the body, but both are part of that infinite supreme space which envelops them.

If my beloved and I are separated by some mishap, and while wandering in search of one another she happens to hear the melodies which we sang together, she will at once be drawn or pulled in the direction of those melodies. In the same way, on hearing the inner melody the energy within the senses and the mind recognizes it as the sound of its beloved. In search of this beloved, which is the supreme consciousness, the energy is propelled into shoonya, the inner space from which it has separated in order to emerge into existence.

## 42. Bija mantra dharana

पिण्डमन्त्रस्य सर्वस्य स्थूलवर्णक्रमेण तु ।
अर्धेन्दुबिन्दुनादान्त:शून्योच्चाराद्भवेच्छिव: ॥ 42 ॥

*Pindamantrasya sarvasya sthoolavarnakramena tu;*
*Ardhendubindunaadaantah shoonyochchaaraad bhavech chhivah.*
(42)

### Anvay

*Pindamantrasya*: of bija mantras; *Sarvasya*: of all; *Sthoola varna*: gross letters; *Kramena*: successively; *Tu*: also; *Ardhendu bindu*: half-moon and bindu or point; *Naadaantah*: within the sound; *Shoonyah*: void; *Uchchaaraat*: by repetition; *Bhavet shivah*: becomes Shiva.

### Translation

By repetition of all the gross letters of the bija mantras successively, including the 'M', (and meditating thus) on the void within each sound, one verily becomes Shiva.

### Commentary

The bija, or seed mantras, include all the letters of the Sanskrit alphabet with an 'M', or makara, at the end of each. The main ones commonly used for meditative purposes are: Aum, Aim, Hrim, Klim, Shrim, Vam, Lam, Ham and Ksham.

These bija mantras are all storehouses of energy. By chanting and meditating on them, the void, or shoonya, can be experienced. For example, if you repeat the mantra Aum loudly and meditate on each of its gross letters one by one, the mind gradually attains the frequencies of those letters. As these frequencies are stabilized in the mind by continuous repetition of the mantra, there comes a point where the vibration becomes so subtle that the awareness is attuned to the same sound reverberating in the atmosphere. For these

197

sounds are forever vibrating throughout the universe at the paravak level.

So when that frequency is attained, you can tune into the cosmic sound and the awareness becomes that sound. As this experience deepens, the mind is gradually transcended and the void is experienced.

*Universal Om Yantra*

## 43. Dharana on the directions

निजदेहे सर्वदिक्कं युगपद्भावयेद्वियत् ।
निर्विकल्पमनास्तस्य वियत्सर्वं प्रवर्तते ॥ 43 ॥

*Nijadehe sarvadikkam yugapad bhaavayed viyat;*
*Nirvikalpamanaas tasya viyat sarvam pravartate.* (43)

### Anvay

*Nijadehe*: in one's own body; *Sarvadikkam*: all directions; *Yugapad*: simultaneously; *Bhaavayet*: contemplate; *Viyat*: space, void; *Nirvikalpamanaah*: the mind being free from any thoughts; *Tasya*: his; *Viyat sarvam*: all dissolved; *Pravartate*: becomes.

### Translation

All the directions should be contemplated upon simultaneously in one's own body as space or void. The mind (too) being free from all thoughts becomes dissolved (in the vacuous space of consciousness).

### Commentary

Direction is an important indicator of space which must be observed, because the moment you enter into space you begin to lose the sense of direction. This is why the directions have to be well defined before you set out on your journey into space. The same principle applies for a journey you may undertake in your car down the road, for a trip into outer space as an astronaut or for the inner journey of meditation. The only difference is that in meditation the journey is inwards, so the directions are delineated within your own body.

Therefore, before starting the practice of dharana on the internal space, you should first define the directions within yourself and then mentally conceptualize those directions as nothing but empty space or void. By doing so you will find that gradually the mind ceases to identify with the gross body. Then, as the experience intensifies, the mind and body are separated and the thoughts cease. Having transcended the body and mind, the awareness identifies with the vast expanse of consciousness, which pervades the space all around it.

*Bhairava Yantra*

## 44. Sushumna and daharakasha dharana

पृष्ठशून्यं मूलशून्यं युगपद्भावयेच्च यः ।
शरीरनिरपेक्षिण्या शक्त्या शून्यमना भवेत् ॥ 44 ॥

*Prishthashoonyam moolashoonyam yugapad bhaavayech cha yah;*
*Shareeranirapekshinyaa shaktyaa shoonyamanaa bhavet.* (44)

### Anvay

*Prishtha shoonyam*: void of the back; *Moola shoonyam*: void of
the root; *Yugapad bhaavayet cha yah*: one who simultaneously
contemplates; *Shareera*: body; *Nirapekshinyaa*: independent
of; *Shaktyaa*: by the energy; *Shoonya-manaa*: void-minded;
*Bhavet*: becomes.

### Translation

One who contemplates simultaneously on the void of the
back (spinal column) and the void of the root becomes void-
minded (completely free of all thought constructs or vikalpas)
by that energy which is independent of the body.

### Commentary

This physical body is made up of five tattwas, which are the
gross form of consciousness condensed into flesh, blood,
bones and marrow. If we can transcend the physical matter
of the body and experience that from which it has evolved,
then we will be able to perceive the essence behind the form.
Beyond the physical body is the pranic body which, although
linked to the physical body, is also independent of it. That
pranic body is known as the pranamaya kosha and it envelops
the physical body in much the same way as the peel surrounds
an orange. This pranic body is made up of prana, just as the
physical body, which is known as annamaya kosha, is made
up of anna, or food. By contemplating on the space within
sushumna and on the space at the root as the essence

201

behind the physical form, one experiences the void in the mind with the aid of the energy field which is reverberating in the pranamaya kosha.

By contemplating both on the space within sushumna and on the space at the root at the same time, one experiences the void of shoonya in the mind with the aid of the energy field, which is reverberating in the pranamaya kosha independent of this physical body.

This sloka describes two important akasha dharanas. The void of the back refers to the practice of *sushumna darshan*, which is one of the most subtle dharanas where the awareness is engulfed in the transcendental space within the sushumna passage. The void of the root refers to *daharakasha dharana*, concentration on the lower or deep space between the navel and the perineum. This is a space where the deep psychic and archetypal symbols manifest, which includes the chakra and tattwa yantras. Both of these spaces are pervaded by the potentiality of pranashakti, which makes them very powerful forms of dharana. By concentrating on both of these spaces simultaneously, the mind is transcended and becomes free from all thoughts or void-minded.

# 45. Sushumna, daharakasha and hridayakasha dharana

पृष्ठशून्यं मूलशून्यं हृच्छून्यं भावयेत्स्थिरम् ।
युगपन्निर्विकल्पत्वान्निर्विकल्पोदयस्ततः      ॥ 45 ॥

*Prishthashoonyam moolashoonyam hrichchhoonyam bhaavayet sthiram;*
*Yugapan nirvikalpatvaan nirvikalpodayas tatah.* (45)

## Anvay

*Prishtha shoonyam*: void of the back; *Moola shoonyam*: void of
the root; *Hrit shoonyam*: void of the heart; *Bhaavayet*:
contemplate, concentrate, think; *Sthiram*: steady; *Yugapat*:
simultaneously; *Nirvikalpatvaat*: from the nirvikalpa;
*Nirvikalpah*: free from thought constructs; *Udayah*: arises;
*Tatah*: there.

## Translation

By steady contemplation on the void of the back (sushumna),
the void of the root and the void of the heart simultaneously,
there arises the state of nirvikalpa, which is free from thought
constructs.

## Commentary

This sloka again reiterates the importance of the two akasha
dharanas described previously, and adds one more. The
void of the heart refers to hridayakasha dharana. Similar
dharana practices are referred to in the Yoga Upanishads.
Hridayakasha is the space of the heart which is permeated
with the vibrations and pulsations of the physical organs of
the heart and lungs, as well as the emotional and psychic
vibrations associated with the heart. This is a very deep and
powerful space in itself, as the emotions are directly linked
to the pranas and to the psyche. By focusing the awareness
within hridayakasha, dharana occurs spontaneously due to
the energy field generated within this space.

This sloka says to focus on the space within sushumna, on the lower space, or daharakasha, and on the heart space, or hridayakasha, simultaneously. This is a very powerful form of dharana which catapults the mind out of its normal patterns and associations into the experience of nirvikalpa, or the void, which is free from all thought patterns. By disassociating the mind from all thoughts, and focusing the awareness on these three spaces which are permeated with the energy and vibration of the chakras and sushumna, one can become totally free of the vikalpas, or thought constructs, and experience that transcendental state of awareness, which is nirvikalpa.

This practice can also be related with the practices of kriya and kundalini yoga, where the mind is attuned to the vibrations of the chakras and thus transcends thought and body identification.

## 46. Antarakasha dharana

तनूदेशे शून्यतैव क्षणमात्रं विभावयेत् ।
निर्विकल्पं निर्विकल्पो निर्विकल्पस्वरूपभाक् ॥ 46 ॥

*Tanoodeshe shoonyataiva kshanamaatram vibhaavayet;*
*Nirvikalpam nirvikalpo nirvikalpasvaroopabhaak.* (46)

### Anvay

*Tanoodeshe*: the body; *Shoonyataa iva*: like a void; *Kshanamaatram*: even for a moment; *Vibhaavayet*: concentrates; *Nirvikalpam*: thoughtlessness; *Nirvikalpah*: mind free from vikalpas; *Nirvikalpa*: void; *Svaroopa bhaak*: verily becomes that form.

### Translation

If one concentrates on the body as a void, even for a moment, with the mind free from thought, then one attains thoughtlessness and verily becomes that form of void.

### Commentary

The limitations of consciousness trapped in the physical body are difficult to transcend. What holds you back from the experience of that supreme state is your identification with the body and the thoughts, which assail you throughout the day, concerning the experiences of the body. If you can concentrate on your body as void or space and transcend all thoughts, even for a moment, your mind will be liberated and will take on the form of that void. It is important to note that you do not have to concentrate for hours and hours in order to experience this state. Even if you focus the mind for just a moment, it is enough to give you the experience of a heightened state of awareness.

This sloka describes the practice of *antarakasha dharana*, concentration on the inner space, in which every part of the body is conceived of as void. At first it may be difficult to perceive the body as space due to our material identifications and associations. However, in time it becomes a natural experience, and by developing this form of concentration the mind also takes on that form of void, because the body and mind are not separate. When we concentrate on anything, the mind takes on that form, even for a moment. So, if we concentrate on the body, the mind becomes that form of the body. In this way, when we see the body as space, the mind also becomes space, and thus the vikalpas, or thought constructs, are immediately transcended.

## 47. Antarakasha dharana (cont.)

सर्वं देहगतं द्रव्यं वियद्व्याप्तं मृगेक्षणे ।
विभावयेत्ततस्तस्य भावना सा स्थिरा भवेत् ॥ 47 ॥

*Sarvam dehagatam dravyam viyadvyaaptam mrigekshane;*
*Vibhaavayet tatas tasya bhaavanaa saa sthiraa bhavet.* (47)

### Anvay

*Sarvam*: all; *Dehagatam*: in the body; *Dravyam*: matter, constituents; *Viyat vyaaptam*: pervaded by void; *Mrigekshane*: gazelle eyed; *Vibhaavayet*: concentrate, feel; *Tatah tasya*: there his; *Bhaavanaa*: thought; *Saa*: that (she); *Sthiraa*: steady; *Bhavet*: becomes.

### Translation

O gazelle-eyed one, concentrate upon all the constituents of the body pervaded by space, so that the thought becomes steady.

### Commentary

This sloka is a continuation of the previous one, and describes how the practice of antarakasha dharana is to be performed. All the parts of the body, one by one, should be visualized as pervaded by space, until the whole body appears as nothing but space. In this way the thought process is gradually stabilized and the mind becomes steady and one-pointed.

*Shoonya bhava* is an altered state of consciousness, where the mind becomes totally supportless. In order to experience the entire body as void, the aspirant should be proficient at attaining shoonya bhava effortlessly. Otherwise, one can focus on the constituents which the body is made up of, such as flesh, blood, bone, marrow, etc., as shoonya or vacant space. Gradually, as this dharana is perfected and the physical matter of the body is seen as shoonya, steadiness in concentration is attained.

## 48. Antarakasha dharana (cont.)

देहान्तरे त्वग्विभागं भित्तिभूतं विचिन्तयेत् ।
न किञ्चिदन्तरे तस्य ध्यायन्नध्येयभाग्भवेत् ॥ 48 ॥

*Dehaantare tvagvibhaagam bhittibhootam vichintayet;*
*Na kinchid antare tasya dhyaayan na dhyeyabhaag bhavet.* (48)

### Anvay

*Dehaantare*: on the body; *Tvak-vibhaagam*: skin-part; *Bhitti bhootam*: like a wall or partition; *Vichintayet*: should be contemplated; *Na kinchit*: nothing; *Antare tasya*: inside it; *Dhyaayan*: by meditating thus; *Na*: cannot; *Dhyeya*: meditated upon, i.e., the void; *Bhaak*: like; *Bhavet*: becomes.

### Translation

One should contemplate on the skin of the body as a mere wall or partition with nothing inside it. By meditating thus, he becomes like the void, which cannot be meditated upon.

### Commentary

This sloka describes a further aspect of antarakasha dharana. Here the body is imagined or visualized as empty space covered by a wall or partition of skin, like an empty shell, and the space inside the body is not differentiated from the space outside the body. The walls of a house give a shape to the space that is inside. If the walls are demolished, the interior and exterior space becomes one and the same. Similarly, if one imagines that the skin of the body is merely a wall separating the space inside the body from the outer space, then the objective experience is also transcended.

## 49. Dharana on the mantra in the heart space

हृद्याकाशे निलीनाक्ष: पद्मसम्पुटमध्यग: ।
अनन्यचेता: सुभगे परं सौभाग्यमाप्नुयात् ॥ 49 ॥

*Hridyaakaashe nileenaakshah padmasamputamadhyagah;*
*Ananyachetaah subhage param saubhaagyam aapnuyaat.* (49)

### Anvay

*Hridyaakaashe*: in the space of the heart; *Nileenaakshah*: closed eyes; *Padma samputa madhyagah*: on the mantra in the middle of the lotus; *Ananyachetaah*: one-pointed concentration; *Subhage*: embodiment of good fortune; *Param*: highest; *Saubhaagyam:* spiritual realization; *Aapnuyaat*: achieved.

### Translation

O embodiment of good fortune, one who contemplates with closed eyes and one-pointed concentration on the mantra in the middle of the lotus in the heart space achieves the highest spiritual realization.

### Commentary

This sloka describes the dharana on mantra in hridayakasha, the heart space. If one can visualize the space of the heart cavity and focus on the samput in the middle of the heart lotus with one-pointed concentration, the highest grace is attained in the form of inner spiritual realization. The heart lotus is anahata chakra, which is the seat of the jivatman, or individual consciousness, and therefore a powerful point for meditation. *Samput* means 'repetition' and here refers to the mantra ceaselessly emanating from anahata chakra, which has to be revealed to the sadhaka through a guru or seer of the mantra. It repeats itself again and again and becomes the samput mantra of that centre.

209

## 50. Dharana on dwadashanta

सर्वतः स्वशरीरस्य द्वादशान्ते मनोलयात् ।
दृढबुद्धेर्दृढीभूतं     तत्त्वलक्ष्यं     प्रवर्तते ॥ 50 ॥

*Sarvataha svashareerasya dvaadashaante manolayaat;*
*Dridhabuddher dridheebhootam tattvalakshyam pravartate.* (50)

### Anvay

*Sarvatah*: everywhere; *Svashareerasya*: of one's own body;
*Dvaadashaante*: in dwadashanta; *Manolayaat*: from (as a result
of) the dissolution of mind; *Dridha buddheh*: with steady
awareness; *Dridhee bhootam*: steady practice; *Tattva lakshyam*:
essence or true nature of the goal; *Pravartate*: is present,
manifests.

### Translation

When the mind is dissolved in dwadashanta by steady
awareness and steady practice, the true nature or essence of
the goal manifests everywhere in one's body.

### Commentary

Here dwadashanta refers to hridaya chakra, which is one
of the important dwadashantas in the body. When the
awareness becomes steady through practice, it overrides
the outgoing and dissipating tendencies of the mind. As it
reaches the heart centre, which is the abode of the
individual consciousness, the awareness is further intensified, which results in dissolution of the mind, as it merges
back into its source.

This dissolution takes place only when two important
requisites are met. The aspirant must develop steady
awareness by means of regular and established practice.
This, in turn, leads to the experience of the tattwa, or
essence, from which one has evolved. Thus one experiences

210

the characteristics of reality in oneself, which happens to be the true nature of the spiritual goal.

As the energy which ascends from the base of the spine becomes more rarefied, it pierces through the subtle energy centres one by one, until it enters the dwadashanta of hridaya. This is the point of the first union, where the individual energy and consciousness become one after their long separation. After this point the consciousness and energy ascend together in one steady stream of awareness in a state of intoxicated bliss, which manifests and spreads throughout the body. This final ascent leads to the mega-merger with the supreme awareness at sahasrara, the thousand-petalled lotus at the crown of the head, which is the abode of Shiva.

## 51. Result of dharana on dwadashanta

यथा तथा यत्र तत्र द्वादशान्ते मन: क्षिपेत् ।
प्रतिक्षणं क्षीणवृत्तेर्वैलक्षण्यं दिनैर्भवेत् ॥ 51 ॥

*Yathaa tathaa yatra tatra dvaadashaante manah kshipet;*
*Pratikshanam ksheenavritter vailakshanyam dinair bhavet.* (51)

### Anvay

*Yathaa tathaa*: however; *Yatra tatra*: wherever; *Dvaadashaante*: in dwadashanta; *Manah*: mind; *Kshipet*: bring forcibly; *Pratikshanam*: each moment; *Ksheena vritteh*: when the fluctuations of the mind diminish; *Vailakshanyam*: extraordinary state; *Dinaih*: day by day; *Bhavet*: becomes.

### Translation

By bringing the mind forcibly to dwadashanta again and again, however and wherever possible, the fluctuations of the mind diminish day by day, so that each moment becomes an extraordinary state.

### Commentary

Here the process of dharana on the dwadashanata of hridaya chakra is further elaborated. Generally speaking, it is not easy to focus the awareness on one point due to the dissipated and fragmented condition of the mind. However, this sloka says that the mind can be forcibly focused on dwadashanta. If one were to force the mind to focus on itself or on any of its mental tendencies or patterns, this same advice could lead to mental disturbance. But the dwadashanta of the heart cavity is a powerful point of luminosity, which attracts and holds the mind without further effort, once it has been brought there.

Moreover, at that stage the mind has developed from moodha (dull) and kshipta (scattered) to spells of vikshipta

212

(oscillation) and moments of ekagrata (one-pointedness). Thus it is possible to direct the awareness forcibly to the dwadashanta in the hridaya chakra, again and again. In this way, the fluctuation of awareness gradually diminishes day by day, and one experiences each moment as extraordinary. This is the very same state of expanded mind mentioned in the introduction, which is inherent in the word tantra itself.

The word tantra is made up of two roots: *tanoti,* expansion and *trayati,* liberation. It is an expanded mind, which has broken away from the fetters or clutches of matter and entered the realm of the spirit, that experiences every moment as extraordinary. This also leads the sadhaka to the realization of the illusory and transient nature of the world and his role within it.

The sloka advises that this dharana should be done again and again, however and wherever it may be possible. This implies that the awareness may be focused on dwadashanta at any time during the day or night, in any place, whether at home or away, in seclusion or amongst people, and also in any condition, whether old or young, weak or strong, happy or sad.

## 52. Dharana on Kaalagni

कालाग्निना कालपदादुत्थितेन स्वकं पुरम् ।
प्लुष्टं विचिन्तयेदन्ते शान्ताभासस्तदा भवेत् ॥ 52 ॥

*Kaalaagninaa kaalapadaad utthitena svakam puram;*
*Plushtam vichintayed ante shaantaabhaasas tadaa bhavet.* (52)

### Anvay

*Kaala*: time; *Agninaa*: by the fire; *Kaala padaat*: movement of
time; *Utthitena*: arising; *Svakam*: one's own; *Puram*: body
(city); *Plushtam*: burnt; *Vichintayet*: concentrate, contemplate;
*Ante*: at last; *Shaanta*: tranquillity; *Aabhaasah*: feeling; *Tadaa*:
then; *Bhavet*: becomes.

### Translation

One should contemplate that one's own body has been
burnt by Kaalagni, arising from the movement of time.
Then at last one will experience tranquillity.

### Commentary

Kaalagni is the manifestation of Shiva as universal destroyer.
Kaala, or time, is the great destroyer. Just as fire destroys
and consumes everything it comes in contact with, so also
time destroys everything that manifests. Shiva, the universal
consciousness, is known as *Mahakaala,* the great time. In
this dharana, time, which is a category of the finite mind, is
personified to such an extent that one gradually focuses on
the movement within it and imagines that it is consuming
the matter which composes the physical body. Once this
dharana is perfected and the physical body is consumed,
what remains will be pure consciousness, whose nature is
tranquillity.

This is the most famous concept of tantra, which has
similarities with the theories in modern physics related to

214

the movement of time. The truths about time are that: it exists only in the present, here and now; it is never static; it has a spiralling motion, and it is deeply related to your existence or yourself. The truth about the self is that: it is shoonya, or space, which is eternal, expanding and moving outwards in each and every direction.

Regarding the concept of time, Swami Satyananda has said that: "Time and space are equal and opposite forces. But when their movements are reversed and they begin to travel towards each other, they meet at one point and an immense explosion takes place. Tremendous heat is generated by this explosion, which completely overrides the mundane mind and gives birth to a very extraordinary state of awareness."

Kaalagni, the fire of time, refers to the great heat of that explosion which takes place when time and space collide with each other. In order to reverse the movements of time and space so that they unite at the centre, concentration on these two equal and opposite forces is required. The flow of time has to become linear and one-dimensional, and the flow of space must be focused rather than dispersed in all directions.

*Ante shanta abhasa* refers to the result of this tremendous explosion, which is that of tranquillity. Just as the surface of a pond or lake which has no ripples appears tranquil, similarly the steady stream of awareness that emerges out of this explosion appears tranquil because it is not broken, fragmented or dissipated, but one composite whole or mass of awareness. This corresponds very closely to the prajna state of consciousness referred to in the Introduction, in the section describing the four stages of consciousness.

## 53. Result of dharana on Kaalagni

एवमेव जगत्सर्वं दग्धं ध्यात्वा विकल्पत: ।
अनन्यचेतस: पुंस: पुंभाव: परमो भवेत् ॥ 53 ॥

*Evam eva jagat sarvam dagdham dhyaatvaa vikalpatah;*
*Ananyachetasah pumsah pumbhaavah paramo bhavet. (53)*

### Anvay

*Evam-eva*: in the same way; *Jagat sarvam*: the entire universe;
*Dagdham*: burnt; *Dhyaatvaa*: having meditated; *Vikalpatah*:
without wavering; *Ananya chetasah*: one-pointed; *Pumsah*:
the man; *Pumbhaavah*: manhood; *Paramah*: supreme; *Bhavet*:
becomes.

### Translation

In the same way, having meditated with an unwavering and
one-pointed mind on the entire universe being burnt (by
Kaalagni), that man becomes a godman or attains a supreme
state of manhood.

### Commentary

Here the dharana from the previous sloka is extended from
the individual body to the universe. You can then focus
your unwavering awareness on Time, the great destroyer,
which ultimately transforms by burning everything in the
manifest and finite world. Visualize the *pralaya*, or great
dissolution, taking place, where everything that has been
created is dissolving back into Shiva, who is known as the
destroyer.

Imagine that all the mountains, oceans, skies, plants,
animals and humans are being consumed by the universal
fire of dissolution and are disappearing back into that
supreme consciousness. This vision was given by Lord
Krishna to Arjuna, during the Mahabharata war right in the

216

midst of the battlefield, when he granted him *divya drishti*, or divine vision, in order to make him aware of the truth of this impermanent existence. Needless to say, this dharana is for the *viras*, who are strong-minded and courageous, and not for the weak-hearted.

As time and space merge and begin to ascend upwards in unison as one steady stream of awareness, not just the individual body but the entire manifest existence is consumed by the fire of that sacrifice. The sadhaka then begins to perceive the object of his worship, or *ishta*, even in its absence. That is the ultimate human state, and only after attaining that is one fit to be called a man, or *manushya*. According to tantra, prior to this state one comes under the category of *pashu*, or animal nature. It is the transformation of man to Godman.

This dharana has its basis in the concept of the trinity which is upheld by vedic and tantric philosophy. The supreme consciousness manifests as three universal principles: Brahma, the creator, Vishnu, the preserver, and Shiva, the destroyer. Together they are the three faces of the one supreme consciousness.

## 54. Tattwa dharana

स्वदेहे जगतो वापि सूक्ष्मसूक्ष्मतराणि च ।
तत्त्वानि यानि निलयं ध्यात्वान्ते व्यज्यते परा ॥ 54 ॥

*Svadehe jagato vaapi sookshmasookshmataraani cha;*
*Tattvaani yaani nilayam dhyaatvaante vyajyate paraa.* (54)

### Anvay

*Svadehe*: in one's own body; *Jagatah*: whole world or universe; *Vaa api*: or else; *Sookshmasookshmataraani*: from subtle to subtlest; *Cha*: and; *Tattvaani*: tattwas and tanmatras; *Yaani*: those which; *Nilayam*: source; *Dhyaatvaante*: at the end of meditation; *Vyajyate*: leads to; *Paraa*: supreme.

### Translation

Dharana on those constituents which comprise one's own body and the whole universe, such as the tattwas and tanmatras, from subtle to subtlest, leads to the source of existence. (In this way) Paradevi, the supreme goddess, (is revealed) at the end of meditation.

### Commentary

This sloka refers to *tattwa shuddhi*, which is a tantric practice of dharana on the elements or tattwas and their subtle forms, the tanmatras.

In this dharana, through a process of involution one has to recreate that from which one has evolved into the physical body. It is interesting to note that Paradevi is revealed to the aspirant through this dharana. This substantiates the claim of tantra that devi, shakti or energy is responsible for the manifest world. It is Shakti who through her threefold powers of iccha (the power to desire all), jnana (the power to know all) and kriya (the power to do all) sets the wheel of creation into motion.

218

In the scheme of creation these three powers first transform themselves into sattwa, rajas and tamas, the three gunas that are present in each and every cell of our physical body. The gunas then evolve into the individual consciousness, the four components of mind, the five organs of knowledge, the five organs of action, the five tanmatras and the five tattwas. In tattwa dharana each of these elements is used as a focus of concentration until finally one arrives back at the source of creation, which is Paradevi or the cosmic energy principle. These tattwas, along with the organs of knowledge and action, are in complete symphony with the mind. They act like a fantastic chain whereby there is immediate and spontaneous transference of knowledge and experience.

However, their gaze is outwards because that is how you have trained them to behave since your birth. Now, if you want to develop the transcendental experience, you will have to redirect their gaze inwards to experience the paradevi from which they have evolved. In order to do this it is necessary to isolate each of these components, such as the five tattwas, five tanmatras, five karmendriyas and five jnanendriyas, as well as the four components of mind from each other so that the chain reaction is broken.

## 55. Dharana on the indriyas, or senses

पीनां च दुर्बलां शक्तिं ध्यात्वा द्वादशगोचरे ।
प्रविश्य हृदये ध्यायन् मुक्त: स्वातन्त्र्यमाप्नुयात् ॥ 55 ॥

*Peenaam cha durbalaam shaktim dhyaatvaa dvaadashagochare;*
*Pravishya hridaye dhyaayan muktah svaatantryam aapnuyaat.* (55)

### Anvay

*Peenaam*: gross; *Cha*: and; *Durbalaam*: weak; *Shaktim*: shakti;
*Dhyaatvaa*: having meditated; *Dvaadashagochare*: range of
twelve; *Pravishya*: entering; *Hridaye*: in the heart; *Dhyaayan*:
meditate; *Muktaha*: free; *Svaatantryam*: liberation; *Aapnuyaat*:
attains.

### Translation

Having meditated on the gross and weak shakti in the
dwadash indriyas (thus making it subtle), one who enters
the heart space and meditates there attains mukti and
becomes liberated.

### Commentary

This dharana refers to the energy inherent in the senses or
indriyas, which is to be meditated upon. Here *dwadash
gochare,* or the range of twelve, implies the senses. The
indriyas are more subtle than the tanmatras and tattwas
mentioned in the previous dharana. The indriyas are
generally described as ten in number: five karmendriyas,
senses of action, and five jnanendriyas, senses of knowledge.
However, this sloka refers to twelve indriyas, as it includes
manas, the lower mind, and ahamkara, the individual
identification, as the last two senses.

The word *go* has been used extensively in relation to the
indriyas or senses. Thus the word Gopal, a name for Lord
Krishna, means 'Lord of the senses' and *gochar* is the field of

operation for the indriyas. The word *char* literally means 'to graze', so gochar is the field of the senses on which the mind grazes.

Due to the mundane associations of these twelve indriyas, the shakti, or energy, inherent in them also appears gross, slow, weak and dissipated. As the awareness is focused on the indriyas, the energy is liberated from its gross association with the sense objects and thus becomes more subtle. By mentally directing that subtle energy liberated from the senses into the heart cavity, one attains mukti, or freedom, from the dominance of the sensory tendencies and nature.

This sloka makes it very clear that the very same energy, which appears weak while moving in the gross and mundane senses, is transformed through concentration into refined inner states that can even penetrate the extremely subtle heart cavity. They are not two different energies. By the practice of steady and unbroken concentration, which culminates in meditation, this *durbal*, or weak energy, is transformed and liberated.

## 56. Dharana on universal dissolution

भुवनाध्वादिरूपेण चिन्तयेत्क्रमशोऽखिलम् ।
स्थूलसूक्ष्मपरस्थित्या यावदन्ते मनोलय: ॥ 56 ॥

*Bhuvanaadhvaadiroopena chintayet kramasho' khilam;*
*Sthoolasookshmaparasthityaa yaavadante manolayah.* (56)

### Anvay

*Bhuvana*: universe; *Adhvaadi*: course, time and space;
*Roopena*: through the form; *Chintayet*: meditating; *Kramashah*:
gradually; *Akhilam*: entire, whole; *Sthoola sookshma*: gross
and the subtle; *Parasthityaa*: being beyond; *Yaavat ante*: at
the end of which; *Manolayah*: dissolution of mind.

### Translation

By meditating on the entire form of the universe and the
course of its development through time and space, gradually
dissolve the gross into the subtle and the subtle into the
state of being beyond, until the mind is finally dissolved
(into pure consciousness).

### Commentary

Here the dharana on dissolution of the tattwas, tanmatras
and antahkarana within the individual mind and body structure is further extended to the entire universe. The awareness
is projected to the evolution of the entire universe as it came
into existence through time and space. Then gradually the
course of evolution is followed in reverse order, from gross
to subtle, from jagat, the manifest world, to the unmanifest
dimension before creation. In this process, as the experience
becomes more and more subtle, dissolution of mind
gradually takes place and pure consciousness is experienced.

Dharana is the mental projection of a thought or idea as
well as an object. Success in dharana depends on one's

222

ability to follow that projection to its natural conclusion. Through this dharana the sadhaka can understand his connection with the universe by experiencing himself as an integral part of it, thus realizing his unity with the pure consciousness that is all pervading. *Manolaya* refers to the state of mind which this dharana induces. Once again, dissolution of mind here does not just mean the conscious mind, but all levels of mind that are indicated by the states of jagrat, swapna and sushupti.

## 57. Shiva tattwa dharana

अस्य सर्वस्य विश्वस्य पर्यन्तेषु समन्ततः ।
अध्वप्रक्रियया तत्त्वं शैवं ध्यात्वा महोदयः ॥ 57 ॥

*Asya sarvasya vishvasya paryanteshu samantatah;*
*Adhvaprakriyayaa tattvam shaivam dhyaatvaa mahodayah.* (57)

### Anvay

*Asya*: of this; *Sarvasya*: of all; *Vishvasya*: of the universe; *Paryanteshu*: up to; *Samantatah*: on all sides; *Adhva*: method; *Prakriyayaa*: by the way; *Tattvam*: tattwa; *Shaivam*: shaiva; *Dhyaatvaa*: meditate; *Maha-udayah*: rise of the highest or greatest.

### Translation

By this method one should meditate on all the sides or aspects of the universe up to the shiva tattwa (which is the quintessence) of all. In this way the experience of the supreme reality arises.

### Commentary

This sloka describes the progression of the previous dharana in which the whole universe that has evolved through time and space was dissolved back into the unmanifest. Shiva tattwa refers to the source from which all creation ensues. Technically it is the state prior to manifestation when the consciousness is described as *shuddha tattwa*, the pure nature of consciousness, where there is no notion of duality. This essence of the entire universe, which exists within each and every speck of creation, as well as independently beyond creation, is to be meditated or concentrated upon through a process of involution.

To understand this process in a simpler way, suppose you want to remember the period in your childhood when

224

you were in your mother's lap. You will have to travel backwards in time from your present age to the moment when you were a little toddler. In this process you will have to focus your awareness on each and every moment you have experienced and thus gradually wind your way back to that moment. In the same way, you should reverse the process of evolution and travel back in time and space to the period before the universe was created. At this point, just before the emanation of the primary evolute of creation, the awareness can be focused on the shiva tattwa, which is the essence of supreme reality from which the universe has evolved. This is a dharana of jnana yoga, which requires a discerning awareness.

## 58. Vishwa shoonya dharana

विश्वमेतन्महादेवि शून्यभूतं विचिन्तयेत् ।
तत्रैव च मनो लीनं ततस्तल्लयभाजनम् ॥ 58 ॥

*Vishvam etan mahaadevi shoonyabhootam vichintayet;*
*Tatraiva cha mano leenam tatas tallayabhaajanam.* (58)

### Anvay

*Vishvam*: universe; *Etat*: this; *Mahaadevi*: O great Goddess; *Shoonya bhootam*: as void; *Vichintayet*: should concentrate; *Tatra-eva*: there, like this; *Cha*: also; *Manah*: mind; *Leenam*: dissolves; *Tatah tat*: then there; *Laya*: dissolution; *Bhaajanam*: experiences.

### Translation

O great Goddess, one should concentrate on this universe as nothing but void. Dissolving the mind also like this, one then experiences the state of laya, or total dissolution.

### Commentary

*Laya* means the state of 'dissolution'. Here, as in the previous dharanas, the universe is first dissolved into the void through a process of annihilation of everything that is contained within it. Thus the concept of the universe is transformed into nothing but the void of consciousness. When the universe is nothing but void, or shoonya, the mind is dissolved in the same way. By focusing the awareness on the void or empty space, the mind, which acts as a barrier to the higher experience on account of its continuous movement into the past, present and future, begins to lose its support and also dissolves. This leads to a totally new dimension of awareness, known as shoonya, which is all pervading stillness.

The concept of shoonya, or the great void, is very important in vedic and tantric philosophy, as well as all other philosophies that have originated from them, such as Buddhism and Jainism. In these philosophies, shoonya, or void, is considered to be the attribute of that supreme consciousness and in many practices is meditated on as being that supreme consciousness. Time and space are categories of the mind. The moment they dissolve and become one, the mind too fades away and ceases to exist. These dharanas reveal how shoonya is conceptualized both within and without the body. In the earlier dharanas the physical attributes such as skin, etc. were the barriers to be transcended for the shoonya within to merge with the shoonya pervading all around. In this dharana it is the mind that has to be dissolved into shoonya to experience total dissolution.

## 59. Dharana on an empty pot

घटादिभाजने दृष्टिं भित्तीस्त्यक्त्वा विनिक्षिपेत् ।
तल्लयं तक्षणाद्गत्वा तल्लयात्तन्मयो भवेत् ॥ 59 ॥

*Ghataadibhaajane drishtim bhittees tyaktvaa vinikshipet;*
*Tallayam tatkshanaad gatvaa tallayaat tanmayo bhavet.* (59)

### Anvay

*Ghata aadi bhaajane*: inside the pot; *Drishtim*: sight; *Bhitteeh*: enclosure; *Tyaktvaa*: leaving aside; *Vinikshipet*: should fix; *Tat-layam*: that dissolution; *Tat kshanaat*: at once; *Gatvaa*: being gone; *Tat-layaat*: through that laya; *Tanmayah*: absorbed completely; *Bhavet*: becomes.

### Translation

One should fix his sight (on the empty space) inside the pot, leaving aside the enclosing structure. Thus, the pot being gone, the mind will at once be dissolved (into the space). Through that laya the mind becomes completely absorbed (in the void).

### Commentary

This sloka is a continuation of shoonya dharana, utilizing the expedient of an empty pot to focus the mind on the space within. In this dharana the barrier which obstructs the individual awareness from merging into the great shoonya is conceptualized by the empty pot. The analogy of the *kumbha,* or mud pot, is commonly used in tantra to denote or explain the amalgamation of inner and outer space. In actual fact, the space inside the pot is not different to the space outside it.

The inner and outer space are simply separated by the mud walls of the pot. If the pot breaks, the space inside will automatically merge with the space outside to become one space. This concept is utilized very effectively by focusing the gaze on the void or empty space inside the pot. By concentrating in this way, the walls of the pot gradually disappear and the awareness merges into the empty space. Thus the mind dissolves into shoonya as the partition between the inner and outer space is transcended. This leads to absorption in the total void.

Kumbha is an important concept of tantra from which the word kumbhaka, or retention, arose. This term was used earlier in relation to the dharanas on pranayama. The word kumbha literally means that which retains something and thus the word kumbhaka signifies the process whereby the vayus and breath are retained, either inside or outside the body. In the same way in this dharana you are asked to focus on the space retained within the kumbha and then experience that the walls of the kumbha have broken to allow the inside space to merge with the space outside.

Once you have perfected this process you can apply it in many places such as the breath, the symbol of your concentration or any point that you wish to concentrate on. This is based on the idea that whatever exists outside is also within you. The macrocosmos is inherent in the micro-cosmos. You are a replica of the universe. Each cell of your body has the universal experience enshrined in it. You are Shiva.

## 60. Dharana on a deserted place

निर्वृक्षगिरिभित्त्यादि-देशे दृष्टिं विनिक्षिपेत् ।
विलीने मानसे भावे वृत्तिक्षीण: प्रजायते ॥ 60 ॥

*Nirvrikshagiribhittyaadideshe drishtim vinikshipet;*
*Vileene maanase bhaave vrittiksheenah prajaayate.* (60)

### Anvay

*Nirvriksha*: treeless; *Giri*: rocks or mountains; *Bhitti aadi*: support for the mind to dwell on; *Deshe*: place; *Drishtim*: gaze; *Vinikshipet*: cast, fix; *Vileene*: being dissolved; *Maanase*: in the mind; *Bhaave*: feeling or thought; *Vritti*: modification, fluctuation; *Ksheenah*: becoming less; *Prajaayate*: takes place.

### Translation

One should fix his gaze on a treeless place, like bare mountains or rocks, where there is no support for the mind to dwell on. Then the modifications of the mind become less and the experience of dissolution takes place.

### Commentary

The same process of the pot can be applied to meditation on deserted, lonely and barren places. This dharana is unique because it gives us two perfect hints about the practice of dharana and the state of dhyana. The first is that these practices require spontaneity and alertness, and the second, that they can be achieved even through the simple act of gazing at a barren mountain. You may well wonder how dissolution of the mind is possible by fixing the gaze on a barren mountain. It is the absence of stimuli in deserted spots which leads to cessation of the *vrittis*, or fluctuations of the mind, for there is nothing to attract or draw it in different directions. Perhaps this is why yogis and hermits have always chosen deserted and uninhabited places to practise their sadhana. In other traditions too recluses often retired into seclusion for years at a time to perfect their spiritual vision.

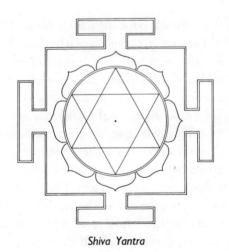

*Shiva Yantra*

## 61. Dharana on the space in between two objects

उभयोर्भावयोर्ज्ञाने ध्यात्वा मध्यं समाश्रयेत् ।
युगपच्च द्वयं त्यक्त्वा मध्ये तत्त्वं प्रकाशते ॥ 61 ॥

*Ubhayor bhaavayor jnaane dhyaatvaa madhyam samaashrayet;*
*Yugapach cha dvayam tyaktvaa madhye tattvam prakaashate.* (61)

### Anvay

*Ubhayoh*: of both; *Bhaavayoh*: think; *Jnaane*: in the event of such knowledge; *Dhyaatvaa*: having meditated; *Madhyam*: in the middle; *Sam-aashrayet*: dwell; *Yuga pat-cha*: to be matured; *Dvayam*: both; *Tyaktvaa*: leaving; *Madhye*: in the middle; *Tattvam*: element, essence; *Prakaashate*: arises.

### Translation

One should think of two objects, and in the event of such knowledge being matured, then cast both aside and dwell (on the gap or space) in the middle. Having meditated in the middle, the experience of the essence arises.

### Commentary

This is a very interesting concept which is used a lot in Zen Buddhism. It can be practised with objects, feelings, thoughts, ideas and even with the breath. The basis of this dharana is that duality has to be transcended by focusing on what lies in-between any two objects. For instance, take the gap between love and hate, night and day, two dogs, two clouds, you and me; any example can be picked up. In that gap neither object exists. Take the example of night and day, in the gap in between, it is neither night nor day. By meditating on that gap, you transcend both and arrive at a new experience, the awareness of the middle state. The split moment between the two equal and opposite forces is an extremely significant point on which dharana is practised in

232

order to catapult the awareness into a higher dimension. It is an extremely subtle moment which, if the sadhaka is able to catch, can propel him to great heights of awareness in which the essence is realized.

Sri Yantra

## 62. Dharana on one object

भावे त्यक्ते निरुद्धा चिन् नैव भावान्तरं व्रजेत् ।
तदा तन्मध्यभावेन विकसत्यति भावना ॥ 62 ॥

*Bhaave tyakte niruddhaa chin naiva bhaavaantaram vrajet;*
*Tadaa tanmadhyabhaavena vikasatyati bhaavanaa.* (62)

### Anvay

*Bhaave*: awareness or feeling; *Tyakte*: casting aside or leaving aside; *Niruddhaa*: restrained; *Chit*: mind; *Na-eva*: not like; *Bhaava-antaram*: from one thought to another; *Vrajet*: takes place; *Tadaa*: then; *Tat-madhya bhaavena*: then inside that feeling; *Vikasatyati*: blossoms; *Bhaavanaa*: awareness.

### Translation

When the mind is restrained to one object of awareness, casting all others aside and not allowing movement to take place from one to another, then inside that perception the awareness blossoms.

### Commentary

This dharana refers to focusing the awareness on a symbol. The symbol is an object that is conducive to concentration. Ideally it is obtained from a guru who has attained mastery over the science of consciousness. Such a guru is able to determine the specific symbol, which will accelerate the evolution of consciousness in the aspirant, according to his personality type, mental, emotional and intellectual nature, as well as subconscious and unconscious tendencies. These deeper realms eventually have to be influenced and awakened in order to progress in this direction.

The symbol used in dharana has the power to influence the deepest levels of mind. Therefore, once it has been chosen, the symbol should not be changed. This is clearly emphasized in this dharana: no other symbol should replace the chosen one. Through protracted and continuous dharana on the chosen symbol, the awareness assumes the form of that symbol. At that point there is perfect awareness of the symbol. The fruit of perfect awareness is dhyana, or spontaneous meditation, where the concentration becomes continuous and unbroken. The fruit of meditation is samadhi, or realization, and the fruit of realization is mukti, or liberation, which leads to the blossoming of the supreme awareness.

This symbol is the support on which the evolution of your awareness depends, so do not take this concept lightly. You may think that the awareness can ascend without the aid of a symbol and that is perfectly right, but perhaps only one in a million can progress in dharana without a foundation for the mind. Moreover, although the gross object is transcended in the process of dharana and later in dhyana, or meditation, the symbol remains with the sadhaka in subtle form. In other words the same symbol you have chosen, such as the shivalingam, candle flame, Sri yantra, your guru, or whatever becomes the form of your awareness, does not disappear.

The symbol is simply transformed as the awareness passes from gross to subtle to causal dimensions of consciousness. Finally, the state of duality ceases as the awareness merges into the symbol. So one may say that the symbol is never transcended; it remains until the final moment of samadhi. This is why it must be chosen with great care by one who has a discerning eye and can see beyond the gross and mundane associations.

## 63. Dharana on all existence as consciousness

सर्वं देहं चिन्मयं हि जगद्वा परिभावयेत् ।
युगपन्निर्विकल्पेन मनसा परमोदय: ॥ 63 ॥

*Sarvam deham chinmayam hi jagad vaa paribhaavayet;*
*Yugapan nirvikalpena manasaa paramodayah.* (63)

### Anvay

*Sarvam*: all; *Deham*: body; *Chinmayam*: consciousness; *Hi*: also; *Jagat-vaa*: even the world; *Paribhaavayet*: should concentrate; *Yugapat*: simultaneously; *Nirvikalpena*: unwavering; *Manasaa*: mind; *Paramah*: supreme; *Udayah*: arises.

### Translation

One should concentrate with an unwavering mind on all existence, the body and even the universe simultaneously as nothing but consciousness, then the supreme consciousness arises.

### Commentary

This sloka is pure Vedanta, and shows the similarity between Tantra and Vedanta. Vedantic philosophy proclaims that the universe is unreal and illusory. *Jagat mithya, Brahman satya*: "the world is false, pure consciousness is truth", is the basic premise of Vedanta. What this implies is that there are grades of consciousness and awareness, and the perception changes as you experience them. For example, what you perceive as the ultimate reality in your present state of awareness may appear false, temporary and illusory when you transcend that state.

Tantra, however, expresses this reality differently. It does not advocate that the universe is unreal; instead it emphasizes that the source of the universe is that all-pervading consciousness which has assumed these forms through the power of its shakti, or energy. A sadhaka has to realize this for himself and experience his strong connection with that source.

This dharana asks you to toss away the idea that everything is real, including your body and the universe around you. Throwing away this idea will generate a sense of detachment towards the objective existence. As the mind becomes established in the idea that it is spirit and not matter which is the substratum of this body and the entire universe, you will experience that consciousness which resides within the body and the universe, but is independent of them. That conscious force which continues to live on when the body and the universe are dissolved is the supreme consciousness.

## 64. Dharana on the fusion of vayus

वायुद्वयस्य संघट्टादन्तर्वा बहिरन्तत: ।
योगी समत्वविज्ञानसमुद्गमनभाजनम् ॥ 64 ॥

*Vaayudvayasya sanghattaad antarvaa bahir antatah;*
*Yogee samatvavijnaanasamudgamanabhaajanam.* (64)

### Anvay

*Vaayu dvayasya*: of both the vayus, prana and apana; *Sanghattaat*: from the fusion; *Antah-vaa*: inside or; *Bahih-antatah*: or outside; *Yogee*: the yogi; *Samatva*: equilibrium; *Vijnaana*: consciousness; *Samudgamana*: for proper manifestation; *Bhaajanam*: able.

### Translation

From the fusion of both vayus (prana and apana) inside or outside (the body), the yogi attains equilibrium and becomes fit for the proper manifestation of consciousness.

### Commentary

This sloka shows the interdependence of prana and consciousness, as the fusion of pranas results in equilibrium or balance, which allows the yogi to enter higher states of consciousness. Prana is the first evolute of the ever-expanding consciousness from which we have evolved into this physical body. At the cosmic level, prana still has all the cosmic properties of pure consciousness intact, such as omnipotence, omnipresence and omniscience. As prana evolves into the manifest world, it becomes the creative force and the life force at different stages. For example, pranashakti manifests in the physical body as kundalini, which is the seed of cosmic energy sown in man. In order to conduct the different activities of the body, pranashakti evolves further into grosser forms, known as prana vayus.

This dharana refers to the two vayus, prana and apana, which flow upward and downward in the body. Here prana and apana represent the inhalation and exhalation respectively. The fusion of these vayus takes place at dwadashanta: the point inside where inhalation reverses and becomes exhalation and the point outside where exhalation reverses and becomes inhalation. The point of fusion inside is twelve finger widths down from the nostrils at the heart and represents the length of inhalation. The fusion point outside is twelve finger-widths from the nose tip and represents the length of exhalation.

The two vayus, which represent the ingoing and outgoing breath, merge at these points of dwadashanta during kumbhaka, or breath retention, which takes place in the gap after one vayu ends and before the other vayu begins. This gap between the two breaths, or vayus, is the point of concentration in this dharana. The sloka further states that this fusion results in equilibrium, which means that it balances the entire pranic and physical structure, and thereby makes the mind fit for the manifestation of higher consciousness.

## 65. Dharana on ananda

सर्वं जगत्स्वदेहं वा स्वानन्दभरितं स्मरेत् ।
युगपन्स्वामृतेनैव परानन्दमयो भवेत् ॥ 65 ॥

*Sarvam jagat svadeham vaa svaanandabharitam smaret;*
*Yugapan svaamritenaiva paraanandamayo bhavet. (65)*

### Anvay

*Sarvam*: all; *Jagat*: universe; *Svadeham*: one's own body; *Vaa*: or; *Sva-aananda*: bliss of Self; *Bharitam*: filled; *Smaret*: contemplate; *Yugapat*: simultaneously; *Sva-amritena-iva*: through one's own nectar; *Paraa-nanda mayaha*: live the supreme bliss; *Bhavet*: becomes.

### Translation

One should contemplate simultaneously on the entire universe or on one's own body filled with the bliss of the self. Then through one's own nectar, one becomes alive with the supreme bliss.

### Commentary

Imagination is a very important tool of the mind. You can create heaven or hell for yourself through imagination. To be imaginative you require a great deal of conceptual power as well as sensitivity. Sensitivity improves the quality of perception and thereby the imagination. There is a saying in English, "As you think, so you become." Similarly, in tantra the mind is described as a *kalpa vriksha*, or wish-fulfilling tree. There is an apt story to illustrate this.

One day a poor old villager was returning home after a hard day at the market. None of his wares had been sold that day and he was feeling weary and dejected. Half way home he decided to stop for a while and rest under a shady tree. He did not know that he had settled under the mythical kalpa vriksha, or wish-fulfilling tree. As he sat there, he began to wish that he could have food and drink, as he was feeling hungry and thirsty. Instantly the most sumptuous meal appeared before him. After he finished his meal he wanted to sleep, so he thought of a bed and immediately a bed appeared. In this way, whatever he wished for appeared before him instantaneously. By now night had descended and this poor old man had not thought of returning home, as he was completely engrossed in this affair of wishing. Suddenly a fear descended on him and he thought, it is night and I am in a lonely place. What if a tiger or lion appears and devours me? As soon as he thought that, a tiger appeared, pounced on him and tore him to pieces.

This is a simple story, but it represents the conceptual power of the mind which is used in this dharana to imagine that one's body or the universe is filled with bliss. Bliss, or ananda, is a quality of the self. The bliss of the self is different from ordinary bliss because it is eternal, whereas the ordinary bliss is transient. The bliss of the self is all pervasive, homogeneous and consistent. To experience this bliss, sit back, relax and imagine that your whole body is filled with nectar. See your legs, arms, head, flesh, blood, bones, marrow, nerves, brain, and breath; every cell and atom that you are made up of is filled with ambrosia and you are alive with bliss.

## 66. Dharana on austerity

कुहनेन प्रयोगेण सद्य एव मृगेक्षणे ।
समुदेति महानन्दो येन तत्त्वं प्रकाशते ॥ 66 ॥

*Kuhanena prayogena sadya eva mrigekshane;*
*Samudeti mahaanando yena tattvam prakaashate.* (66)

### Anvay

*Kuhanena*: performance of austerities; *Prayogena*: by applying; *Sadya*: immediately; *Eva*: indeed, verily; *Mrigekshane*: gazelle-eyed; *Sam-udeti*: then arises; *Mahaa-aanandah*: supreme bliss; *Yena*: by which; *Tattvam*: element, essence; *Prakaashate*: illumines.

### Translation

O gazelle-eyed one, verily by applying the performance of austerities, great bliss arises immediately, by which the essence is illumined.

### Commentary

Denial of the level of comfort that you are accustomed to is austerity. It is a way of controlling the forces of the mind. Instead of allowing the mind to guide your thoughts and actions, you pave the way for the mind to follow a pattern that you impose on yourself in the form of austerity. Therefore, austerity is also a form of dharana, and it has always been a very important spiritual practice down through the ages. Austerity strengthens the willpower and focuses the mind. It increases the *tejas,* or inner heat, and bestows brilliance and inner lustre on the aspirant.

Austerity should be undertaken by those with strong willpower and unfailing resolve. The form of austerity can be physical, such as exposing the body to extreme heat or cold, fasting, sleeping on the bare floor and other such

242

difficulties, or it can be mental. Pratyahara, dharana and dhyana are mental austerities because they starve the mind of external stimuli and offer only a diet of subtle and psychic objects, which the mind creates through self-effort and discipline.

These austerities are a way to tune into the inner self. They lead us within and through them we experience a rare delight which we could never experience in our interactions with the world. They give us an experience of balance, equipoise and harmony within our being without the aid of any object, person or event. In this way, we discover that, in fact, true happiness and joy can only be experienced by looking within. Through this realization we get a glimpse of the reality, which serves as an encouragement for us to pursue and develop this type of experience further.

The Sanskrit word for austerity is *tapas*, which means 'to sharpen' or 'to whet'. The blacksmith sharpens a piece of metal, fashioning it in such a way that it becomes an article of utility for a definite purpose. In the same way, through the fire of tapas the inner instrument of man, known as antahkarana, is refined and tuned to uncover the essence, which is hidden within.

Yogis impose austerity on themselves because they are fully aware that it is through the fire of austerity, or tapasya, alone that the purity of inner experience can be developed. My guru, Swami Satyananda, performed the Panchagni tapasya at Rikhia for nine long years. This vidya is described in the ancient texts such as *Satpatha Brahman* and *Brihadaranyaka Upanishad*. It is a tapasya by which one can reach the heavenly abode whilst still in this physical body. It was taught by Yama, the lord of death, to a young lad known as Nachiketas who had implored him to describe what happened after death.

Swami Satyananda's guru, Swami Sivananda, described him as having the vairagya of Nachiketas, which is perhaps why he was able to successfully endure this arduous sadhana. He said, "Verily, few could exhibit such an intense vairagya at such an early age. Swami Satyananda is full of Nachiketa vairagya. He does the work of four people yet he never complains. Whatever job he takes up is bound to be perfect in every way."

Panchagni is a spiritual austerity. This dharana speaks of austerity of any kind which, when applied through the mind, becomes a source of bliss. There are religious austerities too, which are a combination of both physical and mental practices. This includes a vast array of *vratas* (vows), such as *upavas* (fasting), *yatra* (pilgrimages to holy places), *anushthanas* (repetition of a specific number of mantras), *yajna* (fire sacrifice), *pooja* (worship of the divine forces abounding in the universe), *kirtan* (chanting of the Lord's name), *swadhyaya* (study of the scriptures), *seva* (service to the destitute) and *satsang* (association with saints).

## 67. Dharana on the ascent of pranashakti

सर्वस्रोतोनिबन्धन प्राणशक्त्योर्ध्वया शनै: ।
पिपीलस्पर्शवेलायां प्रथते परमं सुखम् ॥ 67 ॥

*Sarvasrotonibandhana praanashaktyordhvayaa shanaih;*
*Pipeelasparshavelaayaam prathate paramam sukham.* (67)

### Anvay

*Sarva*: all; *Srotah*: channels; *Nibandhana*: blocking; *Praana shakti*: vital energy; *Oordhvayaa*: upwards; *Shanaih*: slowly; *Pipeela sparsh*: feeling the sensation of an ant moving in the body; *Velaayaam*: at the time; *Prathate*: enhances; *Paramam*: supreme; *Sukham*: bliss, happiness.

### Translation

By blocking all the channels (of perception) the pranashakti moves slowly upwards (through the spinal column). At that time, feeling the sensation of an ant crawling in the body, one experiences the supreme bliss.

### Commentary

The channels referred to in this dharana are the ten senses of action and perception. The channels of external action are the karmendriyas, which are five in number, and the channels of internal perception are the jnanendriyas, also five in number. These ten channels of action and perception are continually feeding the mind, causing it to perceive, cogitate, analyze, respond and react to a constant stream of incoming and outgoing impressions and stimuli. In this way they are continually influencing the mind to gaze outwards, thus destroying the fine balance between the inner and outer gaze.

If these channels of perception can be blocked, the mind, being starved of external stimuli, will then enter

245

madhyadasa, or the middle state, the gap between the inner and outer. At that point, one should have a stimuli or point of focus, which may be a symbol of your choice such as an idea, thought, feeling or object, but it is not gross. Rather, it comprises the effulgence of pure consciousness. Moreover, as the full force of mental energy is focused and dissipation is reduced, it becomes a very powerful tool in the hands of the practitioner. This focused mental force can be used to propel the awakening of pranashakti or kundalini, which resides in its abode at the base of the spine.

By blocking the sensory channels and focusing the mental energy on pranashakti at the base of the spine, the coiled kundalini is given a severe jolt. This causes it to raise its head, straighten itself and move upwards through the sushumna, a thin fibre-like nadi situated at the centre of the spinal canal. This nadi alone is strong enough to carry the high voltage current of kundalini energy. The upward movement of kundalini through sushumna has been experienced in many ways by different people. But the first feeling encountered is that of an ant crawling upwards along the spine, creating a tingling sensation of the highest bliss.

Many events take place in this dharana. First of all, the practitioner blocks the sensory channels and accomplishes pratyahara. This may be performed either mentally by withdrawing the senses and focusing them inward, or by application of shanmukhi mudra (sl. 36) whereby the sensory organs are systematically closed with the fingers. The conserved mental energy thus acts as a powerful catalyst to awaken the pranashakti. As kundalini arises, it moves upwards through the channel of sushumna, opening the different psychic energy centres situated alongside it. This movement in the pranic body is perceived in the physical body as ants crawling along the spine. This dharana focuses on the upward movement of energy, which in turn elevates the awareness so that intense inner bliss is experienced.

246

## 68. Dharana on manipura and anahata

वहनेर्विषस्य मध्ये तु चित्तं सुखमयं क्षिपेत् ।
केवलं वायुपूर्णं वा स्मरानन्देन युज्यते ॥ 68 ॥

*Vahaner vishasya madhye tu chittam sukhamayam kshipet;*
*Kevalam vaayupoornam vaa smaraanandena yujyate.* (68)

### Anvay

*Vahaneh*: of fire, from fire; *Vishasya*: fibre of lotus stalk; *Madhye*: in the middle; *Tu*: and; *Chittam*: mind; *Sukhamayam*: blissful; *Kshipet*: throw; *Kevalam*: only; *Vaayu poornam*: full of air; *Vaa*: or; *Smara-aanandena*: remembrance of bliss; *Yujyate*: joined, united.

### Translation

One should throw the blissful mind into the fire (manipura chakra) in the middle of that fibre-like lotus stalk (sushumna) or into that which is only full of air (anahata chakra). Then one is united with the remembrance of bliss.

### Commentary

As mentioned earlier, the kundalini passes through six pranic centres, known as chakras, on its upward journey. In the lower centres of mooladhara and swadhisthana, the experiences are of the jagrat, or conscious, and swapna, or subconscious, states of mind. These are the same experiences that you face in everyday life; the only difference is that in daily life they are mild, whereas with the movement of kundalini they become intense and explosive. You experience the full force of your inherent passions, desires, fears, neuroses and psychoses in one single shot. If the awareness has not been purified and refined by preliminary methods, it can go completely berserk at this point of awakening and even destroy the individual.

The important thing to know, and this is what this dharana points out indirectly, is that while the kundalini is moving through these two centres, the resulting experience is a heightened reflection of the gross experience. Therefore, the kundalini often reverts back to its base, especially if the practitioner is not free from attachment. This causes the awareness to regress back to the dormant level, thus losing its *gati*, or momentum. But once the kundalini reaches the midpoint of sushumna, which is the manipura chakra, representing the element of fire, those gross experiences which were so overwhelming previously are completely burnt and consumed.

After that the kundalini never returns back, but continues moving upwards to anahata chakra, which represents the element vayu, or air, thus generating experiences relating to the sushupti, or unconscious state of mind. When the kundalini reaches anahata, the practitioner begins to remember the bliss which he has known before assuming the physical body or before the consciousness became entrapped in matter. The words *smara ananden* refer to a bliss that you have remembered or known before. It is not new, but you have simply forgotten it because you were so immersed in the gross experience.

A connection to the previous dharana is implied here by the words *chittam sukham,* which refer to the blissful mind attained through the previous dharana when kundalini begins to move upwards. The practitioner is now asked to fix the blissful mind he has attained on manipura and anahata. However, it in no way implies that this dharana is dependent on the previous dharana and cannot be practised by itself. This is a continuation of the previous dharana and yet it is independent and complete in itself as well.

248

## 69. Dharana on union with shakti

शक्तिसङ्गमसंक्षुब्ध-शक्त्यावेशावसानिकम् ।
यत्सुखं ब्रह्मतत्त्वस्य तत्सुखं स्वाक्यमुच्यते ॥ 69 ॥

*Shaktisangamasamkshubdha-shaktyaaveshaavasaanikam;*
*Yat sukham brahmatattvasya tat sukham svaakyam uchyate.* (69)

### Anvay

*Shakti*: energy; *Sangama*: union; *Samkshubdha*: excited; *Shakti*: shakti; *Aavesha*: absorbed into; *Avasaanikam*: forming the end; *Yat sukham*: that bliss which is; *Brahma tattvasya*: of the nature of Brahman; *Tat sukham*: that bliss; *Svaakyam*: one's own kin or self; *Uchyate*: said.

### Translation

By the union with shakti there is excitation and in the end one is absorbed into shakti. That bliss (of union) which is said to be the nature of Brahman (ever-expanding consciousness), that bliss is (in reality) one's own self.

### Commentary

This dharana is a further development of the previous two dharanas, although it can be practised by itself as well. Once again there is a reference to union as in the previous dharana. There union referred to the remembrance of bliss, but in this dharana there is union with shakti, or energy. This union takes place between mind and energy when the kundalini reaches ajna, at the point where the awareness enters the all-pervasive akasha. This is also the point where ida and pingala, the two major nadis emanating from the base of the spine, merge with sushumna after intersecting each of the six psychic centres.

Ida carries the lunar or mental energy, which is feminine in nature, while pingala carries the solar or vital energy, which is masculine in nature. Together they represent the polar opposites and all the resulting experiences of duality, such as night and day, cold and hot, desire and repulsion, passive and active, subject and object, and so on. Their union at ajna, the sixth psychic centre at the mid-brain, is the union of opposites and therefore, marks the end of duality. Ajna is also the point where the channel of sushumna becomes *vyapak,* or all pervasive, spreading in all directions. Therefore, the union of ida and pingala with sushumna at this point has a powerful impact on the kundalini shakti, propelling it upward to its final destination at sahasrara.

Remember, it is only when the flows of ida and pingala are balanced that kundalini awakens, so this process happens simultaneously with the arising of kundalini. As the mental and vital energy flow upward to ajna through ida and pingala, so also the kundalini energy flows through sushumna. However, their union takes place only at ajna, as they meet only briefly before that while intersecting at the chakras, and then go their separate ways.

Ajna chakra is the point where ida and pingala unite with sushumna nadi and fuse into shakti. This state of fusion with shakti, although in fact metaphysical, alludes to the sexual union between man and woman. Just as there is intense excitement in the union between a man and woman, so also the metaphysical union is described as a state of deep excitation. Ultimately the mental and vital forces are absorbed into shakti and the bliss of that union is none other than the bliss of one's own Self.

## 70. Dharana on sexual bliss in the absence of shakti

लेहनामन्थनाकोटै: स्त्रीसुखस्य भरात्स्मृते: ।
शक्त्यभावेऽपि देवेशि भवेदानन्दसंप्लव: ॥ 70 ॥

*Lehanaamanthanaakotaih streesukhasya bharaat smriteh;*
*Shaktyabhaave'pi deveshi bhaved aanandasamplavah.* (70)

### Anvay

*Lehanaa*: kissing; *Manthanaa*: embracing; *Aakotaih*: pressing;
*Streesukhasya*: bliss of a woman; *Bharaat smriteh*: remembering
fully; *Shakti-abhaave*: even in the absence of shakti; *Api*: also;
*Deveshi*: queen of gods; *Bhavet*: becomes, takes place;
*Aananda*: bliss; *Samplavah*: swells.

### Translation

O Queen of Gods, the bliss of a woman is attained even in
the absence of shakti. By fully remembering and absorbing
the mind in the experience of kissing, hugging and embracing, the bliss swells.

### Commentary

In this dharana the allusion to sexual union is more explicit.
What better way can union be explained than by comparing
it to the physical union between man and woman, an act in
which both lose themselves to become one. Although this
union happens for just a brief moment, its outcome is so
powerful that it influences the thoughts, emotions, desires
and actions for the rest of one's life. This dharana is for
those who have known and enjoyed the bliss of that experience. That bliss can be replicated even in the absence of a
woman if you intensely focus your awareness on the embrace,
touch, kiss and warmth of a woman whom you have loved.

Just as you remember the bliss experienced with a woman
you can contemplate on that bliss which results from the

251

union with shakti. This dharana can be further developed until the bliss swells within you. In this way, even in the absence of shakti you can experience the bliss of spiritual union. This dharana clearly illustrates the unique concept of tantra, which is so simple yet so profound. Other spiritual systems have misunderstood and therefore rejected the affinity of sexual union and spiritual union. In fact, some religions regard the sexual act as sinful, while others ignore it altogether or declare it a mundane act which has to be transcended in order to evolve spiritually.

However, tantra has not discarded this vital aspect of man's psyche and, therefore, of his evolution. When the intensity of sexual experience has such a great impact on the mind and emotions, how can it be overlooked? What tantra works with is the focus of the mind in its totality, not the fragmented and dissipated mind, but the complete mind and everything that it is comprised of, including the thoughts, ideas, impressions, emotions, memories, experiences and so on. To ignore, deny or suppress the sexual act would be tantamount to developing a locked compartment within the mind. If there are locked compartments in the mind, how can homogeneity of awareness develop?

As you go deeper into dharana and dhyana, these locked compartments will explode and break the awareness, bringing it back to the mundane level. This obstacle in sadhana has got to be recognized. Dealing with the mind is a very serious matter. In order to progress in sadhana, one has to eradicate all the compartments or boundaries of the mind that have been created. Otherwise there can be no steady progress. In order to align man with the divine and break down these sexual taboos and boundaries, shakti and shiva are defined as energy and consciousness. Although this definition negates all gender, still shakti is personified as feminine and shiva as masculine. However, as opposed to the feminine role in society, here shakti plays the active and dynamic part while shiva remains passive and inert.

The practices of tantra are classified under three categories known as vamachara, dakshinachara and kaulachara. *Vama* means 'left' and *vamachara* are those practices which deal with the awakening of ida, or the left swara, which has been described as feminine energy. *Dakshina* means 'right' and *dakshinachara* are those practices which deal with the awakening of the right swara, which has been described as masculine energy. *Kaula* is derived from the word *kula*, which means 'lineage', or the line in which you are born. *Kaulachara*, which is regarded as the most superior tantra, is related to those practices that lead to the awakening of sushumna and the ascent of kula-kundalini. The term *kula-kundalini* is used here to infer that kundalini is the lineage of man. Each of us is born with kundalini, whether we are Indian, Chinese, American or European. Kundalini is our heritage, which distinguishes us from other forms of life.

This dharana is a practice of vamachara tantra, which utilizes the analogy of sexual union to elevate the awareness. But more than that, this dharana makes it absolutely clear that heightened awareness is achieved only when the two opposite principles of shakti and shiva, or energy and consciousness, unite and merge into one another.

## 71. Dharana on joy

आनन्दे महति प्राप्ते दृष्टे वा बान्धवे चिरात् ।
आनन्दमुद्गतं ध्यात्वा तल्लयस्तन्मना भवेत् ॥ 71 ॥

*Aanande mahati praapte drishte vaa baandhave chiraat;*
*Aanandam udgatam dhyaatvaa tallayas tanmanaa bhavet.* (71)

### Anvay

*Aanande*: in the bliss of joy; *Mahati*: great; *Praapte*: obtained;
*Drishte*: having seen; *Vaa*: or; *Baandhave*: relatives; *Chiraat*:
ever; *Aanandam*: bliss; *Udgatam*: arises, produces, is born;
*Dhyaatvaa*: meditating; *Tat-layah*: in that one-pointedness;
*Tat-manaa*: merging the mind like that; *Bhavet*: becomes.

### Translation

When great joy is obtained (through any event such as)
meeting with relatives, one should meditate on that with
one-pointedness, until the mind becomes absorbed and the
bliss ever arises.

### Commentary

In the previous dharana the focus was on the memory of
union; here it is on the memory of joy. In fact, now it is
becoming clear that remembrance of any intense experience
with clarity and one-pointedness, as if it were actually taking
place right at that moment, leads to total absorption and
heightened inner awareness. In this elevated state, the
consciousness is altered and different dimensions of existence
reveal themselves to the aspirant. This kind of absorption in
the memory of joy is illustrated by the following story.

One day a young girl was going to the market place to
secretly meet her lover. So engrossed was she in the memory
of her sweetheart that she accidentally stepped on the prayer
mat of a devotee, who was praying to God. The young girl

never even saw him and continued to walk on. But the man ran after her in a rage, yelling that she had rudely disturbed his prayers. On hearing someone shouting behind her, the girl turned around and noticed him for the first time. She was quite surprised when she heard his accusations, as she was so immersed in thoughts of her beloved that she did not even know she had disturbed him.

All the while she had been remembering her lover and the joy she had felt when she looked into his eyes, speaking sweet and tender words to him. So enamoured was she that she simply could not wait to see him once again. She stopped for a minute and listened to the devotee, who was shouting, "I was immersed in prayers to my Lord, and you dared to step on my mat and break my meditation!" When she heard that, the girl apologized for her behaviour, but she also expressed her surprise that he could be so easily distracted when thinking of his Lord, whereas she was so deeply immersed in the memory of her lover that she did not even notice him or his mat!

This story emphasizes that the quality of remembrance is paramount, not so much the object of remembrance. Even the remembrance of a joyful meeting with someone you love intensely can take you to sublime heights. In this dharana the focus is on the feeling of joy, which is an emotion; it has no form. So, in order to focus on joy what exactly are you to do? First of all, you have to remember the joy you felt with utmost clarity. Step by step that experience is recreated in the mind, until you actually begin to relive it. The only difference is that this joy is felt in the absence of the object or person who originally caused it.

This dharana enables the mind to transcend objective form and enter the dimension of experience. That experience is purely subjective because it takes place in the absence of any object. As explained earlier, an experience without the aid of the senses and objects is only possible through an expanded mind, and only such a mind can experience unity.

## 72. Dharana on enjoyment of food and drink

जग्धिपानकृतोल्लास-रसानन्दविजृम्भणात् ।
भावयेद्भरितावस्थां महानन्दस्ततो भवेत् ॥ 72 ॥

*Jagdhipaanakritollaasa-rasaanandavijrimbhanaat;*
*Bhaavayed bharitaavasthaam mahaanandas tato bhavet.* (72)

### Anvay

*Jagdhipaana*: eating and drinking; *Kritah-ullaasa*: happiness obtained by that; *Rasa-aananda*: joy of taste; *Vijrimbhanaat*: from such contemplation of enjoyment arises; *Bhaavayed*: concentrates; *Bharitaa-avasthaam*: the state of fullness; *Mahaanandah*: supreme joy or bliss; *Tatah*: then; *Bhavet*: becomes.

### Translation

If one concentrates on eating and drinking and the happiness obtained by that joy of taste, from such contemplation of enjoyment arises the state of fullness, which then becomes supreme joy or bliss.

### Commentary

This is the dharana for gourmets! Here the state of fullness and supreme bliss is obtained by concentrating on the enjoyment of food and drink. In tantra every aspect of life is used as a tool to elevate the consciousness. Every thought, word and act is a potential dharana which can induce superconscious and altered states of mind, if utilized in the appropriate manner. The same objective experiences, which normally externalize the awareness, can also be used to internalize the awareness. After all, your thoughts, words and actions are part and parcel of your being. They arise from within you and are an outcome of the sum total of what you are.

Moreover, the senses of taste, hearing, touch, sight and smell are born out of the *tanmatras*, which are the subtle qualities through which the *tattwas,* or elements, are perceived. Taste is the quality of *apas*, the water element. Hearing is the quality of *akasha*, the ether element. Touch is the quality of *vayu,* the air element. Sight is the quality of *agni*, the fire tattwa. Smell is the quality of *prithvi,* the earth element. These five tattwas are the grossest form of consciousness. By practising dharana on any one of the qualities or tanmatras of the tattwas, one can experience the source from which they have evolved.

Tantra has a very special way of making us realize that the entire life is sacred and can be used as a means to approach that divine state.

## 73. Dharana on sensual pleasures

गीतादिविषयास्वादा - समसौख्यैकतात्मन: ।
योगिनस्तन्मयत्वेन मनोरूढेस्तदात्मता ॥ 73 ॥

*Geetaadivishayaasvaadaa-samasaukhyaikataatmanah;*
*Yoginas tanmayatvena manoroodhes tadaatmataa.* (73)

### Anvay

*Geeta aadi*: song, etc.; *Vishaya-aasvaadaa*: pleasures of the
senses; *Sama*: equal; *Saukhya*: happiness; *Ekataatmanah*: as a
result of concentration; *Yoginah*: yogis; *Tanmayatvena*: by
being absorbed; *Manah-aaroodheh*: from the ascent (of the
yogi) beyond the mind; *Tat-aatmataa*: become one with that.

### Translation

As a result of concentration on the pleasures of the senses,
such as music or song, the yogis experience equal happiness
(or pleasure) within. By being (thus) absorbed the yogi
ascends beyond the mind and becomes one with that
(supreme).

### Commentary

This dharana describes the process of absorption by
concentrating on the pleasures of the senses, such as music
and song. Music relates to the tanmatra of sound, the
quality of akasha, or ether element. Akasha is also the vehicle
of consciousness and, therefore, sound is a powerful medium
for concentration, especially if the song or melody is
appealing. However, any of the pleasures derived from the
senses can be utilized in this way, for example, a beautiful
landscape, a fragrant flower or a loving touch.

Again we see the paradox of tantra, vedanta and yoga.
Whereas vedanta and yoga advocate abstention from the
sensual pleasures, tantra says there is no need to reject or

renounce, as every experience is potentially divine. Through concentration on the pleasures of sensory experience, even in the absence of the objects which cause them, pratyahara and dharana are attained effortlessly. The awareness ascends to great heights beyond the mind and is absorbed in that experience.

Whereas other philosophies speak in terms of annihilation, transformation or transcending the senses, tantra stipulates that the senses are active even in the deepest state of meditation. The only difference is that in the meditative state they are turned inwards rather than outwards to the gross object. When describing the expanded state of mind, tantra explains that in this state you can see, taste, smell, hear and touch, in the absence of any object to cause that perception. This reveals that the activities of the senses are active even in that hypo-sensitive state of total illumination, but they assume a different dimension, as they do not rely on the gross object. Rather they become a dynamic expression of the effulgent consciousness that is beyond the limiting boundaries of the mind.

## 74. Dharana on satisfaction of mind

यत्र यत्र मनस्तुष्टिर्मनस्तत्रैव धारयेत् ।
तत्र तत्र परानन्दस्वरूपं सम्प्रवर्तते ॥ 74 ॥

*Yatra yatra manas tushtir manas tatraiva dhaarayet;*
*Tatra tatra paraanandasvaroopam sampravartate.* (74)

### Anvay

*Yatra yatra*: whenever; *Manah*: of mind; *Tushtih*: satisfaction;
*Manah*: mind; *Tatra-eva*: there alone; *Dhaarayet*: to hold;
*Tatra tatra*: there; *Paraa-aananda*: supreme bliss; *Svaroopam*:
nature; *Sam-pravartate*: manifests.

### Translation

Whenever there is satisfaction of mind and the mind is held
there alone, the nature of supreme bliss manifests.

### Commentary

According to this dharana, you can concentrate on satisfaction of mind alone. Anything that gives the mind
satisfaction can be utilized, because when you are satisfied
with something concentration becomes easier. When concentration takes place, the mind and object of experience are
transcended through a natural and spontaneous process
without too much mental effort. This dharana says that by
concentrating the mind on satisfaction, or anything that
gives satisfaction, the supreme bliss is revealed. This is a
very interesting and unique concept which gives the sadhaka
immense freedom to experiment with what suits his temperament best.

Tantra is not a religious doctrine; it is a scientific way to
deal with the mind and thereby discover higher and higher
states of awareness. Not one of the methods described so far
relates to any religious or sectarian doctrine. Joy, passion,

pleasure and satisfaction are all universal feelings, which each and everyone has experienced intimately. They are not alien to anybody. One does not have to be introduced to them. In this way, tantra is a universal science which views life from each and every angle, and should not be passed off as mere religion intended for certain factions of people.

Everyone in the world experiences satisfaction, joy, good food and physical union. Such experiences can lead to heightened inner awareness, knowledge and bliss. But the Catch 22 is that you have to develop the intensity of experience without the aid of the object. For example, it is very easy to experience passion when you are with a man or woman you love, but it is hard to develop that same intensity of experience in his or her absence. Even if you are able to build up the same intensity through remembrance, it is hard to remain in control and not be physically and mentally disturbed by that experience. Only an adept can remain a master of that situation.

You may well wonder about the relevance of these mundane feelings to that highest and most sublime experience. However, this is precisely the point that VBT establishes in this dharana and in the previous dharanas as well. The quality of awareness can be developed through any medium of experience, whether it be mundane or transcendental.

## 75. Dharana on the threshold before sleep

अनागतायां निद्रायां प्रणष्टे बाह्य गोचरे ।
सावस्था मनसा गम्या परा देवी प्रकाशते ॥ 75 ॥

*Anaagataayaam nidraayaam pranashte baahya gochare;*
*Saavasthaa manasaa gamyaa paraa devee prakaashate.* (75)

### Anvay

*Anaagataayaam*: until it arrives; *Nidraayaam*: sleep; *Pranashte*:
being finished; *Baahya*: outer; *Gochare*: sense objects, i.e.,
outer world; *Saavasthaa*: that state; *Manasaa*: by the mind;
*Gamyaa*: entering; *Paraadevee*: supreme goddess; *Prakaashate*:
illuminates.

### Translation

By entering that state preceding sleep, where the awareness
of the outer world has faded, (the mind is absorbed in the
threshold state) which the supreme goddess illumines.

### Commentary

The four classifications of consciousness are: jagrat, swapna,
sushupti or turiya. Jagrat is the waking consciousness related
to the conscious mind. Swapna is dream consciousness
related to the subconscious mind. Sushupti is deep sleep
related to the unconscious mind, and turiya is the
superconscious state beyond the mind. In between each of
these four states is a kind of neutral or threshold state,
which must be transited in order to enter the next state.
These threshold states are neither one state nor the other,
and therefore they are unqualified and void-like.

Normally, we are not aware of transiting these neutral
states, as the awareness is only sustained in the waking or
conscious state. In this dharana the mind focuses on that
neutral state just before sleep, in between jagrat and swapna,

where the awareness has lost touch with the external world but has not yet hibernated into sleep. This is a brief moment when the awareness is in a type of suspended animation. It is neither aware of the external objects nor has it fallen into sleep. If you are able to grasp that moment and penetrate this neutral space with the mind, you can experience the void, which is illumined by parashakti, the supreme goddess.

## 76. Dharana on the luminous space

तेजसा सूर्यदीपादेराकाशे शबलीकृते ।
दृष्टिर्निवेश्या तत्रैव स्वात्मरूपं प्रकाशते ॥ 76 ॥

*Tejasaa sooryadeepaaderaakaashe shabaleekrite;*
*Drishtir niveshyaa tatraiva svaatmaroopam prakaashate.* (76)

### Anvay

*Tejasaa*: by the rays; *Soorya*: sun; *Deepaadeh*: of the lamp, etc.; *Aakaashe*: space; *Shabaleekrite*: variegated; *Drishtih-niveshyaa*: gazing on that sight; *Tatra-eva*: there like; *Sva-aatma-roopam*: one's own self; *Prakaashate*: illuminates.

### Translation

By gazing on the space that appears variegated by the rays of the sun or an oil lamp, there the nature of one's essential self is illumined.

### Commentary

This dharana employs an important practice of tantra and yoga, which is classified as trataka. To fix one's gaze at a particular spot or point and hold it there without blinking is known as trataka. One can practise trataka on many different types of objects, although a luminous object is considered most suitable as it attracts and holds the gaze. For trataka, such objects as an oil lamp, candle flame, crystal, sun, moon or star are recommended, especially in the beginning. Trataka is first practised with the eyes open until the image is established in the mind. Then the eyes are closed and the same form is seen in the space of chidakasha, in front of the closed eyes.

In this dharana, however, the emphasis is slightly different. The gaze is not focused on the object itself, but on the illumined space around the object, which appears multi-

264

coloured due to the refraction of light rays. By gazing on this luminous, variegated space for protracted periods, the illumined void is established in the mind. In this way, even with closed eyes, this luminous space, which is the essential nature of the self, is seen.

This dharana develops many psychic faculties, such as telepathy, clairvoyance, clairaudience and self-projection. But the real objective is the vision, or darshan, of the luminous nature of the self.

## 77. Dharana on the tantric mudras

करङ्किण्या क्रोधनया भैरव्या लेलिहानया ।
खेचर्या दृष्टिकाले च परावाप्ति: प्रकाशते ॥ 77 ॥

*Karankinyaa krodhanayaa bhairavyaa lelihaanayaa;*
*Khecharyaa drishtikaale cha paraavaaptih prakaashate.* (77)

### Anvay

*Karankinyaa*: skeleton; *Krodhanayaa*: anger; *Bhairavyaa*: bhairavi; *Lelihaanayaa*: flame; *Khecharyaa*: khechari, and; *Drishtikaale cha*: at the time of sight or seeing; *Paraavaaptih*: the supreme attainment; *Prakaashate*: illuminates.

### Translation

At the time of intuitive perception (the attitudes of) karankini, krodhana, bhairavi, lelihanaya and khechari are revealed, whereby the supreme attainment manifests.

### Commentary

Mudras are gestures or attitudes of psychic power which attract the divine forces. They are very potent and can completely eliminate any negative effect that the sadhaka may encounter in his sadhana. In hatha yoga, mudra is practised along with asana, pranayama and bandha to channel the energy and induce balance. In kundalini and kriya yoga, mudra is used to awaken the chakras and kundalini. In classical Indian dance forms, mudra is used to convey feeling as well as to add beauty and grace to the dance.

Mudras influence the glands and hormonal secretions in the physical body as well as the pranas, nadis and chakras in the pranic body, thereby assisting the sadhaka to experience altered states of consciousness. They are to be introduced at specific stages of sadhana and in specific sequences. If this is not observed, they can induce opposite and negative effects instead of the desired ones. This knowledge has always been handed down directly from the guru to the disciple in its complete form, whereas in the classical texts mudras are often explained in a coded and incomplete manner. This was done purposely to make it difficult for even the most discerning aspirant to perform these practices without the expert guidance of a guru.

Intuition is a state which manifests beyond the mind when the thoughts have been transcended. Thoughts are the form and substance of the mind. When there are no thoughts, there is no mind. In this state a higher power manifests known as intuition, or prajna, which is beyond the realm of antahkarana. This means that intuition is even higher than buddhi, or intellect. Mind and intellect operate through words, logic and language, which are finite and therefore limited, but the state of intuition transcends all these.

Therefore, higher knowledge is revealed through intuition, or prajna, not intellect or buddhi. When the sadhaka perceives intuitively, he is able to know something which is beyond the mind and intellect, as prajna is the source of unlimited knowledge. At times, such knowledge may seem irrational to a mind that has not transcended the finite boundaries of analytical thought. But the higher mind or super-mind perceives the truth behind intuitive knowledge.

When intuition begins to manifest in the sadhaka, the tantric mudras are revealed to further enhance and elevate his awareness. *Karankini* means 'skeleton' and this mudra induces vairagya, or detachment. Vairagya is a state of non-attachment to the objects and experiences that one has enjoyed, and there is no craving to have them again. In very simple terms, vairagya means absence of raga and dwesha, of like and dislike, which is an absolute prerequisite for experiencing higher states of awareness. One cannot

267

transcend the thoughts and mind without vairagya, as the mind hovers over its attachments and does not let the awareness ascend. This is the mudra of jnana.

*Krodhana* means 'anger' and this mudra is assumed to release the superfluous tensions from the body, mind and psyche, so that a tranquil awareness may descend. This is done by tightening the facial muscles and other muscles of the body and drawing all the elements, or tattwas, to their source, which is nada or mantra. This is the mudra of mantra.

Bhairavi is also known as *unmani mudra*, or the no mind attitude, where the gaze is focused outward, but the awareness is turned inward beyond the mind. In hatha yoga, bhairavi mudra is a hand mudra also known as shoonya mudra. It is practised along with padmasana and siddhasana by placing the hands on the lap with the left palm on top of the right, facing upwards. Bhairavi mudra brings about a swift change in the dimension of awareness by creating a union between the opposite poles of energy within the physical and pranic body. It is the mudra of siddhi.

*Lelihanaya* means 'flame' and it is the mudra by which the sadhaka perceives his consciousness as an extension of the supreme consciousness. It is the mudra of shakti.

*Khechari* means 'roaming in the open space'. This mudra liberates the consciousness from matter and allows the awareness to travel freely in the open space. In other words, it removes the barrier of the physical body and its material associations, so that the 'I' consciousness merges into the supreme consciousness. This is a very important mudra, even in hatha yoga, where the tongue is elongated and rolled back onto the upper palate. With mastery, the tongue is gradually pushed into the opening at the back of the throat, where it tastes the nectar, or amrita, which flows down from bindu visarga. In this way the downward flow of amrit is reversed and sent back up to the brain, thus rejuvenating the sadhaka and allowing the awareness to roam free in the higher space of consciousness.

Khechari mudra is a very important tantric practice. There are many variations of this practice in which there are references to different chakras being influenced, different nadis being affected, different methods being employed to make the tongue flexible and elongated, and different effects arising out of the practice. However, despite all the differences the common factor is that the tongue is inverted and pushed back into the nasal cavity and gradually up into the eyebrow centre, or ajna chakra. When the tongue is inverted and pushed into the nasal cavity, it controls the flow of ida and pingala in sushumna by blocking the left and right cavity as required. By regulating these flows, sushumna nadi is awakened, which leads to the generation of excessive heat in the form of pranic energy. This heat is similar to that generated by the practice of pranayama, but far more intense.

Perfection in khechari mudra enables the inverted tongue to reach the eyebrow centre internally, thus stimulating ajna chakra, the psychic centre corresponding to the pineal gland. As ajna chakra is closely connected to vishuddhi chakra in the throat, lalana chakra in the upper palate, and bindu visarga at the top back of the head, these centres are stimulated as well. These three centres are related with the falling and processing of the amrita, or nectar. Bindu is described as the seed of creation, or the point where amrita is generated and flows down to permeate the entire body. Lalana is the centre where the falling nectar is collected and stored, and vishuddhi is where the collected nectar is purified and processed.

The texts explain that this secretion becomes the nectar of immortality when it is processed and purified in this way, bestowing long life, youthfulness and vitality. Otherwise it falls down to the lower centres where it is dissipated by the physical processes and interactions. On the spiritual level

269

this nectar results in expansion of mind and the experience of shiva consciousness. The perfection of khechari mudra enables the sadhaka to project this expanded consciousness into all the quarters, directions and dimensions of space.

The pranic heat produced by inverting the tongue and inserting it into the nasal cavity increases the flow of nectar, or amrita. Of course, the nectar flows throughout life, but normally a very tiny drop is secreted and it flows for only for a brief moment. From bindu it falls down to the navel centre and is burnt up by the fire of manipura, and then falls further into the lower centres where it is converted into retas, which is responsible for the creation of sperm and ova. Through the practice of khechari mudra, the increased flow of amrita is reabsorbed by the higher centres, generating the experience of tranquillity and expansion of conscious awareness.

These five tantric mudras are the important mudras of Shiva, which lead to inner illumination and supreme attainment.

*Swami Satyananda in Unmani Mudra*

## 78. Dharana in relaxed asana

मृद्वासने स्फिजैकेन हस्तपादौ निराश्रयम् ।
निधाय तत्प्रसङ्गेन परा पूर्णा मतिर्भवेत् ॥ 78 ॥

*Mridvaasane sphijaikena hastapaadau niraashrayam;*
*Nidhaaya tatprasangena paraa poornaa matirbhavet.* (78)

### Anvay

*Mridu aasane*: on a soft seat; *Sphijaikena*: by means of one buttock; *Hasta-paadau*: hands and legs; *Niraashrayam*: relaxed; *Nidhaaya*: placing; *Tat prasangena*: on that occasion; *Paraa poornaa*: full of transcendence; *Matih*: the mind, intellect; *Bhavet*: becomes.

### Translation

Seated on a soft seat, by means of one buttock, with the hands and legs relaxed, at this time the mind becomes full of transcendence.

### Commentary

This sloka refers to a relaxed and comfortable posture in which the knees are bent and the legs are folded, one over the other, so that one buttock rests on the asana, or seat, and the other is slightly raised. This is a natural posture in which one may sit spontaneously, even without thinking of it as an asana. The arms and legs are completely relaxed, rather than locked into a fixed pose. The hands may rest on the knees, feet, floor or even behind. The knees may be placed one over the other or apart. There is no specific instruction for the placement of arms and legs, except that they should be relaxed.

There are several specific poses that fit this description, such as dhyana veerasana, in which the legs are folded and crossed so that the knees are rotated inward, with one knee

271

resting over the other. The hands are then placed on the uppermost knee. In this pose one buttock remains on the seat, while the other is slightly raised. This asana holds the spine upright and is quite easy and comfortable to sustain for short periods of time.

Dhyana Veerasana

BSY©

Another posture which fits this description is ardha matsyendrasana, in which the right knee is bent and the right foot is placed flat on the floor outside the left knee. Then the left knee is bent, bringing the left foot to the right buttock so that only the left buttock remains on the seat. However, here the arms and hands remain relaxed, rather than effecting a twist of the spine. This asana is named after Sage Matsyendranath, a tantric yogi who founded the Natha sampradaya, the first hatha yoga tradition. He sat in this posture for long durations and attained the highest states of consciousness in this way.

The asana, or seat, prescribed for tantric sadhana is also extremely meaningful as it is used as a means to achieve the desired result. Thus you have tiger skins, kusha grass, deer skins and even yantras used as asanas to create a field of energy within which the sadhaka explores the different

272

dimensions of awareness. The choice of asana is an important detail of sadhana which requires a certain amount of deliberation, because the asana acts as a conductor of energy, which may be released at any time during the process of sadhana.

The asana, or seat, is thus an essential item of sadhana in order to avoid any mishap, such as a short circuit of the energy or even to prevent the energy from flowing out of the body into the *dharti,* or earth, and being lost. With continued use the asana even begins to absorb and radiate the vibrations that the sadhaka develops during sadhana. Anyone can receive those vibrations in the form of blessings and grace if they are fortunate to go near the asana.

In this way, the science of tantra takes care of each and every minute detail, so that the correct experience is achieved. These essential details of sadhana can only be known from a guru or master, whose guidance is absolutely necessary before embarking on this path.

This dharana suggests that each and every moment can become a spontaneous act of dharana if one is relaxed and centred, thus implying that relaxation is important in the process of mastering dharana.

## 79. Dharana on shoonya yantra

उपविश्यासने सम्यक् बाहू कृत्वार्धकुञ्चितौ ।
कक्षव्योम्नि मन: कुर्वन् शममायाति तल्लयात् ॥ 79 ॥

*Upavishyaasane samyak baahoo kritvaardhakunchitau;*
*Kakshavyomni manah kurvan shamam aayaati tallayaat.* (79)

### Anvay

*Upavishya-aasane*: sitting in a posture; *Samyak*: correct; *Baahoo*: arms, hands; *Kritvaardha*: made half; *Kunchitau*: curving; *Kaksha*: orbit, area; *Vyomni*: in the space; *Manah*: mind; *Kurvan*: do; *Shamam*: peace; *Aayaati*: comes; *Tatlayaat*: from that laya.

### Translation

Sitting in a correct posture and curving the arms and hands into a circle, fix the gaze inside this space. The mind becomes peaceful by this laya.

### Commentary

The correct posture for meditation is to ensure that your spinal column and head are erect and straight. This is important as it allows the energy to move upwards without any difficulty or obstruction. Of course, if you are able to adopt padmasana, the lotus posture, or siddhasana, the perfect posture, that is even more conducive to attaining a meditative state of mind, as these asanas create a balance in the pranic flows of the body, which induces equanimity.

Then the arms and hands are raised in front and curved to form a circle. The yantra, or symbol, for shoonya is a circle, which represents infinity because it has no beginning and no end. By creating this yantra of shoonya with the body, the mind also takes on the same form because the body and mind are not separate. By gazing into the space

274

inside this circle, the thoughts are dissolved and the mind becomes peaceful.

The beauty of this dharana is that it brings the subtle and complex concept of shoonya within the grasp of every sadhaka. Here, we again see the unique vision of tantra. While other systems ask you to transcend the body consciousness and negate the body in order to attain spiritual experience, tantra shows you how to convert it into a mandala in order to transcend the mind.

## 80. Dharana on an object

स्थूलरूपस्य भावस्य स्तब्धां दृष्टिं निपात्य च ।
अचिरेण निराधारं मन: कृत्वा शिवं व्रजेत् ॥ 80 ॥

*Sthoolaroopasya bhaavasya stabdhaam drishtim nipaatya cha;*
*Achirena niraadhaaram manah kritvaa shivam vrajet.* (80)

### Anvay

*Sthoola roopasya*: of the gross form, object; *Bhaavasya*: feeling or thinking; *Stabdhaam*: steady; *Drishtim*: gaze in sight; *Nipaatya cha*: transfix; *Achirena*: without any delay, at once; *Niraadhaaram*: supportless, without any base; *Manah*: mind; *Kritvaa*: making, doing, performing; *Shivam*: shiva; *Vrajet*: acquires.

### Translation

One should steady the gaze (without blinking) on the gross form of any object. When the mind is transfixed and made supportless (without any other thought or feeling), it at once acquires the state of shiva (transcendence).

### Commentary

This dharana utilizes the practice of trataka and is one of the simplest methods, which can be practised quite easily by anyone. Gradually, dharana is accomplished by focusing the awareness on a gross object until no other thought arises in the mind and only the object remains. At this point there is only the awareness of subject and object, i.e., the meditator and object of meditation. Perfection of this dharana leads the sadhaka to a point where subject and object merge and become one. The awareness assumes the form of the object on which it has been focusing. As a consequence, the mind loses its support or base and dissolves. In this state of no-mind, the sadhaka acquires the transcendental state of awareness.

276

The same gross awareness that one functions with in daily life has to ultimately be transformed into awareness of spirit. Matter has to be transcended and spirit has to be realized. The lowest point of evolution is matter and the highest point is spirit. In each individual this spirit manifests as the physical body and then lives within it as pure consciousness. However, on account of the doshas, or impurities, that arise during the process of manifestation, the consciousness loses its identification with the spirit and turns its attention towards matter. This dharana utilizes form to turn the gross awareness back towards the effulgence of the spirit.

## 81. Dharana on 'Ha'

मध्यजिह्वे स्फारितास्ये मध्ये निक्षिप्य चेतनाम् ।
होच्चारं मनसा कुर्वंस्ततः शान्ते प्रलीयते ॥ 81 ॥

*Madhyajihve sphaaritaasye madhye nikshipya chetanaam;*
*Hochchaaram manasaa kurvams tatah shaante praleeyate.* (81)

### Anvay

*Madhya jihve*: the middle of the tongue; *Sphaaritaasye*: in that which has been opened widely; *Madhye*: in the middle; *Nikshipya*: thrown; *Chetanaam*: consciousness; *Hah-uchchaaram*: pronouncing 'Ha'; *Manasaa*: in the mind; *Kurvan tatah*: should be done there; *Shaante*: peace, tranquillity; *Praleeyate*: dissolved.

### Translation

(Placing) the middle of the tongue in that which has been opened widely and throwing the consciousness in the middle, mentally repeating 'Ha', the mind will be dissolved in tranquillity.

### Commentary

This sloka refers to dharana on ajna chakra, which is induced by khechari mudra (sl. 77). The tongue is rolled back and the middle of the tongue tip is placed inside the opening or cavity of the cranium, where a tiny gland known as lalana chakra (sl. 30) is located. *Madhya jihve sphaaritasya* refers to the act of placing the tongue at this point. In this way the nadis are opened and the brain channels are cleared, creating a mild pressure at the point of *bhrumadhya*, the eyebrow centre, which is the trigger point for ajna chakra and also the point of convergence of the three main nadis: ida, pingala and sushumna.

The term *madhye* is used here for ajna chakra. In fact, as placing the tongue at the point of lalana chakra is mastered, you will find that the consciousness is thrown to the point of ajna without any effort on your part. At that moment the sound 'Ha' arises spontaneously in the mind, which releases a great deal of tension and pressure in the frontal region of the brain, thus dissolving the mind in tranquillity.

Ajna chakra, which has been referred to as the third eye, is also the point where the commands of the guru are heard. Thus it is an extremely important centre for transmission of knowledge. At this point the awareness becomes *vyapak*, or all-pervading, and is no longer confined or restricted within a particular dimension or space. It is here that the spiritual experiences begin. There is an important tantric mudra known as shambhavi which relates to this chakra and this mudra may occur spontaneously when you perform this dharana.

This is a rejuvenating dharana which results in peace and tranquillity. It strengthens the electro-magnetic circuits in the brain by rechannelling the energy which flows downward from bindu chakra back upward to the higher centres (sl. 77). In this process it also provides a rest and respite from the continuous dissipation of mental energy in the form of unnecessary thoughts and chatter, which diminish the frequencies of the brainwaves.

## 82. Dharana on suspension of the body

आसने शयने स्थित्वा निराधारं विभावयन् ।
स्वदेहं मनसि क्षीणे, क्षणात् क्षीणाशयो भवेत् ॥ 82 ॥

*Aasane shayane sthitvaa niraadhaaram vibhaavayan;*
*Svadeham, manasi ksheene, kshanaat ksheenaashayo bhavet. (82)*

### Anvay

*Aasane*: in the posture or on a seat; *Shayane*: while sleeping; *Sthitvaa*: remaining; *Niraadhaaram*: supportless, suspended; *Vibhaavayan*: should think or concentrate; *Svadeham*: one's own body; *Manasi*: in the mind; *Ksheene*: being reduced; *Kshanaat*: at once; *Ksheena-aashayah*: ceases to be a reservoir; *Bhavet*: becomes.

### Translation

While sitting or lying down, one should think of one's own body as being supportless (suspended in space). Then, in a moment (the samskaras or thought constructs) of the mind being reduced, it ceases to be a reservoir (of old mental dispositions).

### Commentary

This dharana is also very simple and can be practised anywhere, by anyone, at any time. All that is required is the capacity to imagine the body suspended in space. By developing that concept, the mind will gradually become suspended and at that point illumination takes place. The idea of one's body being suspended in space without any support develops a corresponding state of mind, where there are no thoughts for support. This happens by itself because the mind and body are closely interconnected.

Any idea that is imposed on the body also influences the mind and vice-versa. The mind and body are continually

280

influencing each other. When the mind is excited, the heart and respiratory rate increase, the blood circulates faster, the face becomes flushed and sweating may even occur. When the mind is sad, it shows at once on the face, in the eyes and in the walk. Similarly, when the body is sick, the mind becomes depressed, negative and dull. These are simple examples which everyone has experienced.

This dharana can be utilized very effectively by imagining that the body is suspended without any support, floating in space. Gradually this supportless feeling will extend itself to the mind. In this way, the thoughts which are the support for the mind will decrease and eventually cease altogether. Thoughts are mental forms and they have their own existence. Just as you can hand an apple to someone and then take it back, in the same way you can hand a thought to someone and also take it back. If thoughts are forms, they also have to be contained and preserved in something. The mind is the reservoir which contains the thoughts in the form of samskaras, or archetypes.

These samskaras are the source of bondage and keep man forever chained to the cycle of birth and death. There is only one way to exhaust the reservoir of samskaras and that is through the practice of dharana and dhyana, which relieves one of this burden. This is why a feeling of lightness is felt on both the physical and mental dimensions after meditation. This dharana is an extremely effective way of clearing out the reservoir of old and useless samskaras, or mental dispositions, that bind the mind, enabling the consciousness to experience its own essential nature.

## 83. Dharana on swinging the body

चलासने स्थितस्याथ शनैर्वा देहचालनात् ।
प्रशान्ते मानसे भावे देवि दिव्यौघमाप्नुयात् ॥ 83 ॥

*Chalaasane sthitasyaatha shanair vaa dehachaalanaat;*
*Prashaante maanase bhaave devi divyaughamaapnuyaat.* (83)

### Anvay

*Chalaasane*: rocking, rotating; *Sthitasya-atha*: (being) placed like this; *Shanaih-vaa*: slowly; *Deha*: body; *Chaalanaat*: from moving, as a result of moving; *Prashaante*: in the tranquil; *Maanase*: in the mind; *Bhaave*: feeling; *Devi*: O Goddess; *Divya*: divine; *Augham*: flood, stream; *Aapnuyaat*: achieves.

### Translation

O Goddess, as a result of slowly swinging or rocking the body, one attains a tranquil state of mind and floats into the stream of divine consciousness.

### Commentary

Once again, in this dharana the physical body is used to influence the mind. This process is frequently seen in the bhakti marga as well as in the Sufi tradition. The Sufis are known to have large gatherings where the participants whirl around and around, gradually raising the tempo. Then suddenly they bring the body to an abrupt halt and hold it completely still. The rapid movement of the body shakes and rearranges the atoms, cells and molecules of the physical structure, creating a sense of harmony and tranquillity. Symbolically, it is done to shake off the impurities that prevent the free flow of energy between mind, body and spirit.

In bhakti marga, Radha and Krishna are depicted on the *jhoolan*, or swing, in a state of spiritual rapture. Swinging, swaying and twirling the body in harmony with the melodious chants of kirtans is also used very efficaciously to allow the devotee to flow with the stream of divine consciousness that begins to permeate the body through prolonged practice of this method.

This form of swinging dharana brings about relaxation and tranquillity. In that state of harmony all the extraneous tensions drop away and the awareness floats into the stream of divine consciousness, which is all-pervading but which one had become disconnected from. Many meditation techniques have evolved around this dharana and, in fact, all dance forms, especially modern dance, can be easily compared to this technique. Today the world over everyone enjoys dance immensely. Some may even freak out on the dance floor. One can say they get a glimpse of that ecstasy which, if developed further, could even lead them to enlightenment.

## 84. Dharana on the sky

आकाशं विमलं पश्यन् कृत्वा दृष्टिं निरन्तराम् ।
स्तब्धात्मा तत्क्षणाद्देवि भैरवं वपुराप्नुयात् ॥ 84 ॥

*Aakaasham vimalam pashyan kritvaa drishtim nirantaraam;*
*Stabdhaatmaa tatkshanaad devi bhairavam vapur aapnuyaat.* (84)

### Anvay

*Aakaasham*: the sky, space; *Vimalam*: clean; *Pashyan*: having seen; *Kritvaa*: having done; *Drishtim*: gaze, sight; *Nirantaraam*: continuous; *Stabdha-aatma*: steady awareness; *Tatkshanaat*: at once; *Devi*: O Devi; *Bhairavam*: of Bhairava; *Vapuh*: body; *Aapnuyaat*: achieves.

### Translation

O Devi, having fixed the gaze continuously on the clear sky (without blinking) and with a steady awareness, at once the nature of Bhairava is achieved.

### Commentary

In this dharana the sky signifies endless and limitless space, with no beginning and no end. The key to this practice is continuous and steady gazing into the empty sky. By gazing continuously at the infinity of space in the sky, one can transcend the finite nature and acquire the infinite nature of Bhairava. Finite and infinite are two concepts which conjure certain images and ideas in the mind. As long as our gaze is directed towards the finite, our experiences are material, but as soon as we turn the gaze towards the infinite, the awareness perceives infinity and starts to identify with that.

## 85. Dharana on chidakasha

लीनं मूर्ध्नि वियत्सर्वं भैरवत्वेन भावयेत् ।
तत्सर्वं भैरवाकार - तेजस्तत्त्वं समाविशेत् ॥ 85 ॥

*Leenam moordhni viyat sarvam bhairavatvena bhaavayet;*
*Tat sarvam bhairavaakaara-tejastattvam samaavishet.* (85)

### Anvay

*Leenam*: absorbed; *Moordhni*: in the forehead; *Viyat*: space, sky; *Sarvam*: all; *Bhairavatvena*: by the state of bhairava; *Bhaavayet*: contemplate; *Tatsarvam*: all that; *Bhairava-aakaara*: in the form of bhairava; *Tejas-tattvam*: the essence of luminous light; *Samaavishet*: entered.

### Translation

One should contemplate on the sky as the form of bhairava (until it is) all absorbed in the forehead. Then all that (space) will be entered by the essence of light in the state of bhairava.

### Commentary

This practice is related to chidakasha dharana. The word *chid* means 'consciousness' and *akasha* is 'space', so *chidakasha* is the space of consciousness. It refers to the empty space in front of the closed eyes, which occupies the region of the forehead. This is where the element of ether, or akasha, is situated. Ether is one of the five tattwas of the body and is responsible for the conscious and spiritual experiences in man. All the experiences of dharana and dhyana take place in the akasha, or ether, of consciousness. This is a very important point in relation to sadhana and many references are found to it in both tantra and yoga.

In this dharana the sky is absorbed into the forehead or chidakasha as the *akara* or form of bhairava. The ether

285

element is depicted as black in colour because in deep space there is only darkness and no light prevails. However, as you practise dharana in chidakasha, a faint light gradually becomes discernible, which becomes brighter and clearer until everything enters into that light and is absorbed by it. That light is the state of bhairava.

This dharana can further be correlated to the concept of *ashta bhairava*, or the lords of the eight quarters of space. When the open space or sky is conceived as the ashta bhairavas, and that open space becomes delineated instead of diffused, it reveals the essence of light, which is energy.

## 86. Dharana on reality

किंचिज्ज्ञातं द्वैतदायि बाह्यालोकस्तम: पुन: ।
विश्वादि, भैरवं रूपं ज्ञात्वानन्तप्रकाशभृत् ॥ 86 ॥

*Kinchij jnaatam dvaitadaayi baahyaalokas tamah punah;*
*Vishvaadi bhairavam roopam jnaatvaanantaprakaashabhrit.* (86)

### Anvay

*Kinchit-jnaatam*: knowing a bit; *Dvaitadaayi*: duality; *Baahya-aalokah*: outer light; *Tamah*: dark; *Punah*: again; *Vishva-aadi*: manifest world, etc.; *Bhairavam*: of Bhairava; *Roopam*: form; *Jnaatvaa*: knowing, experiencing; *Ananta*: immense, endless, infinite; *Prakaashabhrit*: procures splendour.

### Translation

Knowing a bit about duality, the outer light and darkness in the manifest world and so on, one who again experiences the infinite form of Bhairava procures illumination.

### Commentary

This sloka describes the different perspectives of reality. In order to understand the absolute reality, one must also know a bit about the relative reality. Before one can transcend duality, it must be clear what duality means. Duality relates to the external light which is produced by objective sources, such as the sun, moon, stars, fire, lamp, and so on. In the absence of light, there is darkness, or tamas. This condition of duality comprises all the experiences in the manifest world and always leads to suffering. Where there is light, there must also be darkness; where there is birth, there must also be death, and so on.

Knowing this, one who again experiences the infinite form of Bhairava, which is beyond duality, attains inner illumination. He procures the highest knowledge, who

287

understands both the relative and the absolute reality simultaneously. Consciousness is effulgent, one and without divisions. However it is experienced differently in waking, dream and sleep. So much so that it appears fragmented and we cease to see it as unified awareness. If the sadhaka is able to experience these three states as extensions of the one consciousness, he begins to feel the splendour of pure and infinite consciousness within himself, which is the form of Bhairava.

## 87. Dharana on the darkness of night

एवमेव दुर्निशायां कृष्णपक्षागमे चिरम् ।
तैमिरं भावयन् रूपं भैरवं रूपमेष्यति ॥ ८७ ॥

*Evam eva durnishaayaam krishnapakshaagame chiram;*
*Taimiram bhaavayan roopam bhairavam roopam eshyati.* (87)

### Anvay

*Evam-eva*: like this indeed; *Durnishaayaam*: in the terrible
night; *Krishnapaksha-aagame*: during the dark fortnight;
*Chiram*: ever; *Taimiram*: the darkness; *Bhaavayan*: contemplate; *Roopam*: form; *Bhairavam*: of bhairava; *Roopam-eshyati*:
desires the form.

### Translation

Like this, one should ever contemplate on the terrible
darkness of night during the dark fortnight of the moon, if
he desires to attain the form of bhairava.

### Commentary

This dharana relates to the lunar cycles, which are very
significant in all tantric sadhana. The lunar cycles consist of
fourteen days each, when the moon waxes or wanes. The
waxing of the moon is known as *shuklapaksh*, the bright
fortnight, and the waning is known as *krishnapaksh*, the dark
fortnight. These two cycles of bright and dark fortnight
affect the rhythms of the body, mind and consciousness in a
very significant and pronounced way.

It is natural, therefore, that the effects of sadhana done
during shuklapaksh or krishnapaksh will differ according
to the day and the fortnight in which the sadhana is practised.
For example, *poornima*, full moon, and *amavasya*, no moon,
are considered to be very special days, and any sadhana
done on these days takes on a more significant meaning.

There are certain practices that can only be done on amavasya or on poornima to receive the desired effects of the sadhana.

These lunar cycles also dramatically affect the swara, or flow of the nadis in relation to the breath. As explained earlier, there are two main swaras that flow in the body throughout the entire lifespan. These swaras are ida or *chandra swara*, which flows through the left nostril, and pingala or *surya swara*, which flows through the right nostril. They also control the nervous system and the left and right hemispheres of the brain. These two swaras flow alternately for one hour and twenty minutes throughout the day and night. At the time when the swara is changing over from ida to pingala or vice versa, there is a brief interval when both swaras flow together in equal balance. This awakens the third important nadi, known as sushumna, which flows up the centre of the spinal column and is the channel for the ascent of kundalini.

There are prescribed methods in tantra to increase the duration of flow in ida or pingala or to make them flow together in perfect rhythm and balance. This dharana is to be practised during the dark fortnight, or krishnapaksh, between *ekadashi* (eleventh day) and *amavasya* (fourteenth day), preferably at midnight. It is a dharana for nature lovers, because it is best practised out in the open in the mountains, forests or near the sea, any place where nature appears awesome, splendid and terrible. Of course, if you have a very vivid imagination, you can even practise in your room in an apartment amidst the hustle and bustle of city life, but being outside in natural surroundings stimulates and aids the awareness to dive deep into this contemplation

The shrine to the river Yamuna at Yamnotri in the Himalayas is the perfect setting for this dharana. If you ever get the opportunity to sit outside there at night and contemplate on the awesome surroundings, you are sure to experience the magnitude of this dharana. Intense fear, terror and awe can alter the brain structure. They can make you lose your memory, go into a coma, have a heart attack, or even develop psychosis or neurosis. On the other hand, they can also serve as a catalyst for the quantum leap of consciousness into a higher dimension altogether.

This dharana states that if you can face the intensity of contemplation on the terrible darkness of night, your awareness will assume the form of bhairava. With this aim and belief, the tantrics engage in contemplation and intense *anushthana*, or sadhana for a stipulated period, at isolated and horrifying places, such as the *smashan*, or funeral pyre, even to the extent of sitting on top of a dead body. As you progress in sadhana, the forms which the consciousness assumes will not always be beautiful and pleasant, so you must be ready for that.

Moreover, as the consciousness passes from one stage to another, the transition period before the next stage is stabilized can be very unnerving, unsettling and disturbing. It is like being poised in mid-air with one foot on one rung of the ladder, but the other foot is not yet firmly placed on the next. Until you get the grip, there is always a fear of losing your balance and falling.

## 88. Dharana on the dark form of bhairava

एवमेव निमील्यादौ नेत्रे कृष्णाभमग्रतः ।
प्रसार्य भैरवं रूपं भावयंस्तन्मयो भवेत् ॥ 88 ॥

*Evam eva nimeelyaadau netre krishnaabham agratah;*
*Prasaarya bhairavam roopam bhaavayans tanmayo bhavet.* (88)

### Anvay

*Evam-eva*: like this; *Nimeelyaadau*: while closing both; *Netre*: eyes; *Krishnaabham*: extreme darkness; *Agratah*: in front; *Prasaarya*: spreading; *Bhairavam*: of bhairava; *Roopam*: form; *Bhaavayan*: contemplating; *Tanmayah*: being one with that; *Bhavet*: becomes.

### Translation

Similarly, while closing the eyes, one should contemplate on the profound darkness spreading in front as the form of bhairava. Thus he becomes one with that.

### Commentary

Whatever the self identifies with becomes the form of consciousness. This is known as self-identification. When you identify yourself with the pleasures of the world, the mundane relationships, the material objects, that is the form your consciousness assumes. But if the self identifies with transcendental awareness, the consciousness assumes the form of divinity. Consciousness is pure and effulgent in each one of us. Just as the rays of the sun illumine whatever is in its path, in the same way the consciousness illumines whatever the self turns towards. Just as water collected from the ocean assumes the form of the container in which it is stored, be it a jar, a bucket or a pitcher, in the same way consciousness becomes whatever it is projected on.

This is the concept applied in every form of dharana. However, in this dharana you are asked to focus your awareness on the vast darkness spreading out in front of the closed eyes. As you gaze into this profound darkness, it takes the form of bhairava, which means you are actually identifying yourself with that idea or state of consciousness. This will lead to identification with the state of bhairava consciousness, until you merge into that state and become that. Then you are no different from bhairava.

## 89. Dharana on restraint of the senses

यस्य कस्येन्द्रियस्यापि व्याघाताच्च निरोधतः ।
प्रविष्टस्याद्वये शून्ये तत्रैवात्मा प्रकाशते ॥ 89 ॥

*Yasya kasyendriyasyaapi vyaaghaataach cha nirodhatah;*
*Pravishtasyaadvaye shoonye tatraivaatmaa prakaashate.* (89)

### Anvay

*Yasya kasya*: whoever; *Indriyasya-api*: even of the same sense organ; *Vyaaghaataat-cha*: from the obstruction; *Nirodhatah*: restraining; *Pravishtasya*: of one who has entered; *Advaye*: without any second; *Shoonye*: void; *Tatraiva-aatmaa*: there the atma, or self; *Prakaashate*: illumines.

### Translation

Whoever restrains even the same sense organ enters the one void without a second by this obstruction and there the atma, or self, is illumined.

### Commentary

In this dharana the stress is on restraint of the senses, which enables one to transcend the awareness of duality and enter the non-dual state of atman. The senses are restrained through the practice of pratyahara, the state which immediately precedes dharana. Unless pratyahara is perfected, concentration or dharana will not occur. Pratyahara literally means to withdraw or turn inwards that which is moving outwards. It is a term used to describe the reversal of awareness from outside to inside.

Pratyahara can be achieved by many means. The system of hatha yoga prescribes asana (steady postures that regulate the overall functions of the body and mind), pranayama (awareness of breath) and trataka (fixed gazing at a point). The system of raja yoga prescribes sensory control and withdrawal. The system of bhakti yoga prescribes love for the Lord. The system of jnana yoga prescribes contemplation on the truth. The system of karma yoga prescribes *nishkama seva* (service without thought of reward) and *samarpan* (surrender of one's actions).

In all these systems the aim is to transcend the notion of duality and realize the pure effulgent atman, or self. When pratyahara or restraint of the senses is achieved, concentration begins to take place. As the mental rays are focused and concentrated, illumination begins. Self-restraint and self-effort must be enforced only up to the point of concentration. Illumination happens by itself after that, and there is no effort involved in that. If concentration is achieved for only a flicker of the eyelid, illumination has to occur. If winter comes, spring cannot be far behind; it is as sure as that.

## 90. Dharana on akaara

अबिन्दुमविसर्गं च अकारं जपतो महान् ।
उदेति देवि सहसा ज्ञानौघः परमेश्वरः ॥ 90 ॥

*Abindum avisargam cha akaaram japato mahaan;*
*Udeti devi sahasaa jnaanaughah parameshvarah.* (90)

### Anvay

*Abindum*: absence of bindu; *Avisargam*: absence of visarga; *Cha*: and; *Akaaram*: letter 'A'; *Japatah*: recitation; *Mahaan*: great; *Udeti*: arises; *Devi*: O Devi; *Sahasaa*: at once; *Jnaanaughah*: the torrent of knowledge; *Parameshvarah*: of the supreme Lord.

### Translation

O Devi, by recitation of akaara, the letter 'A', in the absence of bindu and visarga, a great torrent of knowledge of the supreme Lord, Parameshvara, at once arises.

### Commentary

The concept of *akshara*, or letters, is peculiar to the tantras and vedas, where they are declared as a form of Brahman, the highest reality. Akshara means imperishable sound forms and originally this term was used in relation to the sound syllables which comprise mantras. The meaning of mantra is difficult to explain because it does not work on an intellectual principle. Mantras are sound formations which have been realized by the seers in deep states of meditation. By continual repetition they create immensely charged circuits of energy and thereby induce heightened states of awareness. Suffice it to say that mantra is purely metaphysical and each mantra corresponds to a particular form of energy.

The *varna*, or letters, evolved out of the complex array of sounds which represent them in written form. Being fifty-four in number, they were known as *varna mala,* or the garland of letters. These letters were later combined to form words and subsequently the language evolved known as Sanskrit. However, unlike other languages which are linguistic and solely for communication, Sanskrit was and still is purely phonetic. Therefore, the pronunciation of each Sanskrit letter and word creates friction in different centres situated in the mouth, which directly influence the higher centres of the brain. This is precisely why great emphasis is laid on correct pronunciation, so that the effect may be experienced in its entirety. There is an extremely technical and classical tantric text by Sir John Woodroffe, entitled *Garland of Letters,* which deals with this subject.

In this dharana, the *akaara,* or letter 'A', which is the first letter of the Sanskrit alphabet and also the first sound to emanate in the etheric space, or akasha, at the beginning of creation, is repeated. This opens up centres in the brain, releasing a torrent of knowledge which is transcendental in nature. Akaara is also the first letter of the most sacred and primordial mantra Aum, which is considered to be the source of all sounds and the cosmic vibration of the universe. There is an analysis of this mantra and the three sounds 'A', 'U' and 'M' which comprise it in the *Mandukya Upanishad.* Therein it is stated that the Aum mantra alone covers the four states of consciousness, namely: conscious, subconscious, unconscious and superconscious. The first letter 'A' represents jagrat, the conscious state.

In this dharana the letter 'A' is to be repeated without the bindu or visarga which form the 'M' sound. The intonation changes when bindu or visarga are added to any letter of the alphabet, either together or separately. When the akaara, letter 'A', is repeated without bindu or visarga, the sound produces friction in the upper throat just below the epiglottis, where a minor psychic centre known as *lalana* is situated. These vibrations are easily transmitted to ajna

297

chakra behind the eyebrow centre in the mid-brain, as there is a deep connection between these two centres. Ajna chakra is known as the third eye, which is the eye of knowledge. It is here that the divine commands of the guru are realized. Thus, by stimulating this centre a torrent of knowledge pours into the sadhaka.

## 91. Dharana on visarga

वर्णस्य सविसर्गस्य विसर्गान्तं चितिं कुरु ।
निराधारेण चित्तेन स्पृशेद्ब्रह्म सनातनम् ॥ 91 ॥

*Varnasya savisargasya visargaantam chitim kuru;*
*Niraadhaarena chittena sprished brahma sanaatanam.* (91)

### Anvay

*Varnasya*: of a letter; *Sa-visargasya*: joined with visarga; *Visarga-antam*: at the end of visarga; *Chitim*: mind; *Kuru*: make or do; *Niraadhaarena*: being supportless; *Chittena*: by the mind; *Sprished*: touched; *Brahma*: Brahma, or supreme consciousness; *Sanaatanam*: eternal.

### Translation

When the mind is joined with the visarga, at the end of the visarga it is made supportless. In this way the mind is touched by the eternal Brahma, or the supreme consciousness.

### Commentary

In this dharana the visarga is used as a jumping off point for the void. In the Sanskrit alphabet, the visarga is the last letter to be added to a word or a sentence. So, when the mind is focused on visarga, which marks the ending point, naturally it becomes supportless after the visarga.

Tantric philosophy also states that the two dots of visarga represent purusha and prakriti. Purusha is the manifest form of supreme consciousness and prakriti the manifest form of supreme energy. Visarga represents the proximity of these two cosmic forces within the individual, which brings about an intermediary state just before the awareness is propelled into the next dimension.

The sound represented by the visarga is 'Ha'. For example, if visarga were coupled with the letter 'Aa' it would

299

become the sound 'Aaha'. This 'Ha' sound is very important as its intonation touches a centre where a group of nadis converge and spread out to different parts of the head. Thus its vibration is transmitted to all corners of the brain, which brings about immediate pratyahara. In this state of introversion the mind becomes *niradhara*, or supportless, and is thereby touched by Brahma, the supreme consciousness.

## 92. Dharana on oneself in the form of space

व्योमाकारं स्वमात्मानं ध्यायेद्दिग्भिरनावृतम् ।
निराश्रया चिति: शक्ति: स्वरूपं दर्शयेत्तदा ॥ 92 ॥

*Vyomaakaaram svam aatmaanam dhyaayed digbhir anaavritam;*
*Niraashrayaa chitih shaktih svaroopam darshayet tadaa.* (92)

### Anvay

*Vyoma-aakaaram*: into the form of space, ether; *Svam-aatmaanam*: one's own self; *Dhyaayet*: when one meditates; *Digbhih*: directions; *Anaavritam*: unlimited; *Niraashrayaa*: being supportless; *Chitih shaktih*: shakti in the form of consciousness; *Svaroopam*: form of one's own self; *Darshayet-tadaa*: is then revealed.

### Translation

When one meditates on one's own self in the form of unlimited space (in all) directions, the mind is suspended and shakti in the form of consciousness is revealed as the form of one's own self.

### Commentary

In this dharana the vast, unlimited space assists you in transcending the mind. First of all, the imagery is so striking. Just think of yourself out in space with no boundaries. In whichever direction you gaze, there is nothing but endless space. There are no horizons, no reference points, no landmarks, no objects and no definitions. In that state every thought is nullified because there is no prop to support it. This leads to suspension of the mind because the downward movement is prevented or the pull of energy is halted. If this imagery is further developed into suspended animation, the mental energy begins to move upward to the higher centres, touching each one, until

301

*chitishakti*, the supreme energy of consciousness, is revealed as one's own self.

Akasha, or ether, is also the most refined of the five elements that constitute the body. It is located in the region from the mid-eyebrow centre to the top back portion of the head. Its form is unending space in which there is absence of light. In the tantric practice of *tattwa shuddhi*, or refinement of the elements, meditation on this element leads to the experience of that creative energy from which the physical body has evolved.

## 93. Dharana on piercing of the skin

किञ्चिदङ्गं विभिद्यादौ तीक्ष्णसूच्यादिना ततः ।
तत्रैव चेतनां युक्त्वा भैरवे निर्मला गतिः ॥ 93 ॥

*Kinchidangam vibhidyaadau teekshnasoochyaadinaa tatah;*
*Tatraiva chetanaam yuktvaa bhairave nirmalaa gatih.* (93)

### Anvay

*Kinchit:* a little or a bit; *Angam*: limbs of the body; *Vibhidya-aadau*: pierces at first; *Teekshna*: sharp, pointed; *Soochi-aadinaa*: by a needle, etc.; *Tatah*: there; *Tatraiva*: verily there; *Chetanaam*: consciousness; *Yuktvaa*: joined, projecting; *Bhairave*: in bhairava; *Nirmalaa*: pure, clean, fresh; *Gatih*: movement.

### Translation

At first one should pierce any limb of the body a little bit with a sharp, pointed needle or any other instrument. Then projecting the consciousness there, verily there is movement towards the pure nature of bhairava.

### Commentary

It is important to reflect on and understand this dharana. In very simple language it conveys what extraordinary philosophies, debates and discussions have failed to resolve. The point in question is: where do you experience pleasure and pain? Is it at the physical point where you receive the injury or the pleasant sensations? Supposing that the nerves connecting the mind to the body were severed and then your head was chopped off, you would not feel the slightest pain. When you enter surgery under anaesthesia, the surgeon cuts open the body but you do not feel anything at all.

This means that the source of pain and pleasure is not located at the point where you experience it, but elsewhere in the brain. This is why the capacity to bear pain or pleasure differs from person to person. What is extremely painful to you may not evince the slightest reaction in another on account of the quality of the brain and the DNA structure of the person. In this dharana you are asked to concentrate first on the spot which causes pain and then with the same intensity of awareness move your consciousness towards the source of that pain. If you are able to follow it to the source, you will find that it is none other than the pure nature of bhairava.

## 94. Dharana on no-mind

चित्ताद्यन्तः कृतिर्नास्ति ममान्तर्भावयेदिति ।
विकल्पानामभावेन विकल्पैरूज्झितो भवेत् ॥ 94 ॥

*Chittaadyantahkritir naasti mamaantar bhaavayed iti;*
*Vikalpaanaam abhaavena vikalpair ujjhito bhavet.* (94)

### Anvay

*Chittaadi*: mind, etc. (manas, buddhi, chitta, ahamkara); *Antah-kritih*: antahkarana, inner instrument; *Naasti*: not; *Mama-antah*: inside me; *Bhaavayet-iti*: contemplating like this; *Vikalpaanaam*: of the vikalpas (thought constructs); *Abhaavena*: in the absence of; *Vikalpaih*: from the vikalpas; *Ujjhitah*: getting free, rid of; *Bhavet*: becomes.

### Translation

By contemplating thus, the antahkarana, or inner instrument of mind, and so on is non-existent within me, then, in the absence of vikalpas (thought constructs), one becomes free from the vikalpas.

### Commentary

In this dharana we are asked to contemplate on the non-existence of mind. In the absence of mind, the vikalpas, or thoughts, are also absent. This is a way in which we trick the mind to go beyond the mind, because in the absence of the vikalpas we become free from them. When we are free from the vikalpas, the pure self, or atman, is experienced. Atman is the substratum of all existence, the source of everything. The big mango tree is hidden in the seed, although you cannot see it even if you dissect the seed. In the same way atman is hidden in everything that you are, including the mind, buddhi, chitta and ahamkara. Together these four aspects of mind are known as the antahkarana *chatushtaya*, or the four inner instruments, through which atman enacts the game, or *lila*, of life.

This relates to the purely experiential philosophy of Vedanta. How can we verify this statement that atman is the source of everything? Tantra asserts that it can only be verified through experience. It is experience alone that gives birth to real knowledge. We may read volumes on the taste of chocolate, the smell of lavender, the colour of the rising sun or the sound of birds chirping. But unless and until we experience these for ourselves, we will never really know what the volumes we have read were talking about. Of course, the quest for atman is much more abstract and intangible than the taste of chocolate and, therefore, we have to rely solely on our own experience, inner intuition and firm belief or faith in that.

In this dharana we contemplate on the negation of the antahkarana, which comprises everything that we perceive through the mind, buddhi, ego and memory, and through a process of inference arrive at the experience of who we really are. This dharana is pure jnana yoga. It is important to understand and implement jnana yoga in any sadhana you undertake and even in the way you live your life. The basis of jnana yoga is reflection through viveka and vairagya. Concentration alone is not enough to transform the mind of an individual. You may sit for three hours in concentration, but when you emerge from that state, your mind will still exhibit the same base emotions it always has. In the final analysis, unless transformation of the mind takes place, all sadhanas are futile.

A sadhaka should undoubtedly observe the simple aspects of jnana yoga, known as *shravana* – to hear, *manana* – to contemplate and *niddhidhyasana* – to meditate. Out of this two qualities will emerge which have the potential to transform the mind. They are viveka, or discrimination, and vairagya, or absence of craving for past enjoyments. In this way the

306

identification with the antahkarana, or components of the mind, and the resulting vikalpas will be lessened. At this point, by a process of negation of the mind and all the mental processes, the awareness is freed from the vikalpas and merges into the pure consciousness, or atman, which is its real nature.

## 95. Dharana on the nature of the elements

माया विमोहिनी नाम कलाया: कलनं स्थितम् ।
इत्यादिधर्मं तत्त्वानां कलयन्न पृथग्भवेत् ॥ 95 ॥

*Maayaa vimohinee naama kalaayaah kalanam sthitam;*
*Ityaadidharmam tattvaanaam kalayan na prithag bhavet.* (95)

### Anvay

*Maayaa*: illusion; *Vimohinee*: delusive; *Naama*: name;
*Kalaayaah*: activity; *Kalanam*: causing; *Sthitam*: residing;
*Ityaadi dharmam*: thus the nature or functions; *Tattvaanaam*:
of different elements; *Kalayan*: considering, reflecting; *Na
prithak*: not separate; *Bhavet*: becomes.

### Translation

Maya is the delusive principle residing (in manifest
existence), causing name and limited activity. Considering
thus the nature or functions of the various elements, one
(realizes that he) is not separate (from the supreme reality).

### Commentary

Maya is the veiling power inherent in the five unconditioned
shiva tattwas, namely: shiva, shakti, iccha, jnana and kriya.
The illusory power of maya operates through five limiting
aspects, known as kanchukas. The word *kanchuka* literally
means 'sheath' or 'envelope'. Together the five kanchukas act
as a shell, which obscures or limits the kernel. Each kanchuka
limits the cosmic power of shiva/shakti in one aspect. The five
kanchukas are *kalaa*, which limits the power to do all, *avidya
vidya*, which limits the power to know all, *raga*, which creates
like and dislike, *kaala*, which limits perpetual existence by
creating the notion of time, and *niyati*, which limits free will.

These five kanchukas veil the omnipresence, omniscience
and omnipotence of the unified consciousness and create

the notion of duality in every sphere of life. If the sadhaka wakes up to this reality and maintains his awareness of the restrictions imposed on him by the power of maya, which prevents him from experiencing the unified existence, then gradually he will perceive that he is not separate from the supreme reality.

## 96. Dharana on ending desires

झगितीच्छां समुत्पन्नामवलोक्य शमं नयेत् ।
यत एव समुद्भूता ततस्तत्रैव लीयते ॥ ९६ ॥

*Jhagiteechchhaam samutpannaam avalokya shamam nayet;*
*Yata eva samudbhootaa tatas tatraiva leeyate.* (96)

### Anvay

*Jhagit*: flash; *Ichchaam*: desire; *Samutpannaam*: sprung;
*Avalokya*: observing, seeing; *Shamam*: to put an end; *Nayet*:
brings; *Yata eva*: whenever, verily; *Samudbhootaa*: produced,
arises; *Tatah-tatraiva*: then there alone; *Leeyate*: absorbed.

### Translation

Observing the desires, which spring up in a flash, put an
end to them. Then verily (the mind) will be absorbed in the
very source from which they have arisen.

### Commentary

In this dharana you will have to conduct an in-depth study
on desire. First of all, you must observe your desires and the
source from which they arise. After all, to put an end to
something you have to know where it resides, what it looks
like, how it behaves and how it occurs. The root of desire is
attachment, which springs from *raga*, or intense liking. The
opposite of raga is *dwesha*, or intense dislike. Although they
appear opposite, raga and dwesha are actually two sides of
the same coin. They always co-exist together. Where one
exists, you are sure to find the other.

Raga is one of the powers of maya which limits the
power of *icchashakti*, or willpower, by creating intense
attachment and repulsion, thus giving rise to increasing
discontentment. Maya is the veiling power of unified
consciousness, which springs into action during the course

310

of evolution from spirit to matter and becomes the cause for the notion of duality and difference in unity. Once you realize that desire keeps you in bondage, you can set about uprooting it from its very source. However, that is easier said than done because desires spring from the storehouse of past impressions which you carry with you in the form of samskaras, or archetypes.

The storehouse for these samskaras is the subconscious and unconscious realms of the mind, and it is difficult to know what lies there unless you can delve into those spheres. Even if you come to know what lies down there by some quirk of fate, and you do not like what you see, how are you going to eliminate it? This is precisely what can be achieved through this dharana. Concentration on desire is an effective way to work out the samskaras on the mental plane, where they appear as psychic forms.

These psychic experiences are often regarded as spiritual because of their subtle nature, but in fact they are a process of cleansing or purging, which clears the conscious field for the spiritual experience to blossom. Until and unless these samskaras are rooted out, one remains on the periphery without ever entering the spiritual dimension. So the answer lies in focusing on the desire itself. Practise dharana on the desires which arise from the subconscious and unconscious in a flash. Gradually, through concentration and focus on the desire itself, you will be able to put an end to it. This will take you to the source of the desire, which is the unified consciousness beyond the mind.

## 97. Dharana on 'Who am I?'

यदा ममेच्छा नोत्पन्ना ज्ञानं वा, कस्तदास्मि वै ।
तत्त्वतोऽहं तथाभूतस्तल्लीनस्तन्मना भवेत् ॥ 97 ॥

*Yadaa mamechchhaa notpannaa jnaanam vaa kas tadaasmi vai;*
*Tattvato'ham tathaabhootas talleenas tanmanaa bhavet.* (97)

### Anvay

*Yadaa*: when; *Mama-ichchhaa*: my desire; *Na utpannaa*: not
produced; *Jnaanam vaa*: or knowledge; *Kah-tadaa-asmi*: then
what am I? *Vai*: indeed; *Tattvatah-aham*: in essence I am;
*Tathaa bhootah*: being like that; *Talleenah*: absorbed there;
*Tanmanaa*: identifying (with that); *Bhavet*: becomes.

### Translation

(One should contemplate thus:) when my desires do not
produce knowledge, then what am I? Indeed being absorbed
in the essence I am, and identifying with that, one becomes
that.

### Commentary

This dharana is based on one of the fundamental principles
of Vedanta. The word *veda* means 'knowledge' and *anta*
means 'end', thus signifying that Vedanta is the culmination
of knowledge. This is not ordinary knowledge, but special
or transcendental knowledge. Vedanta is not mere specula-
tion. It is an authentic record of the direct realization of the
vedic seers, which they achieved through intense self-enquiry
along the lines mentioned above.

The question you ask yourself in this dharana is: in the
absence of my desires and perceptions of knowledge, then
who or what am I? By following this process you will arrive
at your conclusion through a process of denial and negation
of everything that you are not. You are not desire nor are

312

you thought or the knowledge which arises out of it. Gradually, you will come to realize the mahavakya of Vedanta: *Aham Brahmasmi,* "I am That", and with this realization comes total identification with the source.

Reflection of this sort is a yearning of the soul, which we all have at some time or other, to recognize our true identity. This yearning forms the basis of one's spiritual quest and the answer reached is the culmination. My guru, Swami Satyananda, has written a poem published in his early years of sadhana in which he raises this same question with such intensity that it will compel you to question yourself in the same manner.

The poem written in Hindi is titled, "Who am I", and it says in exquisite terms that this question is resounding every moment in the void, or shoonya, compelling you to ask your inner self, "Who am I, who am I, who am I?" Am I this body whose end is destined, or am I the breath whose numbers are destined? Am I space, fire, water, earth or air? Who am I, who am I? Oh! Who am I?

## 98. Dharana on desire

इच्छायामथवा ज्ञाने जाते चित्तं निवेशयत् ।
आत्मबुद्ध्यानन्यचेतास्ततस्तत्त्वार्थदर्शनम् ॥ 98 ॥

*Ichchhaayaam athavaa jnaane jaate chittam niveshayat;*
*Aatmabuddhyaananyachetaas tatas tattvaarthadarshanam.* (98)

### Anvay

*Ichchhaayaam*: in desire; *Athavaa*: or; *Jnaane*: knowledge;
*Jaate*: appears, arises; *Chittam*: mind; *Niveshayat*: should fix;
*Aatma buddhyaa*: thinking as the very self; *Ananya chetaah*:
making the mind absolutely one-pointed; *Tatah*: there;
*Tattvaartha*: essence of the tattwas; *Darshanam*: realize, sees.

### Translation

When desire or knowledge arises, one should fix the mind
there, thinking that to be the very self. Making the mind
absolutely one-pointed (in this way), he realizes the essence
of the tattwas.

### Commentary

In this dharana an important principle of tantra is expressed.
Desires are powerful thought forms and you should not try
to negate or suppress them. Instead learn to transform
them through dharana. By concentration on the desire or
knowledge that arises from within, develop total self-
identification with that. Become the desire or the knowledge.
This does not mean that you have to enact the desire; rather
you express it through dharana by totally identifying your
awareness with it. In this way, as you focus on the desire,
you will soon find that it undergoes a process which
transforms it into a more subtle experience.

Of course, if you are not trained in dharana, the desires
which arise may take some other form, such as anger, hatred,

314

vengeance or jealousy. But when desire is transformed through dharana by utilizing this systematic and scientific method, then the same craving will elevate you to a higher awareness rather than dragging you down to more mundane levels. This dharana reveals the means to root out desire in a way which frees the mind, rather than obstructing or suppressing it further. When desire arises, focus the mind on that desire, just as you would on any other point of concentration. Then by thinking that desire to be the very self, you can experience the subtle essence of the desire through the inner eye of knowledge.

## 99. Dharana on knowledge

निर्निमित्तं भवेज्ज्ञानं निराधारं भ्रमात्मकम् ।
तत्त्वत: कस्यचिन्नैतदेवंभावी शिव: प्रिये ॥ 99 ॥

*Nirnimittam bhavej jnaanam niraadhaaram bhramaatmakam;*
*Tattvatah kasyachin naitad evambhaavee shivah priye.* (99)

### Anvay

*Nirnimittam*: without cause; *Bhavet-jnaanam*: the knowledge becomes; *Niraadhaaram*: baseless; *Bhramaatmakam*: knowledge whose self is deception; *Tattvatah*: in reality; *Kasya chit*: of any person; *Na-etat*: not this; *Evam bhaavee*: contemplating like; *Shivah*: Shiva; *Priye*: O dear one.

### Translation

O dear one, (compared to absolute knowledge, all relative) knowledge is without cause, and thus becomes baseless and deceptive. In reality, knowledge does not belong to any one person. Contemplating like this, one becomes Shiva.

### Commentary

In this dharana one is asked to discern the truth regarding absolute and relative knowledge. For this type of questioning and contemplation, the sadhaka must have an undaunted intellect, strong willpower and unfailing honesty. He should have mental stamina to question, reason and reject many conclusions that may be arrived at before he reaches the final truth. The intellect should be so sharp that it can cut through all deception and falsehood, without any faltering, doubt or dissension.

Knowledge of the ultimate reality is universal; it is not limited to any one person, sect, nationality, class, creed or religion. It belongs to all mankind and is the heritage bestowed on each and every one of us. Unlike relative forms

316

of knowledge, this knowledge of reality has a cause and that cause is the creator. Therefore, in relation to absolute knowledge, all other forms of knowledge are baseless, deceptive and without cause. At the end of this questioning process, only the knowledge of absolute reality, which is universal, remains.

Transcendental knowledge is timeless and eternal, thus it is applicable to each and every one of us, whether we are old or young, rich or poor, black or white, male or female. Other forms of knowledge relate to particular groups of people, in particular places and at particular times, after which they lose their viability and cease to exist. Contemplation on such lofty ideas results in an experience of universality, wherein each and every speck of creation is realized as a part of the whole. In this way, the consciousness becomes one with Shiva.

## 100. Dharana on undifferentiated consciousness

चिद्धर्मा सर्वदेहेषु विशेषो नास्ति कुत्रचित् ।
अतश्च तन्मयं सर्वं भावयन्भवजिज्जन: ॥ 100 ॥

*Chiddharmaa sarvadeheshu vishesho naasti kutrachit;*
*Atashcha tanmayam sarvam bhaavayan bhavajij janah.* (100)

### Anvay

*Chit-dharmaa*: of the nature of consciousness; *Sarva deheshu*: in all the bodies; *Visheshah*: specially, particularly; *Naasti*: not; *Kutra chit*: anywhere; *Atah-cha*: therefore; *Tanmayam*: pervaded by that; *Sarvam*: all; *Bhaavayan*: contemplate; *Bhavajit*: transcend relative existence; *Janah*: persons.

### Translation

He (Bhairava) is of the nature of undifferentiated consciousness in all embodied forms. Therefore, those persons who contemplate on all creation pervaded by that consciousness, transcend relative existence.

### Commentary

The focus of this dharana is the undifferentiated consciousness, which pervades all the different forms of beings in existence. In this sense, there is relative or differentiated existence and there is also absolute or undifferentiated existence. When we limit our awareness to the individual body and mind by relating to that only, we experience relative existence. Most of us exist in this realm, but a few have dared to step out of this relative awareness and realize the absolute nature of existence.

Such persons realize that everything in the universe is intimately connected and forms a composite whole. This is akin to the unified field theory of modern physics. Consciousness does not differ in different bodies; it is the same in every being. Until this is realized, the differences appear to be vast and we experience separation in every aspect of life. This separation cuts us off from the source of life, knowledge, experience and fulfilment. But when we experience oneness with everything, this separation or relative existence is transcended.

When we become one with the whole of existence, this is the ultimate experience. This state is known as *jivanmukta,* or liberation in the body. When liberation takes place out of the body, this state is known as *videhamukta.* Swami Sivananda, the guru of Swami Satyananda, experienced this state prior to his *mahasamadhi* at Rishikesh in the year 1963. Before he entered his final samadhi, a pen was placed in his hand and he wrote the following words, "God is the only Truth." After attaining videhamukti, the body lives for barely ten to twelve days, as the liberated consciousness does not identify with any one body, but with all bodies and beings and can inhabit any space or sphere.

In this way, we can understand that by focusing the awareness on the undifferentiated consciousness, which pervades all beings, at all times, the relative existence is transcended. This leads to liberation, allowing one to move about freely in the undifferentiated and unlimited dimensions of consciousness.

## 101. Dharana on the negative qualities

कामक्रोधलोभमोहमदमात्सर्यगोचरे     ।
बुद्धिं निस्तिमितां कृत्वा तत्तत्त्वमवशिष्यते ॥ 101 ॥

*Kaamakrodhalobhamohamadamaatsaryagochare;*
*Buddhim nistimitaam kritvaa tat tattvam avashishyate.* (101)

### Anvay

*Kaama*: lust; *Krodha*: anger; *Lobha*: greed; *Moha*: delusion;
*Mada*: pride; *Maatsarya*: jealousy; *Gochare*: dwells, seen;
*Buddhim*: the intellect; *Nistimitaam*: motionless, fixed;
*Kritvaa*: having done; *Tat-tattvam*: that tattwa; *Avashishyate*:
remains.

### Translation

When lust, anger, greed, delusion, arrogance and jealousy
are seen (within), having fixed the mind completely (on
these), the underlying tattwa, or essence, alone remains.

### Commentary

In this dharana the focus of awareness is on the fires raging
within. These are the negative qualities which torture and
torment you throughout life, until you are completely burnt
out and withered by their onslaught. This can be seen in the
life all around you as well. However, you can gradually
change this situation by becoming aware of these internal
forces and focusing your attention on them. In this process
the faculty of buddhi, or proper discrimination, develops,
allowing you to regain control or balance of the mind. This
is the main sadhana that everyone has to undergo in life,
whether on the spiritual path or not. Spirituality is knowledge
about life; it is not anti-life, as many people may think.
Those who tread the spiritual path labour very hard to
understand their true nature and all the facets that govern it.

In this way, *kama* (desire), *krodha* (anger), *lobha* (greed), *moha* (delusion), *mada* (pride) and *matsarya* (jealousy) are the negative and limiting qualities present in each and everyone. They are the product of the gunas and everyone is subject to them, no matter who or what you are. These qualities are the devils that create a living hell for you. The only difference is that some people are more aware of these qualities within themselves than others, and thereby they are able to manage them. So, in fact, what determines your level of self-control and humanness is this awareness.

Therefore, the object of this dharana is to develop awareness of these qualities. Whenever anger, jealousy or delusion arise, step back and observe it, just as you would look at your own face in the mirror. If you observe how you are thinking, behaving, looking, laughing or talking at that time, you will notice a difference in yourself that will not appeal to you. Basically you do not like to see these qualities within yourself and you feel uncomfortable when they arise. Moreover, they cause a great deal of imbalance and you tend to lose control of yourself and the situations you are in at those times.

Thus, this dharana shows how the defects of the human personality can be used as a means to liberate the consciousness. This is the very principle of tantra which sets it apart from other religions and philosophies. They ask you to eradicate anger, greed, jealousy, passion and pride, but they do not tell you how to go about it effectively. Over time you develop a guilt complex because of the inability to manage these negative attributes, which causes further imbalance in your behaviour and personality.

Tantra, on the other hand, says that these negative traits are also a part of the mind, so utilize them just as you would use the assistance of another thorn to remove a thorn which is deeply embedded in your foot. It would be a lie to say that you never feel anger or jealousy. Accept that these feelings do arise within you, and they are also part of nature's law. Wherever there is love, there will be hatred; this is natural. You cannot stop this process, but you can become aware of it.

For example, whenever jealousy arises, focus your mind on it. Develop total awareness of this quality through one-pointed attention and penetrate it with your sharp intellect. If you are able to do this, you will suddenly find that your awareness goes beyond the jealousy and enters a subtler dimension, which brings you closer to the essence. In reality, jealousy and all the other negative qualities are nothing but subtle forms of energy. When you realize the essence of these qualities, you will realize yourself as well as develop the ability to convert negative energy into positive energy.

The energy is the same in all experiences, whether they are positive or negative, material or spiritual. It is just a question of how streamlined the flow of that energy is. If the flow is scattered, dissipated and disturbed, then it is certain that your experience and subsequently your expression will be unbalanced. On the other hand, a positive, confident and focused person will exhibit a steady, unbroken and streamlined flow of energy.

## 102. Dharana on the illusive nature of life

इन्द्रजालमयं विश्वं व्यस्तं वा चित्रकर्मवत् ।
भ्रमद्वा ध्यायतः सर्वं पश्यतश्च सुखोद्गमः ॥ 102 ॥

*Indrajaalamayam vishvam vyastam vaa chitrakarmavat;*
*Bhramad vaa dhyaayatah sarvam pashyatashcha sukhodgamah.* (102)

### Anvay

*Indrajaalamayam*: like jugglery, magic; *Vishvam*: universe;
*Vyastam*: imagined; *Vaa*: or; *Chitra karmavat*: like a painting;
*Bhramadvaa*: transient; *Dhyaayatah*: meditating; *Sarvam*: all;
*Pashyatashcha*: seeing; *Sukha-udgamah*: happiness arises.

### Translation

Meditating on the manifest world as imagined or illusive,
like a magic show or a painting, and seeing all existence as
transient, happiness arises.

### Commentary

In this dharana the focus is on the illusive nature of all
manifest existence. As the awareness of the internal dimensions of consciousness develops, the external world appears
to be more and more unreal. At present most people in the
world would not accept this idea at all. In fact, if you tell the
average person that this world is maya, or illusion, he has
every reason not to believe you because this is the only
reality he has ever known. But, if by chance, effort or grace,
he gets out of this lower gravitational field and enters a
higher dimension of consciousness, this world will appear
unreal to him. At this time the perception of everything
around him will alter, and he will see the essence behind the
form. In modern terms this is described as an altered state
of consciousness. A person who has this vision or realization
is known as a seer.

This dharana also asks you to contemplate on the transience of all existence. Even if you are not able to experience the essence behind the form, your everyday experiences indicate the impermanence of everything you are and all that is around you. Disease, old age and death snatch everything away from you, even if you possessively hang onto it. So, imagining the world like a magic show, contemplate on the transience of life. All manifest existence has a beginning and an end. Therefore, it is not eternal, permanent or real. Then the thought will arise that, instead of chasing the illusive and finite, why not try to discover that which is infinite and real, which has no beginning and no end. Such a seer is sure to experience true happiness.

## 103. Dharana on the middle path

न चित्तं निक्षिपेदुःखे न सुखे वा परिक्षिपेत् ।
भैरवि ज्ञायतां मध्ये किं तत्त्वमवशिष्यते ॥ 103 ॥

*Na chittam nikshiped duhkhe na sukhe vaa parikshipet;*
*Bhairavi, jnaayataam madhye kim tattvam avashishyate.* (103)

### Anvay

*Na*: not; *Chittam*: mind or consciousness; *Nikshipet*: thrown upon; *Duhkhe*: pain; *Na*: not; *Sukhe*: pleasure; *Vaa*: or; *Parikshipet*: thrown upon; *Bhairavi*: O Goddess; *Jnaayataam*: it should be known; *Madhye*: middle; *Kim*: what; *Tattvam*: tattwa, essence; *Avashishyate*: remains.

### Translation

O Goddess, the mind should not dwell on pain or pleasure, but the essence that remains in the middle (in between the opposites) should be known.

### Commentary

This dharana describes concentration on the middle path and how it is to be performed. The middle path means that state beyond duality. One might think that this state is found several levels above duality, but actually it is entered exactly in the middle, in-between the two opposites. That is why the middle path is said to be very narrow and difficult to follow. Of course, once the awareness of the middle way develops, this path opens out and then the path of the opposites seems to diminish or lose its attraction.

The wise have said that pleasure leads to pain and pain leads to pleasure. These two are like the opposite directions of the swinging pendulum. First it swings one way, and when it reaches the maximum height, the momentum propels it in the opposite direction. In this way, the

325

pendulum goes on swinging from one side to the other endlessly, until it stops exactly in the middle, which is the process indicated by this dharana.

Of pain and pleasure, Swami Sivananda has said that excess pleasure weakens the mind, but pain is the crucible into which nature throws a man whenever it wants to make him into a sublime superman. If this is true, perhaps it would it be wise to seek pain and avoid pleasure. Both pleasure and pain are the experiences of the antahkarana. They are relative experiences, not absolute. This dharana says to dwell on that essence in-between pleasure and pain, which is a witness to both but remains unaffected by them.

Ordinarily the gap between dual and opposite forces is quite great. For instance, pain and pleasure seem to be poles apart, so too are night and day, love and hate, heat and cold. They are not only poles apart, they move in opposite directions too, as in the case of prana and apana. This gap has to be reduced until they merge into one another, as in the dharana of prana and apana. This can be done by dwelling on the gap in-between, rather than on the opposite forces of pain or pleasure.

In that gap before pain turns into pleasure or pleasure into pain, there is stillness, shoonya, the void and then again it turns into the movement of energy which you experience in the form of pain or pleasure, according to the quality of your mind. Pain and pleasure are not absolute but relative terms. What you may find painful may not appear the same to another. It is the gap between them that is absolute. So pain and pleasure are forms of energy in constant motion. In the gap between them is the essence or experience of consciousness. It is in this light that shakti is the doorway to Shiva.

## 104. Dharana on 'I am everywhere'

विहाय निजदेहास्थां सर्वत्रास्मीति भावयन् ।
दृढेन मनसा दृष्ट्या नान्येक्षिण्या सुखी भवेत् ॥ 104 ॥

*Vihaaya nijadehaasthaam sarvatraasmeeti bhaavayan;*
*Dridhena manasaa drishtyaa naanyekshinyaa sukhee bhavet. (104)*

### Anvay

*Vihaaya*: abandon; *Nija dehaasthaam*: consideration of one's own body; *Sarvatra-asmeeti*: I am everywhere; *Bhaavayan*: contemplate; *Dridhena*: firmly, determined; *Manasaa*: by the mind; *Drishtyaa*: seen; *Na-anyekshinyaa*: not seeing another, i.e. (through concentration); *Sukhee*: happy; *Bhavet*: becomes.

### Translation

Abandoning consideration for one's own body, one should contemplate with a firm mind that 'I am everywhere'. When this is seen (by means of concentrated insight) one does not see another and thus becomes happy.

### Commentary

In this dharana the concept of one's body or limited individuality, which forms the basis of duality, is abandoned. The root cause for identification with the body is ego, which gives rise to the notion of individual existence and then to the concept of 'I' and 'other'. Although extremely difficult to eradicate, this notion of individuality must be uprooted with a firm and concentrated mind. This is done by projecting the idea that I am not separate from or different to other forms of existence. I am one and the same everywhere and in everything. There is a deep connection which links me to the rest of creation.

With this idea of unity, mental insight is developed and you will see everything as an extension of yourself. This will generate immense joy in your heart, because you will feel united with everything in existence. The deep-rooted unhappiness you carry with you throughout life, despite all that you have accomplished, possessed and enjoyed, is on account of your sense of separation. When you experience total unity within and without, not just with one or two others, but with each and every being in creation, then you will experience sublime happiness.

*Na anyekshinya* refers to a state when you see no other, which implies that it is a state of total oneness and unity with creation. In other words it is the pure I-ness, or *aham*, which you are able to experience. Forgetfulness of your real self leads you to the experience of difference and division from others. You begin to perceive yourself as a man or woman, a professor or doctor, American or English and so on. This is the result of that pure I-ness, or aham, being transformed into the gross ego, because the darkness of ego does not permit you to know your real nature. But if the I-ness remains pure, then you do not have this difficulty, because the pure aham is none other than the self, which gives rise to the notion "I am that", or *Aham Brahmasmi*.

This dharana reveals the sattwic transformation of ego, or aham, into that principle, or tattwa, of pure ego, which is the catalyst for self-realization.

## 105. Dharana on higher knowledge

घटादौ यच्च विज्ञानमिच्छाद्यं वा ममान्तरे ।
नैव सर्वगतं जातं भावयन्निति सर्वग: ॥ 105 ॥

*Ghataadau yach cha vijnaanam ichchhaadyam vaa mamaantare;*
*Naiva, sarvagatam jaatam bhaavayann iti sarvagah.* (105)

### Anvay

*Ghataadau*: jar or pot; *Yat-cha*: which; *Vijnaanam*: special knowledge; *Ichchhaadyam*: desires, etc.; *Vaa*: or; *Mama-antare*: inside me; *Na-eva*: not verily; *Sarvagatam*: everywhere; *Jaatam*: born; *Bhaavayan*: contemplate; *Iti*: thus; *Sarvagah*: all-pervading.

### Translation

Contemplating on that special knowledge, for example, the analogy of the jar, or that the desires, etc. exist not only within me but everywhere, one thus becomes all-pervasive.

### Commentary

This dharana describes concentration on higher knowledge using such analogies as the jar. If you fill a jar with water from the river and then place the jar of water in the river, is the water in the jar any different from the water flowing in the river? If you break the jar, the water in the jar again merges with the water from the river. In the same way, we think of ourselves as individual beings, but the same consciousness and energy which pervades our bodies and minds pervades all beings in creation. So how are we different from all other forms of existence? Contemplating on the truth of this analogy, the dharana says to develop a unified awareness which is all-pervasive in nature, rather than limited to one particular area or field.

329

The history of the world tells us that only a chosen few have transcended duality and attained oneness with the supreme spirit. Duality, and not unity, is the order of the day. We do not have unified awareness. Each of us perceives duality, not unity. We may be proud of our success in meditation, our psychic experiences or other attainments, but in reality we are all still rotating in the gravitational pull of duality. The moment we transcend duality it will reflect in everything we think, say, do or accomplish. We will have no more questions, only answers. One day I met a man who wanted to seek advice from my guru. He said that he had reached the highest state of consciousness and needed guidance about that. I was a bit surprised because to my mind one who has reached the highest stage of consciousness has no questions; in fact, he is in a position to provide all the answers.

The seeds of individuality and desire exist in me and in everyone. This thought leads to a sense of identification with others despite the awareness of duality. Identification with others, in turn, leads to a sense of being an intimate part of this creation, where everyone is like you, and you are no different to others. This enlarges your vision and broadens the scope of your horizon to include others in your awareness. Thus your awareness becomes all-pervasive. The definition of all-pervasive is that which includes everyone and everything within itself, and does not exclude anything. One of the qualities of God is also omnipresence or all-pervasiveness, which means that He is present in everything and everything is present in Him. That is the result of this dharana, when you identify yourself with all beings and consciously apply this principle to yourself.

## 106. Dharana on the subject-object relationship

ग्राह्यग्राहकसंवित्ति: सामान्या सर्वदेहिनाम् ।
योगिनां तु विशेषोऽस्ति संबन्धे सावधानता ॥ 106 ॥

*Graahyagraahakasamvittih saamaanyaa sarvadehinaam;*
*Yoginaam tu vishesho'sti sambandhe saavadhaanataa.* (106)

### Anvay

*Graahya*: objects; *Graahaka*: subject; *Samvittih*: consciousness;
*Saamaanyaa*: common; *Sarvadehinaam*: in everybody;
*Yoginaam*: yogis; *Tu visheshah-asti*: however, especially are;
*Sambandhe*: regarding relation; *Saavadhaanataa*: carefulness,
alertness.

### Translation

The subject-object consciousness is common to everybody.
Yogis, however, are especially alert regarding this relationship.

### Commentary

The focus of this dharana is the subject-object relationship,
which is an important concept in tantra and yoga. Most
people live in accordance with the subject-object perspective
of duality without ever realizing that there is any other way
of viewing life. However, a yogi or adept is very careful about
making this distinction, because he is able to perceive the
unity behind the diversity. Although he understands the
absolute truth, he also accepts the relative truth of the
subject-object relationship and the purpose for this
awareness. If the awareness of duality is common to
everybody, it must have some definite purpose; it cannot
exist by accident or coincidence. Yogis say that the perception
of duality is a stage of evolution, which every individual
must pass through on his journey to enlightenment.

Of course, they also say that this subject-object awareness of duality is the cause of division, disharmony, unhappiness and sorrow. We are born to experience unity, not separation. That is our birthright and the sooner we realize it the better. For this reason, the yogis are very alert about how they view life and interact in the world. Although they understand the mundane experiences in relation to duality, at the same time they see the transcendental reality and so they are never identified with or confused by the events of life. In this way, the yogis live in the world but remain untouched by it, like a lotus leaf on the water. Although people think that human birth is meant for achieving many things in the material world, the real purpose of our birth as a human being is to rise above the perception of duality and experience unity.

## 107. Dharana on consciousness

स्ववदन्यशरीरेऽपि    संवित्तिमनुभावयेत् ।
अपेक्षां स्वशरीरस्य त्यक्त्वा व्यापी दिनैर्भवेत् ॥ 107 ॥

*Svavad anyashareere'pi samvittim anubhaavayet;*
*Apekshaam svashareerasya tyaktvaa vyaapee dinair bhavet.* (107)

### Anvay

*Sva-vat*: like one's own; *Anya-shareere-api*: even in another's body; *Samvittim*: consciousness; *Anubhaavayet*: contemplate; *Apekshaam*: expectation; *Sva-shareerasya*: of one's body; *Tyaktvaa*: abandoning; *Vyaapee*: all-pervasive; *Dinaih:* in course of time; *Bhavet*: becomes.

### Translation

Contemplate on consciousness, such as one's own and even in another's body as well. Thus abandoning all physical expectation, one becomes all-pervasive in the course of time.

### Commentary

The focus of this dharana is on the consciousness which exists within oneself and within others as well. Concentrating on this conscious principle, which pervades all beings, one should leave the body awareness and identification. Body consciousness is the main thing that limits or obstructs one's entry into the realm of spirit. This dharana suggests a way to overcome the physical barrier, so that one can soar high into the spiritual realms. The body is just a vehicle for consciousness to enact its *lila*, or game plan.

Just as consciousness is embodied in oneself to fulfil some purpose, in the same way consciousness is present in all bodies to fulfil different goals. But the common goal of consciousness in each one of us is self-realization. Keeping this in mind one should cease to consider the body as important. Rather one should realize that the body is a puppet in the hands of consciousness, which pulls the strings. This is true, not just in oneself, but in everybody. When consciousness, and not matter, becomes the focus of attention, then one develops an all-pervasive nature in the course of time.

## 108. Dharana on the unsupported mind

निराधारं मन: कृत्वा विकल्पान्न विकल्पयेत् ।
तदात्मपरमात्मत्वे    भैरवो    मृगलोचने ॥ 108 ॥

*Niraadhaaram manah kritvaa vikalpaan na vikalpayet;*
*Tadaatmaparamaatmatve bhairavo mrigalochane.* (108)

### Anvay

*Niraadhaaram*: supportless, suspends; *Manah*: mind; *Kritvaa*:
having done; *Vikalpaan*: the vikalpas; *Na*: not; *Vikalpayet*:
should think; *Tat-aatma*: that self; *Paramaatmatve*: in the
supreme self; *Bhairavah*: state of bhairava; *Mrigalochane*: O
deer-eyed one.

### Translation

O gazelle-eyed one, having freed the mind of all supports,
one should refrain from all the vikalpas (thoughts/counter-
thoughts). Then, the self becomes one with the supreme
Self in the state of bhairava.

### Commentary

The focus in this dharana is the unsupported or suspended
mind, which remains tranquil and undisturbed by the
thoughts and counter-thoughts. The mind needs some
support in order to exist. Those supports are known as
*vikalpas*, thoughts and counter-thoughts. Every thought that
arises in the mind is invariably followed by a counter-thought,
which either compliments or contradicts it, and thus the
thought process continues. Thoughts are dissipated energy
forms and each thought gives rise to multiple thoughts.
This process goes on all day long without ceasing and
continues even into sleep where it takes the form of dreams,
which are nothing but dormant and unexpressed thought
forms.

The sensory impressions are received by the mind from outside, but the thoughts arise from chitta, the storehouse of past impressions, which is closely connected to the mind. The mind continually draws information from chitta and analyzes whether it is good or bad, right or wrong, useful or useless, with the aid of buddhi, or intellect. Then the mind identifies each thought as its own through ego and is thus affected and influenced by it. This mental process is a continuous cycle. In order to stop this process you have to dissociate the mind from the thoughts. This separation results in a disconnection between the mind and ego.

This separation of the mind from the thoughts and the mind from the ego is an extremely rare accomplishment and results in a much heightened state of awareness. When the mind is freed from the thoughts, it enters a state of suspension, or no mind, which is just pure concentrated energy. In that state the individual self is revealed and becomes one with the supreme Self or spirit in the state of bhairava.

## 109. Dharana on identification with Shiva

सर्वज्ञ: सर्वकर्ता च व्यापक: परमेश्वर: ।
स एवाहं शैवधर्मा इति दाढर्याद्भवेच्छिव: ॥ 109 ॥

*Sarvajnah sarvakartaa cha vyaapakah parameshvarah;*
*Sa evaaham shaivadharmaa iti daardhyaad bhavechchhivah.* (109)

### Anvay

*Sarvajnah*: omniscient; *Sarvakarttaa cha*: and omnipotent; *Vyaapakah*: omnipresent; *Parameshvarah*: supreme Lord; *Sa*: he; *Eva-aham*: verily, I; *Shaiva-dharma*: shiva-nature; *Iti*: thus; *Daardhyaat*: firmly; *Bhavet-shivah*: becomes Shiva.

### Translation

The supreme Lord, who is omnipresent, omniscient and omnipotent, verily, I am He and I have the same shiva-nature. Contemplating thus with firm conviction, one becomes Shiva.

### Commentary

In this dharana the focus of concentration is the identification of the individual self with the supreme Self or Shiva. In the *Taittiriya Upanishad* (Shikshavalli 1:10), there is a declaration by the seer Trishanku in a beautiful verse of just three lines, which can make ones hair stand on end on account of the boldness of the statement and the power it emits. He says, "I am the power, the wealth and the light of the divine intuition. I have realized the true knowledge. Imperishable and immortal have I become." This is the declaration of knowledge made by the seer Trishanku after his self-realization.

Swami Satyananda, in one of his most memorable poems, 'An Ode to Tapasya', has said, "This creation will be sent to destruction with just a flutter of my eyelids." These are not

337

just empty statements. During the journey from matter to spirit, there is an experience when the powers of the Lord filter through to the aspirant. When sugar is mixed with milk, it becomes sweet and takes on that quality. It no longer has a separate existence. In the same way, when the individual self merges with the supreme, it takes on those attributes, becoming omnipotent, omniscient and omnipresent, the three qualities of the Divine. Christ also said, "My father and I are one."

A sadhaka should develop this identification with firm conviction on the basis of the experience of the seers of the past. The scriptures say that a sadhaka who wants to realize the truth should follow the path that great and mighty beings have walked upon, then he is sure to reach the destination. Gradually this belief will begin to manifest and become a reality for him, leading to the discovery that he is indeed Shiva.

## 110. Dharana on identification with the source

जलस्येवोर्मयो वह्नेर्ज्वालाभङ्ग्य: प्रभा रवे: ।
ममैव भैरवस्यैता विश्वभङ्ग्यो विभेदिता: ॥ 110 ॥

*Jalasyevormayo vahner jvaalaabhangyah prabhaa raveh;*
*Mamaiva bhairavasyaitaa vishvabhangyo vibheditaah.* (110)

### Anvay

*Jalasya-iva-oormayah*: like waves arise out of water; *Vahneh-jvaalaabhangyah*: flames from fire; *Prabhaa raveh*: rays of the sun; *Mama-eva*: mine indeed; *Bhairavasya-etaa*: these (waves) of bhairava; *Vishvabhangyah*: emanations of the universe; *Vibheditaah*: differentiated.

### Translation

Just as waves arise from water, flames from fire and light rays from the sun, similarly the waves of bhairava, which produce the different emanations of the universe, are verily my source.

### Commentary

The similes in this dharana are so aptly illustrated that it really needs no further elucidation. It is just another way of saying that each one of us has emanated from the whole. My mother and father may have created my physical body, but the cause of my birth is inherent in the creator. The will to create is His and I am an expression of it. He is the director of this mega movie, and I am playing a role in it. My entry into this world is decided by Him and so too is my exit; neither are in my hands. Not even the simple act of digestion is within my control. If today my stomach fails to digest, I would not know what to do.

The body moves, sleeps, thinks, acts, ages, all by itself. I do not play any part in that process. Just as waves are born

339

out of water, flames from fire and light from the sun, I am born out of Him, along with the rest of creation. We are all differentiated waves of energy, emanating from the universe. Although having diverse forms, we arise from the same source, which is bhairava. If we have arisen from the same source, then just as every ray of light carries the brilliance, heat and glow of the sun, in the same way all the different forms of bhairava carry the attributes or nature that characterize the supreme consciousness.

## 111. Dharana on whirling around

भ्रान्त्वा भ्रान्त्वा शरीरेण त्वरितं भुवि पातनात् ।
क्षोभशक्तिविरामेण परा संजायते दशा ॥ 111 ॥

*Bhraantvaa bhraantvaa shareerena tvaritam bhuvi paatanaat;*
*Kshobhashaktiviraamena paraa sanjaayate dashaa.* (111)

### Anvay

*Bhraantvaa bhraantvaa*: whirling round and round; *Shareerena*: body; *Tvaritam*: at once; *Bhuvi*: on the ground; *Paatanaat*: from falling; *Kshobha-shakti*: energy causing commotion; *Viraamena*: by cessation; *Paraa*: the supreme; *Sanjaayate*: appears, arises; *Dashaa*: state.

### Translation

Whirling the body round and round until it falls on the ground makes the energy causing commotion at once (become static). By that cessation the supreme state appears.

### Commentary

Although this dharana appears illogical, there is a great deal of logic in it. The nature of energy is motion. It is always moving, spreading and dissipating, on account of which it is easily exhausted and frittered away, instead of becoming a concentrated and powerful force. In material life this becomes the main cause for the onset of disease, and in spiritual life it drains the momentum for higher experience. Just as a dam collects water in a reservoir and transforms its power into electricity, similarly for physical, mental, emotional and spiritual health, the energy has to be channelled, conserved, concentrated, and transformed. This is only possible when you create a build-up of energy at the appropriate points within the body and then stop its movement.

How do you stop the motion of this force, which is constantly moving? One way to do this quite effectively is described in this dharana. By whirling the body round and round until it falls down, the sudden cessation of physical energy is spontaneously transferred to the dimension of mental energy, and the mind too becomes still. When the physical and mental energies stop their outward movement, there is no dissipation or loss of energy. At this point of cessation, the energies become concentrated, which generates the necessary quantum to transform the physical and mental experiences into spiritual experience. Hence, during this moment of cessation, the supreme state manifests.

This method has been used by the mystics of the Sufi tradition to enter high states of ecstasy and trance and attain union with the Divine. The *tandav nritya*, or dance of destruction, performed by Shiva when he gyrated non-stop until the whole universe began to resound with the vibrations of that dance is an apt illustration of this dharana.

## 112. Dharana on erroneous perception

आधारेष्वथवाऽशक्त्याऽज्ञानाच्चित्तलयेन वा ।
जातशक्तिसमावेश-क्षोभान्ते भैरवं वपु: ॥ 112 ॥

*Aadhaareshvathavaa' shaktyaa'jnaanaachchittalayena vaa;*
*Jaatashaktisamaaveshak-shobhaante bhairavam vapuh.* (112)

### Anvay

*Aadhaareshu*: in support, objects to be perceived; *Athavaa*: or; *Ashaktyaa*: being helpless or powerless; *Ajnaanaat*: from ignorance; *Chitta-layena vaa*: dissolution of mind or; *Jaata shakti*: shakti, or energy, produced by commotion; *Samaavesha*: absorption, totality; *Kshobhaante*: at the end of commotion, disturbance; *Bhairavam*: Bhairava; *Vapuh*: body form.

### Translation

Being powerless to perceive objects due to ignorance or wrong perception, if one is able to dissolve the mind by absorbing it on the erroneous perception of objects, then at the end of commotion brought about by that absorption, there the form of Bhairava appears.

### Commentary

Concentration on any form leads to a heightened state of awareness. Absorption in any form catapults the awareness to an altered state. Erroneous perception or ignorance about the real nature of an object or an event often leads to disturbance in the mental patterns or thoughts of an individual. If concentration is achieved at that time, even if one is unable to perceive the object or event correctly, still he can enter a higher dimension.

This sloka reveals that even periods of commotion and upheaval due to erroneous perception lead to a heightened state of awareness. Sometimes due to ignorance one becomes

343

agitated, confused and disturbed and, in that state, is not able to perceive objects, persons and situations correctly. Even in that state of mental commotion, although one may be dazed and confused and unable to perceive the external objects or situation correctly, one can enter an altered state where a different dimension of existence is experienced.

This is a dharana which each of us can try, because we all face situations where our mental patterns are disturbed and we are forced to experience internal commotion and upheaval. Often this upheaval is overpowering and we become immobilized, stunned and shocked. The mind loses its balance and enters a state of laya, or suspension of the thought process, as it is unable to think clearly. This is a natural form of dissolution, which can be utilized through dharana to enter into a higher dimension of experience. Even though the mind and energy have gone into suspension, if one is aware of what is happening at that moment and is able to utilize the energy generated by the commotion to focus the mind, he can enter into an altered state of consciousness.

In fact, this sloka says that in this way one can experience the form of Bhairava. This is an important concept which throws light on the laws that govern the unfoldment of the spiritual reality within us. This dharana indicates that even during times of commotion and upheaval when the faculties of perception and cognition are impaired, one can have an intense spiritual experience. This means that the faculties of external perception, although useful in our daily lives, are not at all essential for the highest experience. The spiritual experience does not belong to the realm of the head; it is governed by the heart and defies all logic. It can neither be understood by the mind, nor expressed in words.

It is often said that in order to have spiritual experience, you have to be innocent like a child. A child is not logical; he does crazy things. The child often does not perceive objects as they really are. He can pick up an expensive object and throw it down, as if it were worth nothing. He can put his hand in fire or jump from a great height while playing. He can shout, scream, cry and do all sorts of things which grownups would hesitate to do, simply because he has not yet started living through the head. The child is pure feeling and his actions are dominated by the heart; he does not have any trace of the devious mind. When you operate through the heart, it is easy to become absorbed in anything, even if you do not understand it correctly. It is only when you operate through the head that you have difficulty in concentration, because the mind always dissipates and distracts you.

Moreover, when you are in a state of mental upheaval, the emotions are very high and volatile and the heart comes into play more than the head. Thus it is easier to slip into a higher dimension, as the awareness is automatically catapulted wherever you focus it. You can utilize this dharana the next time you have a quarrel or separation from someone you love very much. At that moment the mind becomes tired and dejected, allowing the heart to rule the thought, speech and actions. Instead of becoming despondent at such times and submitting to the circumstance, use that situation for spiritual experience and upliftment.

## 113. Dharana of steady gazing

संप्रदायमिमं देवि शृणु सम्यग्वदाम्यहम् ।
कैवल्यं जायते सद्यो नेत्रयो:स्तब्धमात्रयो: ॥ 113 ॥

*Sampradaayam imam devi shrinu samyag vadaamyaham;*
*Kaivalyam jaayate sadyo netrayoh stabdhamaatrayoh.* (113)

### Anvay

*Sampradaayam*: tradition; *Imam*: this; *Devi*: O Devi; *Shrinu*: listen; *Samyak*: entire, whole; *Vadaami-aham*: I am telling; *Kaivalyam*: highest samadhi; *Jaayate*: arise; *Sadyah*: immediately; *Netrayoh*: both the eyes; *Stabdha-maatrayoh*: merely by making the eyes steady, fixed gaze.

### Translation

Listen, O Devi, as I am telling you about this (mystic) tradition in its entirety. If the eyes are fixed in a steady gaze (without blinking), kaivalya will arise immediately.

### Commentary

The tradition that deals with this knowledge is mystic and occult because it reveals that which cannot be understood by the mind or intellect. This form of knowledge is far too subtle to be perceived by the mental faculties. They have to be transcended in order to allow this knowledge to flow into you. In order to have this experience, you have to let go of the mind, ego and intellect. That is the real renunciation, and until those are renounced you cannot have that experience.

The method employed by tantra for revealing knowledge to the deserving seeker is transmission. The knowledge is transmitted directly through the mind in waves, not in words. This is why it is pure and untainted, because the medium through which it travels is unobstructed, and the

346

reception is immediate and clear. In this sloka Bhairava asks Devi to listen carefully, as he is transmitting the mystic knowledge of the tantric tradition in its entirety to her directly, in the same way that it has been transmitted down through the ages from guru to disciple.

The dharana which follows is the basic method for developing one-pointed concentration. It says that by fixing the eyes in a steady gaze, the state of kaivalya arises immediately. Steady and fixed gazing with the eyes open or closed is the main requisite for the practice of trataka, which is an important form of tantric meditation. Steadiness of the eyes leads to steadiness of the brain waves and subsequently the mind, as the rapid eye movement is eliminated.

The rapid eye movement continuously disturbs the brainwaves, even during sleep, which subsequently disturbs the mind and emotions. Even in character analysis it is observed that a person who moves his eyes rapidly is easily distracted and lacks concentration and willpower. Since concentration is the basis of dharana, it is easy to understand that steadiness of the eyes will gradually lead to success in dharana.

Kaivalya is the highest state of samadhi beyond the conscious, subconscious and unconscious mind. Kaivalya comes from the word *kevala*, meaning 'one only'. It is the superconscious state, where all duality is transcended and only the one universal consciousness remains. In the upanishadic texts kaivalya is the realization attained by establishing the awareness in the fourth state of consciousness known as turiya, the transcendental state. Kaivalya has many synonyms, for example, the Hindus call it moksha, or liberation, and the Buddhists call it nirvana.

This sloka asserts that by merely fixing the eyes in a steady gaze, the highest state of samadhi, known as kaivalya, can be attained. Although this may sound overstated, as you may feel that steady gazing is not at all difficult, it would be

347

better to try this dharana first before making that judgement. Steady and fixed gazing can be perfected for short durations through constant and repeated practice, but it is not easy to maintain for extended periods. The duration of the steady gazing is most important, because when it continues for protracted periods the brain waves are altered and the experience of kaivalya, or oneness with the highest reality, takes place.

Although this sloka does not specify whether the eyes should remain open or closed, one may assume that at the commencement of this dharana the eyes are made steady while they are open and fixed on a point, object, person or scene. Later that steadiness of the eyes is maintained even with the eyes closed, and the object or point of concentration is observed and experienced internally. This internal gaze is gradually developed until the awareness is dissolved into the object and becomes one with it. Then that object appears as the form of Bhairava, the supreme consciousness. The tantric practice of trataka, which Swami Satyananda has highlighted in his teachings, is a way to perfect this dharana.

## 114. Dharana on anahad nada

संकोचं कर्णयो: कृत्वा ह्यधोद्वारे तथैव च ।
अनच्कमहलं ध्यायन्विशेद्ब्रह्म सनातनम् ॥ 114 ॥

*Samkocham karnayoh kritvaa hyadhodvaare tathaiva cha;*
*Anachka mahalam dhyaayan vished brahma sanaatanam.* (114)

### Anvay

*Samkocham*: plugging; *Karnayoh*: of the ear; *Kritvaa*: having done; *Hi-adho-dvaare*: also the lower opening; *Tathaa-eva-cha*: in the same way; *anachka*: (unstruck sound); *Mahalam*: place or palace; *Dhyaayan*: meditating; *Vishet*: enters; *Brahma*: Brahma; *Sanaatanam*: eternal.

### Translation

Contracting (or closing) the openings of the ears and also the lower opening (reproductive/excretory organs) in the same way, and then meditating on the palace of the anahad (unstruck) sound within, one enters the eternal Brahma.

### Commentary

Suppose you are sitting in your room and you want to listen to your favourite kirtan but there is a loudspeaker playing film songs just outside, what will you do? You will shut the windows, close the doors, draw the curtains and fully insulate your room against outside intervention, so that you can listen to the music of your choice. This dharana asks you to do the same by closing the openings of the ears and lower openings.

The ears are closed by inserting the tips of the index fingers into the apertures. After plugging the ears in this way, the external sounds are no longer heard distinctly and the inner sounds become more prominent. The lower openings are closed by application of moola bandha, vajroli

349

mudra and ashwini mudra. Moola bandha is contraction of the perineum; vajroli mudra is contraction of the urinary passage, and ashwini mudra is contraction of the anal sphincter. By closing these three openings, the energies which are dissipated in the lower centres are rechanneled upward to the brain.

The sloka goes on to say that after closing the ears and the lower openings, one should meditate on the palace of anahad nada in order to hear the transcendental sound. Although the anahad nada emerges from the heart chakra, it is heard most vividly at bindu chakra, at the top back of the head. This inner music has been described in the songs of Mirabai, and in the couplets of Kabir, Surdas, Tulsidas and many other saints throughout the ages in whom the anahad nada was experienced. Mirabai heard it as the song of the peacock and the melody of the flute. Others have heard the roar of thunder, the clashing of cymbals, the blowing of the conch and the beating of drums.

These internal sounds can be heard only when the external perceptions are momentarily switched off by closing the doors through which they enter, so that the awareness tunes into the higher and more subtle frequencies of the inner ear. Nada is the first evolute of supreme consciousness when it begins to vibrate with the movement of energy, and thus is considered to be as refined as Brahman itself. Therefore, by meditating on the anahad nada, that eternal reality can be experienced.

## 115. Dharana on a deep well

कूपादिके महागर्ते स्थित्वोपरि निरीक्षणात् ।
अविकल्पमते: सम्यक् सद्यश्चित्तलय:स्फुटम् ॥ 115 ॥

*Koopaadike mahaagarte sthitvopari nireekshanaat;*
*Avikalpamateh samyak sadhyash chittalayah sphutam.* (115)

### Anvay

*Koopaadike*: in well, etc.; *Mahaagarte*: deep hole; *Sthitvaa-upari*: remaining at the top; *Nireekshanaat*: looking steadily; *Avikalpa mateh*: being free from vikalpas; *Samyak*: entirely; *Sadhyah*: immediately; *Chittalayah*: dissolution; *Sphutam*: manifest.

### Translation

Standing above a deep hole or well and looking steadily downward (into the abyss), the mind becomes entirely free of vikalpas and dissolution immediately manifests.

### Commentary

This dharana involves gazing down into a deep hole or well. Dharana is not a process of thinking, but of seeing and imagining. Imagination is the faculty through which you can create images out of thoughts and ideas, or even out of nothing. Suppose you are looking down into a deep hole or well and the end is not in sight. Being unable to determine the end, if you have developed the power of imagination, you can easily develop the image of infinity or eternity, where there is no beginning or end. As the awareness remains focused on this image, gradually the mind loses its customary support of thoughts and ideas, and becomes deep, hollow and endless, like the hole or well into which you are gazing.

With the development of this image, dissolution immediately manifests. The mind dissolves into the void, taking the ahamkara, buddhi and chitta along with it. This is the *mahayajna,* in which the individual chatushthaya antahkarana is offered as *ahuti,* or oblation, into the fire of consciousness. It is the greatest sacrifice and the greatest tapasya, which reaps the thousand-fold blessings in this life, as well as after it, and brings everlasting bliss.

## 116. Dharana on the omnipresent reality

यत्र यत्र मनो याति बाह्ये वाभ्यन्तरेऽपि वा ।
तत्र तत्र शिवावस्था व्यापकत्वात्क्व यास्यति ॥ 116 ॥

*Yatra yatra mano yaati baahye vaabhyantare'pi vaa;*
*Tatra tatra shivaavasthaa vyaapakatvaat kva yaasyati.* (116)

### Anvay

*Yatra yatra*: wherever; *Manah*: mind; *Yaati*: moves; *Baahye*: outwards; *Vaa*: or; *Abhyantare-api vaa*: inwards also; *Tatra tatra*: there; *Shiva-avasthaa*: state of shiva; *Vyaapakatvaat*: all-pervasiveness; *Kva*: where; *Yaasyati*: will go.

### Translation

Wherever the mind moves, whether outwards or inwards, there the all-pervasive state of shiva will go.

### Commentary

The object of this dharana is the omnipresent state, which is everywhere, outside and inside, at the same time. Since Shiva is omnipresent, where will the mind go to avoid Him? Shiva is the name given to that all-pervading reality. In 'Chamakam', an ancient vedic invocation to that omnipresent reality, its presence has been acknowledged in everything from inert matter to the highest creation. *Chamakam* means 'that which shines' and here it alludes to that reality which shines in everything. There is nothing in this world in which it is not present. We shine on account of its presence.

This dharana once again emphasizes that the object of concentration does not need much deliberation. Wherever your mind goes, whether inward or outward, you will find that reality. But in order to perceive it, you need to develop philosophical attention. Otherwise it will just pass you by, and you will never know it. Many people have seen an apple fall from the tree, but Newton alone had the philosophical attention to perceive the law of gravity when he observed that. It is that type of attention which you have to acquire in order to perceive Shiva wherever the mind wanders, whether outside or inside. That type of attention is only possible if you perfect the art of dharana.

## 117. Dharana on poornatva

यत्र यत्राक्षमार्गेण चैतन्यं व्यज्यते विभो: ।
तस्य तन्मात्रधर्मित्वाच्चिल्लयाद्भरितात्मता ॥ 117 ॥

*Yatra yatraakshamaargena chaitanyam vyajyate vibhoh;*
*Tasya tanmaatradharmitvaach chillayaad bharitaatmataa. (117)*

### Anvay

*Yatra yatra*: wherever; *Akshamaargena*: way or medium through sight; *Chaitanyam*: consciousness; *Vyajyate*: to lead, to go; *Vibhoh*: omnipresent, being everywhere; *Tasya*: of that; *Tanmaatra*: that alone; *Dharmitvaat*: from contemplation of that (object) being of the same nature as the supreme; *Chitlayaat*: from the absorption of the mind; *Bhritaa-aatmataa*: state of full consciousness, or poornatva.

### Translation

Wherever the consciousness leads through the channel of the eyes, by contemplation on that object alone being of the same nature as that of the supreme, absorption of mind and the state of poornatva are experienced.

### Commentary

It is important to realize that the very same senses which draw the awareness outwards and bind it to the gross experience lead it to the realization of the highest consciousness. It is only a matter of converting the gross perception of the senses into a subtle form of the same energy. It is wrong to believe that the indriyas, or senses, have to die before that transcendental experience is realized. The senses are not extinguished, instead they are transformed. Whereas in the gross experience the senses are illumined by the antahkarana, comprising manas, chitta, buddhi and ahamkara, in the transcendental experience the

355

senses are illumined by the Self. They shine with the light of consciousness. Thus, even in the transcendental state, one still sees, hears, smells, tastes and touches, although this happens in the absence of an object to cause it.

This dharana leads to *poornatva*, the state of fullness. While describing that state the first mantra of *Ishavasya Upanishad* says, "If you take out the full from the full, the full alone remains." That highest reality is *poorna*, or the nature of fullness. Although all creation, animate and inanimate, has emerged from it, still it retains its fullness and completeness. Ordinarily, when you remove a part of any substance, the original mass is depleted. It does not remain full or whole anymore. In giving something out, it loses its completeness, but this is not the case with Brahman. Although the supreme reality resides in each and every speck of creation, it ever remains whole, undivided and complete. It is never diminished or depleted.

This is inconceivable to the finite mind because it is out of the range of objective experience. This mind has never witnessed such a phenomenon. Everything perceived by this mind diminishes, decays and dies from moment to moment. So how can it draw a parallel? Therefore, it is said that in order to have that range of experience, the mind has to be absorbed into a higher state. According to this dharana, the mind can be absorbed by focusing on those very sense perceptions that bind the mind to the finite world. Those sense perceptions are also forms of that supreme reality and are pervaded by its essence. By focusing on that sense experience and realizing it to be of the same essence as the supreme, the doorway opens to the experience of poornatva, or completeness.

## 118. Dharana on the state of Brahma

क्षुताद्यन्ते भये शोके गह्वरे वा रणाद्द्रुते ।
कुतूहले क्षुधाद्यन्ते ब्रह्मसत्तामयी दशा ॥ 118 ॥

*Kshutaadyante bhaye shoke gahvare vaa ranaad drute;*
*Kutoohale kshudhaadyante brahmasattaamayee dashaa.* (118)

### Anvay

*Kshut-aadi-ante*: at the beginning and end of sneezing; *Bhaye*: in terror; *Shoke*: in sorrow; *Gahvare*: in confusion; *Vaa ranaat drute*: or fleeing from the battlefield; *Kutoohale*: in curiosity; *Kshudhaa-aadi-ante*: at the beginning and end of hunger, etc.; *Brahmasattaa-mayee*: the external existence of Brahma; *Dashaa*: state.

### Translation

At the beginning and end of sneezing, in terror, sorrow or confusion, when fleeing from a battlefield, during (keen) curiosity, or at the onset or appeasement of hunger, that state is the external existence of Brahma.

### Commentary

This dharana illustrates that no experience is devoid of the essence of Brahman. In fact, everything that you experience in life, from the simple act of sneezing to the feeling of curiosity, can lead you to that supreme realization. In fact, you can achieve that state this very moment, no matter what you are doing. Here and now, in a split second, you can reach that state of awareness. That experience is more intimate than your breath, without which you cannot live for even a second. All you have to do is learn how to focus into that ever-present state through the practice of dharana. Through dharana your awareness or inner eye is trained to focus on a chosen object or situation, as well as to remain

357

focused for an extended period of time. Once you are able to do this, it does not matter what you meditate on, whether you practise with the eyes open or closed, or whether you are looking inwards or outwards. The result is the same experience of the ever-expanding state of Brahman. The important point is that you should learn to direct and fix the awareness on the present moment, no matter what that moment holds for you. If it is a sneeze, direct the totality of your awareness to it and you will find there the eternal existence of Brahman or that ever-expanding consciousness.

The analogy of milk and its derivatives may be used to explain this further. No matter what product you make out of milk, whether it is cheese, chocolate, butter or yoghurt, you will discover the presence of milk when you subject it to scrutiny, although it may not be apparent at first. In the same way, *Brahma satta*, as stated in the sloka, is the pervading reality of all your experiences, both subjective and objective.

## 119. Dharana on memories

वस्तुषु स्मर्यमाणेषु दृष्टे देशे मनस्त्यजेत् ।
स्वशरीरं निराधारं कृत्वा प्रसरति प्रभुः ॥ 119 ॥

*Vastushu smaryamaaneshu drishte deshe manas tyajet;*
*Svashareeram niraadhaaram kritvaa prasarati prabhuh.* (119)

### Anvay

*Vastushu*: in objects; *Smaryamaaneshu*: memorable; *Drishte*: seen; *Deshe*: land, country; *Manah-tyajet*: leave the mind; *Sva-shareeram*: one's own body; *Niraadhaaram*: supportless; *Kritvaa*: making; *Prasarati*: pervades (all); *Prabhuh*: mighty Lord.

### Translation

Leave the mind aside when memorable objects of the past, such as one's country or land arise, making one's body supportless; then the omnipresent and mighty Lord manifests.

### Commentary

In this dharana the idea is to leave the mind aside by taking the help of memories, which are larger than life. For example, ones country or homeland generates feelings of brotherhood, universality of spirit and oneness with a cause. It is easy to lose oneself in memorable experiences about one's nation, birthplace, family or any such objects. For example, soldiers willingly go into battle and die for their motherland because they rise above the limited mind. All of their fears and attachments are set aside and they remain one-pointed in their duty.

In the same way, one should lose oneself in dharana on any memorable object one has known in the past. By losing oneself in such memories, the body and mind become

359

supportless, as the mind is absorbed in another reality. When one ceases to project oneself in any way, either through the body or mind, then the Lord, who is the real ruler of the body and mind, reveals himself. Thus one begins to perceive how he is present in each and every cell and atom of one's body and mind.

## 120. Dharana on unmani

क्वचिद्वस्तुनि विन्यस्य शनैर्दृष्टिं निवर्तयेत् ।
तज्ज्ञानं चित्तसहितं देवि शून्यालयो भवेत् ॥ 120 ॥

*Kvachid vastuni vinyasya shanair drishtim nivartayet;*
*Taj jnaanam chittasahitam devi shoonyaalayo bhavet.* (120)

### Anvay

*Kvachit-vastuni*: in some objects; *Vinyasya*: imposing, placing;
*Shanaih drishtim*: momentary gaze; *Nivartayet*: withdrawn;
*Tat-jnaanam*: that knowledge (impression); *Chitta-sahitam*:
with the consciousness or with the thought and impression;
*Devi*: O Goddess; *Shoonya-aalayah*: abode of the void; *Bhavet*:
becomes.

### Translation

O Goddess, momentarily casting the gaze on some object
and slowly withdrawing it with the knowledge and impression
of that object, one becomes the abode of the void.

### Commentary

This dharana describes a tantric mudra known as unmani,
where the eyes are open, gazing outward, but the awareness
or attention is turned inward. At that moment one is looking
inside and seeing something invisible to others present.
This mudra is also known as bhairavi mudra in some tantric
texts.

This may have happened to you many times. While
looking at something, the awareness slips into another
dimension and you take your mental impression of that
object into that other dimension. However, there the
impression of that object alters and you may perceive it
differently. If you continue to hold on to the impression of
that object, it will continue to change, as the mind goes

361

deeper and deeper, until gradually you enter the abode of the void.

In this dharana once again the medium of sense impression is utilized to enter an altered state of mind, such as the experience of shoonya within oneself. The trick lies in transforming the impression of the object you cast your gaze on into an eternal reality, where it is not subject to death and decay. This is only possible when the awareness, which is infinite and immortal, assumes the form of that object through dharana, or concentration.

## 121. Dharana on intuition

भक्त्युद्रेकाद्विरक्तस्य यादृशी जायते मतिः ।
सा शक्तिः शाङ्करी नित्यं भावयेत्तां ततः शिवः ॥ 121 ॥

*Bhaktyudrekaad viraktasya yaadrishee jaayate matih;*
*Saa shaktih shaankaree nityam bhaavayet taam tatah Shivah. (121)*

### Anvay

*Bhakti-udrekaat*: from intense devotion; *Viraktasya*: of the detached one; *Yaadrishee*: that which; *Jaayate*: arises, emerges; *Matih*: intuition; *Saa shaktih*: that shakti; *Shaankaree*: of Shankara; *Nityam*: regularly, perpetually; *Bhaavayet-taam*: contemplating on that (shakti); *Tatah*: there; *Shivah*: Shiva.

### Translation

That intuition which emerges from the intense devotion of one who is perfectly detached is known as the shakti of Shankara. By contemplating regularly on that (shakti), Shiva (is revealed) there.

### Commentary

The faculties of perception bestowed on man are many layered. As you develop one layer you are led to another, and with each unfolding the source of perception becomes more and more subtle.

The first level of perception is instinct, which belongs to the realm of the senses. Knowledge gained through instinct is an automatic process that does not involve thinking, analysis or logic. Instinct is an inbuilt system of perception in all living beings from the mineral and plant to animal and human life. Intelligence is higher than instinct and belongs to the realm of the mind. It incorporates a high level of understanding as well as the ability to apply knowledge in a constructive and progressive manner. Beyond intelligence is intellect, a discriminating faculty, which belongs to the realm of buddhi.

Above these faculties is intuition, or prajna, which belongs to the realm of the higher mind and has access to the unlimited knowledge abounding in the universe. Intuition is able to grasp waves and frequencies that are far too subtle for the senses, mind or intellect. It is a higher source of knowledge and in this realm there is no barrier of past, present and future. Through intuition one can even know what will happen in the distant future or what has happened in the distant past. Abhinavgupta, the famed pundit of Kashmir Shaivism, in his magnum opus on tantra known as *Tantraloka*, has termed this intuitive awareness as *pratibha samvitti*, a term which implies that this state is full of the excellence of the Divine.

Intuition is the form of energy which is known as *shankara*, and this state can be developed by practising intense devotion, or bhakti, on a person who is perfectly detached, such as the guru. Intense devotion is a state of total oneness and unity with the object of devotion. The act of worship alone is not devotion unless it is accompanied by surrender, which leads to unity and to the birth of intuition. Regular contemplation on the shakti, known as prajna. or intuition, leads to *chaitanya,* or illumination of the shiva-like nature.

This is the first dharana to utilize the powerful tool of bhakti, or intense devotion. About bhakti, Swami Satyananda has said that the brain waves of a person who is absorbed in intense devotion are phenomenal. Bhakti grips you and supercedes everything that you may have been feeling, wanting, desiring or thinking about in your life. It is a state of total one-pointedness, which enables the achievement of anything you set your mind upon. The only prerequisite for bhakti is purity of heart and feelings. When you feel bhakti towards a person who is totally detached, you become detached as a consequence. This leads to intuition, because detachment, or vairagya, is the breeding ground for intuition. Attachment leads to clouding of vision and perception, but the detached mind has a higher range of faculties at his disposal.

## 122. Dharana on a particular object

वस्त्वन्तरे वेद्यमाने सर्ववस्तुषु शून्यता ।
तामेव मनसा ध्यात्वा विदितोऽपि प्रशाम्यति ॥ 122 ॥

*Vastvantare vedyamaane sarvavastushu shoonyataa;*
*Taam eva manasaa dhyaatvaa vidito'pi prashaamyati.* (122)

### Anvay

*Vastu-antare*: in a particular object; *Vedyamaane*: perceives;
*Sarva-vastushu*: in all objects; *Shoonyataa*: void; *Taam-eva*:
that verily; *Manasaa*: by the mind; *Dhyaatvaa*: contemplating;
*Viditah-api*: even when known; *Prashaamyati*: rests in
tranquillity.

### Translation

When one perceives a particular object, vacuity is established
regarding all other objects. Contemplating on that (vacuity)
verily, even though the particular object is still known or
perceived, the mind rests in tranquillity.

### Commentary

Dharana on one particular object or symbol leads to vacuity
and the exclusion of all other objects, thoughts or ideas
from the mind. The mind which is accustomed to experiencing many conflicting and complementary thoughts,
feelings, ideas and responses at the same time begins to feel
empty and vacuous. Through concentration on an object
the mind becomes calm and its normal chatter is reduced.
Although the mind is focused on one particular object, still
some thoughts may arise in relation to that object. However,
the vacuum created by the absence of all other objects leads
to a state of *shanti*, or tranquillity and peace, as the ripples of
energy created by several objects are absent.

## 123. Dharana on purity

किंचिज्ज्ञैर्या स्मृता शुद्धि: सा शुद्धि: शाम्भुदर्शने ।
न शुचिर्ह्यशुचिस्तस्मान्निर्विकल्प: सुखी भवेत् ॥ 123 ॥

*Kimchijjnair yaa smritaa shuddhih saa shuddhih shambhu darshane;*
*Na shuchir hyashuchis tasmaan nirvikalpah sukhee bhavet. (123)*

### Anvay

*Kinchit-jnaihyaa*: knowing a little, which; *Smritaa*: remembered;
*Shuddhih*: purity; *Saa shuddhih*: that purity; *Shambhu darshane*:
in the experience of shambhu or shiva; *Na*: not; *Shuchih hi
ashuchih*: neither pure nor impure; *Tasmaat*: of that; *Nirvikalpah*: without any vikalpas; *Sukhee bhavet*: attains happiness.

### Translation

What people of little understanding believe to be purity is
neither pure nor impure to one who has experienced shiva.
Nirvikalpa, or freedom from vikalpas, is the real purification
by which one attains happiness.

### Commentary

In order to progress in dharana it is very necessary to
understand vikalpa and how it obstructs the flow of awareness. Only the person who has mastered dharana is free of
vikalpa, and such a person is rare. Vikalpa literally means
'option', which implies that it is never single. It always has a
dual implication, such as pure and impure, good and bad,
hot and cold, love and hate, beautiful and ugly, fat and thin,
short and tall. As soon as you think of purity, automatically
the notion of impurity will come up in your mind. Whenever
you think of something beautiful, the notion of ugliness will
spontaneously spring up. This thought and counter-thought
process is a natural mechanism, which prevents the mind
from becoming one-pointed.

You can immediately attain the state of dhyana or meditation by ridding the mind of these vikalpas. Thus great emphasis is laid on developing a state of mind which is devoid of vikalpas. The lower mind is full of vikalpas and the higher mind is able to rise above vikalpas. According to the Shaivite philosophy, the term 'purity' implies precisely this: a state of mind devoid of vikalpas. Those of little knowledge understand purity and impurity as social and moral values, but one who has understood the state of shiva attributes purity to a state of mind. One who controls the vikalpas and influences the nature of the mind transcends these ideas and attains inner peace.

## 124. Dharana on the non-dual reality

सर्वत्र भैरवो भाव: सामान्येष्वपि गोचर: ।
न च तद्व्यतिरेकेण परोऽस्तीत्यद्वया गति: ॥ 124 ॥

*Sarvatra bhairavo bhaavah saamaanyeshvapi gocharah;*
*Na cha tadvyatirekena paro'steetyadvayaa gatih.* (124)

### Anvay

*Sarvatra*: everywhere; *Bhairavah-bhaavah*: reality of bhairava;
*Saamaanyeshu-api*: even in ordinary people; *Gocharah*: dwells;
*Na cha parah*: nothing other than; *Tat vyatirekena*: with the
exception of that; *Asteeti*: exists; *Advayaa*: one without a
second, non-dual; *Gatih*: attains.

### Translation

The reality of bhairava dwells everywhere, even in ordinary
people. By contemplating thus, "There is nothing other
than Him," one attains the non-dual state (of homogenous
awareness).

### Commentary

Here the focus of dharana is on the one reality without a
second, which is everywhere and in all beings. By rising
above the state of duality, we attain homogenous awareness.
In this state the energy flows freely and the concentration
remains unbroken and one-pointed. This realization leads
to a feeling of unity with all beings because the idea of
difference is lost. Gradually, we are able to perceive this
reality in all beings, even in the most ordinary or wretched
person.

This is a very high state of awareness, which brings
about the state of total emancipation. Ordinarily each of us
perceives ourselves as different from others. Even if we have
a deep affinity for, feel in tune with or love someone very

369

much, this feeling of difference persists. We are unable to transcend this differentiation because our understanding of unity is merely intellectual. It is a concept that we may have understood and accepted but are unable to apply ourselves, even with conscious effort.

Swami Sivananda, an enlightened sage of the twentieth century, who had attained this unified state of mind during his lifetime, exhibited many of the rare tendencies such a person may have. He had *sama drishti*, or equal vision for all. He was free from raga and dwesha, like and dislike, and was full of compassion and love. He was always in a state of divine ecstasy and bliss, and had a magnetic charm which attracted others to him, like bees are attracted to honey. He had absolute vairagya, or absence of craving of any sort, and was simple and pure. The divine grace flowed freely through him and he became a channel or medium of transmission of the transcendental knowledge, which he gave to others. He became a *videhamukta*, or liberated soul, while living. This was recounted by his disciple and my guru, Swami Satyananda, who lived with him and served him in Rishikesh for twelve years.

When there is total emancipation of the individual, he is able to perceive his ties with each and every being in creation. Just as a river merges into the ocean and loses its individuality and limitations, in the same way the emancipated individual loses his individuality or ego when the finite mind expands into the cosmic mind. Even while living in the physical body, he is able to transcend the body and becomes pure awareness, to the extent that the limitations of the body no longer apply to him, and he transcends all the physical barriers and boundaries.

This sloka reiterates that by contemplation on the non-dual nature of your existence, you will gradually realize your universal nature.

## 125. Dharana on equality

सम: शत्रौ च मित्रे च समो मानावमानयो: ।
ब्रह्मण: परिपूर्णत्वादिति ज्ञात्वा सुखी भवेत् ॥ 125 ।

*Samah shatrau cha mitre cha samo maanaavamaanayoh;*
*Brahmanah paripoornatvaad iti jnaatvaa sukhee bhavet.* (125)

### Anvay

*Samah*: equality; *Shatrau cha mitre cha*: either in friend or foe;
*Samah*: equal; *Maana-avamaanayoh*: in honour and dishonour;
*Brahmanah*: the Brahma (supreme consciousness); *Pari-poornatvaatiti*: full in itself; *Jnaatvaa*: knowing; *Sukhee*: happy;
*Bhavet*: becomes.

### Translation

One who makes no distinction between friend and foe, honour and dishonour, knowing Brahman to be full in itself (all pervading), becomes supremely happy.

### Commentary

In this dharana the focus is on non-distinction or equality of vision, even amidst opposites. To distinguish between friend and enemy or honour and dishonour is the quality of the ordinary mind and the average person. But exceptional minds experience equality in all beings and in all acts, whether they are beneficial or detrimental, pleasant or unpleasant. This means that such a mind has surpassed the influence of raga and dwesha, like and dislike, and experiences everything and everybody as a receptacle of that all-pervading Brahman.

This realization leads to the ultimate happiness because one experiences eternity. The notion of death is replaced with the firm conviction that, although the body ultimately decomposes, there exists within it the tattwa known as atman,

371

or self, which is immortal. Each individual atman is connected to every other, as well as to the universal atman. This
understanding results in completeness, wholeness and
happiness, because the very cause of unhappiness is the
belief that you are mortal and subject to death and decay.
But once you experience the immortal atman which resides
within, all unhappiness, fear and apprehension will be
eradicated.

## 126. Dharana in between two opposites

न द्वेषं भावयेत्क्वापि न रागं भावयेत्क्वचित् ।
रागद्वेषविनिर्मुक्तौ मध्ये ब्रह्म प्रसर्पति ॥ 126 ॥

*Na dvesham bhaavayet kvaapi na raagam bhaavayet kvachit;*
*Raagadveshavinirmuktau madhye brahma prasarpati.* (126)

### Anvay

*Na*: not; *Dvesham*: enmity; *Bhaavayet kva-api*: should ever think; *Na raagam*: nor the friendship; *Bhaavayet kvachit*: should think ever; *Raaga dvesha vinirmuktau*: being free from friendship and enmity; *Madhye*: in between; *Brahma*: Brahma (supreme consciousness); *Prasarpati*: blooms.

### Translation

One should never think in terms of friendship or enmity. Being free from (this idea) of friend and foe, in between the brahma bhava, or nature of supreme consciousness, blooms.

### Commentary

In this dharana the awareness is focused in the middle, in-between the two opposites. A liberated mind is never attached to any idea or concept. It has a broader vision and is not bound by persons, places and events like the ordinary mind. This is the quality of a universal mind. *Brahma bhava*, or the nature of supreme consciousness, is sure to blossom in such a mind because it is free-flowing like a river, forever moving, expanding, experiencing and learning.

In this dharana once again the concept of the gap between the two opposites is used to effectively eliminate the idea of difference and duality. This concept is extremely popular in tantra, which has always advocated that it is unwise to widen the gap between two opposites, such as love and hate, life and death, etc. On the other hand, it has recommended uniting the two opposites in the middle, so that you can experience unity. This principle is applied by tantra to every facet of existence, whether it is the breath in the form of inhalation and exhalation, the two vayus of prana and apana that flow in opposite directions within the body, the concepts of time and space or energy and consciousness.

## 127. Dharana on bhairava as the unknowable void

यदवेद्यं यदग्राह्यं यच्छून्यं यदभावगम् ।
तत्सर्वं भैरवं भाव्यं तदन्ते बोधसंभव: ॥ 127 ॥

*Yad avedyam yadagraahyam yach chhoonyam yad abhaavagam;*
*Tat sarvam bhairavam bhaavyam tadante bodhasambhavah.* (127)

### Anvay

*Yat-avedyam*: that which cannot be known; *Yat-agraahyam*: that which cannot be grasped; *Yat-shoonyam*: that which is void; *Yat-abhaavagam*: that which cannot be imagined; *Tat sarvam*: all that; *Bhairavam*: bhairava; *Bhaavyam*: contemplating; *Tadante*: at the end; *Bodha sambhavah*: realization takes place.

### Translation

By contemplating on bhairava as all that which is void and cannot be known, grasped or imagined, at the end realization takes place.

### Commentary

In order to become self-realized you have to step out of yourself. It is a bit like committing suicide. You take the decision to jump into the ocean without knowing what lies in store for you. You may drown or you may not; both are acceptable. You have no conditions. In the same way, by contemplating on that supreme reality without any preconceived or preconditioned notions, self-realization takes place. In other words through a process of negation or realizing what the state of bhairava is not, you arrive at the realization of what it actually is, the great void, which cannot be qualified by the mind.

The word *bhavyam* is more than just contemplation, as it implies a combination of understanding and feeling. The

375

head and heart combine to arrive at an experience of the void, which is bhairava, by inferring what it is not and thereby developing an intuitive awareness of the state of bhairava. For example, suppose a blind man was asked to describe an object which he had never seen, grasped, known or imagined. How would he achieve this?

First of all, he would go through a process of inference, trying to understand that object through whatever sensory faculties he could use, such as hearing, touching, tasting and smelling. If the senses prove inadequate, he would try to understand the object through the mind on the basis of his past experiences in relation to other objects by comparing it with them and negating what it is not. If that proved inadequate, he would try to reason through his intellect and discrimination in order to arrive at a conclusion. If even that proved inadequate, he would try to understand it through his intuitive awareness, which can know without the medium of the senses, mind, or intellect. In the same way this dharana asks you to awaken the intuitive awareness, which alone gives the experience of bhairava.

## 128. Dharana on outer space

नित्ये निराश्रये शून्ये व्यापके कलनोज्झिते ।
बाह्याकाशे मन: कृत्वा निराकाशं समाविशेत् ॥ 128 ॥

*Nitye niraashraye shoonye vyaapake kalanojjhite;*
*Baahyaakaashe manah kritvaa niraakaasham samaavishet.* (128)

### Anvay

*Nitye*: eternal; *Niraashraye*: supportless; *Shoonye*: void;
*Vyaapake*: omnipresent; *Kalana-ujjhite*: beyond estimation or
calculation; *Baahya-aakaashe*: in the outer space; *Manah
kritvaa*: placing the mind; *Niraakaasham*: formless, unmanifest dimension; *Samaavishet*: enters.

### Translation

Fixing the mind in the outer space, which is eternal, without
support, void, omnipresent and beyond estimation or calculation, one enters into the formless, unmanifest dimension.

### Commentary

In this dharana the awareness is focused on outer space, the
vast and limitless void from which the entire universe emanates.
The moment you set a definite boundary to any object within
space and time, it becomes finite, with a beginning and an
end. In other words it becomes limited. But when you
concentrate your mind on the external space or void, which
has no beginning or end, it assumes an omnipresent quality,
which is beyond any calculation or estimate. This is an
extremely useful method for attaining laya, or dissolution, of
mind. By fixing the mind on that space, which is endless and
limitless, the awareness enters that void and experiences the
formless, unmanifest dimension.

This practice is also known as *bahyakasha* dharana,
concentration on the external or outer space.

## 129. Dharana on thoughtlessness

यत्र यत्र मनो याति तत्तत्तेनैव तत्क्षणम् ।
परित्यज्यानवस्थित्या निस्तरङ्गस्ततो भवेत् ॥ 129 ॥

*Yatra yatra mano yaati tattat tenaiva tatkshanam;*
*Parityajyaanavasthityaa nistarangas tato bhavet.* (129)

### Anvay

*Yatra yatra*: wherever; *Mano yaati*: mind dwells; *Tat tat*: that, that; *Tenaiva*: that verily; *Tatkshanam*: that moment; *Parityajya*: leaving aside; *Anavasthityaa*: by being supportless; *Nistarangah*: free from commotion; *Tatah-bhavet*: then becomes.

### Translation

Wherever the mind dwells, casting that aside that very moment, the mind becomes supportless and free from disturbance.

### Commentary

This dharana is a great mental exercise intended for those who have superfluous and unending thoughts. Cast aside every thought that arises in your mind at the very moment it springs up. The mind thrives on thoughts and will gradually weaken, faint and collapse due to starvation, just as the physical body would if it were deprived of food. Thoughts nourish the mind, giving it vigour and life, so it is natural that the mind craves for thoughts. But in this dharana you have to wilfully deny the thoughts. In this way the commotion caused by the generation of thoughts gradually ceases, and because there is no movement of mental energy, the mind becomes still. Wherever there is stillness, peace and tranquillity descend.

At another level this dharana is also intended for the sadhaka who has already developed a focused and concentrated mind and is able to conceptualize or visualize an object of meditation clearly within. When this stage of dharana is attained, then one should merge with the object or concept on which the mind dwells. In this way, the mind that is supported by the object will immediately become supportless and will enter into a state of suspension. At this level of dharana, after painstakingly developing the image, concept or sound of the internal object, one endeavours to dissolve the mind into it. It is something like sugar dissolving into milk. The mind becomes the object. In this way, the mental waves which generate the object cease and the mind becomes absolutely still, free from any modification.

## 130. Dharana on the word Bhairava

भया सर्वं रवयति सर्वदो व्यापकोऽखिले ।
इति भैरवशब्दस्य सन्ततोच्चारणाच्छिव: ॥ 130 ॥

*Bhayaa sarvam ravayati sarvado vyaapako' khile;*
*Iti bhairavashabdasya santatochchaaranaach chhivah.* (130)

### Anvay

*Bhayaa*: fear and terror; *Sarvam*: all; *Ravayati*: crying and howling; *Sarvadah*: all giver; *Vyaapakah*: all-pervading; *Akhile*: entire universe; *Iti*: like this; *Bhairavashabdasya*: of the word Bhairava; *Santatah*: constant, uninterrupted; *Uchchaaranaat*: from pronouncing; *Shivah*: Shiva.

### Translation

The word Bhairava denotes he who dispels all fear and terror, who howls and cries, who gives all, and who pervades the entire universe (manifest and unmanifest). He who constantly repeats the word bhairava becomes one with Shiva.

### Commentary

This dharana utilizes the word Bhairava as a mantra to focus the awareness upon. Shiva and Bhairava are one and the same. They are both manifestations of that supreme consciousness in different stages of experience. Bhairava is derived from the root *ravayati*, which literally means 'to howl' or 'to cry'. A person who enters this state is likely to experience these blood-curdling sounds or may emit such sounds himself. The howling of Bhairava is the cry of separation from that universal consciousness, which one perceives within his reach, but not yet totally in his grasp.

Bhairava is that state of consciousness which one enters just before the ultimate experience, which is known as Shiva.

In tantric allegory, Bhairava is the chief security officer of Shiva, whose scrutiny must be faced before one can meet Shiva face to face. In this state all fear is dispelled and the sadhaka becomes fearless and able to face anything. This state gives the experience of everything that exists in the universe being pervaded by Bhairava. In this dharana one attains that state through repetition of the word Bhairava, which leads to Shiva.

This dharana is based on the practice of japa and the sloka asserts that the word Bhairava is itself a mantra, which can induce the bhairava awareness, if repeated continuously. The same principle applies to the words Shiva, Durga or Kali, because they are made up of akshara or matrika, indestructible creative energy of the divine. According to Shaivism the manifest world is made up of different vibrations, which are produced through different combinations of sounds. These sounds are the fifty-two letters of the Sanskrit alphabet, known as matrikas, that collectively form the basis of the manifest world.

When the supreme consciousness assumes the form of letters, it is known as *matrika shakti,* or the power of letters. In the second sloka of this text Devi asks Shiva if he is the power contained in the letters or sounds from which all the mantras have been formed. Shiva replies to this question in the negative, because *shabda rasi,* or the garland of letters, is not the Divine itself, but a form which it assumes in the process of manifestation to enact the process of creation in its entirety. Although these letters are not the Divine itself, the Divine can be realized through their medium, because they are the form which the divine consciousness has assumed and thus are full of its creative power.

The sacred science of Shiva, known as Shaivism, further says that these matras or letters, known as matrika, are the cause of all knowledge and understanding as well as the source of limited knowledge. The letters combine to form

381

words and words combine to form sentences, which convey meaning, and thus understanding is born through the power of matrika. This understanding gives rise to feelings. All that we feel is born through the power of these words, so you can say that it is through these matrikas that we feel the dualities of life, such as good and bad, pleasure and pain, insult and praise.

This is how the world of duality is born through the power of matrika, on account of which you enjoy or suffer in this world. The moment you are able to understand the true nature of matrika, you rise above its limitations and it can no longer keep you bound to the world of duality. This is how repetition of the word Bhairava liberates you from bondage and ignorance of the true nature of Shiva, the supreme consciousness.

## 131. Dharana on Tat (that highest reality)

अहं ममेदमित्यादि प्रतिपत्तिप्रसङ्गत: ।
निराधारे मनो याति तद्ध्यानप्रेरणाच्छमी ॥ 131 ॥

*Aham mamedam ityaadi pratipattiprasangatah;*
*Niraadhaare mano yaati taddhyaanapreranaach chhamee.* (131)

### Anvay

*Aham*: I; *Mama-idam*: this is mine; *Ityaadi*: and so on; *Pratti-patti*: assertion; *Prasangatah*: at the time of; *Niraadhaare*: supportless; *Manah*: mind; *Yaati*: goes; *Tat-dhyaana*: meditation on That; *Preranaat-shamee*: from inspiration.

### Translation

At the time of asserting, "I am," "This is mine," and so on, by inspired meditation on Tat (that highest reality), the mind becomes supportless.

### Commentary

Ego is the asserting influence in our lives. If we did not have ego, we would cease to assert ourselves on any issue. We would simply exist, not knowing that we do so, in much the same way as vegetables, plants and animals do. On account of aham, the sense of 'I-ness', we begin to know ourselves and identify with each and everything around us. Ego is the basis of our relationship with the world and gives us the identity which separates us from others. Thus, we begin to feel our separation from the rest of creation and under the influence of ego we develop the ideas of ownership, possessiveness and attachment.

Ironically, that very ego which gives rise to separation has to be exploded in order to have the experience of unified existence. In other words, awareness of ego leads to that supreme tattwa that does not depend on anything for support. Ego stays with the sadhaka for a long time on his spiritual journey. Traces of ego are found even in the heightened state of savikalpa samadhi on account of which the consciousness returns to the earthly plane. It is only when the consciousness reaches nirvikalpa samadhi that the ego is dissolved into that supreme tattwa.

This theory is the basis of this dharana, which asks one to look beyond the ego to discover the subtler tattwas of which it is composed. In this way the mind becomes supportless and the Self is realized. In applying this dharana, one should understand that the ego is under the influence of the gunas and thus has three shades of manifestation. Tamasic ahamkara is responsible for dwesha, or repulsion, which intensifies the painful and negative experiences, creating feelings of doubt, insecurity, fear, procrastination and apprehension.

Rajasic ahamkara is responsible for raga, or attraction, and is thus a self-motivated force that kindles dynamic activity through the feeling of I-ness or individuality within the person. Eventually this dynamism of rajasic ahamkara leads to dissipation of thought and action. Sattwic ahamkara is a balanced state in between rajas and tamas, attraction and repulsion, which is responsible for the notion of 'I am'. This form of ahamkara acts as a catalyst in the process of self-realization, as it is closest to that highest reality. In other words the pure form of aham, or the ego principle, is very near to the experience of transcendence.

## 132. Dharana on divine attributes

नित्यो विभुर्निराधारो व्यापकश्चाखिलाधिपः ।
शब्दान् प्रतिक्षणं ध्यायन् कृतार्थोऽर्थानुरूपतः ॥ 132 ॥

*Nityo vibhur niraadhaaro vyaapakash chaakhilaadhipah;*
*Shabdaan pratikshanam dhyaayan kritaartho'rthaanuroopatah.* (132)

### Anvay

*Nityah*: eternal; *Vibhuh*: omnipresent; *Niraadhaarah*: support-less; *Vyaapakah-cha*: all-pervasive; *Akhila-adhipah*: master of the entire universe; *Shabdaan*: words; *Pratikshanam*: every moment; *Dhyaayan*: meditating; *Kritaarthah*: fulfilment; *Artha-anuroopatah*: according to the meaning of.

### Translation

Meditating every moment on the words: eternal, omnipresent, supportless, all-pervasive, master of the universe, one attains fulfilment in accordance with their meaning.

### Commentary

In this dharana the awareness is focused on the words which describe the divine attributes of the Lord of the universe. By concentrating on those qualities which describe his nature, such as eternal, omnipresent, all-pervading and devoid of support, one gradually develops experiences in accordance with the meaning of these words. There is a saying in English, "As one thinks, so one becomes." Thoughts make or break a man. If you think or contemplate on the divine attributes with total attention, then you can attract those qualities to manifest in you. This is a simple way of developing the divine experience, which any aspirant can try.

# 133. Dharana on the illusory nature of the world

अतत्त्वमिन्द्रजालाभमिदं सर्वमवस्थितम् ।
किं तत्त्वमिन्द्रजालस्य इति दार्ढ्याच्छमं व्रजेत् ॥ 133 ॥

*Atattvam indrajaalaabham idam sarvam avasthitam;*
*Kim tattvam indrajaalasya iti daardhyaach chhamam vrajet.* (133)

## Anvay

*Atattvam*: non-essence; *Indrajaalah-aabham*: jugglery, magical spectacle; *Idam*: this whole (world); *Sarvam*: all; *Avasthitam*: exists; *Kim*: what; *Tattvam*: tattwa, essence; *Indrajaalasya*: of the magic; *Iti*: like this; *Daardhyaat*: firmly, determined; *Shamam*: silence, peace; *Vrajet*: achieves.

## Translation

This world is (illusory) like magic, devoid of any essence. What essence exists in magic? Being firmly convinced of this, one attains peace.

## Commentary

This dharana reaffirms the vedantic aphorism: *Brahma satya; jagat mithya*: "Brahman alone is real; this world is illusion." This is the experience of those who have transcended the gross mind and entered into the dimension beyond form. Every object has a concrete form, but behind that form, which is visible to the naked eye, there is a subtle form that can be perceived only when the mind transcends the gross experience. In that state the same object will appear differently. Many seers attained that state and experienced the transcience of the world; thus they became truly detached from it.

They have given us details of their experiences, as the scientists today give us details of their experiments with matter. Just as we do not ignore the findings of the modern

386

scientists, it would be unwise to ignore the experiences of the seers who explored the uncharted regions of the consciousness. However, we have an advantage over them because we do not need to experiment. We can accept the illusory nature of this world and have no need to prove it. Being firmly convinced of the pronouncements of the sages, we can attain peace through this understanding alone.

## 134. Dharana on the changeless atman

आत्मनो निर्विकारस्य क्व ज्ञानं क्व च वा क्रिया ।
ज्ञानयत्ता बहिर्भावा अतः शून्यमिदं जगत् ॥ 134 ॥

*Aatmano nirvikaarasya kva jnaanam kva aacha vaa kriyaa;*
*Jnaanayattaa bahirbhaavaa atah shoonyam idam jagat.* (134)

### Anvay

*Aatmanah*: of the self, or atman; *Nirvikaarasya*: changeless;
*Kva*: how; *Jnaanam*: knowledge; *Kva cha vaa kriyaa*: what is
action; *Jnaanayattaa*: under the control of knowledge; *Bahih-
bhaavaa*: external objects; *Atah*: therefore; *Shoonyam-idam*:
this void; *Jagat*: universe.

### Translation

How can there be knowledge or activity of the changeless
atman, or self? All external objects are under the control of
knowledge. Therefore, this world is void.

### Commentary

In order to gain knowledge about something, it must exist
as a separate entity, which can be identified, qualified and
thus described. Only then can you gain knowledge about
any object. All external objects come under this category.
Thus they are controlled by knowledge in the sense that you
cannot perceive or experience anything without that relevant
knowledge. You can only know that which you have knowledge
about.

However, the atman does not exist as a separate entity.
The sum total of you is your atman. If there is no atman, then
you cease to exist. Your atman and you are not separate
entities, just as your body and you, or your mind and you, are
not separate entities. This atman is forever the same. It does
not grow old or die, nor does it get fat or thin; it is changeless.

In this dharana you are asked to go beyond the limitations of objective knowledge and perceive that changeless atman, or self, which has no action and cannot be known by any qualification. This atman, or self, is therefore only experienced as void, and the same applies in relation to the objects in this world. If we go beyond the external action and objective knowledge, this universe and all that it contains are also nothing but void. Again this reiterates the vedantic principle that *Ayam Atma Brahma*: "Atman is Brahman". The individual self and the cosmic self are one and the same.

## 135. Neither bondage nor liberation

न मे बन्धो न मोक्षो मे भीतस्यैता विभीषिका: ।
प्रतिबिम्बमिदं बुद्धेर्जलेष्विव विवस्वत: ॥ 135 ॥

*Na me bandho na moksho me bheetasyaitaa vibheeshikaah;*
*Pratibimbam idam buddher jaleshv iva vivasvatah.* (135)

### Anvay

*Na me*: not to me; *Bandhah*: bondage; *Na mokshah me*: neither liberation to me; *Bheetasya etaa*: of the cowards, these; *Vibheeshikaah*: scare; *Pritibimbam*: reflection; *Idam*: of this; *Bhuddheh*: of buddhi (intellect); *Jaleshu iva*: like in the water; *Vivasvatah*: of the sun.

### Translation

There is neither bondage nor liberation for me. These scare cowards and are the reflections (projections) of the intellect, just as the sun is reflected in water.

### Commentary

This sloka is a continuation of the previous dharana. The atman is not bound by time, space or matter. It sees and knows all. It is free like the wind and travels everywhere, not just to Japan, America and China, but to all the lokas, or planes of existence. These planes of existence are seven in number: bhuh – earthly plane, bhuvah – intermediary plane, svahah – heavenly plane, followed by mahah, janah, tapah and satya, which are progressively subtler planes of divinity, where the rishis, munis, siddhas and realized souls dwell.

We are only aware of the first plane of existence, which is the earth on which we live. At the time of death the atman gains momentum and travels to other planes, according to the degree of awareness it has attained during its time here on earth. However, it is possible to travel into other realms while still in this physical body, if one can transcend the objective awareness. This is possible through dharana, and VBT reveals the way to transcend this awareness.

Bondage and liberation are mental projections of the deluded intellect that is caught in the dimension of time, space and object. Buddhi, influenced by the samskaras which are stored in chitta, associates with the ideas of bondage, liberation or both. But just as the sun's rays reflected in water are not real, in the same way these reflections of intellect are not real. The atman is pure, untainted awareness, ever effulgent, homogenous and liberated. Dharana on such an idea leads one to the experience of atman as the all-pervading indweller of oneself.

## 136. Withdrawal of the senses

इन्द्रियद्वारकं सर्वं सुखदुःखादिसङ्गमम् ।
इतीन्द्रियाणि संत्यज्य स्वस्थः स्वात्मनि वर्तते ॥ 136 ॥

*Indriyadvaarakam sarvam sukhaduhkhaadisangamam;*
*Iteendriyaani samtyajya svasthah svaatmani vartate.* (136)

### Anvay

*Indriya dvaarakam*: doors of perception; *Sarvam*: all; *Sukha-duhkha-aadi*: pain and pleasure, etc.; *Sangamam*: contact; *Iti-indriyaani*: thus the senses; *Samtyajya*: leaving or casting aside; *Svasthah*: stationed in oneself, withdrawing within; *Sva-aatmani*: in one's own self; *Vartate*: stays.

### Translation

All the doors of perception produce pain and pleasure through contact with the senses. Thus, casting aside (the sensory objects) and withdrawing (the senses) within, one abides in one's own self.

### Commentary

This sloka describes the stage of *pratyahara,* or sensory withdrawal. Our lives are ruled by the senses, which constantly produce pain and pleasure. Like a pendulum we swing from one to the other. There is hardly a moment in our lives when we are not in the grip of either pain or pleasure. This obsession with the senses has to be cast aside if we want to abide in the self. For that experience, we have to withdraw the senses and transcend both pain and pleasure. Sensory withdrawal is difficult to achieve, even for those who are extremely aware, and impossible for those who are not. Can we cast aside our senses of smell, touch, taste, sight and sound, and the experiences which continually arise from their contact with the sensory objects?

In normal life this would be known as sensory depriva-
tion. In meditative terms it is known as pratyahara, or
withdrawal of the senses, which is an important requisite for
dharana and other higher stages of meditation. These five
senses are forever pulling the mind towards sensorial
experience, and preventing it from looking within. In order
to dive deep into that centre where perfect inner stillness is
experienced, the sensory objects must be cast aside and the
senses withdrawn. If we are able to do that, nothing can
disturb our poise and equanimity; nothing can shake our
mental balance.

Constant and diligent practice of pratyahara also leads
to the extrasensorial range of experience. Without perfecting
this practice, it is not possible to experience the inner senses
and their objects, which are comprised of mind-stuff.
Pratyahara is the stage of meditation which just precedes
dharana, or concentration, and it becomes easier if the
object of concentration spontaneously absorbs the mind. In
this way the stage of pratyahara can be entered almost
immediately.

In the *Bhagavad Gita*, the five senses are described as five
wild horses, and the mind as the chariot. If the charioteer is
not ruled by viveka, or discrimination, these horses pull the
chariot in five different directions and are bound to cause
an accident. The senses do not operate independently; they
operate only in tandem with the mind. However, if you
disconnect the senses from the mind, pratyahara will occur
automatically and the mind will become quiet. One very
effective way to induce pratyahara is restraint of the breath.
This thins the sensory impressions and controls the senses
so that they do not come in contact with objects.

## 137. Dharana on knowledge and knower

ज्ञानप्रकाशकं सर्वं सर्वेणात्मा प्रकाशक: ।
एकमेकस्वभावत्वात् ज्ञानं ज्ञेयं विभाव्यते ॥ 137 ॥

*Jnaanaprakaashakam sarvam sarvenaatmaa prakaashakah;*
*Ekam ekasvabhaavatvaat jnaanam jneyam vibhaavyate.* (137)

### Anvay

*Jnaana prakaashakam:* knowledge reveals; *Sarvam:* all; *Sarvena-aatmaa:* by all the atma; *Prakaashakah:* revealer; *Ekam-eka:* each other; *Svabhaavatvaat:* from the nature of being the same; *Jnaanam:* knowledge; *Jneyam:* that which is known; *Vibhaavyate:* should contemplate.

### Translation

Knowledge reveals all and the self of all is the revealer (knower). One should contemplate on the knowledge and the knower as being one and the same.

### Commentary

This dharana refers to the heightened state of samadhi. Although there are many stages of samadhi, the two main categories are sabija and nirbija, or samprajnata and asamprajnata. The difference between these two states is that in samprajnata samadhi the awareness of duality is still present and therefore the consciousness returns back to the normal awareness after having experienced samadhi. In asamprajnata samadhi, however, all dualities cease and the consciousness remains steady, equipoised and balanced despite the absence of any *alambana*, or support, in the form of thoughts or samskaras.

In this state the knower and known, the meditator and object of meditation merge and become one. They are not separate entities. In other words you experience that you are the supreme consciousness. At this point the vedantic mahavakya, *Aham Brahmasmi*: "I am Brahman," becomes a reality.

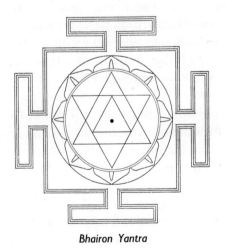

*Bhairon Yantra*

## 138. Dissolution of the set of four

मानसं चेतना शक्तिरात्मा चेति चतुष्टयम् ।
यदा प्रिये परिक्षीणं तदा तद्भैरवं वपुः ॥ 138 ॥

*Maanasam chetanaa shaktir aatmaa cheti chatushtayam;*
*Yadaa priye pariksheenam tadaa tad bhairavam vapuh.* (138)

### Anvay

*Maanasam*: mind; *Chetanaa*: awareness; *Shaktih*: energy;
*Aatmaa*: individual self; *Cha-iti*; and this; *Chatushtayam*: set
of four; *Yadaa*: when; *Priye*: dear one; *Pariksheenam*: dissolve;
*Tadaa*: then; *Tat*: that; *Bhairavam*: bhairava; *Vapuh*: state.

### Translation

O dear one, when the mind, awareness, energy and individual
self, this set of four dissolves, then the state of bhairava
manifests.

### Commentary

According to tantra, during the course of evolution the
cosmic consciousness and energy manifest in the physical
body as atma and prana. Atma is the principle of intelligence,
a silent witness that sees and knows all in the past, present
and future. Prana is the principle of action that sets your life
into motion, the power through which you think, speak and
act. As they evolve into grosser forms, the atma reflects
through buddhi and governs it, and prana rules the mind.
If you want to influence the mind, you can easily do so by
controlling the prana in your body and vice versa. Similarly,
if you want to influence buddhi, then you have to reach out
for the self.

The mind is the gross form of prana, and grosser still
than the mind are the senses. However, atma cannot be seen
or experienced beyond the range of buddhi. In the physical

body buddhi is the closest to pure consciousness. The senses and mind simply have no access to that dimension or range of experience. So long as you function through the senses, you can never hope to reach the self. This dharana asks you to dissolve the set of four, i.e., mind, awareness, energy and individual self. The resulting experience through this process of alchemy is the state of bhairava, or roaring consciousness, that represents immense power.

In order to experience that state, you have to give up everything that is individual, which includes the self. That same self which you have been trying to experience and know through sadhana also has to be transcended for that ultimate experience. So, the individual mind is poured as an oblation into the chetana, or individual awareness, and awareness into energy and energy into the self, or atma. When only the atma remains and everything else has faded, extinguished and dissolved, then the self shines by its own light and becomes self-illumined.

## 139. Means of cessation

निस्तरङ्गोपदेशानां शतमुक्तं समासतः ।
द्वादशाभ्यधिकं देवि यज्ज्ञात्वा ज्ञानविज्जनः ॥ 139 ॥

*Nistarangopadeshaanaam shatam uktam samaasatah;*
*Dvaadashaabhyadhikam devi yajjnaatvaa jnaanavij janah.* (139)

### Anvay

*Nistarangah*: without any surge in the mind; *Upadeshaanaam*: advice, instructions, teachings; *Shatam-uktam*: told hundred; *Samaasatah*: in brief; *Dvaadashaabhih-adihikam*: more by twelve; *Devi*: O Goddess; *Yat-jnaatvaa*: knowing which; *Jnaanavit-janah*: people become wise.

### Translation

O Goddess, I have briefly told you more than one hundred and twelve ways whereby the mind (is rendered still) without any surge of thought, knowing which people become wise.

### Commentary

Here Bhairava sums up that one hundred and twelve dharanas have been given. Each of these methods will eradicate the mental modification or surges, which disturb the brain waves and keep the mind constantly in a state of flux. Sometimes, when the main transformer which supplies electricity is faulty, the electrical circuits in your home have a sudden surge or increase in the voltage of power, which damages your sensitive equipment. In the same way the mind also has surges of thoughts throughout the life. These surges damage the circuits in the brain and deplete the energy, leaving one incompetent and exhausted.

In fact, all the thoughts are unwanted electrical surges. They carry waves of energy that shock and tire the brain. Therefore, it is important to protect the mind from these surges, so that it gradually becomes surge-free. This is necessary for spiritual experience as well as for a healthy, happy and long life. Therefore, Bhairava has described these one hundred and twelve dharanas, which are a means to become free from mental surges and thus attain wisdom, because you cannot access wisdom unless the thoughts cease.

## 140. Perfection of one dharana

अत्र चैकतमे युक्तो जायते भैरव: स्वयम् ।
वाचा करोति कर्माणि शापानुग्रहकारक: ॥ 140 ॥

*Atra chaikatame yukto jaayate bhairavah svayam;*
*Vaachaa karoti karmaani shaapaanugrahakaarakah.* (140)

### Anvay

*Atra cha*: here also; *Ekatame*: even in one of these (practices);
*Yuktah*: joining; *Jaayate*: becomes; *Bhairavah*: bhairava;
*Svayam*: self; *Vaachaa*: speech; *Karoti*: does; *Karmaani*: action;
*Shaapa*: curse; *Anugraha kaarakah*: boons.

### Translation

One attains the state of bhairava, if established even in one
of these (one hundred and twelve dharanas), and by his
speech he confers blessings or curses.

### Commentary

In this sloka the importance of practice is emphasized. The
one hundred and twelve dharanas that have been described
in this text are so effective that, even if one of them is
mastered, the state of bhairava is experienced. That state of
consciousness is so powerful that the words uttered by such
a person inevitably come true. In this way, speech confers
blessings or curses, as one becomes a medium for the
transmission of divine energy in this world.

## 141. Master of yogis and siddhas

अजरामरतामेति सोऽणिमादिगुणान्वित: ।
योगिनीनां प्रियो देवि सर्वमेलापकाधिप: ॥ 141 ॥

*Ajaraamarataam eti so'nimaadigunaanvitah;*
*Yogineenaam priyo devi sarvamelaapakaadhipah.* (141)

### Anvay

*Ajarah*: free from old age; *Amarataam eti*: free from mortality;
*Sah-animaadi*: he, anima, etc.; *Gunaanvitah*: endowed,
decorated; *Yogineenaam*: of the yoginis; *Priyah*: darling; *Devi*:
Goddess; *Sarva*: all; *Melaapakaah*: gathering of siddhas and
yogins; *Adhipah*: master.

### Translation

O Goddess, (by virtue of even one of these dharanas) the
sadhaka becomes free from old age, attains immortality and
is endowed with siddhis, such as anima, etc. He becomes
the darling of all yoginis and master of all siddhas.

### Commentary

This is a continuation of the previous sloka and describes the
wondrous results of these dharanas, each of which has the
potential power to completely alter the molecular structure
and transform the awareness. Today everyone seeks that state
which is free from the effects of ageing and makes one immortal.
Cessation of mind and senses is the key to attaining that state.
If this is the reality, then it would seem that everything in our
lives goes against us in some way. The worries, anxieties,
desires, and thoughts that assail us are the cause of ageing,
ignorance and impotence in our lives. But one who has
transcended these becomes the favourite amongst the
enlightened and attains the most favoured status, in much the
same way as nations today are granted most favoured nation
status by those who rule the world.

## 142. Liberated while living

जीवन्नपि विमुक्तोऽसौ कुर्वन्नपि न लिप्यते ।
श्रीदेवी उवाच
इदं यदि वपुर्देव परायाश्च महेश्वर॥ 142 ॥

*Jeevann api vimukto'sau kurvannapi na lipyate;*
*Shree Devee uvaacha:*
*Idam yadi vapur deva paraayaash cha maheshvara.* (142)

### Anvay

*Jeevannapi*: while alive; *Vimuktah-asau*: liberated; *Kurvannapi*:
while active; *Na lipyate*: not affected; *Shree devee uvaacha*:
Goddess said; *Idam yadi vapuh-deva*: if this is the body; *Paraayaah-cha*: of the supreme; *Maheshvara*: great Lord (Shiva).

### Translation

The Goddess said, O great Lord, if this is the nature of the
supreme reality, he is liberated while living and not affected
(by the activities of the world) while active.

### Commentary

This sloka continues to expound the results of the dharanas
given in this text. Normally, death brings *moksha*, or liberation,
but you lose your physical body at that time. However, by
mastery of any one dharana you can enjoy moksha while still
living in the body. Why strive to attain moksha while living
when death will bring it anyway? This is because while living
there is awareness of this state, whereas after death you may
attain moksha, but you will not know that you have attained it
because there is no self-awareness. Furthermore, once moksha
has been attained in the physical body, the activities of the
world do not taint or affect you in any way. You remain ever
pure and effulgent, despite interactions with the world.

Now Devi is curious to know more about the nature of
this supreme reality.

## 143. Who is the worshipper and who is worshipped?

एवमुक्तव्यवस्थायां जप्यते को जपश्च क: ।
ध्यायते को महानाथ पूज्यते कश्च तृप्यति ॥ 143 ॥

*Evamuktavyavasthaayaam japyate ko japash cha kah;*
*Dhyaayate ko mahaanaatha poojyate kash cha tripyati.* (143)

### Anvay

*Evam-ukta*: thus said; *Vyavasthaayaam*: in the established order; *Japyate kah*: who would be invoked; *Japah-cha kah*: what is the recitation; *Dhyaayate kaha*: whom to be meditated; *Mahaanaatha*: O great Lord; *Poojyate kah*: who is to be worshipped; *Cha tripyati*: and who is to be satisfied.

### Translation

Thus (Devi) said, O great Lord, (tell me) in the established order, who would be invoked and what would be the invocation? Who is to be worshipped or meditated upon and who is to be gratified by that worship?

### Commentary

In order to know more about the nature of the supreme reality, Devi asks the Lord the following questions: Who is to be invoked and what should the invocation be? Who is the worshipper and who is to be worshipped or gratified by that worship, because in reality they are both one and the same?

In heightened states of trance Paramahamsa Rama-krishna would often wave the lights over himself instead of the Goddess Kali, whom he was worshipping. He would put the garland on himself rather than on the statue of Kali. He would put the prasad of sweets into his own mouth, instead of placing them in front of her. He did not see any difference between himself and the Goddess. This is precisely what

Devi is implying when she asks: when that state arises then who is the worshipper and who is the worshipped? What is the distinction or difference between the two?

*Kali Yantra*

## 144. Gross forms of worship

हूयते कस्य वा होमो याग: कस्य च किं कथम् ।
श्रीभैरव उवाच
एषात्र प्रक्रिया बाह्या स्थूलेष्वेव मृगेक्षणे ॥ 144 ॥

*Hooyate kasya vaa homo yaagah kasya cha kim katham;*
*Shree Bhairava uvaacha:*
*Eshaatra prakriyaa baahyaa sthooleshveva mrigekshane.* (144)

### Anvay

*Hooyate*: invoking or summoning (either ancestors or gods);
*Kasya vaa*: whom; *Homah*: oblation; *Yaagah*: sacrifices; *Kasya cha*: of whom; *Kim katham*: how is done; *Shree Bhairava uvaacha*: Sri Bhairava said; *Eshaa Atra*: this here; *Prakriyaa*: performance; *Baahyaa*: outer, external; *Sthooleshu eva*: gross indeed; *Mriga eekshane*: O deer-eyed.

### Translation

(Devi continues), to whom should the invocations be made; to whom should oblations be offered during the sacrifice and how should these be done? Sri Bhairava said, O gazelle-eyed one, these acts are verily the gross forms of worship.

### Commentary

Devi is inquiring how the supreme reality is to be known through the rites and rituals of yajna, or sacrifice. This is not a negation of *karmakanda*, or ritualistic worship; rather it is an explanation of the level of realization that is accomplished through it. Rituals help to focus the mind at the gross level, but they also leave you there. Ultimately, the gross and physical awareness of objects and worship is to be transformed into mental, psychic, subtle and causal states of awareness corresponding to the sapta bhumikas, or seven lokas, which are: *bhuh* (physical plane), *bhuvah* (intermediate plane), *svahah* (divine plane), *mahah* (plane of saints and siddhas), *janah* (plane of rishis and munis), *tapah* (plane of liberated souls) and *satya* (plane of ultimate truth).

These are the seven planes of higher awareness that we have to cross in relation to our practices. At one level the object is gross, but as the awareness ascends the same gross object is successively transformed until it is perceived through the effulgence of the ultimate truth, or satya.

This experience has been described as nirguna, or without quality. This does not mean that the gunas are absent in this state; instead it indicates that they do not exist as a separate entity but are merged or contained within that ultimate experience of truth.

## 145. Japa dharana on the supreme consciousness

भूयो भूय: परे भावे भावना भाव्यते हि या ।
जप: सौऽत्र स्वयं नादो मन्त्रात्मा जप्य ईदृश: ॥ 145 ॥

*Bhooyo bhooyah pare bhaave bhaavanaa bhaavyate hi yaa;*
*Japah so'tra svayam naado mantraatmaa japya eedrishah.* (145)

### Anvay

*Bhooyah-bhooyah*: being, again and again; *Pare bhaave*: in the supreme consciousness; *Bhaavanaa*: thought; *Bhaavyate*: contemplate; *Hi yaa*: is also; *Japah*: recitation; *Sah-atra*: that have; *Svayam*: self; *Nadah*: sound; *Mantraatmaa*: atma of mantra; *Japya*: recitation; *Eedrishah*: like this.

### Translation

Contemplate on the thought of being in the supreme consciousness again and again; this is also japa. That self-sound (which is spontaneously produced) is verily the soul of mantra. Japa is done like this.

### Commentary

*Japa* literally means 'repetition'. Due to constant association with mantra, japa now implies the idea of mantra repetition. However, one can practise japa of anything. One can practise repetition of the remembrance of an idea or thought. For example, it can be said that by remembering your beloved the whole day, you are practising japa on her/him. In the same way one can continuously remember the Lord or contemplate on the idea that one is in the supreme conscious state, experiencing the anahad nada, which is the sound of the soul, or the atma of all mantras. This is the real japa because all mantras have emanated from that anahad, or unstruck cosmic sound, that is reverberating throughout the universe.

*Svayam nado* refers to the ajapa japa mantra Soham or Hamso that emanates from the heart centre, or anahata chakra, with each inhalation and exhalation of the breath, and is regarded as the soul or source of all mantras. Hence this dharana equates the act of breathing and the subsequent sound that is emitted as the real japa which has been infused in each and every being. Soham is the self-born mantra. The divine consciousness initiates us into this mantra at the very beginning of our existence in the mother's womb. After birth it is the guru who reminds us of this inborn treasure we have received as our natural heritage, for it is these two mantras which once again bring us in touch with our creator.

## 146. Verification of meditation

ध्यानं हि निश्चला बुद्धिर्निराकारा निराश्रया ।
न तु ध्यानं शरीराक्षिमुखहस्तादिकल्पना ॥ 146 ॥

*Dhyaanam hi nishchalaa buddhir niraakaaraa niraashrayaa;*
*Na tu dhyaanam shareeraakshimukhahastaadikalpanaa.* (146)

### Anvay

*Dhyaanam*: verify the meditation; *Hi nishchalaa*: absolutely steady; *Buddhih*: intellect; *Niraakaaraa*: formless; *Niraashrayaa*: supportless; *Na tu dhyaanam*: meditation is not; *Shareera-akshi-mukha-hasta-aadi*: body, eyes, face, hands, etc.; *Kalpanaa*: imagination.

### Translation

When the intellect becomes steady, formless and without any support, meditation is verified. Imagination of the form of the divine with a body, eyes, mouth, hands, etc. is not meditation.

### Commentary

In these last few slokas the entire text of VBT and the gist of the one hundred and twelve dharanas are neatly summed up. First it was said that ritualistic worship is gross. Then it was said that the real japa is contemplation on the sound of the self. Now we learn what true meditation is. Meditation is not concentration on the sakara aspect, which is limited to the imaginary form of a body with hands, feet, mouth, etc. Meditation, or dhyana, is that state where the awareness remains steady, even in the absence of an object, and has no support in the form of thoughts. It is formless or nirakara, thoughtless or nirvichara, supportless or nirbija, and steady or samprajnata.

*Dhyanam hi nishchala buddhi* supports the idea that the same intellect you use in daily life has to be transformed through dhyana into a steady stream of awareness.

## 147. True worship

पूजा नाम न पुष्पाद्यैर्या मति: क्रियते दृढा ।
निर्विकल्पे महाव्योम्नि सा पूजा ह्यादराल्लय: ॥ 147 ॥

*Poojaa naama na pushpaadyair yaa matih kriyate dridhaa;*
*Nirvikalpe mahaavyomni saa poojaa hyaadaraallayah.* (147)

### Anvay

*Poojaa naama*: name of worship; *Na pushpaadyaih*: not by offering of flowers, etc.; *Yaa matih*: one's mind; *Kriyate*: making; *Dridhaa*: firm; *Nirvikalpe*: in nirvikalpa; *Mahaavyomni*: in mahakasha, or the supreme void; *Saa-poojaa hi*: that is worship indeed; *Aadaraat*: from respect, reverence; *Layah*: dissolution.

### Translation

Offering of flowers, etc. is not pooja, or worship, but making one's mind steady in mahakasha, the great void, (and thoughtless) in nirvikalpa is worship indeed. From such reverence, dissolution (of mind) takes place.

### Commentary

Pooja and ritual offerings are not the ultimate form of worship. Through the practice of dharana the mind is made steady and firm. When the mind is firm as a rock and does not waver or dissipate with thoughts, then it should be placed on the altar of shoonya in the temple of *mahakasha*, the great void, which is the absence of everything. This should be done with the bhava, or attitude, of reverence and respect. Only then will the great dissolution of mind and the mega-merger of individual consciousness with the supreme consciousness take place.

## 148. Complete fulfilment or satisfaction

अत्रैकतमयुक्तिस्थे योत्पद्येत दिनादिनम् ।
भरिताकारता सात्र तृप्तिरत्यन्तपूर्णता ॥ 148 ॥

*Atraikatamayuktisthe yotpadyeta dinaad dinam;*
*Bharitaakaarataa saatra triptir atyantapoornataa.* (148)

### Anvay

*Atra-ekatama-yukti-sthe*: being established in any one of the practices here; *Yaa-utpadyeta*: whatever being produced; *Dinaat dinam*: day by day; *Bharitaakaarataa*: develop, the state of fullness; *Saa-atra*: that here; *Triptih*: satisfaction; *Atyanta poornataa*: absolute fullness.

### Translation

By being established in any one of the practices (described) here, whatever (experience) is produced, develops day by day until the state of absolute fullness or satisfaction is attained.

### Commentary

This is a continuation of the previous slokas which describe the results of being established in any one of the dharanas described in this text. The experience produced by the practice of dharana develops day by day, gradually bringing about a state of complete fullness or satisfaction, known as *tripti*. Ordinary satisfaction wanes and one can easily become dissatisfied and full of craving again, but tripti is a fulfilment that does not reduce, wane or die. Thus tripti gives rise to santosha, or contentment.

## 149. Real oblation

महाशून्यालये वह्नौ भूताक्षविषयादिकम् ।
हूयते मनसा सार्धं स होमश्चेतनास्रुचा ॥ 149 ॥

*Mahaashoonyaalaye vahnau bhootaakshavishayaadikam;*
*Hooyate manasaa saardham sa homash chetanaa-sruchaa.* (149)

### Anvay

*Mahaa-shoonya-aalaye*: in the abode of the great void; *Vahnau*: in fire; *Bhootah*: the five elements; *Aksha-vishayaadikam*: the sense organs (eyes, etc.) and their respective sense objects; *Hooyate*: poured as oblation; *Manasaa*: with the mind; *Saardham*: together, along with; *Sa homah*: that is homa (oblation); *Chetanaa*: consciousness; *Sruchaa*: ladle.

### Translation

The real oblation is (made) when the elements and sense perceptions along with the mind are poured as oblation into the fire of the great void (i.e. bhairava or supreme consciousness) using the consciousness as a ladle.

### Commentary

This is the great sacrifice mentioned in the Vedas, Tantras, Puranas, Upanishads, Brahmanas and Itihasas. It is a purely metaphysical concept, which can be realized only through experience. In order to pay homage to that supreme consciousness, or bhairava, the individual self offers as oblation all the faculties it has enjoyed, such as the tattwas (elements), indriyas (senses), manas (mind), ahamkara (ego) and buddhi (intellect), into the fire of the supreme consciousness.

412

## 150. Saviour of all

यागोऽत्र परमेशानि तुष्टिरानन्दलक्षणा ।
क्षपणात्सर्वपापानां त्राणात्सर्वस्य पार्वति ॥ 150 ॥

*Yaago'tra parameshaani tushtir aanandalakshanaa;*
*Kshapanaat sarvapaapaanaam traanaat sarvasya paarvati.* (150)

### Anvay

*Yaagah atra*: here the sacrifice; *Parama-eeshaani*: O supreme goddess; *Tushtih*: satisfaction; *Aananda lakshanaa*: characterized by bliss; *Kshapanaat*: from destruction; *Sarva paapaanaam*: of all the sins; *Traanaat*: protects; *Sarvasya*: of all; *O Paarvati*: (consort of Shiva).

### Translation

O supreme Goddess, Parvati, here the sacrifice characterized by bliss and satisfaction becomes the saviour of all by the destruction of all sins.

### Commentary

This sacrifice of the individual mind, senses and objects of the senses into the great void results in spiritual bliss and satisfaction of the soul, spirit, or atma. Until now you have known only the satisfaction derived from the senses and mind. This is characterized by pain and pleasure, happiness and unhappiness, satisfaction and dissatisfaction. Through this sacrifice you can know the satisfaction of the atma, which is accompanied by ananda, or unending bliss. By destroying all the negative elements or attributes that hamper the evolution of consciousness, this sacrifice saves the soul from becoming entangled in the bondage of worldly experience and attachments.

413

## 151. Highest contemplation

रुद्रशक्तिसमावेशस्तत्क्षेत्रं भावना परा ।
अन्यथा तस्य तत्त्वस्य का पूजा कश्च तृप्यति ॥ 151 ॥

*Rudrashaktisamaaveshas tat kshetram bhaavanaa paraa;*
*Anyathaa tasya tattvasya kaa poojaa kash cha tripyati.* (151)

### Anvay

*Rudra shakti*: shakti of Rudra; *Samaaveshah*: being absorbed into it; *Tat kshetram*: that state; *Bhaavanaa paraa*: greatest contemplation; *Anyathaa*: otherwise; *Tasya*: of that; *Tattvasya*: of tattwa; *Kaa poojaa?*: what worship?; *Kashcha tripyati?*: who is to be gratified?.

### Translation

The greatest contemplation is that state where one is absorbed into the shakti of Rudra. Otherwise how can there be any worship of that element and who is it that is to be gratified?

### Commentary

Contemplation is different from meditation. In contemplation the subject-object awareness is still present. It has not been transcended, whereas in meditation, or dhyana, the subject and object become one. Once that happens, that supreme tattwa cannot be worshipped because the duality of subject and object, seer and seen, worshipper and worshipped, is lost.

Therefore, just as the greatest meditation is to become one with the object of worship, which is the supreme consciousness, in the same way the greatest contemplation is that state where one is absorbed in the tattwa that is an essential part of the supreme consciousness, which is none other than Shakti. If the shuddha tattwa of shakti did not emerge from the supreme consciousness, how would it be

414

possible to worship that highest tattwa, Rudra? Absorption into the shakti of Rudra is indeed worship of that supreme reality, for they are one and the same.

*Sri Yantra*

415

## 152. Real purification

स्वतंत्रानन्दचिन्मात्रसार: स्वात्मा हि सर्वत: ।
आवेशनं तत्स्वरूपे स्वात्मन: स्नानमीरितम् ॥ 152 ॥

*Svatantraanandachinmaatrasaarah svaatmaa hi sarvatah;*
*Aaveshanam tatsvaroope svaatmanah snaanam eeritam.* (152)

### Anvay

*Svatantraananda*: bliss of independence; *Chinmaatra saarah*: essence of consciousness; *Svaatmaa*: one's own atma (self); *Hi*: verily; *Sarvatah*: everywhere; *Aaveshanam*: absorption; *Tat-svaroope*: in that nature or form; *Svaatmanah*: of one's own self; *Snaanam-eeritam*: said to be a bath.

### Translation

One's own self is verily the all-pervasive bliss of freedom and the essence of consciousness. Absorption into that nature or form of one's own self is said to be the real bath (purification).

### Commentary

This sloka clearly defines the concept of purification according to tantra. In this interpretation tantra stands miles apart from other philosophies which have conformed to a social approach, while tantra has maintained a spiritual understanding of purity. Absorption into one's own self, which is the essence of consciousness characterized by the bliss of freedom, is purity in actual fact. Independence and freedom are its qualities as the bliss one experiences in that state is not dependent on anything or anyone. Ordinarily one is happy on account of external events, persons, objects and so on, but this bliss is essentially characterized by the fact that it is independent of all these factors. This is the real freedom which money, name and fame cannot bestow.

## 153. What is worship?

यैरेव पूज्यते द्रव्यैस्तर्प्यते वा परापर: ।
यश्चैव पूजक: सर्व: स एवैक: क्व पूजनम् ॥ 153 ॥

*Yair eva poojyate dravyais tarpyate vaa paraaparah;*
*Yash chaiva poojakah sarvah sa evaikah kva poojanam.* (153)

### Anvay

*Yaireva poojyate*: by that is worshipped; *Dravyaih-tarpyate*: oblations with the objects; *Vaa paraaparah*: transcendental and the immanent; *Yah-cha-eva*: by which verily; *Poojakah*: worshipper; *Sarvaha*: all; *Sa*: that; *Evaikah*: only one; *Kva*: what; *Poojanam*: worship.

### Translation

The oblations and the worshipper by which verily the transcendental reality is worshipped are all one and the same. What then is this worship?

### Commentary

Shiva and shakti, the cosmic consciousness and energy, are the transcendental reality which exists in everyone and everything, for their nature is all pervasive. Therefore, the worshipper and the worshipped are of one and the same essence. What then is the purpose and outcome of this worship? Of course, this refers to the ultimate experience or realization where all differences are dissolved along with the sense of separation from one's true nature. When that state is attained, then worship performed by offering of flowers, incense, lights and so on becomes irrelevant as the awareness has transcended the dualistic perspective.

417

## 154. Supreme place of pilgrimage

व्रजेत्प्राणो विशेज्जीव इच्छया कुटिलाकृति: ।
दीर्घात्मा सा महादेवी परक्षेत्रं परापरा ॥ 154 ॥

*Vrajet praano vishej jeeva ichchhayaa kutilaakritih;*
*Deerghaatmaa saa mahaadevee parakshetram paraaparaa.* (154)

### Anvay

*Vrajet*: having moved; *Praano*: prana; *Vishet-jeeva*: apana moved swiftly (in a distinct direction); *Ichchhayaa*: by wish; *Kutilaakritih*: curvilinear form, kundalini; *Deergha-aatmaa*: when stretched, elongated (kundalini); *Saa mahaadevee*: that supreme goddess; *Para-kshetram*: supreme abode for pilgrimage; *Para-aparaa*: manifest and unmanifest.

### Translation

Prana and apana, having moved swiftly in a distinct direction, by the wish of kundalini, that great goddess stretches (elongates herself) and becomes the supreme place of pilgrimage of both manifest and unmanifest.

### Commentary

The real worship is to awaken the goddess kundalini. She is the witness, or sakshi, to the para and apara, immanent and transcendental, bestowing knowledge and experience of both states of consciousness. So her abode is the most sacred place of pilgrimage. While resting in the cavity, or *kunda,* at the base of the spine, she bestows the experience of para, or manifestation. By paying obeisance to her, she is pleased and stretches herself, ascending to the abode of supreme consciousness in sahasrara, so that the sadhaka can attain the transcendental experience.

In the physical body she flows as prana and apana, which manifest as the gross breath in the form of inhalation

418

and exhalation and, according to her wish, give rise to the sensorial experience. When worshipped in this form, she favours the sadhaka by reversing the movement of prana and apana so that they merge at the centre, paving the way for the ascent of kula kundalini to the higher transcendental centres.

## 155a. Blissful sacrifice

अस्यामनुचरन् तिष्ठन् महानन्दमयेऽध्वरे ।
तया देव्या समाविष्ट: परं भैरवमाप्नुयात् ॥ 155a ॥

*Asyaam anucharan tishthan mahaanandamaye'dhvare;*
*Tayaa devyaa samaavishtah param bhairavam aapnuyaat.* (155a)

### Anvay

*Asyaam*: in this; *Anucharan*: following; *Tishthan*: stay; *Maha-aanandamaye*: full of supreme bliss; *Adhvare*: in the sacrifice; *Tayaa*: by that; *Devyaa*: by the Devi; *Samaavishtah*: well instructed, entered, absorbed; *Param*: supreme; *Bhairavam-aapnuyaat*: attains bhairava.

### Translation

One who pursues and abides in this sacrifice which is full of supreme bliss attains by (the grace of) that goddess the supreme state of bhairava.

### Commentary

The sadhaka or seeker who diligently pursues this blissful sacrifice and abides in it day after day attains that supreme state of bhairava by the grace of Devi. In order to arouse the divine energy one has to sacrifice the pleasures associated with the sensorial world. It is the senses that keep kundalini grounded in mooladhara by dissipating the awareness and the quantum of energy required to arouse her. Sensorial addictions deplete the energy and expend it without regenerating fresh energy to compensate for the loss.

Gradually, in the course of time one pays the toll for this misuse and careless waste of energy, suffering degeneration, disease and death. Attachment to the sensorial experiences keeps one forever ignorant of the higher experiences that regenerate and give new life, vigour, happiness, bliss, freedom, knowledge and awareness. In order to achieve these, the seeker has to make a great sacrifice of the pleasures he is accustomed to and turn his attention to the tattwas, or essence of reality, which lie beyond the senses, or indriyas.

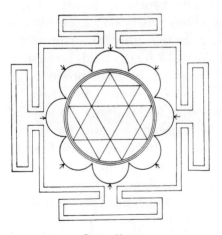

*Durga Yantra*

421

## 155b. Hamsa dharana

सकारेण बहिर्याति हकारेण विशेत् पुन: ।
हंसहंसेत्यमुं मंत्रं जीवो जपति नित्यश: ॥ 155b ॥

*Sakaarena bahir yaati hakaarena vishet punah;*
*Hamsahamsetyamum mantram jeevo japati nityashah.* (155b)

### Anvay

*Sakaarena*: making the sound 'Sa'; *Bahir-yaati*: goes outside; *Hakaarena*: with the sound 'Ha'; *Vishet*: enters or comes inside; *Punah*: again; *Hamsa hamseti*: mantra Hamsa; *Amum*: this particular; *Mantram*: mantra; *Jeevo*: individual; *Japati*: recites; *Nityashah*: always.

### Translation

The breath is exhaled with the sound 'Ha' and inhaled again with the sound 'Sa'. Thus the individual always repeats this particular mantra Hamsa.

### Commentary

'Ha' and 'Sa' together form the mantra of ajapa japa, which means 'spontaneous repetition'. Even without your knowledge you have been repeating this mantra from the moment you were born because this sound is created by the outgoing and ingoing breath. Exhalation produces the sound 'Ha' and inhalation 'Sa'. This sound of the breath is an intimate aspect of your being, and is thus a natural and spontaneous way to turn the awareness towards the inner self. *Hamsa* is the self-born mantra which you receive from the Divine, and is the utterance of that supreme consciousness. If you could perceive this with total understanding, you would realize the truth this very moment. Through understanding the mystery of Soham or Hamsa, you come to know the self.

This dharana is also related to the first dharana in sloka 24, because the prana and apana vayus mentioned there further manifest as the breath. You can join the inhalation to the exhalation by repeating the mantra Soham, or the exhalation to the inhalation by repeating Hamso. Eventually, however, an awareness of the gap between them should be developed by focusing at the point where the inhalation turns into exhalation or exhalation turns into inhalation. There the mind dissolves spontaneously.

This generates the experience of the pancha vayus as they flow in the body, which subsequently leads to awareness of the cosmic prana or supreme source of the breath.

## 156. Continuous japa of the breath

षट्-शतानि दिवा रात्रौ सहस्राण्येकविंशति: ।
जपो देव्या: समुद्दिष्ट: सुलभो दुर्लभो जडै: ॥ 156 ॥

*Shat shataani divaa raatrau sahasraanyekavimshatih;*
*Japo devyaah samuddishtah sulabho durlabho jadaih.* (156)

### Anvay

*Shat shataani*: six hundred; *Divaa raatrau*: day and night; *Sahasraani*: thousand; *Eka vimshatih*: twenty-one; *Japah*: japa; *Devyaah*: of the Devi; *Samuddishtah*: indicated or mentioned; *Sulabhah*: easily available; *Durlabhah*: difficult; *Jadaih*: by the ignorant.

### Translation

This japa of the Devi which was previously indicated, (being repeated) twenty-one thousand six hundred times during the day and night, is easily available and difficult only for the ignorant.

### Commentary

This japa is easily available if you know that you have been repeating it with each breath twenty-one thousand six hundred times every day since you were born. There has not been a single moment since you were born when you were not repeating this mantra. However, this knowledge is secret and thus difficult to avail oneself of without initiation from a guru into the conscious knowledge of this process. The secret Hamsa mantra is para, or transcendental knowledge, because it is the japa of Devi, and its repetition bestows the supreme experience on the sadhaka. This japa is most easy to accomplish because it is already going on spontaneously. All you have to do is become aware of the process by turning the mind inward and focusing the attention on the sound of the breath which flows in and out continuously.

424

## 157. Need for secrecy

इत्येतत्कथितं देवि परमामृतमुत्तमम् ।
एतच्च नैव कस्यापि प्रकाश्यं तु कदाचन ॥ 157 ॥

*Ityetat kathitam devi paramaamritam uttamam;*
*Etach cha naiva kasyaapi prakaashyam tu kadaachana.* (157)

### Anvay

*Ityetat kathitam*: it is said like this; *Devi*: O Goddess; *Param-aamritam*: supreme nectar, an immortal state; *Uttamam*: best; *Etat cha*: all this; *Na-eva*: not, verily; *Kasyaapi*: to anybody; *Prakaashyam*: reveal; *Tu kadaachana*: forever.

### Translation

O Goddess, this most excellent teaching, which is said to lead to the immortal state, should verily not be revealed to anybody.

### Commentary

In previous times, the esoteric knowledge of all spiritual traditions was highly revered and always kept secret. It was only the yogic renaissance in the latter half of the twentieth century that gave access to many of the higher forms of tantric and yogic practice to ordinary people. Therefore, all esoteric texts still uphold this instruction to maintain absolute secrecy, regarding the knowledge and practices revealed in the text.

This revelation of VBT can lead to the supreme nectar that brings immortality; therefore, it is advised to avail oneself of it in secret. Anything which is of great power and value should never be broadcast indiscriminately. There are two important reasons why secrecy is advised here. First of all, the practices and knowledge contained in VBT are of the highest order and will be useless to the ordinary person

425

who is not prepared for the subtlety of these concepts. So it would be a waste of time to discuss this text with people who are not able to understand or value this level of teaching and may even misuse or malign it.

The second reason for secrecy relates to the actual spiritual progress of the practitioner. When one embarks on an inner journey, this is not a matter to be discussed openly in society. This is a very private affair, which concerns oneself and one's spiritual teacher alone. No one else needs to know or should know about the inner journey that the spiritual aspirant undertakes. By discussing one's spiritual understanding and experiences with many people, the inspiration or higher momentum is lost and one may even fall back on the path. Pride is also engendered in this way, which obstructs the subtle receptivity necessary for higher spiritual realization.

## 158. Qualification for tantric practice

परशिष्ये खले क्रूरे अभक्ते गुरुपादयो: ।
निर्विकल्पमतीनां तु वीराणामुन्नतात्मनाम् ॥ 158 ॥

*Parashishye khale kroore abhakte gurupaadayoh;*
*Nirvikalpamateenaam tu veeraanaam unnataatmanaam.* (158)

### Anvay

*Parashishye*: to other disciples; *Khale*: evil; *Kroore*: cruel; *Abhakte*: not devotional; *Guru paadayoh*: at the feet of the guru; *Nirvikalpa-mateenaam*: whose mind becomes free from vikalpas; *Tu veeraanaam*: vira sadhaka; heroic, self-controlled; *Unnata-aatmanaam*: to the higher advanced soul.

### Translation

(These teachings should not be disclosed) to other disciples, to those who are evil and cruel, or to those who have not surrendered to the feet of the guru. (They should only be revealed) to advanced souls, who are self-controlled and whose minds are free of vikalpas.

### Commentary

This sloka is a continuation of the previous one, giving a further word of caution about whom this knowledge should and should not be revealed to. Unless the practitioner is self-controlled, disciplined, devoted and thus a suitable recipient for this esoteric knowledge, he could destroy himself through the powers attained by these practices. The recipient of such knowledge must be fully deserving and qualified; otherwise both the giver and the receiver may suffer the consequences. Observation of this directive also ensures that the esoteric knowledge and practices will be preserved and passed on intact, and thus will remain available for future generations of spiritual seekers.

427

Just as you guard the precious jewels or wealth that you have amassed, in the same way, this knowledge has to be guarded from the undeserving. Those who protect knowledge are regarded as protectors of the dharma. The sannyasins of India have always been regarded in this light. They are not merely religious monks or priests, but the protectors of the transcendental knowledge. It is solely on account of the sannyasa tradition in India that this knowledge is still available to us even today. It is the sannyasins who have preserved it down through the ravages of history.

## 159 & 160. Tantric initiation

भक्तानां गुरुवर्गस्य दातव्यं निर्विशङ्कया ।
ग्रामो राज्यं पुरं देश: पुत्रदारकुटुम्बकम् ॥ 159 ॥
सर्वमेतत्परित्यज्य ग्राह्यमेतन्मृगेक्षणे ।
किमेभिरस्थिरैर्देवि स्थिरं परमिदं धनम् ॥ 160 ॥

*Bhaktaanaam guruvargasya daatavyam nirvishankayaa*
*Graamo raajyam puram deshah putradaarakutumbakam.* (159)
*Sarvam etat parityajya graahyam etan mrigekshane*
*Kim ebhir asthirair devi sthiram param idam dhanam.* (160)

### Anvay

*Bhaktaanaam*: to the devotees; *Guruvargasya*: of the gurus;
*Daatavyam*: should be given; *Nirvishankayaa*: without any
doubt or hesitation; *Graamo raajyam puram deshah*: village,
country, homeland; *Putra daara kutumbakam*: sons, wife and
relatives; *Sarvam etat*: to all these; *Parityajya*: renouncing;
*Graahyam-etan*: should accept initiation; *Mriga-eekshane*: deer-
eyed one; *Kim-ebhih*: what, with these; *Asthiraih*: oscillating;
*Devi*: O Goddess; *Sthiram*: everlasting; *Param-idam dhanam*:
this supreme wealth.

### Translation

Those devotees of the guru who are without the slightest
doubt or hesitation, O gazelle-eyed one, having renounced
son, wife, relatives, home, village, kingdom and country,
should be accepted for initiation. The (worldly accoutrements) are all temporary, O Goddess, but this supreme
wealth is everlasting.

### Commentary

This sloka elucidates the qualified recipient for initiation
into the knowledge and practices of VBT. One who has
vairagya (detachment), bhakti (devotion), and vishvas (faith)

429

should receive initiation into this knowledge. It is necessary to discard the temporary pleasures and security of son, wife, relatives and homeland in search of the permanent reality through initiation. The importance of initiation is emphasized here, and rightly so, because the knowledge becomes fruitful and turns into experience only through the grace of guru in the form of initiation.

Tantric initiations depend more on direct transmission than on verbal instructions. Often the knowledge is transmitted through dream or by thought projection. Many times the disciple may not even be consciously aware of the transmission from the guru, but the knowledge flows into him if he is a fit receptacle.

## 161. Never give up this knowledge

प्राणा अपि प्रदातव्या न देयं परमामृतम् ।
श्रीदेवी उवाच
देवदेव महादेव परितृप्तास्मि शङ्कर ॥ 161 ॥

*Praanaa api pradaatavyaa na deyam paramaamritam*
*Shree Devee uvaacha:*
*Devadeva mahaadeva paritriptaasmi shankara.* (161)

### Anvay

*Praanaa api*: even one's prana; *Pradaatavyaa*: should be given; *Na deyam*: should not be given; *Parama-amritam*: the supreme nectar; *Shreedevee uvaacha*: auspicious goddess said; *Deva deva*: O God of gods; *Mahaadeva*: O great Lord; *Paritripta*: completely satisfied; *Asmi*: I am; *Shankara*; O Shankara.

### Translation

One may give up even one's prana (life energy), but this teaching which is the supreme nectar should never be given up. The auspicious goddess said: O great Lord Shankara, God of gods, I am now fully satisfied.

### Commentary

Here Lord Shankara tells Devi that all the things of this world which are of a transitory nature, even one's own prana, or life force, may be given up. But this teaching, which is the supreme nectar or highest teaching leading to the realization of absolute truth, must never be given up. And Devi, being the most qualified disciple, replies that all of her questions have now been answered and she is satisfied.

## 162. Devi's understanding

रुद्रयामलतन्त्रस्य सारमद्यावधारितम् ।
सर्वशक्तिप्रभेदानां हृदयं ज्ञातमद्य च ॥ 162 ॥

*Rudrayaamalatantrasya saaram adyaavadhaaritam*
*Sarvashaktiprabhedaanaam hridayam jnaatam adya cha.* (162)

**Anvay**

*Rudrayaamala tantrasya*: of the Rudrayamala Tantra; *Saaram-adya*: essence today; *Avadhaaritam*: understood; *Sarva shakti*: of all the shaktis; *Prabhedaanaam*: difference; *Hridayam*: heart; *Jnaatam-adya cha*: today I know.

**Translation**

Today I have understood the quintessence of Rudrayamala Tantra and also the heart (innermost core) of all the different shaktis.

**Commentary**

This sloka completes the previous one and describes Devi's understanding of the Rudrayamala, of which VBT is a major text. Rudrayamala is an important part of Kashmir Shaivism, which is a synthesis of Tantra and Vedanta. This synthesis is very difficult to grasp completely. Thus Devi had many questions, which the Lord answered by relating the one hundred and twelve dharanas to her, pointing out that the ultimate truth is beyond intellect and must be experienced in order to be known.

The heart of all the different shaktis refers to the essence of the different elements and dimensions of creation, which must be known and transcended in order to finally merge with the unmanifest, supreme consciousness.

## 163. Union of Shiva and Shakti

इत्युक्त्वानन्दिता देवी कण्ठे लग्ना शिवस्य तु ॥ 163 ॥

*Ityuktvaananditaa devee kanthe lagnaa shivasya tu.* (163)

**Anvay**

*Iti-uktvaa*: thus saying; *Aananditaa*: being delighted; *Devee*: Goddess; *Kanthe lagnaa*: embraced; *Shivasya tu*: of Shiva.

**Translation**

Thus saying, the Goddess being steeped in delight embraced Shiva.

**Commentary**

After Devi has received and realized the highest knowledge, she once again resumes her embrace with Shiva and becomes one with him.

# Appendices

# Sanskrit Text

## विज्ञानभैरव तन्त्र

1. श्री देव्युवाच
   श्रुतं देव मया सर्वं रुद्रयामलसम्भवम् ।
   त्रिकभेदमशेषेण सारात्सारविभागशः ॥

2. अद्यापि न निवृत्तो मे संशयःपरमेश्वर ।
   किं रूपं तत्त्वतो देव शब्दराशिकलामयम् ॥

3. किं वा नवात्मभेदेन भैरवे भैरवाकृतौ ।
   त्रिशिरोभेदभिन्नं वा किं वा शक्तित्रयात्मकम् ॥

4. नादबिन्दुमयं वापि किं चंद्रार्धनिरोधिकाः ।
   चक्रारूढमनच्कं वा किं वा शक्तिस्वरूपकम् ॥

5. परापरायाः सकलम् अपरायाश्च वा पुनः ।
   पराया यदि तद्वत्स्यात् परत्वं तद्विरुध्यते ॥

6. नहि वर्ण-विभेदेन देहभेदेन वा भवेत् ।
   परत्वं, निष्कलत्वेन, सकलत्वे न तद्भवेत् ॥

7. प्रसादं कुरु मे नाथ निःशेषं छिन्धि संशयम् ।
   भैरव उवाच
   साधु साधु त्वया पृष्टं तन्त्रसारमिदं प्रिये ॥

8. गूहनीयतमं भद्रे तथापि कथयामि ते ।
   यत्किञ्चित्सकलं रूपं भैरवस्य प्रकीर्तितम् ॥

9. तदसारतया देवि विज्ञेयं शक्रजालवत् ।
मायास्वप्नोपमं चैव गन्धर्वनगरभ्रमम् ॥

10. ध्यानार्थं भ्रान्तबुद्धीनां क्रियाडम्बरवर्तिनाम् ।
केवलं वर्णितं पुंसां विकल्पनिहतात्मनाम् ॥

11. तत्त्वतो न नवात्मासौ शब्दराशिर्न भैरवः ।
न चासौ त्रिशिरा देवो न च शक्तित्रयात्मकः ॥

12. नादबिन्दुमयो वापि न चंद्रार्धनिरोधिकाः ।
न चक्रक्रमसम्भिन्नो न च शक्तिस्वरूपकः ॥

13. अप्रबुद्धमतीनां हि एता बालविभीषिकाः ।
मातृमोदकवत्सर्वं प्रवृत्त्यर्थमुदाहृतम् ॥

14. दिक्कालकलनोन्मुक्ता देशोद्देशाविशेषिणी ।
व्यपदेष्टुमशक्यासावकथ्या परमार्थतः ॥

15. अन्तः स्वानुभवानन्दा विकल्पोन्मुक्तगोचरा ।
यावस्था भरिताकारा भैरवी भैरवात्मनः ॥

16. तद्रूपस्तत्त्वतो ज्ञेयं विमलं विश्वपूरणम् ।
एवंविधे परे तत्त्वे कः पूज्यः कश्च तृप्यति ॥

17. एवंविधा भैरवस्य यावस्था परिगीयते ।
सा परा, पररूपेण परादेवी प्रकीर्तिता ॥

18. शक्तिशक्तिमतोर्द्वत् अभेदः सर्वदा स्थितः ।
अतस्तद्धर्मधर्मित्वात् पराशक्तिः परात्मनः ॥

19. न वन्हेर्दाहिका शक्तिः व्यतिरिक्ता विभाव्यते ।
केवलं ज्ञानसत्तायां प्रारम्भोऽयं प्रवेशने ॥

20. शक्त्यवस्थाप्रविष्टस्य निर्विभागेन भावना ।
तदासौ शिवरूपी स्यात् शैवी मुखमिहोच्यते ॥

21. यथालोकेन दीपस्य किरणैर्भास्करस्य च ।
    ज्ञायते दिग्विभागादि तद्वच्छक्त्या शिव: प्रिये ॥

22. श्रीदेव्युवाच
    देव देव त्रिशूलाङ्क, कपालकृतभूषण ।
    दिग्देशकालशून्या च व्यपदेशविवर्जिता ॥

23. यावस्था भरिताकारा भैरवस्योपलभ्यते ।
    कैरूपायैर्मुखं तस्य परादेवी कथं भवेत् ।
    यथा सम्यगहं वेद्मि तथा मे ब्रूहि भैरव ॥

24. श्रीभैरव उवाच
    ऊर्ध्वे प्राणो ह्यधो जीवो विसर्गात्मा परोच्चरेत ।
    उत्पत्तिद्वितयस्थाने, भरणाद्भरिता स्थिति: ॥

25. मरुतोऽन्तर्बहिर्वापि वियद्युग्मानिवर्तनात् ।
    भैरव्या भैरवस्येत्थं भैरवि व्यज्यते वपु: ॥

26. न व्रजेन्न विशेच्छक्ति-र्मरुद्रूपा विकासिते ।
    निर्विकल्पतया मध्ये तया भैरवरूपता ॥

27. कुम्भिता रेचिता वापि पूरिता या यदा भवेत् ।
    तदन्ते शान्तनामासौ शक्त्या शान्त: प्रकाशते ॥

28. आ मूलात्किरणाभासां सूक्ष्मात् सूक्ष्मतरात्मिकाम् ।
    चिन्तयेत्तां द्विषट्कान्ते शाम्यन्तीं भैरवोदय: ॥

29. उद्गच्छन्तीं तडिद्रूपां प्रतिचक्रं क्रमात्क्रमम् ।
    ऊर्ध्वं मुष्टित्रयं यावत् तावदन्ते महोदय: ॥

30. क्रमद्वादशकं सम्यग् द्वादशाक्षरभेदितम् ।
    स्थूलसूक्ष्मपरस्थित्या मुक्त्वा मुक्त्वान्तत: शिव: ॥

31. तयापूर्याशु मूर्धान्तं भङ्क्त्वा भ्रूक्षेपसेतुना ।
    निर्विकल्पं मन: कृत्वा सर्वोर्ध्वे सर्वगोद्गम: ॥

32. शिखिपक्षैश्चित्ररूपैर्मण्डलै: शून्यपञ्चकम् ।
ध्यायतोऽनुत्तरे शून्ये प्रवेशो हृदये भवेत् ॥

33. ईदृशेन क्रमेणैव यत्र कुत्रापि चिन्तना ।
शून्ये कुड्ये परे पात्रे स्वयं लीना वरप्रदा ॥

34. कपालान्तर्मनो न्यस्य तिष्ठन्मीलितलोचन: ।
क्रमेण मनसो दार्ढ्यात् लक्षयेल्लक्ष्यमुत्तमम् ॥

35. मध्यनाड़ी मध्यसंस्था बिससूत्राभरूपया ।
ध्यातान्तर्व्योमया देव्या तया देव: प्रकाशते ॥

36. कररुद्धदृगस्त्रेण भ्रूभेदाद् द्वाररोधनात् ।
दृष्टे बिन्दौ क्रमाल्लीने तन्मध्ये परमा स्थिति: ॥

37. धामान्त: क्षोभसंभूतसूक्ष्माग्नितिलकाकृतिम् ।
बिन्दुं शिखान्ते हृदये लयान्ते ध्यायतो लय: ॥

38. अनाहते पात्रकर्णेऽभग्नशब्दे सरिद्द्रुते ।
शब्दब्रह्मणि निष्णात: परं ब्रह्माधिगच्छति ॥

39. प्रणवादिसमुच्चारात् प्लुतान्ते शून्यभावनात् ।
शून्यया परया शक्त्या शून्यतामेति भैरवि ॥

40. यस्य कस्यापि वर्णस्य पूर्वान्तावनुभावयेत् ।
शून्यया शून्यभूतोऽसौ शून्याकार: पुमान्भवेत् ॥

41. तन्त्र्यादिवाद्यशब्देषु दीर्घेषु क्रमसंस्थिते: ।
अनन्यचेता: प्रत्यन्ते परव्योमवपुर्भवेत् ॥

42. पिण्डमन्त्रस्य सर्वस्य स्थूलवर्णक्रमेण तु ।
अर्धेन्दुबिन्दुनादान्त:शून्योच्चाराद्भवेच्छिव: ॥

43. निजदेहे सर्वदिक्कं युगपद्भावयेद्वियत् ।
निर्विकल्पमनास्तस्य वियत्सर्वं प्रवर्तते ॥

44. पृष्ठशून्यं मूलशून्यं युगपद्भावयेच्च यः ।
शरीरनिरपेक्षिण्या शक्त्या शून्यमना भवेत् ॥

45. पृष्ठशून्यं मूलशून्यं हृच्छून्यं भावयेत्स्थिरम् ।
युगपन्निर्विकल्पत्वान्निर्विकल्पोदयस्ततः ॥

46. तनूदेशे शून्यतैव क्षणमात्रं विभावयेत् ।
निर्विकल्पं निर्विकल्पो निर्विकल्पस्वरूपभाक् ॥

47. सर्वं देहगतं द्रव्यं वियद्व्याप्तं मृगेक्षणे ।
विभावयेत्ततस्तस्य भावना सा स्थिरा भवेत् ॥

48. देहान्तरे त्वग्विभागं भित्तिभूतं विचिन्तयेत् ।
न किञ्चिदन्तरे तस्य ध्यायन्नध्येयभाग्भवेत् ॥

49. हृद्याकाशे निलीनाक्षः पद्मसम्पुटमध्यगः ।
अनन्यचेताः सुभगे परं सौभाग्यमाप्नुयात् ॥

50. सर्वतः स्वशरीरस्य द्वादशान्ते मनोलयात् ।
दृढबुद्धेर्दृढीभूतं तत्त्वलक्ष्यं प्रवर्तते ॥

51. यथा तथा यत्र तत्र द्वादशान्ते मनः क्षिपेत् ।
प्रतिक्षणं क्षीणवृत्तेर्वैलक्षण्यं दिनैर्भवेत् ॥

52. कालाग्निना कालपदादुत्थितेन स्वकं पुरम् ।
प्लुष्टं विचिन्तयेदन्ते शान्ताभासस्तदा भवेत् ॥

53. एवमेव जगत्सर्वं दग्धं ध्यात्वा विकल्पतः ।
अनन्यचेतसः पुंसः पुंभावः परमो भवेत् ॥

54. स्वदेहेजगतो वापिसूक्ष्मसूक्ष्मतराणि च ।
तत्त्वानि यानि निलयं ध्यात्वान्ते व्यज्यते परा ॥

55. पीनां च दुर्बलां शक्तिं ध्यात्वा द्वादशगोचरे ।
प्रविश्य हृदये ध्यायन् मुक्तः स्वातन्त्र्यमाप्नुयात् ॥

441

56. भुवनाध्वादिरूपेण चिन्तयेत्क्रमशोऽखिलम् ।
स्थूलसूक्ष्मपरस्थित्या यावदन्ते मनोलय: ॥

57. अस्य सर्वस्य विश्वस्य पर्यन्तेषु समन्तत: ।
अध्वप्रक्रियया तत्त्वं शैवं ध्यात्वा महोदय: ॥

58. विश्वमेतन्महादेवि शून्यभूतं विचिन्तयेत् ।
तत्रैव च मनो लीनं ततस्तल्लयभाजनम् ॥

59. घटादिभाजने दृष्टिं भित्तीस्त्यक्त्वा विनिक्षिपेत् ।
तल्लयं तत्क्षणाद्गत्वा तल्लयात्तन्मयो भवेत् ॥

60. निर्वृक्षगिरिभित्त्यादि-देशे दृष्टिं विनिक्षिपेत् ।
विलीने मानसे भावे वृत्तिक्षीण: प्रजायते ॥

61. उभयोर्भावयोर्ज्ञाने ध्यात्वा मध्यं समाश्रयेत् ।
युगपच्च द्वयं त्यक्त्वा मध्ये तत्त्वं प्रकाशते ॥

62. भावे त्यक्ते निरुद्धा चिन् नैव भावान्तरं व्रजेत् ।
तदा तन्मध्यभावेन विकसत्यति भावना ॥

63. सर्वं देहं चिन्मयं हि जगद्वा परिभावयेत् ।
युगपन्निर्विकल्पेन मनसा परमोदय: ॥

64. वायुद्वयस्य संघट्टादन्तर्वा बहिरन्तत: ।
योगी समत्वविज्ञानसमुद्गमनभाजनम् ॥

65. सर्वं जगत्स्वदेहं वा स्वानन्दभरितं स्मरेत् ।
युगपन्स्वामृतेनैव परानन्दमयो भवेत् ॥

66. कुहनेन प्रयोगेण सद्य एव मृगेक्षणे ।
समुदेति महानन्दो येन तत्त्वं प्रकाशते ॥

67. सर्वस्रोतोनिबन्धन प्राणशक्त्योर्ध्वया शनै: ।
पिपीलस्पर्शवेलायां प्रथते परमं सुखम् ॥

442

68. वह्नेर्विषस्य मध्ये तु चित्तं सुखमयं क्षिपेत् ।
केवलं वायुपूर्णं वा स्मरानन्देन युज्यते ॥

69. शक्तिसङ्गमसंक्षुब्ध-शक्त्यावेशावसानिकम् ।
यत्सुखं ब्रह्मतत्त्वस्य तत्सुखं स्वाक्यमुच्यते ॥

70. लेहनामन्थनाकोटै: स्त्रीसुखस्य भरात्स्मृते: ।
शक्त्यभावेऽपि देवेशि भवेदानन्दसंप्लव: ॥

71. आनन्दे महति प्राप्ते दृष्टे वा बान्धवे चिरात् ।
आनन्दमुद्गतं ध्यात्वा तल्लयस्तन्मना भवेत् ॥

72. जग्धिपानकृतोल्लास-रसानन्दविजृम्भणात् ।
भावयेद्भरितावस्थां महानन्दस्ततो भवेत् ॥

73. गीतादिविषयास्वादा - समसौख्यैकतात्मन: ।
योगिनस्तन्मयत्वेन मनोरूढेस्तदात्मता ॥

74. यत्र यत्र मनस्तुष्टिर्मनस्तत्रैव धारयेत् ।
तत्र तत्र परानन्दस्वरूपं सम्प्रवर्तते ॥

75. अनागतायां निद्रायां प्रणष्टे बाह्य गोचरे ।
सावस्था मनसा गम्या परा देवी प्रकाशते ॥

76. तेजसा सूर्यदीपादेराकाशे शबलीकृते ।
दृष्टिर्निवेश्या तत्रैव स्वात्मरूपं प्रकाशते ॥

77. करङ्किण्या क्रोधनया भैरव्या लेलिहानया ।
खेचर्या दृष्टिकाले च परावाप्ति: प्रकाशते ॥

78. मृद्वासने स्फिजैकेन हस्तपादौ निराश्रयम् ।
निधाय तत्प्रसङ्गेन परा पूर्णा मतिर्भवेत् ॥

79. उपविश्यासने सम्यक् बाहू कृत्वार्धकुञ्चितौ ।
कक्षव्योम्नि मन: कुर्वन् शममायाति तल्लयात् ॥

443

80. स्थूलरूपस्य भावस्य स्तब्धां दृष्टिं निपात्य च ।
अचिरेण निराधारं मनः कृत्वा शिवं व्रजेत् ॥

81. मध्यजिह्वे स्फारितास्ये मध्ये निक्षिप्य चेतनाम् ।
होच्चारं मनसा कुर्वंस्ततः शान्ते प्रलीयते ॥

82. आसने शयने स्थित्वा निराधारं विभावयन् ।
स्वदेहं मनसि क्षीणे, क्षणात् क्षीणाशयो भवेत् ॥

83. चलासने स्थितस्याथ शनैर्वा देहचालनात् ।
प्रशान्ते मानसे भावे देवि दिव्यौघमाप्नुयात् ॥

84. आकाशं विमलं पश्यन् कृत्वा दृष्टिं निरन्तराम् ।
स्तब्धात्मा तत्क्षणादेवि भैरवं वपुराप्नुयात् ॥

85. लीनं मूर्ध्नि वियत्सर्वं भैरवत्वेन भावयेत् ।
तत्सर्वं भैरवाकार - तेजस्तत्त्वं समाविशेत् ॥

86. किंचिज्ज्ञातं द्वैतदायि बाह्यालोकस्तमः पुनः ।
विश्वादि, भैरवं रूपं ज्ञात्वानन्तप्रकाशभृत् ॥

87. एवमेव दुर्निशायां कृष्णपक्षागमे चिरम् ।
तैमिरं भावयन् रूपं भैरवं रूपमेष्यति ॥

88. एवमेव निमील्यादौ नेत्रे कृष्णाभमग्रतः ।
प्रसार्य भैरवं रूपं भावयंस्तन्मयो भवेत् ॥

89. यस्य कस्येन्द्रियस्यापि व्याघाताच्च निरोधतः ।
प्रविष्टस्याद्वये शून्ये तत्रैवात्मा प्रकाशते ॥

90. अबिन्दुमविसर्गं च अकारं जपतो महान् ।
उदेति देवि सहसा ज्ञानौघः परमेश्वरः ॥

91. वर्णस्य सविसर्गस्य विसर्गान्तं चितिं कुरु ।
निराधारेण चित्तेन स्पृशेद्ब्रह्म सनातनम् ॥

444

92. व्योमाकारं स्वमात्मानं ध्यायेद्दिग्भिरनावृतम् ।
निराश्रया चिति: शक्ति: स्वरूपं दर्शयेत्तदा ॥

93. किञ्चिदङ्गं विभिद्यादौ तीक्ष्णसूच्यादिना तत: ।
तत्रैव चेतनां युक्त्वा भैरवे निर्मला गति: ॥

94. चित्ताद्यन्त: कृतिर्नास्ति ममान्तर्भावयेदिति ।
विकल्पानामभावेन विकल्पैरूज्झितो भवेत् ॥

95. माया विमोहिनी नाम कलाया: कलनं स्थितम् ।
इत्यादिधर्मं तत्त्वानां कलयन्न पृथग्भवेत् ॥

96. झगितीच्छां समुत्पन्नामवलोक्य शमं नयेत् ।
यत एव समुद्भूता ततस्तत्रैव लीयते ॥

97. यदा ममेच्छा नोत्पन्ना ज्ञानं वा, कस्तदास्मि वै ।
तत्त्वतोऽहं तथाभूतस्तल्लीनस्तन्मना भवेत् ॥

98. इच्छायामथवा ज्ञाने जाते चित्तं निवेशयत् ।
आत्मबुद्ध्यानन्यचेतास्ततस्तत्त्वार्थदर्शनम् ॥

99. निर्निमित्तं भवेज्ज्ञानं निराधारं भ्रमात्मकम् ।
तत्त्वत: कस्यचिन्नैतदेवंभावी शिव: प्रिये ॥

100. चिद्धर्मा सर्वदेहेषु विशेषो नास्ति कुत्रचित् ।
अतश्च तन्मयं सर्वं भावयन्भवजिज्जन: ॥

101. कामक्रोधलोभमोहमदमात्सर्यगोचरे ।
बुद्धिं निस्तिमितां कृत्वा तत्तत्त्वमवशिष्यते ॥

102. इन्द्रजालमयं विश्वं व्यस्तं वा चित्रकर्मवत् ।
भ्रमद्वा ध्यायत: सर्वं पश्यतश्च सुखोद्गम: ॥

103. न चित्तं निक्षिपेदु:खे न सुखे वा परिक्षिपेत् ।
भैरवि ज्ञायतां मध्ये किं तत्त्वमवशिष्यते ॥

445

104. विहाय निजदेहास्थां सर्वत्रास्मीति भावयन् ।
दृढेन मनसा दृष्ट्या नान्येक्षिण्या सुखी भवेत् ॥

105. घटादौ यच्च विज्ञानमिच्छाद्यं वा ममान्तरे ।
नैव सर्वगतं जातं भावयन्निति सर्वग: ॥

106. ग्राह्यग्राहकसंवित्ति: सामान्या सर्वदेहिनाम् ।
योगिनां तु विशेषोऽस्ति संबन्धे सावधानता ॥

107. स्ववदन्यशरीरेऽपि संवित्तिमनुभावयेत् ।
अपेक्षां स्वशरीरस्य त्यक्त्वा व्यापी दिनैर्भवेत् ॥

108. निराधारं मन: कृत्वा विकल्पान्न विकल्पयेत् ।
तदात्मपरमात्मत्वे भैरवो मृगलोचने ॥

109. सर्वज्ञ: सर्वकर्ता च व्यापक: परमेश्वर: ।
स एवाहं शैवधर्मा इति दाढ्यद्द्वेच्छिव: ॥

110. जलस्येवोर्मयो वह्नेज्र्वालाभङ्ग्य: प्रभा रवे: ।
ममैव भैरवस्यैता विश्वभङ्ग्यो विभेदिता: ॥

111. भ्रान्त्वा भ्रान्त्वा शरीरेण त्वरितं भुवि पातनात् ।
क्षोभशक्तिविरामेण परा संजायते दशा ॥

112. आधारेष्वथवाऽशक्त्याऽज्ञानाच्चित्तलयेन वा ।
जातशक्तिसमावेश-क्षोभान्ते भैरवं वपु: ॥

113. संप्रदायमिमं देवि शृणु सम्यग्वदाम्यहम् ।
कैवल्यं जायते सद्यो नेत्रयो:स्तब्धमात्रयो: ॥

114. संकोचं कर्णयो: कृत्वा ह्यधोद्वारे तथैव च ।
अनच्कमहलं ध्यायन्विशेद्ब्रह्म सनातनम् ॥

115. कूपादिके महागर्ते स्थित्वोपरि निरीक्षणात् ।
अविकल्पमते: सम्यक् सद्यश्चित्तलय:स्फुटम् ॥

446

116. यत्र यत्र मनो यातिबाह्ये वाभ्यन्तरेऽपि वा ।
तत्र तत्र शिवावस्था व्यापकत्वात्क्व यास्यति ॥

117. यत्र यत्राक्षमार्गेण चैतन्यं व्यज्यते विभो: ।
तस्य तन्मात्रधर्मित्वाच्चिल्लयाद्भरितात्मता ॥

118. क्षुताद्यन्ते भये शोके गह्वरे वा रणाद्द्रुते ।
कुतूहले क्षुधाद्यन्ते ब्रह्मसत्तामयी दशा ॥

119. वस्तुषु स्मर्यमाणेषु दृष्टे देशे मनस्त्यजेत् ।
स्वशरीरं निराधारं कृत्वा प्रसरति प्रभु: ॥

120. क्वचिद्वस्तुनि विन्यस्य शनैर्दृष्टिं निवर्तयेत् ।
तज्ज्ञानं चित्तसहितं देवि शून्यालयो भवेत् ॥

121. भक्त्युद्रेकाद्विरक्तस्य यादृशी जायते मति: ।
सा शक्ति: शाङ्करी नित्यं भावयेत्तां तत: शिव: ॥

122. वस्त्वन्तरे वेद्यमाने सर्ववस्तुषु शून्यता ।
तामेव मनसा ध्यात्वा विदितोऽपि प्रशाम्यति ॥

123. किंचिज्ज्ञैर्या स्मृता शुद्धि: सा शुद्धि: शम्भुदर्शने ।
न शुचिर्ह्यशुचिस्तस्मान्निर्विकल्प: सुखी भवेत् ॥

124. सर्वत्र भैरवो भाव: सामान्येष्वपि गोचर: ।
न च तद्व्यतिरेकेण परोऽस्तीत्यद्वया गति: ॥

125. सम: शत्रौ च मित्रे च समो मानावमानयो: ।
ब्रह्मण: परिपूर्णत्वादिति ज्ञात्वा सुखी भवेत् ॥

126. न द्वेषं भावयेत्क्वापि न रागं भावयेत्क्वचित् ।
रागद्वेषविनिर्मुक्तौ मध्ये ब्रह्म प्रसर्पति ॥

127. यदवेद्यं यदग्राह्यं यच्छून्यं यदभावगम् ।
तत्सर्वं भैरवं भाव्यं तदन्ते बोधसंभव: ॥

447

128. नित्ये निराश्रये शून्ये व्यापके कलनोज्झिते ।
बाह्याकाशे मन: कृत्वा निराकाशं समाविशेत् ॥

129. यत्र यत्र मनो याति तत्तत्तेनैव तत्क्षणम् ।
परित्यज्यानवस्थित्या निस्तरङ्गस्ततो भवेत् ॥

130. भया सर्वं रवयति सर्वदो व्यापकोऽखिले ।
इति भैरवशब्दस्य सन्ततोच्चारणाच्छिव: ॥

131. अहं ममेदमित्यादि प्रतिपत्तिप्रसङ्गत: ।
निराधारे मनो याति तद्ध्यानप्रेरणाच्छमी ॥

132. नित्यो विभुर्निराधारो व्यापकश्चाखिलाधिप: ।
शब्दान् प्रतिक्षणं ध्यायन् कृतार्थोऽर्थानुरूपत: ॥

133. अतत्त्वमिन्द्रजालाभमिदं सर्वमवस्थितम् ।
किं तत्त्वमिन्द्रजालस्य इति दाढ्र्याच्छमं व्रजेत् ॥

134. आत्मनो निर्विकारस्य क्व ज्ञानं क्व च वा क्रिया ।
ज्ञानयत्ता बहिर्भावा अत: शून्यमिदं जगत् ॥

135. न मे बन्धो न मोक्षो मे भीतस्यैता विभीषिका: ।
प्रतिबिम्बमिदं बुद्धेर्जलेष्विव विवस्वत: ॥

136. इन्द्रियद्वारकं सर्वं सुखदु:खादिसङ्गमम् ।
इतीन्द्रियाणि संत्यज्य स्वस्थ: स्वात्मनि वर्तते ॥

137. ज्ञानप्रकाशकं सर्वं सर्वेणात्मा प्रकाशक: ।
एकमेकस्वभावत्वात् ज्ञानं ज्ञेयं विभाव्यते ॥

138. मानसं चेतना शक्तिरात्मा चेति चतुष्टयम् ।
यदा प्रिये परिक्षीणं तदा तद्भैरवं वपु: ॥

139. निस्तरङ्गोपदेशानां शतमुक्तं समासत: ।
द्वादशाभ्यधिकं देवि यज्ज्ञात्वा ज्ञानविज्जन: ॥

448

140. अत्र चैकतमे युक्तो जायते भैरव: स्वयम् ।
वाचा करोति कर्माणि शापानुग्रहकारक: ॥

141. अजरामरतामेति सोऽणिमादिगुणान्वित: ।
योगिनीनां प्रियो देवि सर्वमेलापकाधिप: ॥

142. जीवन्नपि विमुक्तोऽसौ कुर्वन्नपि न लिप्यते ।
श्रीदेवी उवाच
इदं यदि वपुर्देव परायाश्च महेश्वर: ॥

143. एवमुक्तव्यवस्थायां जप्यते को जपश्च क: ।
ध्यायते को महानाथ पूज्यते कश्च तृप्यति ॥

144. हूयते कस्य वा होमो याग: कस्य च किं कथम् ।
श्रीभैरव उवाच
एषात्र प्रक्रिया बाह्या स्थूलेष्वेव मृगेक्षणे ॥

145. भूयो भूय: परे भावे भावना भाव्यते हि या ।
जप: सोऽत्र स्वयं नादो मन्त्रात्मा जप्य ईदृश: ॥

146. ध्यानं हि निश्चला बुद्धिर्निराकारा निराश्रया ।
न तु ध्यानं शरीराक्षिमुखहस्तादिकल्पना ॥

147. पूजा नाम न पुष्पाद्यैर्या मति: क्रियते दृढा ।
निर्विकल्पे महाव्योम्नि सा पूजा ह्यादराल्लय: ॥

148. अत्रैकतमयुक्तिस्थे योत्पद्येत दिनादिनम् ।
भरिताकारता सात्र तृप्तिरत्यन्तपूर्णता ॥

149. महाशून्यालये वह्नौ भूताक्षविषयादिकम् ।
हूयते मनसा सार्धं स होमश्चेतनास्रुचा ॥

150. यागोऽत्र परमेशानि तुष्टिरानन्दलक्षणा ।
क्षपणात्सर्वपापानां त्राणात्सर्वस्य पार्वति ॥

449

151. रुद्रशक्तिसमावेशस्तत्क्षेत्रं भावना परा ।
अन्यथा तस्य तत्त्वस्य का पूजा कश्च तृप्यति ॥

152. स्वतंत्रानन्दचिन्मात्रसार: स्वात्मा हि सर्वत: ।
आवेशनं तत्स्वरूपे स्वात्मन: स्नानमीरितम् ॥

153. यैरेव पूज्यते द्रव्यैस्तर्प्यते वा परापर: ।
यश्चैव पूजक: सर्व: स एवैक: क्व पूजनम् ॥

154. व्रजेत्प्राणो विशेज्जीव इच्छया कुटिलाकृति: ।
दीर्घात्मा सा महादेवी परक्षेत्रं परापरा ॥

155a. अस्यामनुचरन् तिष्ठन् महानन्दमयेऽध्वरे ।
तया देव्या समाविष्ट: परं भैरवमाप्नुयात् ॥

155b. सकारेण बहिर्याति हकारेण विशेत् पुन: ।
हंसहंसेत्यमुं मंत्रं जीवो जपति नित्यश: ॥

156. षट्-शतानि दिवा रात्रौ सहस्राण्येकविंशति: ।
जपो देव्या: समुद्दिष्ट: सुलभो दुर्लभो जडै: ॥

157. इत्येतत्कथितं देवि परमामृतमुत्तमम् ।
एतच्च नैव कस्यापि प्रकाश्यं तु कदाचन ॥

158. परशिष्ये खले क्रूरे अभक्ते गुरुपादयो: ।
निर्विकल्पमतीनां तु वीराणामुन्नतात्मनाम् ॥

159. भक्तानां गुरुवर्गस्य दातव्यं निर्विशङ्कया ।
ग्रामो राज्यं पुरं देश: पुत्रदारकुटुम्बकम् ॥

160. सर्वमेतत्परित्यज्य ग्राह्यमेतन्मृगेक्षणे ।
किमेभिरस्थिरैर्देवि स्थिरं परमिदं धनम् ॥

161. प्राणा अपि प्रदातव्या न देयं परमामृतम् ।
श्रीदेवी उवाच
देवदेव महादेव परितृप्तास्मि शङ्कर ॥

162. रुद्रयामलतन्त्रस्य सारमद्यावधारितम् ।
सर्वशक्तिप्रभेदानां हृदयं ज्ञातमद्य च ॥

163. इत्युक्त्वानन्दिता देवी कण्ठे लग्ना शिवस्य तु ॥

# Appendix B

# Translation

## Vijnana Bhairava Tantra

1. Sri Devi says:
   O Deva, I have heard in detail all that has been revealed through the union of Rudra and his shakti or what has emerged from the Rudrayamala Tantra. I have also understood Trika, or the three divisions of Shakti, which forms the quintessence of all knowledge.

2. O Supreme Lord, in spite of everything that I have heard, even today my doubts are not dispelled. What is your reality, O Divine One? Are you the power or energy contained in sound from which all the mantras have originated?

3. Can your reality be perceived through the nine different ways by which one can enter the realm of higher consciousness, as enumerated in Bhairava Agama? Is it different from the procedure in Trishira Bhairava Tantra? Or can it be perceived through knowledge of the triple forms of shakti, ie. para, parapara and apara? These are my doubts, O Bhairava!

4. Is it nada and bindu or can it be known by concentrating on the ascending psychic centres or the unstruck sound which emanates without any vibration? Or is it the form of the obstructing half moon or else is it the form of shakti?

5.  (Is your reality) transcendent and immanent or is it completely immanent or completely transcendental? If it is immanent (then the very) nature of transcendence is contradicted.

6.  Paratva, or transcendence, cannot exist in the divisions of varna (colour), shabda (sound) or roopa (form). If transcendence is indivisible, then it cannot be defined or co-exist with composite parts.

7.  O Lord, by your blessings, please destroy all my doubts completely. Then Bhairava says: Good, well spoken, O dear one! What you have asked about is the essence of tantra.

8.  Noble lady, although this is the most secret part of the tantras, yet I will speak to you about what has been expounded regarding the (defined) forms of Bhairava.

9.  O Devi, the sakara aspect of Bhairava is insubstantial and of no spiritual value, like the illusory dream-like web of Indra, and is also like the delusion of celestial musicians.

10. (The sakara sadhanas) are described for those people of deluded intellect, who are prey to distracted thought patterns or are inclined towards the performance of action and ostentatious rituals to traverse the path of meditation.

11. In reality (the essence) of Bhairava is not the nine forms, nor the garland of letters, nor the three flows and not even the three powers of shakti.

12. His (Bhairava's) form (cannot be perceived) in nada and bindu nor even in the obstructed half moon, nor in the piercing of successive chakras, nor does shakti, or energy, constitute his essence.

13. These things have been told (about the form of Bhairava), like the tales used to frighten children, to induce people of immature intellect to follow the spiritual path, just as the mother entices her child with sweets.

14. Ultimately (that state of bhairava) cannot be measured in terms of time, space or direction, nor can it be indicated by any attribute or designation.

15. One can have this inner experience for oneself when the mind is free from modifications or thought patterns. The atman of bhairava, which is known as bhairavi, is then experienced as the bliss of one's own inner awareness, a state whose form is fullness, free from all contradictions (which is the abode of the entire universe).

16. The essence of his nature is known to be free of dross and pervades the entire universe. This being the nature of the highest reality, who is the object of worship and who is to be pacified by worship?

17. In this way the transcendental state of bhairava, which is described or sung of, is known by means of the absolute or highest form that is Paradevi, the highest goddess.

18. Just as shakti, or power, is not different from shaktimaan, the holder of power, similarly parashakti, the highest power, who is the essence of the absolute (and therefore) identical with dharma, can never be separated from Bhairava, the possessor of dharma.

19. (Just as) the power to burn is not separate from fire, (similarly parashakti is not different from Bhairava). However, it is imagined as separate in the beginning, as a preliminary step towards entry into its knowledge.

20. One who enters the state of shakti has the feeling of identification with Shiva, without division. Then one verily

becomes like the form of Shiva. In this context, it is said that Shakti is the face of Shiva.

21. Just as space, direction and form are revealed by the flame of a candle or the rays of the sun, similarly Shiva is revealed by the medium of Shakti, O dear one.

22. Sri Devi said: O Lord of the Gods, who bears the trident and skulls as ornaments, (tell me) of that state (which is) devoid of time, space and direction and free from (any) characteristics.

23. By what means can that state of fullness of Bhairava be achieved, (and) how does Paradevi, the highest Shakti, become the face (or entrance of Bhairava)? Tell me (this), O Bhairava, in the manner (whereby) I shall know it completely.

24. Sri Bhairava said:
Paradevi, whose nature is visarga, or creation, manifests as the upward prana and the downward apana. By fixing the mind at the two points of generation (of prana and apana), the state of fullness results.

25. When the ingoing pranic air and outgoing pranic air are both restrained in their space from their (respective points of) return, the essence of bhairava, which is not different from bhairavi, manifests.

26. When shakti in the form of vayu or pranic air is still and does not move swiftly in a specific direction, there develops in the middle, through the state of nirvikalpa, the form of Bhairava.

27. When kumbhaka takes place after pooraka or rechaka, then the shakti known as shanta is experienced and through that peace (the bhairava consciousness) is revealed.

28. Concentrate on the shakti arising from the root like the rays of the sun, gradually becoming subtler and subtler, until at last she dissolves in the dwadashanta and bhairava manifests.

29. (Meditate on that shakti) moving upwards like lightning through all the chakras one by one to the dwadashanta. Then at last the glorious form of Bhairava dawns.

30. The twelve (centres) should be pierced successively through proper understanding of their (associated) twelve letters. Thus becoming liberated from the gross then the subtle, one by one, at the end (of its journey) the kundalini becomes shiva.

31. Then, having filled the tip of moordha and crossed the bridge between the eyebrows, the mind rises above all dichotomizing thought patterns and omnipresence (prevails).

32. Like the five different coloured circles on the peacock's feathers, one should meditate on the five voids. Then by following them to the end, which becomes the principle void, enter the heart.

33. In this way, wherever there is mindful awareness, either on the void, or on another (object such as a) wall, or on an excellent person (such as guru), gradually the boon of absorption into the self is granted.

34. Having closed the eyes, and fixing the attention at the crown of the head, gradually stabilize the mind and direct it towards the goal, which will become discernible.

35. One should meditate on the inner space of the medial nadi (sushumna) situated in the central axis of the body (the spinal column), which is as slender as a fibre of the

lotus stem, and then by the grace of Devi, the divine (form) is revealed.

36. By using the hands (as tools) to block the entrances in all directions, the eyebrow centre is pierced and bindu (or light) is seen. Being gradually absorbed within that, the supreme state is realized.

37. Whenever one meditates upon the subtle fire, in the form of a tilak (like the mark on the forehead), or on the bindu at the end of the shikha, a condition of agitation and shaking is produced, followed by absorption and dissolution in the cave of the heart.

38. One who is adept in listening to the unstruck sound in anahata, (which is) uninterrupted like a rushing river, attains the supreme state of Brahma by mastery of shabdabrahman, the form of Brahman as sound.

39. O Bhairavi, one who repeats the Pranava (Aum) perfectly, while concentrating on the void for protracted periods, experiences the void, and by that void the transcendental shakti (is revealed).

40. Whoever contemplates even on the matras or letters (of Aum) from first to last, in the form of void, verily that sadhaka by meditation on the void becomes the void.

41. When one-pointed awareness on the prolonged inner sounds of different musical instruments, such as stringed, wind and percussion, is gradually established, in the end the body becomes the supreme space.

42. By repetition of all the gross letters of the bija mantras successively, including the 'M', (and meditating thus) on the void within each sound, one verily becomes Shiva.

43. All the directions should be contemplated upon simultaneously in one's own body as space or void. The mind (too) being free from all thoughts becomes dissolved (in the vacuous space of consciousness).

44. One who contemplates simultaneously on the void of the back (spinal column) and the void of the root becomes void-minded (completely free of all thought constructs or vikalpas) by that energy which is independent of the body.

45. By steady contemplation on the void of the back (sushumna), the void of the root and the void of the heart simultaneously, there arises the state of nirvikalpa, which is free from thought constructs.

46. If one concentrates on the body as a void, even for a moment, with the mind free from thought, then one attains thoughtlessness and verily becomes that form of void (known as Bhairava).

47. O gazelle-eyed one, concentrate upon all the constituents of the body pervaded by space, so that the thought becomes steady.

48. One should contemplate on the skin of the body as a mere wall or partition with nothing inside it. By meditating thus, he becomes like the void, which cannot be meditated upon.

49. O embodiment of good fortune, one who contemplates with closed eyes and one-pointed concentration on the mantra in the middle of the lotus in the heart space achieves the highest spiritual realization.

50. When the mind is dissolved in dwadashanta by steady awareness and steady practice, the true nature or essence of the goal manifests everywhere in one's body.

51. By bringing the mind forcibly to dwadashanta again and again, however and wherever possible, the fluctuations of the mind diminish day by day, so that each moment becomes an extraordinary state.

52. One should contemplate that one's own body has been burnt by Kaalagni, arising from the movement of time. Then at last one will experience tranquillity.

53. In the same way, having meditated with an unwavering and one-pointed mind on the entire universe being burnt (by Kaalagni), that man becomes a godman or attains a supreme state of manhood.

54. Dharana on those constituents which comprise one's own body and the whole universe, such as the tattwas and tanmatras, from subtle to subtlest, leads to the source of existence. (In this way) Paradevi, the supreme goddess, (is revealed) at the end of meditation.

55. Having meditated on the gross and weak shakti in the dwadash indriyas (thus making it subtle), one who enters the heart space and meditates there attains mukti and becomes liberated.

56. By meditating on the entire form of the universe and the course of its development through time and space, gradually dissolve the gross into the subtle and the subtle into the state of being beyond, until the mind is finally dissolved (into pure consciousness).

57. By this method one should meditate on all the sides or aspects of the universe up to the shiva tattwa (which is the quintessence) of all. In this way the experience of the supreme reality arises.

58. O great Goddess, one should concentrate on this universe as nothing but void. Dissolving the mind also like this, one then experiences the state of laya, or total dissolution.

59. One should fix his sight (on the empty space) inside the pot, leaving aside the enclosing structure. Thus, the pot being gone, the mind will at once be dissolved (into the space). Through that laya the mind becomes completely absorbed (in the void).

60. One should fix his gaze on a treeless place, like bare mountains or rocks, where there is no support for the mind to dwell on. Then the modifications of the mind become less and the experience of dissolution takes place.

61. One should think of two objects, and in the event of such knowledge being matured, then cast both aside and dwell (on the gap or space) in the middle. Having meditated in the middle, the experience of the essence arises.

62. When the mind is restrained to one object of awareness, casting all others aside and not allowing movement to take place from one to another, then inside that perception the awareness blossoms.

63. One should concentrate with an unwavering mind on all existence, the body and even the universe simultaneously as nothing but consciousness, then the supreme consciousness arises.

64. From the fusion of both vayus (prana and apana) inside or outside (the body), the yogi attains equilibrium and becomes fit for the proper manifestation of consciousness.

65. One should contemplate simultaneously on the entire universe or on one's own body filled with the bliss of the self. Then through one's own nectar, one becomes alive with the supreme bliss.

460

66. O gazelle-eyed one, verily by applying the performance of religious austerities, great bliss arises immediately, by which the essence is illumined.

67. By blocking all the channels (of perception) the prana-shakti moves slowly upwards (through the spinal column). At that time, feeling the sensation of an ant crawling in the body, one experiences the supreme bliss.

68. One should throw the blissful mind into the fire (manipura chakra) in the middle of that fibre-like lotus stalk (sushumna) or into that which is only full of air (anahata chakra). Then one is united with the remembrance of bliss.

69. By the union with shakti there is excitation and in the end one is absorbed into shakti. That bliss (of union) which is said to be the nature of Brahman (ever-expanding consciousness), that bliss is (in reality) one's own self.

70. O Queen of Gods, the bliss of a woman is attained even in the absence of shakti. By fully remembering and absorbing the mind in the experience of kissing, hugging and embracing, the bliss swells.

71. When great joy is obtained (through any event such as) meeting with relatives, one should meditate on that with one-pointedness, until the mind becomes absorbed and the bliss ever arises.

72. If one concentrates on eating and drinking and the happiness obtained by that joy of taste, from such contemplation of enjoyment arises the state of fullness, which then becomes supreme joy or bliss.

73. As a result of concentration on the pleasures of the senses, such as music or song, the yogis experience equal happiness (or pleasure) within. By being (thus) absorbed

461

the yogi ascends beyond the mind and becomes one with that (supreme).

74. Whenever there is satisfaction of mind and the mind is held there alone, the nature of supreme bliss manifests.

75. By entering that state preceding sleep, where the awareness of the outer world has faded, (the mind is absorbed in the threshold state) which the supreme goddess illumines.

76. By gazing on the space that appears variegated by the rays of the sun or an oil lamp, there the nature of one's essential self is illumined.

77. At the time of intuitive perception (the attitudes of) karankini, krodhana, bhairavi, lelihanaya and khechari are revealed, whereby the supreme attainment manifests.

78. Seated on a soft seat, by means of one buttock, with the hands and legs relaxed, at this time the mind becomes full of transcendence.

79. Sitting in a correct posture and curving the arms and hands into a circle, fix the gaze inside this space. The mind becomes peaceful by this laya.

80. One should steady the gaze (without blinking) on the gross form of any object. When the mind is transfixed and made supportless (without any other thought or feeling), it at once acquires the state of shiva (transcendence).

81. (Placing) the middle of the tongue in that which has been opened widely and throwing the consciousness in the middle, mentally repeating 'Ha', the mind will be dissolved in tranquillity.

82. While sitting or lying down, one should think of one's own body as being supportless (suspended in space). Then, in a moment (the samskaras or thought constructs) of the mind being reduced, it ceases to be a reservoir (of old mental dispositions).

83. O Goddess, as a result of slowly swinging or rocking the body, one attains a tranquil state of mind and floats into the stream of divine consciousness.

84. O Devi, having fixed the gaze continuously on the clear sky (without blinking) and with a steady awareness, at once the nature of Bhairava is achieved.

85. One should contemplate on the sky as the form of bhairava (until it is) all absorbed in the forehead. Then all that (space) will be entered by the essence of light in the state of bhairava.

86. Knowing a bit about duality, the outer light and darkness in the manifest world and so on, one who again experiences the infinite form of Bhairava procures illumination.

87. Like this, one should ever contemplate on the terrible darkness of night during the dark fortnight of the moon, if he desires to attain the form of bhairava.

88. Similarly, while closing the eyes, one should contemplate on the profound darkness spreading in front as the form of bhairava. Thus he becomes one with that.

89. Whoever restrains even the same sense organ enters the one void without a second by this obstruction and there the atma, or self, is illumined.

90. O Devi, by recitation of akaara, the letter 'A', in the absence of bindu and visarga, a great torrent of knowledge of the supreme Lord, Parameshvara, at once arises.

91. When the mind is joined with the visarga, at the end of the visarga it is made supportless. In this way the mind is touched by the eternal Brahma, or the supreme consciousness.

92. When one meditates on one's own self in the form of unlimited space (in all) directions, the mind is suspended and shakti in the form of consciousness is revealed as the form of one's own self.

93. At first one should pierce any limb of the body a little bit with a sharp, pointed needle or any other instrument. Then projecting the consciousness there, verily there is movement towards the pure nature of bhairava.

94. By contemplating thus, the antahkarana, or inner instrument of mind, and so on is non-existent within me, then, in the absence of vikalpas (thought constructs), one becomes free from the vikalpas.

95. Maya is the delusive principle residing (in manifest existence), causing name and limited activity. Considering thus the nature or functions of the various elements, one (realizes that he) is not separate (from the supreme reality).

96. Observing the desires, which spring up in a flash, put an end to them. Then verily (the mind) will be absorbed in the very source from which they have arisen.

97. (One should contemplate thus:) when my desires do not produce knowledge, then what am I? Indeed being absorbed in the essence I am, and identifying with that, one becomes that.

98. When desire or knowledge arises, one should fix the mind there, thinking that to be the very self. Making the mind absolutely one-pointed (in this way), he realizes the essence of the tattwas.

464

99. O dear one, (compared to absolute knowledge, all relative) knowledge is without cause, and thus becomes baseless and deceptive. In reality, knowledge does not belong to any one person. Contemplating like this, one becomes Shiva.

100. He (Bhairava) is of the nature of undifferentiated consciousness in all embodied forms. Therefore, those persons who contemplate on all creation pervaded by that consciousness, transcend relative existence.

101. When lust, anger, greed, delusion, arrogance and jealousy are seen (within), having fixed the mind completely (on these), the underlying tattwa, or essence, alone remains.

102. Meditating on the manifest world as imagined or illusive, like a magic show or a painting, and seeing all existence as transient, happiness arises.

103. O Goddess, the mind should not dwell on pain or pleasure, but the essence that remains in the middle (in between the opposites) should be known.

104. Abandoning consideration for one's own body, one should contemplate with a firm mind that, 'I am everywhere'. When this is seen (by means of concentrated insight) one does not see another and thus becomes happy.

105. Contemplating on that special knowledge, for example, the analogy of the jar, or that the desires, etc. exist not only within me but everywhere, one thus becomes all-pervasive.

106. The subject-object consciousness is common to everybody. Yogis, however, are especially alert regarding this relationship.

107. Contemplate on consciousness, such as one's own and even in another's body as well. Thus abandoning all physical expectation, one becomes all-pervasive in the course of time.

108. O gazelle-eyed one, having freed the mind of all supports, one should refrain from all the vikalpas (thoughts/counterthoughts). Then, the self becomes one with the supreme Self in the state of bhairava.

109. The supreme Lord, who is omnipresent, omniscient and omnipotent, verily, I am He and I have the same shivanature. Contemplating thus with firm conviction, one becomes Shiva.

110. Just as waves arise from water, flames from fire and light rays from the sun, similarly the waves of bhairava, which produce the different emanations of the universe, are verily my source.

111. Whirling the body round and round until it falls on the ground makes the energy causing commotion at once (become static). By that cessation the supreme state appears.

112. Being powerless to perceive objects due to ignorance or wrong perception, if one is able to dissolve the mind by absorbing it on the erroneous perception of objects, then at the end of commotion brought about by that absorption, there the form of Bhairava appears.

113. Listen, O Devi, as I am telling you about this (mystic) tradition in its entirety. If the eyes are fixed in a steady gaze (without blinking), kaivalya will arise immediately.

114. Contracting (or closing) the openings of the ears and also the lower opening (reproductive/excretory organs) in the same way, and then meditating on the palace of the

anahad (unstruck) sound within, one enters the eternal Brahma.

115. Standing above a deep hole or well and looking steadily downward (into the abyss), the mind becomes entirely free of vikalpas and dissolution immediately manifests.

116. Wherever the mind moves, whether outwards or inwards, there the all-pervasive state of shiva will go.

117. Wherever the consciousness leads through the channel of the eyes, by contemplation on that object alone being of the same nature as that of the supreme, absorption of mind and the state of poornatva are experienced.

118. At the beginning and end of sneezing, in terror, sorrow or confusion, when fleeing from a battlefield, during (keen) curiosity, or at the onset or appeasement of hunger, that state is the external existence of Brahma.

119. Leave the mind aside when memorable objects of the past, such as one's country or land arise, making one's body supportless; then the omnipresent and mighty Lord manifests.

120. O Goddess, momentarily casting the gaze on some object and slowly withdrawing it with the knowledge and impression of that object, one becomes the abode of the void.

121. That intuition which emerges from the intense devotion of one who is perfectly detached is known as the shakti of Shankara. By contemplating regularly on that (shakti), Shiva (is revealed) there.

122. When one perceives a particular object, vacuity is established regarding all other objects. Contemplating on that (vacuity) verily, even though the particular object is still known or perceived, the mind rests in tranquillity.

123. What people of little understanding believe to be purity is neither pure nor impure to one who has experienced shiva. Nirvikalpa, or freedom from vikalpas, is the real purification by which one attains happiness.

124. The reality of bhairava dwells everywhere, even in ordinary people. By contemplating thus, "There is nothing other than Him," one attains the non-dual state (of homogenous awareness).

125. One who makes no distinction between friend and foe, honour and dishonour, knowing Brahman to be full in itself (all pervading), becomes supremely happy.

126. One should never think in terms of friendship or enmity. Being free from (this idea) of friend and foe, in between the brahma bhava, or nature of supreme consciousness, blooms.

127. By contemplating on bhairava as all that which is void and cannot be known, grasped or imagined, at the end realization takes place.

128. Fixing the mind in the outer space, which is eternal, without support, void, omnipresent and beyond estimation or calculation, one enters into the formless, unmanifest dimension.

129. Wherever the mind dwells, casting that aside that very moment, the mind becomes supportless and free from disturbance.

130. The word Bhairava denotes he who dispels all fear and terror, who howls and cries, who gives all, and who pervades the entire universe (manifest and unmanifest). He who constantly repeats the word bhairava becomes one with Shiva.

131. At the time of asserting, "I am," "This is mine," and so on, by inspired meditation on Tat (that highest reality), the mind becomes supportless.

132. Meditating every moment on the words: eternal, omnipresent, supportless, all-pervasive, master of the universe, one attains fulfilment in accordance with their meaning.

133. This world is (illusory) like magic, devoid of any essence. What essence exists in magic? Being firmly convinced of this, one attains peace.

134. How can there be knowledge or activity of the changeless atman, or self? All external objects are under the control of knowledge. Therefore, this world is void.

135. There is neither bondage nor liberation for me. These scare cowards and are the reflections (projections) of the intellect, just as the sun is reflected in water.

136. All the doors of perception produce pain and pleasure through contact with the senses. Thus, casting aside (the sensory objects) and withdrawing (the senses) within, one abides in one's own self.

137. Knowledge reveals all and the self of all is the revealer (knower). One should contemplate on the knowledge and the knower as being one and the same.

138. O dear one, when the mind, awareness, energy and individual self, this set of four dissolves, then the state of bhairava manifests.

139. O Goddess, I have briefly told you more than one hundred and twelve ways whereby the mind (is rendered still) without any surge of thought, knowing which people become wise.

140. One attains the state of bhairava, if established even in one of these (one hundred and twelve dharanas), and by his speech he confers blessings or curses.

141. O Goddess, (by virtue of even one of these dharanas) the sadhaka becomes free from old age, attains immortality and is endowed with siddhis, such as anima, etc. He becomes the darling of all yoginis and master of all siddhas.

142. The Goddess said, O great Lord, if this is the nature of the supreme reality, he is liberated while living and not affected (by the activities of the world) while active.

143. Thus (Devi) said, O great Lord, (tell me) in the established order, who would be invoked and what would be the invocation? Who is to be worshipped or meditated upon and who is to be gratified by that worship?

144. (Devi continues), to whom should the invocations be made; to whom should oblations be offered during the sacrifice and how should these be done? Sri Bhairava said, O gazelle-eyed one, these acts are verily the gross forms of worship.

145. Contemplate on the thought of being in the supreme consciousness again and again; this is also japa. That self-sound (which is spontaneously produced) is verily the soul of mantra. Japa is done like this.

146. When the intellect becomes steady, formless and without any support, meditation is verified. Imagination of the form of the divine with a body, eyes, mouth, hands, etc. is not meditation.

147. Offering of flowers, etc. is not pooja, or worship, but making one's mind steady in mahakasha, the great void, (and thoughtless) in nirvikalpa is worship indeed. From such reverence, dissolution (of mind) takes place.

148. By being established in any one of the practices (described) here, whatever (experience) is produced, develops day by day until the state of absolute fullness or satisfaction is attained.

149. The real oblation is (made) when the elements and sense perceptions along with the mind are poured as oblation into the fire of the great void (i.e. bhairava or supreme consciousness) using the consciousness as a ladle.

150. O supreme Goddess, Parvati, here the sacrifice characterized by bliss and satisfaction becomes the saviour of all by the destruction of all sins.

151. The greatest contemplation is that state where one is absorbed into the shakti of Rudra. Otherwise how can there be any worship of that element and who is it that is to be gratified?

152. One's own self is verily the all-pervasive bliss of freedom and the essence of consciousness. Absorption into that nature or form of one's own self is said to be the real bath (purification).

153. The oblations and the worshipper by which verily the transcendental reality is worshipped are all one and the same. What then is this worship?

154. Prana and apana, having moved swiftly in a distinct direction, by the wish of kundalini, that great goddess stretches (elongates herself) and becomes the supreme place of pilgrimage of both manifest and unmanifest.

155a. One who pursues and abides in this sacrifice which is full of supreme bliss attains by (the grace of) that goddess the supreme state of bhairava.

155b. The breath is exhaled with the sound 'Ha' and inhaled again with the sound 'Sa'. Thus the individual always repeats this particular mantra Hamsa.

156. This japa of the Devi which was previously indicated, (being repeated) twenty-one thousand six hundred times during the day and night, is easily available and difficult only for the ignorant.

157. O Goddess, this most excellent teaching, which is said to lead to the immortal state, should verily not be revealed to anybody.

158. (These teachings should not be disclosed) to other disciples, to those who are evil and cruel, or to those who have not surrendered to the feet of the guru. (They should only be revealed) to advanced souls, who are self-controlled and whose minds are free of vikalpas.

159 & 160. Those devotees of the guru who are without the slightest doubt or hesitation, O gazelle-eyed one, having renounced son, wife, relatives, home, village, kingdom and country, should be accepted for initiation. The (worldly accoutrements) are all temporary, O Goddess, but this supreme wealth is everlasting.

161. One may give up even one's prana (life energy), but this teaching which is the supreme nectar should never be given up. The auspicious goddess said: O great Lord Shankara, God of gods, I am now fully satisfied.

162. Today I have understood the quintessence of Rudrayamala Tantra and also the heart (innermost core) of all the different shaktis.

163. Thus saying, the goddess being steeped in delight embraced Shiva.

# Glossary

**Abhyasa** – constant, regular and uninterrupted practice; the basis of sadhana

**Adi guru** – ancient, primordial or original guru; divine source from which the power of initiation and guidance descends to a line of gurus; an epithet of Sri Shankaracharya and sometimes of Dakshinamurti

**Advaita** – literally, 'non dual'; concept of oneness; monistic vision of reality

**Agama** – literally, 'to carry on' or 'go forward'; testimony; revelation; traditional knowledge; esoteric tradition of tantra, appropriate for kali yuga; tantric philosophy and scriptures in which Lord Shiva teaches Parvati, his consort; these texts outline a code of living which includes ritual, worship, discipline, meditation and attainment of siddhis; pre-date the Vedas

**Aghora** – literally, 'one for whom nothing is abominable'; one who is in total tune with nature, having mastered the elements; totally innocent

**Aham** – I, absolute I

**Aham Brahmasmi** – literally, 'I am Brahma' (supreme consciousness); one of the four mahavakyas, or great pronouncements, of Vedanta

**Ahamkara** – faculty of ego, awareness of the existence of 'I'; centre of individual mental, emotional, psychic and physical functioning

**Ahuti** – oblations offered into the fire during yajna, or sacrifice

**Ajapa japa** – spontaneous, unbroken repetition of mantra; meditation practice in which mantra is repeated in coordination with the incoming and outgoing breath; suffix 'a' in front of japa implies that the process of japa becomes spontaneous

**Ajna chakra** – third eye (eye of knowledge); command or guru centre; psychic centre that is the seat of intuition

**Akaara** –first letter of Sanskrit alphabet; first sound to emanate in space at the beginning of creation

**Akara** – form

**Akshara** – indelible sound vibration contained within the letters that make up words and language; fifty in number; written on the lotus petals of the chakras

**Alambana** – support (of awareness) in the form of thoughts or samskaras; base

**Alasya** – laziness; one of the obstacles in sadhana according to Sage Patanjali

**Anahad nada** – literally, 'unstruck sound'; unstruck cosmic sound that is reverberating throughout the universe; sound made without contact of two objects coming together; sound of the soul; although it emerges from anahata chakra, it is heard most clearly at bindu at the top back of the head

**Anahata chakra** – psychic/pranic centre situated in the region of the heart and cardiac plexus; fourth chakra in human evolution

**Anandam (ananda)** – state of supreme or unending bliss; beatitude

**Anandamaya kosha** – body of bliss

**Anavopaya** – means whereby the anu, or empirical individual, uses his own karanas, or instruments, i.e., senses, prana and mind, for self-realization. Includes disciplines concerning regulation of prana, rituals, japa, concentration, etc.; technique through which inner realization dawns; one of the four upaya sadhanas of tantra

**Angula** – finger-width

**Anna** – grain; food

**Annamaya kosha** – material or food body

**Ansha** – part

**Antahkarana** – literally, 'inner tool' or 'inner self'; internal organ of consciousness; comprises manas, chitta, buddhi and ahamkara

**Anu** – prefix representing the subtle dimensions; atom; infinitesimal point; little; limited, conditioned or empirical individual

**Anugraha** – divine grace; transmission of energy or shaktipath; blessing

**Anupaya** – attainment of spiritual experience through little or no means or effort, for very advanced aspirants only

**Apara** – immanent; lower; material; one of the threefold principles of shakti

**Apara para** – both immanent and transcendental

**Ardha sahasrara** – chakra below mooladhara

**Ardhachandrika** – literally, 'half-moon'; psychic centre corresponding to bindu visarga

**Arjuna** – disciple of Sri Krishna who, in the Bhagavad Gita, received the highest knowledge from him; third of the five son's of Kunti and King Pandu

**Arohan** – ascent; used in context of ascent of consciousness; also refers to the ascending scale in music, psychic pathway used in kriya yoga and meditation which runs from mooladhara chakra up the front of the body to sahasrara chakra at the crown of the head

**Asana** – according to Patanjali, a steady and comfortable meditation pose in which one is at perfect ease; a specific position of the body which balances and channels prana, opens the chakras and removes energy blocks; third stage of Patanjali's ashtanga yoga

**Ashtanga yoga** – the eight-limbed yoga of Patanjali: yama, niyama, asana, pranayama, pratyahara, dharana, dhyana and samadhi

**Ashwamedha vidya** – horse sacrifice; elaborate vedic ceremony undertaken by kings or emperors to attain a son or sovereignty; esoteric tantric meditation

**Ashwini mudra** – contraction of the anal sphincter

**Atharva Veda** – last of the four Vedas; named after Sage Atharvan, who classified the agamas that existed under the name of tantra, and consolidated them in the Atharva Veda

**Atma chintan** – reflective thinking

**Atman** – pure consciousness which pervades everything; undying; self; spirit; soul

**Aum** – primordial sound; cosmic vibration of the universe; universal mantra; Pranava; represents the four states of consciousness: conscious, subconscious, unconscious and superconscious; symbol of Brahmin; also spelt Om

**Avarohan** – descent of consciousness; descending psychic pathway used in kriya yoga and meditation which starts at sahasrara and travels down through sushumna to mooladhara chakra

**Avatara** – descent or incarnation of supreme consciousness into human form, e.g., Rama, Krishna, Buddha and the other dashavataras, or ten incarnations, of Vishnu

**Avidya** – ignorance of true reality; complete unawareness; nescience

**Avyakta** – unmanifest; unseen

**Ayama** – dimension

**Batuk** – literally, 'little'; one of the eight bhairavas or states of consciousness

**Bhagavad Gita** – literally, 'Song of God'; discourse on yoga between Sri Krishna and Arjuna on the battlefield at the onset of the Mahabharata war

**Bhairava** – state of consciousness which precedes the ultimate experience of universal consciousness, or Shiva; an order or tradition; name or epithet of Lord Shiva in his fierce aspect; derived from the root 'ravayati', which literally means 'to howl' or 'to wail'; the cry of separation from universal consciousness, which is almost within the aspirant's reach; experience of intoxicated bliss

**Bhairavi** – female counterpart or shakti of Bhairava, the fierce aspect of Lord Shiva

**Bhairavi pooja** – ritual worship performed to invoke Bhairavi

**Bhasmasura** – bhasma means 'ashes' and asura means 'demon'; the demon who had the power to turn anyone to ashes by placing his hand on their head

**Bhava** – intense inner attitude or subtle emotion; state of being

**Bhaya** – fear, especially of the unknown

**Bhrumadhya** – eyebrow centre; kshetram, or contact point, for ajna chakra; also called trikuti

**Bhumika** – stage, level or plane of evolution

**Bija mantra** – seed mantra or syllable

**Bindu** – point of potential energy where the descending consciousness first emerges into multiplicity and diversity; source; substratum of whole cosmos; compact mass of shakti gathered into an undifferentiated point; symbol for creation; psychic centre also known as bindu visarga; concentration point at the back of the head where the hair whorls; nucleus; drop of ojas according to tantra; symbol of Shiva; anusvara, or nasal sound indicated by a dot over a letter

**Brahma** – cosmic creator in Hindu pantheon; one of the holy trinity; manifest force of life and creation; potentiality of mooladhara chakra

**Brahman** – ever-expanding consciousness; absolute reality; derived from the root 'bri', meaning 'to expand'

**Bri** – to expand

**Buddhi** – higher intellect, discrimination; intuitive aspect of consciousness by which the essential self awakens to truth; aspect of mind closest to pure consciousness; part of antahkarana which deals with understanding human nature; higher intelligence

**Chaitanyam atma** – literally, 'awareness is light'; eternal soul

**Chakra** – literally, 'wheel or vortex'; major psychic centre in the subtle body responsible for specific physical and psychic functions

**Chakra arudham** – ascent of kundalini through the chakras

**Chakra bhedan** – literally, 'piercing of the chakras'

**Chausath shaktipeethas** – sixty-four places of Shakti in India

**Chetana** – consciousness (intermediate between the highest level and the ordinary empirical consciousness); that which has the ability to illumine the object on which it is focused

**Chidakasha** – derived from 'chit', consciousness, and 'akasha', space or ether; vast space or ether of individual consciousness where infinite psychic events can be visualized in front of the closed eyes during meditation; mental screen; also likened to a cave into the depths of the mind

**Chitta** – individual consciousness which includes the conscious, subconscious and unconscious dimensions of the mind; one of twenty-four elements constituting the mind; one of four aspects of antahkarana which receives impressions of experiences and stores them for future use in the form of samskaras; empirical mind

**Chitta vritti** – mental fluctuation, movement or modification; five in number: pramana, or sources of right knowledge; viparyaya, or misconception; vikalpa, or unfounded belief; nidra, or the state of sleep; smriti, or memory

**Chitishakti** – supreme energy of consciousness

**Chittam atma** – literally, 'awareness is atma'

**Chittam mantra** – literally, 'awareness is mantra'

**Dakshinayana** – southern path; one of two prescribed paths of meditation

**Dashnam** – ten orders of sannyasa formed by Adi Guru Shankaracharya: Saraswati, Giri, Tirtha, Ashrama, Bharati, Vanam, Aranya, Parvat, Sagar, Puri

**Devata** – literally, 'illumined being'; luminous nature of spirit; god; divine power; deity

**Devi** – luminous nature of spirit in its female aspect; goddess; divine mother

**Dharana** – literally, 'to hold or possess'; practice of concentration; continuity of mental process on an object or idea; sixth stage of Patanjali's ashtanga yoga

**Dharma** – values that complement the laws of nature; right conduct

**Dharma Shastras** – scriptures concerning the inner knowledge of one's duty in relation to all aspects of life

**Dhvani** – sound vibration

**Dhyana** – spontaneous state of meditation which arises out of the perfection of dharana; seventh stage of Patanjali's ashtanga yoga; fusion of mind with the object of contemplation; inner awakening; natural expression of sattwic state

**Dosha** – three humours of the body: phlegm, acid and wind; defect; one of the four main obstacles to sadhana according to Patanjali

**Dvaita** – philosophy of supreme consciousness in which one perceives oneself as separate from the supreme self and aspires for union with it; dualism; philosophical school proposing two original realities; Brahma and Maya

**Dwadashanta** – literally, 'the end of twelve'; two poles or points of rest between which the breath travels

**Dwesha** – repulsion; aversion; dislike

**Ekagra** – one-pointed mind; fourth stage of evolution of mind; state of fixed attention

**Ganapatya** – worshippers of Ganesha

**Ganesha** – God of wisdom and remover of obstacles worshipped before any new undertaking; son of Shiva and Parvati; depicted as being short and fat with a large belly, four hands, riding a mouse and having the head of an elephant; symbol of all that is auspicious; scribe of Mahabharata

**Ganga** – river Ganges, longest and most sacred river in India whose source is in Gangotri

**Gati** – motion; gait

**Gayatri mantra** – vedic mantra of twenty-four syllables: 'Om bhur bhuvah svaha, tat savitur varenyan, bhargo devasya dhimayi, dhiyo yonah prachodayat'; considered to be mother of the Vedas; represents female aspect of the sun

**Gayatri vidya** – knowledge of or meditation on Gayatri

**Guna** – qualities or attributes of nature; threefold aspects of manifest energy, prakriti, or nature, viz., tamas, rajas and sattwa; natural qualities governing life; genetic qualities of universe

**Guru** – literally, 'dispeller of darkness'; spiritual master; realized person who by the light of his own soul, or atma, can rid the disciple's mind of ignorance and delusion

**Hamsa** – swan; third stage of sannyasa; a sannyasin who can discriminate between reality and unreality, as the mythical swan separates milk from water

**Hiranyagarbha** – cosmic subtle body; golden womb of creation; cosmic equivalent of tejas.

**Hridayakasha** – heart space; hridaya means 'heart' and akasha means 'space'

**Ichchha** – desire; will

**Ichchha shakti** – power of will

**Ida nadi** – major nadi running on left side of spine from mooladhara to ajna chakra; pranic channel through which mental energy flows; lunar energy or chitta shakti; passive force; governs the conscious dimension

**Indriya** – sensory organ, ten in number; see karmendriyas and jnanendriyas

**Ishvara** – literally, 'one who rules'; cosmic, causal body of sound, also known as parabindu, parashabda, supreme being or God; state of unchanging transcendental reality, corresponds to western concept of a personal God

**Jagrat** – waking state related to the conscious mind; awake (to the world)

**Jaimini** – sage who wrote the Dharma Shastras

**Japa** – repetition of a mantra or name of God

**Jata** – matted locks worn by sadhus and ascetics

**Jivanmukta** – soul liberated while living

**Jivatma** – individual soul or consciousness; empirical self

**Jnana** – higher knowledge, cognition or wisdom

**Jnanendriyas** – five organs of sense perception and knowledge, viz., ears, eyes, nose, tongue and skin

**Jyotirlinga** – natural oval-shaped stone worshipped as Lord Shiva; symbol of pure consciousness; jyoti means 'light' and linga means 'mark' or 'to be absorbed'; induces concentration of mind

**Jyotsna** – light of the soul; light of consciousness; effulgence

**Kaala** – time in the absolute sense, or eternity; the great destroyer; time principle; one of the five kanchuka, limiting aspects of energy, which creates the dimension of time and restricts the individual within it; one of the eight bhairavas or states of consciousness

**Kaala Bhairava** – Shiva in his fierce aspect; dissolution of time

**Kaalagni** – fire of time; kaala means 'time' and agni means 'fire'; heat which takes place when time and space collide in a great explosion

**Kaivalya** – liberation; comes from the word kevala, meaning 'one only'; superconscious state where all duality is transcended and only the one universal consciousness remains; highest state of samadhi; moksha; nirvana

**Kalaa** – one of the kanchukas; limiting aspect of energy which restricts the creative power of individual consciousness and body; ray or force which emanates from the nucleus of bindu due to vibrations caused by nada; part of letter or word

**Kali** – primal manifestation of Shakti; divine mother; goddess of destruction; destroyer of time, space and object, i.e., ignorance

**Kalpa vriksha** – tree of knowledge; wish fulfilling tree

**Kanchuka** – invisible cloak of maya which limits or restricts consciousness and creates the notion of duality; literally, 'sheath' or 'envelope'; five in number, viz., kalaa, avidya vidya, raga, kaala and niyati

**Kapala** – skull

**Karmendriyas** – five organs of action: hands, feet, vocal cords, tongue, excretory and reproductive organs

**Kashmir Shaivism** – division of Shaivism found in North India

**Kaula Tantra** – sect of tantra in which the mother is recognized as the guru of the family lineage

**Kevala** – spontaneous; only one; beyond duality

**Kevala kumbhaka** – spontaneous cessation of breath which occurs during samadhi, when the consciousness transcends duality

**Khechari mudra** – khechari literally means 'to roam freely in the sky'; this mudra liberates consciousness from matter and allows the awareness to travel freely in space; important mudra of Lord Shiva

**Krishna** – literally, 'black'; an incarnation of Lord Vishnu; an enlightened person who lived in the Dwapara Yuga, 5,000 years ago, whose teachings are given in the Bhagavad Gita

**Kriya** – activity, action, motion; dynamic kundalini yoga practice

**Kshipta** – broken; scattered

**Kula** – family lineage

**Kumari pooja** – worship of virgin girls

**Kumbhaka** – literally, 'breath retention'; pre-meditation technique which steadies the mind and intensifies concentration

**Kundalini** -- spiritual energy; evolutionary force; referred to as serpent power; latent energy in mooladhara chakra;

divine energy that transforms human consciousness; bio-psychic energy

**Loka** – seven planes of existence: bhuh, bhuvah, svahah, mahah, janah, tapah and satya

**Madhushala** – literally, 'place where honey is kept'; refers to amrit, or nectar, within the body of the seeker, which brings about a state of spiritual ecstasy; a place where intoxicating herbs and liquor are served

**Madhyama nada** – literally, 'middle sound'; subtle sound vibration; whispering sound

**Madhye taya** – middle state

**Mahakaala** – literally, 'great or endless time'; timelessness; another name for Shiva, or universal consciousness

**Mahakaleshvara** – one of the twelve jyotirlingas

**Mahashakti** – literally, 'great energy or power'; another name for kundalini which lies coiled like a serpent in mooladhara chakra

**Mahat** – cosmic intelligence; higher individual consciousness

**Mahodaya** – from maha meaning 'great' and udaya meaning 'sunrise'; the great dawning; birth of new consciousness

**Manana** – to contemplate

**Manas** – lower or empirical mind; aspect of manifest mind involved in experiences of sensory perception and thought/counter-thought; mental faculty of comparing, classifying and reasoning; one of the four tools of the antahkarana

**Mandala** – diagram within a circumference symbolizing the deeper aspects of man's psyche, and capable of invoking cosmic power; complex geometrical symbol merging macrocosmic and microcosmic events

**Manipura chakra** – literally, 'city of jewels'; psychic centre situated behind the navel, associated with vitality and energy

**Manomani** – condition of mind devoid of thought

**Manomaya kosha** – mental sheath or body

**Mantra** – literally, 'that which liberates the mind'; subtle sound vibration which liberates mental forces; process of tantra for liberating energy from the limitations of mundane awareness and expanding consciousness

**Matrika** – creative energy concealed in mantra; another name for mantra; little mothers; letters of Sanskrit alphabet

**Maya** – literally, 'illusion'; veiling power of manifest shakti; the illusory nature of the phenomenal world; ignorance of reality

**Moodha** – confused, dull, forgetful state of mind; lowest mental state

**Moola ajnana** – root of ignorance

**Moola bandha** – locking of the perineum; technique for awakening mooladhara chakra and releasing brahma granthi

**Mooladhara chakra** – lowest psychic centre in human body where kundalini shakti emerges; situated in the perineum

**Moordha** – minor psychic centre located above the palate where it opens into the nasal cavity

**Mudra** – literally, 'gesture' or 'attitude' utilized to express or channel cosmic/pranic energy within the mind/body as an aid to concentration

**Muni** – one who has achieved mauna, complete silence or stillness of mind; ascetic; sage

**Nabhi chakra** – energy vortex situated behind navel

**Nada** – subtle sound vibration heard in the meditative state

**Nada yoga** – process of tracing psychic sound back to its original source in order to attain self-realization

**Nadanta** – centre where difference between sound and experiencer dissolves

**Nadi** – flow; river; pranic channel which conducts the flow of energy in the body; 72,000 in number

**Nara** – man; matter

**Nasikagra** – nose tip; also known as nasagra

**Navatma** – nine states of consciousness or higher awareness; nine forms through which the atman can be realized

**Neti neti (na iti)** – literally, 'not this, not this'; a famous exclamation of the Upanishads related to the impossibility of reducing divinity to any explanation or definition

**Nidra** – sleep; isolation from mind and senses; unconscious state

**Nigama** – vedic knowledge; ritual procedures

**Nirakara** – formless; unmanifest

**Nirodha** – mental state in which the mind is blocked or prevented from functioning; beyond three qualities, or gunas;

483

complete cessation of patterns of consciousness when the mind is under perfect control

**Nirodhika** – psychic centre where the experience of form is obstructed

**Nirvikalpa samadhi** – superconscious state where mental modifications cease to exist, resulting in transcendence of the manifest world

**Niyama** – five observances of personal discipline which render the mind tranquil for meditation: shaucha, santosha, tapas, swadhyaya, ishvara pranidhana; second stage of Patanjali's ashtanga yoga

**Pancha makara** – five makaras of tantra: mudra (psychic attitude), mansa (flesh), maithuna (physical union), matsya (fish), madya (wine)

**Panchagni vidya** – sadhana of sitting in the middle of five burning fires with the burning sun overhead acting as the fifth fire

**Para** – supreme; greatest; highest; transcendental; one of the threefold principles of shakti

**Para vidya** – transcendental knowledge

**Paradevi** – supreme goddess; cosmic energy principle

**Paramahamsa** – literally, 'supreme swan'; high order of sannyasins who are able to discriminate between reality and unreality

**Paramatma** – cosmic soul or consciousness; universal or supreme self; highest spirit

**Paramshiva** – supreme consciousness; the absolute; highest reality

**Parapara** – one of the threefold principles of shakti; the intermediate stage between immanent and transcendent; unity in diversity

**Parashakti** – supreme power; kundalini; medium for revealing Shiva

**Paravidya** – supreme or highest knowledge

**Parvati** – consort and first disciple of Lord Shiva; cosmic mother; mahashakti; daughter of Himavan

**Pashu** – animal nature

**Pashyanti nada** – sound vibration in the subtle body; inaudible sound; mental sound

**Patanjali** – sage, or rishi, who codified the Yoga Sutras, propounder of ashtanga yoga

**Pingala nadi** – major pranic channel in the body which conducts the dynamic force, or prana shakti; solar or vital energy channel; emerges from the right of mooladhara chakra and intersects each of the chakras before reaching ajna chakra

**Pooraka** – inhalation

**Prajna** – intuition; source of individual revelation; unconscious mind

**Prakasha** – eternal light, luminosity; internal or subtle illumination; principle of self-revelation

**Prakriti** – manifest and unmanifest nature composed of the three gunas, or attributes; cosmic energy; vehicle of purusha (consciousness) according to Samkhya philosophy

**Pralaya** – dissolution of universe where everything created dissolves back into the unmanifest source of existence

**Prana** – principle of energy that sets life in motion; vital air or energy force, sustaining life and creation; vital air which operates in the chest region

**Pranamaya kosha** – energy sheath or body

**Pranashakti** – creative aspect of pure consciousness

**Pranayama** – yogic practices involving control of inhalation, exhalation and retention of breath; technique for expanding the dimensions of prana

**Pratyabhijna** – doctrine of recognition belonging to Kashmir Shaivism

**Pratyahara** – literally, 'to turn inwards that which moves outwards'; process of withdrawing the senses from external objects; an important prerequisite for dharana and higher stages of meditation; fifth limb of Patanjali's ashtanga yoga

**Raga** – liking; attachment; attraction

**Raja Yoga Sutras** – classical yoga text codified by Sage Patanjali: delineates the system of ashtanga yoga, or eight-fold path of yoga: yama, niyama, asana, pranayama, pratyahara, dharana, dhyana and samadhi

**Rajas/Rajoguna** – one of the three qualities of nature, representing dynamism, mobility, creativity; responsible for desire, ambition, restlessness; term used for menstrual secretions

**Ramana Maharshi** – realized saint and jnana yogi born in Tamil Nadu, South India, who taught atma vichara, or awareness of pure consciousness through self-enquiry

**Rechaka** – exhalation

**Rig Veda** – first of the four Vedas; contains hymns to deities or guardians of the law, such as Agni, Varuna, Indra and Mitra; presents nature as an eternal force working in the interests of humanity

**Rishi** – seer; realized sage who meditates on the self

**Roopa** – form

**Rubaiyat** – poem by Omar Khayam about the experience of enlightenment

**Rudanti** – crying, wailing or howling

**Rudra** – name of Lord Shiva in Rig Veda, meaning 'He who proclaims himself aloud'; signifies transformation through dissolution

**Rudrayamala** – intimate union of Rudra and his shakti, Yamala

**Rudrayamala Tantra** – text of Kashmir Shaivism in which Vijnana Bhairava Tantra is found devoted entirely to esoteric sadhana

**Sadhaka** – spiritual aspirant established in sadhana, or spiritual practice; one who is striving for moksha, or self-realization

**Sadhana** – spiritual practice done regularly for inner experience and liberation; process of internal refinement on path towards perfection.

**Sadvichara** – right or proper thinking

**Sahasrara chakra** – literally, 'thousand-petalled lotus'; spiritual centre situated at crown of head; represents state of enlightenment; abode of Shiva; transcendental consciousness

**Sakara** – with form

**Sakshi bhava** – attitude of silent witness or seer; awareness

**Sama Veda** – third of the four Vedas which deals mainly with devotion, worship and contemplation

**Samadhi** – eighth stage of Patanjali's ashtanga yoga, culmination of meditation; state of union of mind with the object of meditation; supramental consciousness; merging with divine consciousness; total illumination

**Samani** – centre where samprajnata samadhi is experienced

**Sambhavopaya** – direct approach to Shiva; sudden emergence of shiva-consciousness without any vikalpa by a mere hint that one's essential self is Shiva; means of approach which is passive, unsupported alertness or awareness; one of the four upaya sadhanas of tantra

**Sampradaya** – tradition

**Samshaya** – doubt; one of the nine obstacles to sadhana according to Patanjali

**Samskara** – mental impression stored in the subtle body as an archetype; unconscious memories or impressions which set up impulses and trains of thought, and which govern our personality and performance

**Sanatan dharma** – eternal values

**Sankalpa** – spiritual resolve; positive affirmation; willpower, determination or conviction; concept formed in the mind; important tool used in the practice of yoga nidra

**Sannyasa** – literally, 'equable trust', from sam, or equable, and nyasa, or trust; trustee; dedication; renunciation of the world, possessions and attachments

**Sannyasi** – one who has renounced illusion; one who has entrusted his life to the guru; one who is dedicated to spiritual life and service

**Sanyama** – self-restraint; simultaneous occurrence of concentration, meditation and samadhi in a developed yogi

**Saraswati** – divine form of cosmic energy; consort of Brahma; creative power which bestows knowledge of fine arts and power of speech; generally depicted in white dress, holding a vina, or lute, and sitting on a white swan; another name for sushumna nadi; legendary underground river; one of the ten orders of sannyasa

**Satchidananda** – truth, consciousness, bliss; qualities of the supreme

**Sattwa/Sattoguna** – one of the three qualities of nature representing steadiness, purity, harmony and light; balanced expression of inner self; experienced when tamoguna and rajoguna are balanced

**Satyam-Shivam-Sundaram** – truth, consciousness, bliss; qualities of the supreme

**Saura** – worshippers of the sun

**Saura Tantra** – system of tantra related to the sun

**Savikalpa samadhi** – supraconsciousness with traces of thought in dormant or seed state; when there is oneness of mind with the object but dissolution of self is not yet incomplete

**Shaiva Siddhanta** – division of Shaivism found in South India; central doctrine is that Shiva is the supreme reality and the jiva, or individual soul, is of the same essence as Shiva but not identical; distilled essence of Vedanta; rival school of Vaishnavism

**Shaiva Tantra** – system of tantra related to Shiva

**Shaivism** – sect in which Lord Shiva is worshipped as the supreme reality, arguably the most ancient faith in world

**Shaivite** – one who worships Lord Shiva as the supreme reality

**Shakta** – one who worships Shakti, God in the form of Mother, as the supreme power which creates, sustains and withdraws the universe

**Shakti** – vital energy; creative potential force; feminine aspect of creation and divinity; vehicle of consciousness; centre where intense waves of bliss permeate one's being

**Shaktiman** – holder of shakti

**Shaktism** – sect in which Shakti, or the cosmic mother (female creative principle) is worshipped as the supreme reality; the basis of shaktism is the Vedas; one of the oldest and most widespread religions in the world

**Shaktopaya** – means of approach to the divine through Shakti; one of the four upaya sadhanas of tantra

**Shanta** – peaceful, tranquil; one of the eight bhairavas, or states of consciousness.

**Shanti** – inner peace

**Shiva** – literally, 'auspicious one'; destructive aspect of Hindu trinity; destroyer of the ego and duality; Lord of yogis, who is said to dwell on Mount Kailash; archetypal renunciate; symbol of cosmic consciousness

**Shiva Sutras** – text of Kashmir Shaivism in which Lord Shiva instructs Parvati in the path towards realization of supreme consciousness

**Shivalingam** – symbol of consciousness

**Shoonya** – void; state of absolute nothingness in which no object is experienced; mental vacuum; state of darkness referred to as 'the dark night of the soul' prior to enlightenment

**Shrishti** – creation; created universe; letting go; manifestation; emanation

**Shvasa** – breath

**Siddha** – adept, master, perfected soul; one who has fully developed his psychic/pranic capacity of mind/body; one who has control over nature, matter and mind

**Siddhi** – perfection; psychic power associated with awakening of chakras, resulting in control over the physical elements

**Sloka** – scriptural verse

**Smashan sadhana** – tantric practice performed in the graveyard

**Soham** – literally, 'That (supreme consciousness) I am'; mantra of the breath; used in the meditation practice of ajapa japa; 'So' represents cosmic consciousness, 'ham' individual consciousness

**Spanda** – cosmic vibration; dynamic aspect of Shiva; primordial pulsation

**Spanda Shastras** – doctrine of vibration

**Sri** – auspicious; name of Devi; epithet of respect

**Sri Yantra** – geometrical diagram representing Goddess Sri or Lakshmi

**Srimad Devi Bhagavatam** – scriptural text containing the myths and doctrines of Devi

**Sthoola** – gross; relating to the world of matter and the waking state, or jagrat

**Sthita prajna** – stabilized consciousness

**Sukshma** – subtle; relating to the world of the psyche

**Sushumna** – spiritual energy channel flowing from mooladhara to sahasrara; pathway of kundalini, related to transcendental awareness

**Sushumna jagran** – tantric practice for awakening sushumna nadi

**Sushupti** – deep dreamless sleep; unconscious state of mind

**Sutra** – literally, 'thread'; aphorism

**Swabhava** – innate or inherent nature

**Swapna** – dream state; subconscious

**Tamas/tamoguna** – one of the three gunas, or qualities of nature and mind, representing stability and immobility; responsible for inertia, laziness, procrastination, dullness, darkness, fear of change

**Tanmatra** – quality or essence of the five elements; nature; sensory perception; five in number: smell, sight, taste, touch and hearing

**Tanoti** – expansion

**Tantra** – process of expansion of mind and liberation of energy and consciousness from matter; comes from two roots: tanoti meaning 'expansion' and trayati 'liberation'; ancient universal science, philosophy and culture of man dealing with transcendence of gross human nature from the present level of evolution to the highest state of human attainment, liberation; one of the classical Indian philosophies

**Tantric** – practitioner of the esoteric tantric science

**Tapas** – literally, 'to sharpen' or 'to whet'; austerity; derived from tapa, or fire

**Tattwa** – literally, 'thatness'; essential element or principle; five in number: earth, water, fire, air and ether

**Tejas** – literally, 'bright'; that which illuminates subtle objects; subconscious state related to dream whose essence is light

**Traita** – one supreme reality, manifesting as three

**Trataka** – literally, 'steady gazing' at a fixed point or object without blinking; a method of focusing the mind

**Trayati** – liberation

**Trika** – threefold, triple; system or philosophy of the triad: (i) Shiva, (ii) Shakti and (iii) Nara, bound soul; or (i) para, the highest, non-different from Shiva, (ii) parapara, the intermediate state of identity in difference, (iii) apara, the state of difference; basic philosophy of Kashmir Shaivism

**Trishira Bhairava Tantra** – tri means 'three' and shira means 'that which carries'; text dealing with the three flows, or shiras, of prana known as ida, pingala and sushumna

**Trishiropanishad** – upanishad which deals with the three flows, or shiras, of energy known as ida, pingala and sushumna

**Trishul** – three-pronged trident symbolic of the three gunas, or qualities of nature, in equipoise

**Turiya** – fourth dimension of consciousness transcending the waking, dreaming and deep sleep states, and linking these states; integral awareness; sakshi, or witnessing consciousness; superconsciousness

**Udana vayu** – pranic energy current operating above the throat

**Ujjayi pranayama** – psychic breath

**Unmani** – literally, 'no mind'; centre beyond mind or thought, where the mind is completely turned inwards

**Unmani mudra** – psychic attitude in which the eyes are open, gazing outward, but the awareness is fixed within; also known as bhairavi mudra

**Unmesha** – unfoldment; opening (of the eyes); blinking; expansion

**Upanishad** – literally, 'to sit close by'; last part of Vedas, containing their essence; containing dialogues between guru-disciple about the nature of reality and the identity of individual and cosmic consciousness

**Upaya** – means or process

**Uttarayana** – northern path; one of the two prescribed paths of meditation; path of light

**Vaikhari nada** – audible sound or speech

**Vairagi** – one who is not attached to the world of the senses; sect of renunciates who have transcended matter

**Vairagya** – dispassion; non-attachment; state in which one remains internally calm and balanced under all circumstances; absence of sensual craving and desire

**Vaishnavism** – sect that worships incarnations of Lord Vishnu as the supreme reality

**Vaishnavite** – one who worships incarnations of Lord Vishnu as the supreme reality

**Vaishvanara** – Lord of the conscious realm, the material world

**Vajroli mudra** – contraction and release of the urinary passage to stimulate swadhisthana chakra

**Varna** – colour

**Vedanta** – end of the Vedas; Veda means '(transcendental) knowledge' and anta means 'end'; ultimate philosophy of the Vedas; one of the six darshanas, or systems, of vedic philosophy which deals with the transcendental and manifest nature of consciousness

**Vedas** – oldest known spiritual texts of Aryans written more than 5,000 years ago; four in number: Rig Veda, Yajur Veda, Sama Veda and Atharva Veda

**Vi** – prefix meaning separation, disjunction

**Vibhooti** – psychic power; accomplishment of yoga; splendour; purified essence or sacred ash worn on the forehead by devotees of Shiva; subtle, unmanifest power behind creation; perfection; dominion

**Vibhooti Pada** – third chapter of Sage Patanjali's Yoga Sutras

**Vichara** – right enquiry; discernment; path of self-enquiry which implies discrimination between the real and unreal, self and ego

**Vidya** – from the root, 'vid', or inner knowledge

**Vijnana** – essential truth; intuitive ability of mind; higher understanding.

**Vijnana bhairava** – state of consciousness where one achieves union with the cosmic consciousness

**Vijnanamaya kosha** – higher mental sheath or body

**Vikalpa** – imagination, fancy, doubt, error; idea, ideation; thought/counter-thought; thought or conclusion without factual evidence; one of the five vrittis, or modifications of mind

**Vikshipta** – oscillating state of mind between dissipation and one-pointedness

**Vimala** – full of purity (absence of duality or subject/object)

**Vimarsha** – nature, or swabhava, of Shiva; aspect of prakasha by which it knows itself; experience; self-consciousness of the supreme; another name for shakti

**Vira** – brave; hero

**Virat** – literally, 'enormous'; macrocosm; sum total of the entire manifest universe

**Vishaya** – object

**Vishnu** – vedic deity; preserver and sustainer of the universe; one of the Hindu trinity; supreme consciousness; often associated with water

**Vishu** – chakra below mooladhara

**Vishwa** – universe; entire cosmos; external consciousness

**Vishwamitra** – royal sage who became a brahmarishi, or knower of Brahman, the supreme reality

**Viveka** – discernment; the power to discriminate correctly; right knowledge or understanding

**Vritti** – literally, 'circle'; mental fluctuation, modification, wave or pattern

**Vyakta** – manifest universe

**Vyana vayu** – pranic air current pervading whole body

**Vyapika** – centre or abode of shoonya which can be pierced or transcended only by the appearance of jyotsna

**Yajna** – vedic sacrifice; sacrificial rite; offering oblations to the fire

**Yajur Veda** – second of the four Vedas; explains the rituals involved in vedic sacrifices

**Yama** – five self-restraints or rules of conduct pertaining to ethical perfection, designed to remove emotional disorders in preparation for higher yoga practices: ahimsa, satya, asteya, brahmacharya, aparigraha; first stage of Patanjali's ashtanga yoga; period of three hours.

**Yamala** – pair or couple

**Yantra** – geometrical form of mantra used for concentration

**Yoga** – literally, 'union' or 'yoke'; systematic science of body/mind leading to union of individual consciousness with cosmic consciousness; process of uniting opposing forces in body/mind to realize the spiritual essence; one of the six classical Indian philosophies

**Yuga** – age

# Index

Advaita 18
Agama 15, 97, 98
Aghora 20
Ahamkara (see Ego)
Ajapa japa 37, 162, 174, 408
Ajna chakra 249–250, 278–279, 298
Akaara 296–297
Akasha 258, 284, 285, 297, 302, 377
Akasha dharana 202, 203
Akshara 50, 51, 100, 106, 170, 191, 296
Alchemy 6–7, 9
Amrita 159, 269
Anahad nada 7, 105–106, 188–189, 349–350, 407
Anahata chakra 105, 188–189, 209, 247–248
Ananda 240–241, 248
Anandamaya kosha 35, 149, 196
Anavopaya 27
Annamaya kosha 149, 151
Antahkarana 4–5, 42–43, 177, 243, 267, 305–307, 355
Antarakasha dharana 205–208
Anupaya 26
Apana 36, 38, 148, 152–154, 15, 156–158, 160–162, 163–164, 173, 238–239
Ardhachandrika 105
Ardha matsyendrasana 272
Asana 271–273
Ashta bhairava 286

Atma 125, 135, 371–372, 388–389, 390–391, 391, 396–397
Aum 50, 190–192, 193–194, 197, 297
Austerity 242–243
Avatar 5
Awareness 14–15, 33–34, 44–45, 46, 58, 71–72; subliminal 88; mindful 178–179

Bahyakasha dharana 377
Bhagavad Gita 9, 64, 75, 161, 393
Bhairava 21, 72–74, 81, 101–102, 110, 113–114, 125, 126, 127, 129, 130, 131, 134, 135, 136, 137, 146, 157, 164, 168, 293, 339–340, 375–376, 380–382, 400, 420; forms 101–102, 111, 112–114
Bhairava Agama 101
Bhairavi 129, 131, 134–135, 136, 137, 157; forms 102
Bhairavi mudra 268, 361
Bhakti 282–283, 364
Bhasmasura 112
Bhavana 53
Bhrumadhya 172
Bija mantra 169, 170, 197
Bindu 7, 25, 52, 104–105, 152–153, 155, 185, 186–187, 269
Body 280–281, 282
Brahma nadi 182
Brain 5–6, 68–70
Breath 37–39, 155

494

Brahma 357–358
Brahmarandhara 194
Buddhi 4, 320, 391, 396

Chakras 39, 104–105, 166, 170–171
Chetana 14–15, 41, 135
Chidakasha 285–286
Chidakasha dharana 52, 285
Chitta 4
Chittashakti 166
Consciousness 4–9, 18, 74–79, 288, 291, 292–293, 318–319, 318–319, 333–334; continuity of 89; stages of 19–21; states of 63, 262
Contemplation 414
Creation 23, 155

Daharakasha 204
Daharakasha dharana 202
Dakshinachara 253
Dakshinayana 47
Dance 283
Desire 310–311, 314–315
Dharana 29–30, 32–33, 43–45, 46, 47, 50–51, 53–54, 59–62, 65–68, 84–88, 178, 180, 398–399, 400
Dharma 136–137
Dhyana 30, 72, 235 (see Meditation)
Dhyana veerasana 271–272
Direction 199
Dissolution 222–223, 226, 230, 351–352, 344
Dreams 46–47
Duality 13, 138–139, 232, 287, 325–326, 331–332

Dvaita 18
Dwadashanta 38, 165, 166, 167, 210, 212, 239
Dwesha 310, 371, 384

Ego 4, 327–327–328, 383–384
Emotions 66
Energy 341–342
Evolution of consciousness 4–10
Expansion and liberation 9–10, 16

Faith 55
Fear 291

Genetics 61–62
Gravity 82
Gunas 3, 194, 219, 384, 406
Guru-disciple 40–42, 82, 234

Hamsa dharana 422–423
Hatha Yoga Pradipika 162
Heart 344–345
Hiranyagarbha 76
Hridaya chakra 210, 212
Hridayakasha 187, 203–204, 209
Hridayakasha dharana 203–204

Ida 173, 183, 249–250
Imagination 86–87, 240–241
Indriyas (see Senses)
Initiation 429–430
Intuition 365–364
Ishavasya Upanishad 356
Ishvara 77–78

Jagrat 75, 83, 190, 193, 262
Japa 424
Japa dharana 407

Jivatma 7, 177
Jnana yoga 58, 225, 306
Jnanendriyas 245
Joy 254–255

Kaala 28–29, 214
Kaalagni 214–215, 216
Kaivalya 347–348
Kalaa 25
Kali 28
Kalpa vriksha 81, 240–241
Kanchukas 308
Karana sadhana 83–84
Karankini mudra 267
Karmendriyas 245
Kashmir Shaivism 18–19, 24, 25,
    96, 134, 142, 364
Kaulachara 253
Kevala kumbhaka 158, 173
Khechari mudra 268–270, 278,
    163
Knowledge 11–12, 90–91, 316–
    317
Koshas 149, 151
Kriya yoga 174, 183, 204
Krodhana mudra 268
Kumbha 228–229
Kumbhaka 38, 157–158, 160,
    163–164, 229
Kundalini 8, 96, 143, 165, 166,
    167–168, 169–171, 173, 182–
    183, 246, 250, 418–419
Kundalini yoga 174, 183, 204

Lalana chakra 269
Laya 187, 226, 228, 344, 377
Lelihanaya mudra 268
Liberation 48, 319, 402
Lokas 19–20, 390, 405–406

Lunar cycles 289–290

Mahakaala 28–29, 214
Mahashakti 8
Mahat 76
Manas 4, 42
Mandala 45, 113, 275
Mandukya Upanishad 194
Manipura chakra 247
Manomaya kosha 149, 151
Mantra 45, 49–52, 99, 100, 113,
    169, 170, 190–192, 209, 296,
    381, 407–408
Matra 193–194
Matrika 50, 381–382
Maya 25, 308–309, 310, 323, 386
Meditation 6, 47–48, 409 (see
    Dhyana)
Memory 254–255, 359
Manolaya 222–223
Mind 44–45, 76–77, 89–90, 129–
    130, 212–213, 335–336
Mooladhara chakra 39, 165
Moordha 172
Motion 341–342
Mudras 184, 266–270
Music 258

Nachiketas 244
Nada 7, 25, 99–100, 104, 105,
    189, 195–196, 350
Nada yoga 189
Nadi 165
Negative qualities 320–322
Nidra 77
Nirakara 107, 116, 126, 133, 173
Nirodhika 105
Nirvikalpa 204
Nirvikalpa samadhi 79, 141, 384

Opposites 371–374

Panchagni 245–246
Paradevi 134, 135, 148, 149, 152, 165, 218, 219
Paramahamsa 20
Parashakti 143, 153
Paramshiva 24, 148
Paramtattwa 143
Parvati 22–24, 40
Patanjali 6, 46, 57, 105, 129–130, 162
Perception 33, 343–345
Pingala 173, 183, 249–250
Poornatva 355–356
Pooraka 163
Prajna 77–78, 215, 267, 364
Prakasha 24, 134
Prakriti 31, 299
Pralaya 216
Prana 34–39, 148–156, 157–158, 160–162, 163–164, 166, 173, 238–239
Pranamaya kosha 35, 150–151, 201–202
Pranashakti 35–36, 102, 149–150, 166, 184, 238, 245–246
Pranava 190–192
Pranayama 38, 151, 158, 161, 174
Pratyabhijna 19
Pratyahara 16, 43, 54, 246, 259, 294–295, 300, 392–393
Purity 367–368
Purusha 299

Raga 310, 371, 384
Rajas 194, 384
Ramakrishna Paramahamsa 403

Reality: immanent 18, 107–109; transcendent 18, 107–110, 121–122, 124, 383–384, 132, 369–370
Rechaka 163
Rudra 73, 95, 97–98, 415
Rudrayamala Tantra 19, 95–97, 113, 432

Sadhana 10–11, 26–27, 31–32, 83–84
Sahasrara chakra 8, 39, 166, 180–181
Sahita kumbhaka 158
Sakara 107, 116–118, 119–120, 133, 173; meditation 119–120, 126
Samadhi 30, 79, 235, 394
Samani 105
Sambhavopaya 26, 29
Samprajnata samadhi 105
Samskaras 280, 281, 311
Sanatana dharma 136–137
Sannyasa 21, 147, 428
Sanskrit 155, 170, 172, 197, 297, 299
Santosha 147, 411
Sattwa 194, 384
Satya 95
Savikalpa samadhi 71, 79, 141, 384
Self-realization 2–4, 337–338
Senses 33, 44, 220–221, 245–246, 256–257, 258–259, 294–295, 355, 392–393
Sexual union 250, 251–252
Shabdabrahman 188–189
Shakti 7, 17, 19, 22–25, 37, 85, 95–96, 105, 134–135, 140–141,

142–143, 164, 218, 249–250, 414–415
Shaktopaya 27, 29
Shaivism 17, 18
Shambhavi mudra 279
Shanmukhi mudra 184–185, 246
Shanta 163–164
Shiva 17, 22–25, 37, 42, 85, 95–96, 112, 134–135, 140–141, 142–143, 144, 164, 166, 181, 216, 337–338, 342, 353–354, 380–382
Shiva Sutras 50
Shiva tattwa 224, 308
Shoonya 52, 59, 173, 187, 192, 197–198, 205–206, 207, 226–227, 228–229, 274–275
Shoonya dharana 226–227, 228
Shoonya panchaka 173
Shoonya yantra 274
Sleep 262
Space 199, 233, 284
Spandan 35
Spirituality 320
Srimad Devi Bhagavatam 89
Sthita prajna 64
Sthoola sadhana 83–84
Sufi 282, 342
Sukshma sadhana 83–84
Sukshmagni 186
Sushumna 161, 165, 173, 182–183, 201–202, 246, 248, 249–250
Sushumna darshan 202
Sushupti 83, 190, 193, 262
Swami Satyananda 42, 59, 60, 72, 80, 85–86, 162, 174, 183, 215, 244, 348, 364, 370
Swami Sivananda 42, 190–191, 244, 326, 370
Swapna 76, 83, 190, 193, 247, 262
Swara 290
Symbol 45, 55–58, 63–65, 68–69, 86, 234, 235, 366

Taittiriya Upanishad 337
Tamas 194, 384
Tanmatras 175–176
Tantra 4, 9, 10, 12–18, 20, 34, 54, 56, 59, 62–63, 66, 85, 97–98, 110, 111–115, 124, 130, 146, 155, 213, 214–215, 236, 253, 258–259, 260, 306, 321, 374, 416
Tapas (see Austerity)
Tattwas 25, 175, 218, 257, 308, 201
Tattwa shuddhi 218, 302
Tejas 76
Therapy 59–61
Thoughtlessness 378–379
Tilak 186
Time 27–29, 214–215, 216
Traita 18, 19
Transcendence 107–108
Transmission 40–42, 346–347, 430
Trataka 264, 276, 346–348
Trika 19, 26, 95–98, 102, 142
Trikuti 161
Trishira Bhairava Tantra 101–102
Trishul 144
Turiya 59, 60, 63, 78–79, 83, 161, 191, 194, 262

Ujjayi pranayama 172
Unity 327–328, 329–330

Unmani 105
Unmani mudra 268, 361
Upayas 25–27, 29, 83–84, 148
Uttarayana 47–48

Vairagya 20, 147, 267–268, 365
Vaishvanara 75
Vamachara 253
Vedanta 85, 96, 116, 132, 236, 306, 312–313
Vidyas 130
Vijnana bhairava 74, 79–80, 81–82
Vijnana Bhairava Tantra 12, 17–19, 21–22, 79–81, 137, 425; classification of practices 83–86
Vijnanamaya kosha 35, 149, 196
Vikalpa 204, 206, 305–307, 367–368

Vimarsha 24, 134
Virat 75
Visarga 155, 299–300
Vishwa 75
Visualization 86–87
Vrittis 230
Vyapika 105

Witness 70–71
Worship 410, 417

Yajna 5, 145, 161, 352, 405
Yamala 97
Yantra 45, 113, 202, 274
Yoga 17, 30, 59, 130
Yuga dharma 137

Zen Buddhism 232

*Swami Satyasangananda Saraswati with her guru,*
*Swami Satyananda Saraswati, at Vaishnava Devi*